D0760932

A Nation of Veterans

A Nation of Veterans

*War, Citizenship, and the Welfare State
in Modern America*

Olivier Burtin

PENN

UNIVERSITY OF PENNSYLVANIA PRESS

PHILADELPHIA

Published by
University of Pennsylvania Press
Philadelphia, Pennsylvania 19104-4112
www.upenn.edu/pennpress

Printed in the United States of America on acid-free paper

10 9 8 7 6 5 4 3 2 1

Hardcover ISBN 9781512823141
Ebook ISBN 9781512823158

Library of Congress Cataloging-in-Publication Data
Names: Burtin, Olivier, author.
Title: A nation of veterans : war, citizenship, and the
welfare state in modern America / Olivier Burtin.
Description: Philadelphia : University of Pennsylvania Press,
[2022] | Includes bibliographical references and index.
Identifiers: LCCN 2022007571 | ISBN
9781512823141 (hardcover)
Subjects: LCSH: Veterans—Government policy—United
States—History—20th century. | Veterans—Services
for—United States—History—20th century. | Veterans—
Political activity—United States—History—20th century.
| Welfare state—United States—History—20th century.
| Public welfare—Political aspects—United States. |
Veterans—United States—Societies, etc. | Veterans—
Legal status, laws, etc.—United States. | United
States—Social policy—History—20th century.
Classification: LCC UB357 .B865 2022 |
DDC 362.860973—dc23/eng/20220223
LC record available at https://lccn.loc.gov/2022007571

To my family and to the many friends made along the way

CONTENTS

Introduction

Military veterans were at the center of the U.S. welfare state in the mid-twentieth century. The annual cost of their benefits in the 1940s and 1950s represented an average of two-fifths of all federal spending on social welfare, for a total of almost $100 billion over this entire period.[1] Ranging from disability pensions to life insurance to civil service preference, the list of these programs was so extensive that beneficiaries needed self-help manuals to grasp their full scope.[2] Taken as a whole, they formed what I call here the "veterans' welfare state." All these services were managed by a single mammoth agency, the Veterans Administration (VA), which was the predecessor of today's Department of Veterans Affairs. It not only operated the largest hospital system in the nation but also employed more personnel than any other federal entity save the military and the Post Office.[3] VA staff served a clientele of over 20 million former service members in the postwar years, more than ever before in American history.[4] Together with their relatives, veterans represented an estimated 40 percent of the U.S. population during this period, leading some commentators to argue that the country was fast turning into "a nation of veterans."[5] The substantial size of their benefits led the magazine *Fortune* to note in 1952 that the U.S. "welfare state" was really "a veterans' state."[6] Other observers concurred, calling veterans "our biggest privileged class."[7]

This last comment was meant to be provocative, but it was an understatement. There is indeed evidence to suggest that the benefits available to American veterans in the mid-twentieth century were more generous than those accessible not only to other categories of the U.S. population but also to their counterparts overseas. In a report to Congress in 1945, financier and statesman Bernard Baruch found that "in the main the provisions enacted ... for American veterans are more liberal than comparable programs" in other industrialized countries such as Australia, Canada, Britain, New Zealand, and the Union of South Africa.[8] Canadian expert and government official Robert England agreed, noting a few years later that while his country practiced a similar "segregation of the veteran [from the civilian] in all welfare and rehabilitation programmes," the United

States spent far more on benefits for former service members.[9] This gap was the result not just of the larger size of the U.S. economy and population but also of its programs' more liberal eligibility criteria. Where most countries offered benefits only to veterans with war-connected disabilities or to the survivors of those killed in action, the United States granted access to those whose impairment or death was unrelated to service as well.[10] The result was a remarkable irony: even though the United States suffered comparatively less casualties in both world wars than most of the other major belligerents, it ended up spending far more than them on veterans' welfare.[11]

The central place of military veterans within the U.S. welfare state was a frequent topic of policy debates at midcentury.[12] Commentators often remarked on the groundbreaking nature of the benefits available to this group compared to those for the general population. As one political scientist noted in 1945, "the existing veterans legislation is the most advanced welfare legislation yet adopted."[13] In fact, many at the highest levels of the state thought that veterans' benefits had grown so much that they now represented an obstacle to the expansion of more universal welfare programs such as Social Security. President Harry Truman himself recognized publicly that it was "undesirable to have a duplicate or dual system of benefits"—one open only to those who had served in the military and the other to the rest of the population—and that the growth of non-service-connected benefits for veterans should be checked. "What we are trying to do," he added, "is make the social security system so good that nobody will want any special benefits."[14] Following his lead, many social policy experts and journalists criticized former service members as a "military caste" enjoying "special privileges" over other categories of the population and represented by "professional patriots."[15]

Though the connection between veterans and the welfare state was obvious at the time, it has largely faded from popular consciousness. Today, former service members are typically seen as one of a few privileged groups whose deservedness should be assumed rather than questioned, not unlike victims of natural disasters or senior citizens. Our own language offers perhaps the most vivid illustration of this phenomenon. We routinely refer to veterans and service members as "heroes," "warriors," or "fallen angels," terms that not only glorify but also naturalize their separate and superior status.[16] A major think tank even capitalized "Veterans" in a recent report.[17] Because we so often see former service members as an especially deserving group, we tend to think of their benefits as falling into the category of earned rights instead of "welfare" (a term often understood pejoratively as connoting handouts for the undeserving poor), which is why we usually consider veterans' programs to be distinct from the welfare state.

This popular assumption is reflected in the scholarly literature. Most recent works on the welfare state in the midcentury have ignored veterans and focused instead on marginalized groups such as the poor, racial minorities, or single mothers.[18] Scholars of veterans' history have questioned this separation, but the overwhelming majority of those who studied that same period have concentrated on the 1944 "GI Bill of Rights," a landmark piece of legislation in its own right but nevertheless only one part of the larger landscape of veterans' benefits.[19] *A Nation of Veterans* adopts a broader perspective, showing how the vast range of programs that made up veterans' welfare state—including not just the GI Bill but also hospitals, public housing, and retirement pensions—featured centrally in midcentury social policy debates.

In so doing, this book reminds us that we should not assume that veterans have always been treated in the same way that they are now. The assumption of veterans' deservedness that pervades our own public discourse is a recent development. To be sure, the idea that the state should help those with service-connected disabilities or the survivors of those who died in service has never really been controversial. Yet the broader concept that military service itself, rather than just wartime impairment or demise, conferred upon an individual the right to receive special benefits has proved more problematic. Throughout U.S. history, the notion that all veterans should be treated as a separate and select group of citizens has generated a steady stream of debate both inside and outside the veteran community. Critics have argued that some former service members were more deserving than others by pointing to differences between those who saw combat and those who did not, between those who volunteered and those who were drafted, and between those who were disabled and those who left the service able-bodied. Some have even challenged the distinction between veterans and nonveterans by asking why the state should reward service members who never served abroad (as was the case for half of those who served in World War I and a quarter of those in World War II) and not the civilian workers whose contributions to the home front were often just as essential to the war effort.[20] Put simply, the idea that veterans form a unified community whose members are all on an equally superior moral footing compared to civilians has long been controversial.

By following this debate into the midcentury, we can see that veterans' welfare state was the product not of consensus but of conflict. Popular support for their benefits was strong but not unlimited and veterans' advocates were far from omnipotent. In the context of the military buildup of the early Cold War, the competition for resources was fierce. Former service members had to fight to obtain and then defend every single one of their advantages against criticism from both sides of the aisle. On the one hand, liberal voices such as President Truman, the *New York Times*, and even the progressive veterans' group American Veterans Committee opposed the idea of granting privileged treatment to a segment of the population based only on military service. They argued that former service members with non-service-connected disabilities should receive the same benefits as every other citizen. On the other hand, many conservatives not only rejected the very idea of a welfare state but worried—as Austrian economist Friedrich Hayek forcefully argued in his best-selling pamphlet *The Road to Serfdom* (1944)—that mounting government spending would pave the way for a totalitarian regime.[21] Following this logic, right-wing groups and individuals such as the U.S. Chamber of Commerce, the American Medical Association, and ex-president Herbert Hoover counted among the most relentless critics of veterans' welfare state. The combined threat of these two camps led veterans' advocates to complain in the late 1950s that a "cold war on veterans" was under way.[22]

The central question of this book stems from that paradox: how, in the two middle decades of the twentieth century, did U.S. veterans manage to build the world's most generous separate welfare state for themselves despite relentless criticism from across the political spectrum?

The answer is that they formed one of the largest and most important social movements in wartime and postwar America—yet one that scholars have never examined in depth. By rallying behind their advocacy groups in defense of shared interests, former service members managed to permanently embed their privileged status in public policy despite fierce attacks from liberals and conservatives alike. Veterans formed as much of a social movement as other groups making claims on the state during this same period, such as labor unions or civil rights activists.

But what do we mean by "social movement," exactly? According to sociologists Charles Tilly and Sidney Tarrow, the term designates a "sustained campaign of claim-making, using repeated performances that advertise the claim, based on organizations, networks, traditions, and solidarities that sustain these activities." All these criteria apply to former service members. They have long been involved at various levels of politics, not only to defend their own benefits but also to advance their broader vision for the country; they have engaged in various acts of collective claim-making such as signing petitions, writing letters to their representatives, carrying out mass demonstrations, and giving public speeches; they have joined a vast and diverse network of organizations that serve as intermediaries between them and the state; finally, they have shared a common belief in their own distinctiveness vis-à-vis civilians. Tilly and Tarrow further argue that social movements tend to engage in "repeated public displays of worthiness, unity, numbers, and commitment."[23] This was also true of the members of veterans' groups, who wore military-style uniforms, performed elaborate rituals, and maintained strict entry barriers by requiring an honorable discharge from the military.

The reason why we have yet to see veterans for what they are—a social movement—is not because of a lack of attention. There is a wealth of scholarship on the readjustment of World War II veterans, to cite only this specific period.[24] Rather, the problem stems from the same pervasive assumption mentioned earlier, namely that U.S. veterans have always enjoyed the same heralded status in popular culture as they do today. For if there is a consensus that former service members are a deserving category of the population, then why would they need to organize? This notion is particularly strong for the mid-twentieth century: beginning in the 1990s, veterans of World War II have come to be known as the "Greatest Generation," an especially deserving cohort who fought the "Good War" and returned home as heroes. Though historians have long disproven such myths, their grip on our collective consciousness remains firm.[25] They prevent us from seeing that the claims made by veterans on the state have not always met with unqualified approval, and that turning these claims into reality required organizing into a social movement.

Another reason why we have yet to see veterans as such is because we often associate the concept of "social movement" with bottom-up campaigns that seek to bring about change from outside the political structure, whereas we typically see former service members as part of the establishment. There are two problems with this view, however. The first is that it incorrectly assumes, once again, that the past was similar to the present. Though veterans' politics today are mostly the purview of a few interest groups, the repertoire of collective action used by former service members has historically included more radical tactics. Rank-and-file veterans carried out one of the first popular marches on Washington in the early 1930s to demand the Bonus, for instance, while their successors in the late 1940s reacted to the nationwide housing shortage by engaging in acts of collective protest that included sit-ins. The second problem is that social scientists have shown that "not all movements are radical, reject mainstream or institutionalized forms of political contention, or favor wholesale social change."[26] A more productive definition would recognize their diversity and dynamism. Not only can their strategy range from the disruptive to the conventional, but it can also change over time as movements go through successive life cycles. This was the case of the veterans' movement, whose advocates in the midcentury combined confrontational and institutional methods to achieve their goals. Their strength lay precisely in the fact that their movement was neither fully institutionalized nor completely marginal, but rather somewhere in between. In other words, veterans were not fundamentally different from other social movements.

The point of adopting this framework is to acknowledge the importance of hitherto neglected aspects of veterans' politics. The few social scientists who studied this topic have focused on the role of veterans' organizations as national lobbies, and in particular on their close relationship with government officials in Congress and the White House.[27] This perspective is important but incomplete, insofar as it fails to account for the deep roots put down by these groups in thousands of communities across the country. Their local posts organized a wide range of social activities such as junior baseball leagues, high school debates, mock government groups, marching bands, and civics and marksmanship classes. Veterans' relatives could join their own affiliates, such as the Legion Auxiliary for women or the Sons of the American Legion. Their officers helped raise funds for charity, erect war memorials, and maintain cemeteries, among other projects. At the same time as they were interest groups, veterans' organizations were also fraternal orders, social clubs, and welfare rights associations. Their influence in national politics stemmed not primarily from their professional lobbyists but rather from their ability to reach deep into local communities and to use their grassroots infrastructure to translate the support of ordinary citizens into political action (in that sense, they adopted the same strategy that would later make the National Rifle Association so powerful).[28] This is why we should see veterans' politics not just as a collection of pressure groups but instead as a full-fledged social movement.

The core collective frame of this movement was the ideal of martial citizenship, according to which military service set former service members apart from the rest of the population and entitled them to special consideration from the state.[29] The idea was not new, even though its exact outlines have changed over time: Union veterans were already advancing such claims in their campaign to obtain pensions in the late nineteenth century, for instance.[30] Martial citizenship held that veterans' benefits were part of the cost of war and therefore radically different from other types of welfare programs. They amounted to a sacred and inviolable debt, the result of a moral contract between the state and those who served under its banners. This view posited veterans as the creditors of the state, by contrast with recipients of public assistance who were more often seen as its debtors. To avoid tainting veterans' programs with the stigma of charity attached to the label of "welfare," their advocates pushed for these benefits to be placed under a separate administrative entity, the VA. They further insisted that their programs be run at the federal level, not only because soldiers had served the nation as opposed to individual states but also to establish a shared bedrock of rights available to all regardless of where they lived. In sum, veterans advanced a view of the body politic defined by a strict hierarchy between different classes of citizens, with themselves at the top.

If martial citizenship established a distinction between veterans and civilians, it did so within the veteran population as well. Though anyone with an honorable discharge could in theory claim the status of veteran and the benefits attached to it, in practice access was often contingent on matters of race, gender, and sexuality. Martial citizenship in the mid-century was largely understood as applying only to white, heterosexual men. Military service in the United States had long been open only to this specific category of the population, with other groups being either excluded or kept in subordinate positions.[31] Of the 16 million people who served in the U.S. military during World War II, for instance, only 1 million were African Americans and 350,000 women, much less than their respective share of the general population. The Army also adopted explicitly antigay policies.[32] As a result, white men represented the overwhelming majority of military veterans at midcentury, even though they accounted for only about 45 percent of the total U.S. population in 1950.[33] Not until the late 1960s and 1970s would the boundaries of martial citizenship be extended, as the claims of marginalized groups to veteran status began to gain traction. In the earlier period that this book focuses on, martial citizenship largely reflected traditional racial and gender norms.

This ideal did not exist in a vacuum. In many ways, martial citizenship offered an alternative to the ideology of breadwinner liberalism, which was a driving force behind the development of the U.S. welfare state from the late nineteenth century to the New Deal of the 1930s and the Great Society of the 1960s. Many of the welfare programs created for the general population during this period reflected a vision of American society organized around white, middle-class families with men as self-supporting heads of household and women as child-rearing homemakers.[34] Both martial citizenship and breadwinner liberalism were centered on white men, but the former departed from the latter in its insistence that what made individuals deserving of state assistance was military service rather than family making or economic independence. As we will see time and again in this book, behind the attacks on veterans' benefits often lay the fear that granting public support to former service members would encourage idleness and make them dependent on the state for a living. Since veterans' programs were part and parcel of the larger welfare state, it should come as no surprise that they attracted the same kind of criticism that was often leveled at recipients of other types of benefits.

The many organizations that formed the veterans' movement played a key role in defending martial citizenship against these attacks. According to some estimates, there were no less than two hundred veterans' associations on the national stage in the United States after World War II.[35] This large number reflected the heterogeneity of the veteran community, with some groups open only to former service members of a specific conflict (such as the American Veterans of World War II), others to a particular branch of the military (the Marine Corps League) or to a specific religion or ethnicity (the Catholic War Veterans and the Jewish War Veterans), and yet others to a specific sex (the Women's Overseas Service League). The veterans' movement was thus as diverse as any other, even if only a handful of these organizations played a truly important role in national politics throughout the twentieth century. Contemporaries often referred to them as the "Big Three," and this is the term that I will use here to designate the American Legion (initially open only to World War I veterans), the Veterans of Foreign Wars (VFW, created by veterans of the Spanish-American War and later open to all who served abroad), and the Disabled American Veterans (DAV, open to the war-disabled).[36]

As a political history of the veterans' movement in the midcentury, this study centers on these three organizations. With a combined membership of almost 5 million in 1946 (3.3 million for the Legion, 1.5 million for the VFW, and 105,000 for the DAV), they counted among the largest associations of any kind in the United States.[37] They also leaned clearly to the right of the political spectrum, defending a shared conservative and nationalist agenda. Of these three groups, the Legion was not only the largest and the most influential but also the one that kept the most extensive archival records, which is why its internal operations are a focal point of this book.[38] The detailed view afforded by its documents will help us understand the larger dynamics of veterans' politics.

One of the most important of these undercurrents was the relationship of the veterans' movement with the state. As with all other social movements, the nature of this connection changed over time, oscillating between antagonism and partnership depending on the circumstances. The link between veterans and state actors was particularly strong in the 1940s but less so in the following decade, for instance. Nevertheless, throughout the postwar years the leading veterans' organizations largely behaved as what one political scientist has called "parastates": private and voluntary groups that served as intermediaries between individual citizens and the state.[39] This is not to say that veterans never used confrontational tactics, but simply that these instances were more the exception than the norm in this period. More often than not, veterans' leaders collaborated so closely with policymakers at all levels of government that the line between the state and civil society essentially disappeared.

The examples of this phenomenon abound. Not only were the overwhelming majority of VA employees veterans themselves, but service officers of various veterans' groups played a key role in inspecting its facilities and in helping veterans file disability claims.[40] The interpenetration of the VA with the veterans' movement was such that the former issued a circular in the mid-1950s forbidding its personnel to hold offices in veterans' groups, lest this create "divided loyalty" and conflicts of interest.[41] Beyond this agency, individual states and local communities across the country often helped cover the expenses of veterans' groups (the state of Indiana provided $2.5 million for the erection of a new Legion headquarters in its capital after World War II, for instance).[42] Blurring the distinction between the public and the private even further, the most important veterans' groups received a charter from Congress, which among other privileges meant that the federal government was responsible for printing the proceedings of their annual conventions. Finally, the Big Three replicated the federalist structure of the U.S. state by organizing into three semiautonomous levels (national organization, state chapters, and local posts), which made them particularly adept at lobbying public actors. In all of these ways, the veterans' movement acted in symbiosis with the state.

As with any true synergy, the relationship went both ways, for former service members also did the bidding of the state. Veterans' groups enthusiastically offered their services to fulfill various missions essential to the war effort during World War II, for example: their rank-and-file served as aircraft warden observers, first-aid workers, and volunteer police or firemen.[43] This collaboration extended beyond wartime. From the 1940s to the mid-1960s, Legionnaires cooperated with the FBI in a campaign to fight espionage and sabotage.[44] These examples show that the growth of veterans' welfare state was not the result of private actors imposing their wishes on reluctant state officials, but of a mutually beneficial partnership. Accordingly, this study embraces neither a state- nor a society-centered narrative but offers instead a political history of the U.S. state in society.[45]

This perspective reflects the fact that veterans' welfare state left a significant mark on American society. Far from serving only to mitigate wartime handicaps, veterans' benefits also helped set this group apart from nonveterans in ways felt long after war's end. The economic opportunities offered by these programs could indeed translate into significant advantages: former service members of World War I enjoyed an edge in terms of income and occupation distribution over their civilian peers in the same age group as late as the mid-1950s, for instance.[46] Such effects varied over time, depending on the generosity of the benefits granted each cohort. While veterans of World War II and Korea earned more as a group than their civilian peers, for example, the opposite was true for those of the Vietnam War.[47] The situation has changed since then: today, former service members enjoy lower unemployment rates and higher individual incomes and education levels than their civilian counterparts.[48] This should not surprise us. After all, feminist scholars have long shown how the welfare state embodies certain ideological assumptions about how society should function and can thus serve not just to diminish but also to sharpen inequalities between different segments of the population.[49] Some cohorts of service members benefited from this mechanism more than others.

Veterans were hardly exceptional in their ability to shape public policy. Other groups such as big business or farmers have also been adept at creating their own niche within the state.[50] As with these groups, a major reason behind the success of the veterans' movement in the twentieth century had to do with its nonpartisan character. The Big Three steered clear of any firm association with either major party, both to avoid being drawn into partisan warfare and to be able to exert influence on whichever side was in power at any given time.[51] In this sense, the existence of veterans' welfare state points to the limits of the familiar narrative of modern U.S. history as a perennial fight between "small-government" conservatives and "big-government" liberals.[52] Rather than being championed primarily by one camp or the other, the growth of veterans' benefits was the product of a long campaign carried out by a specific group of the population in defense of its own interests. As we will see throughout this book, veterans' groups formed coalitions with both sides of the political spectrum at different times without ever tying their fate too closely to either one. The construction of veterans' welfare state followed a trajectory that resembled that of the "carceral state," the "racial state," the "warfare state," and "the straight state," which other historians have explored in depth: it was a project that cut across partisan divides, electoral time lines, and ideological fault lines.[53]

All these features of the veterans' movement—its defense of martial citizenship, its racial and gender boundaries, its existence on the local and the national levels, its interconnectedness with the state, and its nonpartisan character— remind us that the continued growth of veterans' benefits was the result not of some unchanging cultural tradition, but of specific and contingent factors. Put simply, this study seeks to replace myth with history.

An important step in that direction involves recognizing that the veterans' movement was not representative of all veterans, in the same way that labor unions have never represented all workers or feminist groups all women. This was true in several ways.

First and foremost, not all veterans were organized. A survey undertaken in the mid-1950s indicates that a majority of former service members (53 percent) never belonged to any veterans' group.[54] These numbers varied over time. The veterans' movement tended to be particularly strong in the immediate aftermath of a war, when the need for comradeship and support was most acute.[55] Membership lagged thereafter, with veterans' groups attracting a public more likely to be older, disabled, and less well-off economically.[56]

In addition to the gap between organized and unorganized veterans, there were tensions within veterans' groups themselves. Their leaders often claimed to speak on behalf of all members, but in practice they often clashed with the rank and file. This problem was hardly unique: the struggle of veterans' groups to reconcile grassroots pressure with the constraints imposed by the political system in which they operated was familiar to all large organizations. Such internecine conflicts testified only to the vitality and dynamism of the veterans' campaign.

Understanding who the veterans' movement represented and who it did not also entails taking into account matters of race and gender. We have already seen how these factors were essential to the construction of martial citizenship, and it is only logical that they helped define who could access the leading organizations of the veterans' movement as well. The Legion and the VFW generally prohibited black veterans from joining southern chapters, for instance, and even those who joined northern ones were often segregated and kept out of leadership positions.[57] Women were allowed in the Legion, but they were often forced to create their own posts and excluded from major responsibilities throughout this period (the VFW did not accept them as members until 1978).[58] Moreover, the diversity of the movement was not represented in its public discourse: official Legion and VFW publications virtually always showed former service members as white, male breadwinners, and women as child-rearing, domestic wives.[59] The veterans' movement in the mid-century was therefore largely a white men's movement.

It should not come as a surprise, then, that the separate welfare state built by this movement served not only to set veterans ahead of civilians but also to place white men ahead of other groups in American society. The example of the 1944 GI Bill is particularly illustrative here. This law relied primarily on local institutions, which had to approve applications before the benefits funded by the federal government could be granted. Given the pervasiveness of racism in midcentury U.S. society, a large number of African American veterans were unable to apply for government-guaranteed VA mortgages and thus to access homeownership. This had dramatic implications in the long run, for their children would inherit a smaller amount of capital than those of white veterans, thereby widening the divide between white and black family wealth in the United States.[60] Other kinds of benefits had a similar effect, as revealed by a test case against veterans' preference in civil service brought by feminist groups in the late 1970s. The case argued that this program gave men an undue preference over the other sex in public employment, since women were largely excluded from the military. The Supreme Court recognized the existence of discrimination but ruled against feminists on the ground that the prejudice was not intentional but simply a byproduct of the accidental fact that most veterans were men.[61] In doing so, the justices failed to recognize that the exclusion of certain groups from military service was instrumental in the growth of veterans' welfare state. Even though many of these benefits were nominally race- and gender-blind, they often amounted to what scholars have called an "affirmative action program" for white men.[62]

Martial citizenship was more than just a tool of exclusion, however. It helped both to buttress and to undermine the status quo. As a political scientist noted in 1945, "the emphasis on the unity and commonalty of veterans will tend to break down sex, race, nationality, and religious distinctions."[63] At the same time as certain categories of former service members experienced discrimination in their access to benefits and to the veterans' movement, some of their members were nevertheless able to use their status as veterans to ameliorate both their own condition and that of the group to which they belonged. For instance, the military experience of Mexican American veterans encouraged them to challenge the prejudices that they faced upon their return home. In time, those who could use their benefits took advantage of their improved social standing to become civic leaders in their own right, demanding equal status and opportunity both for themselves and for the larger Hispanic community.[64] The same was true for African American, Native American, and Asian American veterans, all of whom played an important role in the struggle of their own minority group for civil rights.[65] In this sense, the veterans' movement served to inspire and energize many other campaigns. Martial citizenship left a profound mark on U.S. history not only in terms of what it granted those who were able to claim it but also in terms of the aspirations for equal treatment that it unleashed among those to whom it was denied.

Understanding who the veterans' movement spoke for is one way of replacing myth with history. Another important step in that direction involves discerning the larger context in which the movement operated. Like all other social movements, the fate of the veterans' campaign was determined both by its own actions and by circumstances far beyond its control. This is not to say that its outcome was predetermined, but simply that we should avoid the common pitfall of attributing too much causal power to one's own object of study.[66] Former service members were not solely responsible for the growth of their benefits in the mid-twentieth century; they also benefited from an array of external factors.

One of them was fortuitous timing. The fact that World War II began only a little over twenty years after the close of the Great War meant that veterans of the latter still enjoyed considerable clout in national politics, which they could use on behalf of their younger counterparts. The same was true for veterans of the Korean War, who benefited from the influence of their elders from the Second World War. This chronological proximity stood in stark contrast with what had happened during World War I. By the time the United States had joined the fray in April 1917, most of the members of the major advocacy group for Union veterans of the Civil War (the Grand Army of the Republic) had already died of old age. Its decline gave free rein to critics of veterans' benefits, who in the absence of a counterweight were able to implement a much less generous system. In short, the fact that the mid-twentieth century witnessed several major wars in close succession to each other created uniquely favorable conditions for the veterans' movement by allowing new cohorts to rely on the political support of previous ones.

As important as the timing of the wars in which the United States took part in the mid-twentieth century was their location and outcome. The fact that hostilities always occurred outside its continental borders made it easier for veterans to claim that only they (and not civilians) had borne the burden of war and therefore deserved special treatment. This was a very different situation from many European or East Asian countries. In places like Germany or Japan where the civilian population suffered bitterly from warfare, former service members found it more difficult to claim that their experience set them apart from the rest of the population.[67] Moreover, the fact that the United States was a victor in both world wars meant that veterans of these conflicts enjoyed a degree of prestige that reinforced the legitimacy of their claims to special treatment (in contrast to veterans of the Vietnam War, a divisive conflict that ended in a humiliating U.S. defeat and whose veterans were often regarded as undeserving).[68] Finally, the advantageous economic position that the United States enjoyed at the end of both world wars meant that it could afford large outlays on veterans' programs, whereas other victors such as France or Great Britain emerged from these conflicts greatly weakened. In sum, the specific U.S. experience of warfare in the first half of the twentieth century helps explain why veterans' welfare state grew as much as it did.[69]

The peculiar structure of veterans' politics also played a role. For one thing, in the twentieth century former service members were present in virtually every community across the country. Rather than being a sectional interest—as they had been after the Civil War, when Union veterans were concentrated in the North and the West but largely absent from the South—veterans were now a truly national category, able to put pressure on all members of Congress. Former service members likewise benefited from the absence of a coherent countermovement, unlike other groups such as workers who always faced the determined resistance of business. This difference stemmed from the fact that public opinion was generally reluctant to support a full-scale attack on veterans' benefits, even though it was not always fully supportive of them either. As the *New Republic* noted sarcastically, few politicians wanted to run on an "anti-veteran" platform, for they were well aware that "next to voting against God and mother, voting against benefits for veterans comes closer than anything else to being a capital crime on Capitol Hill."[70] This does not mean that politicians never pushed back against veterans' programs, but simply that those who did so lacked a clear popular mandate, which is why the most outspoken attacks on veterans' welfare state described in this book came from unelected experts or interest groups like the First Hoover Commission or the American Medical Association. In sum, the veterans' movement benefited from an asymmetrical balance of power: its foes were hamstrung by a lack of public support while its members cared passionately about their own benefits.[71] This imbalance helps explain why the growth of veterans' welfare state could be temporarily halted or slowed but never fully stopped or rolled back.

Another structural advantage enjoyed by the veterans' movement in the mid-twentieth century had to do with the phenomenon that political scientists call path dependence—the idea that the past conditions the options available in the present.[72] Veterans' advocates were not creating a system from scratch in the 1940s and 1950s, but merely building upon a long-standing legacy. It is indeed hardly an exaggeration to say that the U.S. welfare state was born in military clothing: the first veterans' pensions dated back to the colonial period, when they served to entice recruitment into the militia. They were also among the first pieces of legislation introduced by the Continental Congress in 1776 as a way to support the war with Great Britain. Over time, benefits that were initially limited to monetary payments for war-disabled soldiers or for the relatives of those killed in combat were expanded not just to cover disabilities or deaths unrelated to service but also to take other forms—such as homes for the old and indigent, land grants, and burial assistance. At a time when most welfare programs were still run by state or city governments, veterans' benefits were the first to be administered at the federal level by entities such as the Pension Bureau (created in 1815), which reflected their privileged status.[73] This heritage greatly facilitated the task of veterans' advocates in the mid-twentieth century. Not only were they able to present the costly extension of benefits to new generations as simply a matter of fairness (why should new veterans be denied what their elders were granted?), but they could also rely on the support of preexisting state actors like the VA. In all these ways, the options available to the veterans' movement in the mid-century were shaped by a long history.

It would nonetheless be a mistake to see the story told in these pages as simply another chapter in a centuries-old process. The mid-twentieth century marked a major turning point, for it was during this period that martial citizenship was permanently embedded into public policy. Before then, Congress had granted benefits on an ad hoc and temporary basis, with each new cohort of veterans receiving a separate set of programs that were supposed to expire after the demise of its last member.[74] The World War I pension regime was legally and administratively distinct from that of the Civil War, for instance. A major step toward a less piecemeal and transient framework was taken in 1930 with the creation of a single federal agency with responsibility over the benefits of all veterans without distinction of generation (the VA), but its future remained in doubt until World War II, as we will see. It was likewise not before the midcentury that the structure of the legislative branch came to reflect the permanent separation between civilians' and veterans' programs, with the creation in 1946 of a single House Committee to centralize all legislation for the latter.[75] Though we now take such a division for granted, this book reminds us that it was neither evident nor uncontested and is not even very old.

The institutionalization of martial citizenship was part and parcel of a broader turn in the midcentury whereby "the shadow of war" came to loom ever larger in U.S. life.[76] War novels such as John Hersey's *A Bell for Adano* or Norman Mailer's *The Naked and the Dead* were among the most important works of literature produced in this period. Veterans were key figures in the film noir genre and a movie about their return to civilian life (*The Best Years of Our Lives*) won seven Academy Awards in 1947, including Best Picture.[77] They were everywhere in postwar politics as well: former service members accounted for nearly half of all U.S. senators and representatives that same year, in addition to five cabinet members, three Supreme Court justices, over half of all governors, and the president himself.[78] Their organizations enjoyed unrivaled prestige, as illustrated by a poll from the early 1950s showing that the general public trusted the American Legion more than labor unions, business associations, and churches.[79] Finally, war's shadow engulfed the U.S. economy, with one-half to two-thirds of federal spending allocated to national defense in the decade after 1953. The institutionalization of martial citizenship was thus only one aspect of the broader militarization of U.S. culture, politics, and economics.[80]

The confluence of all these factors—the timing, location, and outcome of American wars; the geographical dispersion of veterans and the asymmetrical nature of their politics; the long legacy of American state building; and the broader shadow of war in American life—created a perfect storm for the veterans' movement in the midcentury.

This window of opportunity was as favorable as it was brief. Just as the veterans' movement achieved some of its most significant victories, it helped unleash the forces that led to its own decline. Ironically, the omnipresence of former service members in postwar society was a mixed blessing for the movement, since in the long run it meant that policymakers were less inclined to buy into martial citizenship. For as many observers noted at the time, if the United States was indeed turning into "a nation of veterans," then who would be left to pay for their special benefits?

The structure of this book seeks to capture this sense of a constantly shifting terrain. While Part I follows the movement's rise to prominence from the interwar period to the late 1940s, Part II chronicles its partial eclipse beginning in the 1950s. The narrative ends in the early 1960s, with the veterans' movement no longer as central to U.S. politics as it once was but with the benefits it had pushed so hard for now firmly cemented into law. The following pages trace the roots of this paradox.

PART I

Ascent

CHAPTER I

Reform and Reaction

Veterans' Politics in the Interwar Years

The two decades between the end of the First World War and the beginning of the Second witnessed several major developments in veterans' politics. A new generation emerged with the return of millions of former "doughboys" (the nickname for members of the American Expeditionary Force in France) who superseded their elders from the Civil and Spanish-American Wars. Not only did they form their own organizations such as the American Legion and the Disabled American Veterans of the World War (DAVWW), but they also rejuvenated older ones such as the VFW. Together, these three groups would go on to dominate veterans' affairs for the rest of the century. This new cohort also took important steps toward the institutionalization of martial citizenship by centralizing the administration of all veterans' benefits into a single agency (the VA) and by obtaining the creation of a House committee responsible for all legislation covering World War I veterans. In this sense, the new cycle of the veterans' movement that began in 1917 further separated veterans' welfare programs from those available to the rest of the population.

The events that took place in the interwar period left a deep mark in collective memory as well. For many years thereafter, veterans' leaders would cite the example of the chaotic demobilization of 1918–19, during which ex-doughboys had to navigate a confusing maze of agencies to get help from the government, as a cautionary tale against efforts to dismantle the VA.[1] Likewise, the role played by President Herbert Hoover in the brutal expulsion of thousands of poor veterans from the federal capital in 1932 would not be easily forgotten: decades later, some Legionnaires drew on this example to call him "the greatest enemy of the ex-service man."[2] Last but not least, one of the primary goals of lawmakers when they began planning for the readjustment of World War II veterans was to pre-empt the passage of another expensive and divisive bonus bill similar to the one voted in 1924.[3]

Any attempt to understand the dynamics of veterans' politics at midcentury must therefore start with their roots in the World War I era. The story of this period can be boiled down to two words: reform and reaction. The impetus for reform came from Progressives, who sought to move away from a Civil War pension system that they saw as hopelessly corrupt by implementing new laws that would treat veterans on the same basis as the rest of the population, thereby breaking with the ideal of martial citizenship. Yet their approach was marred by its own blind spots and inadequate planning, which caused public opinion to turn against them. Veterans' groups used this opening to reaffirm themselves and dismantle the new approach brick by brick. Throughout the 1920s and 1930s, every attempt to bring veterans' programs into the fold of a general welfare structure was defeated. Not only were their benefits separated from those for civilians, but they also remained more generous (and costly) than virtually anywhere else in the world. By the time of Pearl Harbor, reaction had triumphed over reform.

This is not to say that the pendulum simply swung back to its starting position. The veterans' movement pushed back against some Progressive innovations, but not all. The foremost example of this was the introduction of medical benefits, which evolved into a separate hospital system. This program embodied Progressives' belief in the power of modern medicine, which they imagined would be able to "cure" veterans of their disabilities once and for all and thus put an end to their need for public assistance. It proved a quixotic hope. As former service members took advantage of the free health care now available to them, more and more began to demand access to these new hospitals, challenging the view of medical experts as to whether their disabilities required treatment. The result was exactly the opposite of what Progressives had envisioned: instead of a temporary benefit meant to help former service members rapidly readjust to civilian life, hospitals became a permanent and sizable addition to veterans' welfare state.

Aside from responding to Progressive reforms, the veterans' movement also introduced its own. One of the major changes to veterans' policy in the interwar years was indeed the recognition that the state should help not just disabled veterans (as had been the case previously) but also able-bodied ones. Veterans' leaders fought for this idea to be implemented into law through their long campaign for the Bonus, a lump sum that the government would pay them to compensate for the difference between the low wartime wages earned by enlisted personnel and those of defense workers on the home front. The debate took place not just between veterans and their critics but also within the veterans' movement itself, which was divided between a moderate and a populist wing represented respectively by the Legion and the VFW. By 1936, veterans had managed to convince lawmakers that military service itself amounted to a social disability and therefore that all former service members needed assistance.[4]

These developments demonstrated the resilience and dynamism of the veterans' movement. Learning from the experience of their Civil War elders, the leaders of this new cycle were careful to remain nonpartisan. By coordinating grassroots activities with expert guidance at the national level, they wielded pressure effectively on both major parties. Their repertoire of collective action was also remarkably extensive: when traditional lobbying failed to achieve immediate payment of the Bonus, rank-and-file veterans spontaneously engaged in massive street protests, demonstrating that their movement could take a more confrontational approach. This flexibility explains why their benefits grew throughout the interwar period regardless of which party was in power.

As its purview expanded, martial citizenship remained tied to white manhood. Many veterans' programs created during the Great War, such as family allotments, were premised on a maternalistic view of gender roles in which recipients were seen as primarily male breadwinners with child-rearing housewives.[5] The letter of the law never explicitly excluded racial minorities from access, but in practice they were often victims of racist discrimination by the officials in charge of implementing benefits on the local level. This was the case with disabled African American veterans throughout the South, who complained of being given low disability ratings by white doctors or of being directed toward jobs below their qualifications by white rehabilitation officers. Their campaign to achieve equal treatment would be one of the rallying points of the new generation of civil rights groups that emerged at the turn of the twentieth century.[6] The main organizations of the veterans' movement were of little help in this regard, however. To the contrary, the Big Three largely subscribed to the ideals of white supremacy and female domesticity that pervaded American culture in these years.

Still, the possibilities for change seemed boundless as the United States geared up to join the First World War. To understand the enduring legacy of this conflict on veterans' affairs, we need to recapture the background against which it took shape.

The Road to Progressive Reform

On the eve of World War I, the range of policies available to U.S. veterans was remarkably extensive. At the federal level, Union veterans who had been honorably discharged with more than ninety days of service were entitled to a pension after the age of sixty-two, as were the survivors—widows, orphans, or dependent parents—of those who had died. The requirement that the disability or death be connected to service had been abolished in 1890, which is why people often called such payments a "service pension," in the sense that they depended only on military service. Approximately thirty thousand veterans were also living in one of the eleven branches of the National Home for Disabled Volunteer Soldiers and Sailors, an institution created after the Civil War to provide shelter for the elderly poor.[7] Moreover, preferential hiring and retaining policies in place since 1865 meant that more than 10 percent of federal civil service employees were disabled veterans or their survivors.[8] Finally, former service members who sought to settle on public land enjoyed preferential treatment in applying under the Homestead Act.[9]

Administering these benefits was not a minor task. Monetary payments for Union veterans were managed by six thousand clerks at the Bureau of Pensions, which made it one of the largest agencies in the federal government and—according to its commissioner—"the largest executive bureau in the world"[10] (Fig. 1). It was an expensive mission: from 1865 to 1915, the total cost of veterans' pensions at the federal level reached $5 billion, more than was spent on the Civil War itself.[11]

Veterans' welfare state extended beyond the federal level. Confederate veterans were barred from such benefits, but they had access to similar ones provided by their local community and state of residence. For instance, one-fifth of Mississippi's revenues in 1866 was spent on artificial limbs for returning soldiers.[12] Throughout the North and the South, most states exempted veterans from poll taxes, provided them with special relief funds, and paid for the burial of those in need.[13]

This separate welfare state for military veterans had no equivalent abroad. At the same time as the United States was developing a wide range of social policies for former service members, western European nations like Germany and Great Britain were implementing workers' compensation and old-age pension programs open to most wage earners. Though these benefits theoretically targeted a much larger group, U.S. veterans' programs were made so liberal in practice that they came to overshadow more broad-based European safety nets. By 1910, veterans' pensions cost the U.S. federal government nearly $160 million per year and covered almost 30 percent of men aged sixty-five or older.[14] Social

Figure 1. The towering silhouette of the Bureau of Pensions in Washington, D.C., ca. 1925. From Keystone View Company, *United States Pension Office, Washington, D.C.* Washington D.C., ca. 1925 (Meadville, Pa.: Keystone View Co.), Library of Congress Prints and Photographs Division.

insurance experts recognized that U.S. veterans' pensions were much larger than the British pension system in terms of size and cost, for instance.[15] The same applied to other kinds of benefits: though civil service preference also existed for veterans in countries like France, Germany, and Great Britain, its terms were more generous in the United States.[16]

There was no question that the range of benefits available to U.S. military veterans on the eve of the First World War was uniquely large. Observers disagreed as to whether this model should be emulated or repudiated, however. As the country prepared to send a new generation of soldiers to fight in Europe, this old debate assumed new urgency.

The members of the Progressive movement led by President Woodrow Wilson were largely of one mind on the question. They were convinced that the country had to move in a new direction. Veterans' pension reform was one of the many issues that had helped bring these reformers together back in the 1880s, when a small group of elite reformers called "Mugwumps" first coalesced around the progressive wing of the Republican Party. They found common cause in the condemnation of Civil War pensions, whose size and cost were ballooning at that same time.[17] Reflecting their largely middle- and upper-class background, many Progressives feared that such benefits would encourage idleness and dependence among poor veterans instead of encouraging productive and "manly" work habits.[18] This campaign also echoed their larger fight on behalf of expertise and against patronage. In a book published in 1912, for instance, the journalist and descendant of two presidents Charles Francis Adams, Jr., accused the Bureau of Pensions of being a tool of the Republican machine, distributing federal monies in return for votes instead of carefully evaluating the worthiness of applicants. The title said it all: *The Civil War Pension Lack-of-System: A Four-Thousand-Million Dollar Record of Legislative Incompetence Tending to General Political Corruption.*

Such indignation achieved little prior to the outbreak of the war in Europe. As William Henry Glasson noted in his landmark 1918 study, criticism of the pension system found little purchase beyond a small coterie of like-minded experts, as the general public continued to display "a feeling of genuine gratitude towards the men who fought to preserve the Union."[19] Even within the halls of power, Progressives' technical exposés were no match for the political firepower of veterans' groups, the most prominent of which was the Grand Army of the Republic (GAR). This organization of Union veterans defended their pensions as the repayment of a "sacred debt" incurred by the government, a "mortgage written in blood," and they rejected Progressives' accusations of a "raid upon the Treasury."[20] Not only did the GAR enjoy a close working relationship with the Bureau of Pensions, but it also had the ear of Congress, whose members were careful not to antagonize the powerful voting group it represented. Legislative subservience helps explain the rapid growth of the system, which accounted for nearly one million recipients and over 40 percent of the federal budget in the 1890s.[21] Costs began to decline only in the mid-1910s, not as the result of Progressives' efforts but rather of the mounting death rate among Civil War veterans.

With this cohort becoming increasingly irrelevant in national politics, prospects for a wholesale reform improved. After the United States declared war in

1917, Wilson formed a working group to design new programs for the future veterans of this conflict. The result was the War Risk Insurance Act, signed into law a few months after the United States entered the fray. This piece of legislation offered a radical revision of the principles that had formed the backbone of veterans' welfare state for over a century. It created four new benefits: compulsory allotments for the families of service personnel, compensation for service-connected death and disability, medical and rehabilitation services for the war disabled, and subsidized life insurance. In an attempt to wrest control from a Bureau of Pensions seen as being under the thumb of veterans' groups, the law vested control of these programs in three other agencies. The most important of them was the Bureau of War Risk Insurance, established in 1914 to help insure maritime trade in wartime. In addition, the Federal Board of Vocational Education was put in charge of the rehabilitation of disabled veterans and the Public Health Service administered hospitals and medical care. The programs for World War I veterans were therefore legally and administratively separated from those of their elders.

To better understand the ideas behind this Progressive reform, let us take a closer look at some of these programs.

Driven by a firm belief in scientific progress, the new system of medical benefits was part of a larger agenda of rehabilitation, an umbrella term for what one historian has called an "integrated program of physical and social reform combining orthopedics, vocational training, psychological counseling, and industrial discipline" whose goal was "to help disabled veterans reintegrate into postwar society as productive citizens." Convinced as they were that veterans had a duty to become normal civilians again as fast as possible, Progressives saw medical treatment as a way to "cure" war-related disabilities and thus to return veterans to a position where they could be socially and economically useful without relying on pensions. In other words, these benefits promised to "remasculinize" veterans by cutting them off from what was seen as a feminizing dependency on the government. Not incidentally, this scheme also had the advantage of preempting long-running and costly pension outlays.[22]

Life insurance was likewise a way to shift the responsibility for the readjustment process away from the government and toward the injured parties. By having soldiers contribute to a government-subsidized insurance scheme in wartime, Progressives sought to ensure that assistance would not be extended later to those disabled or killed by injuries unrelated to service. They wanted to supersede the old Civil War system: as Congressman Sam Rayburn of Texas argued, "after this war is over, another saturnalia of pension frauds and pension claims will be put up to this Congress" unless the new insurance program was passed.[23] Secretary of the Treasury William McAdoo agreed, seeing the bill as a check against "any future attempts at service-pension legislation."[24] As an extension of a similar program already available to merchant seamen, life insurance was of a piece with Progressives' larger effort to deny veterans special status.

The same desire inspired compensation reform. The idea that the state should provide payments to former service members injured in the line of duty, or to their survivors in case of death, was nothing new. But the choice of a new terminology to designate these payments—"compensation" instead of "pension"—was not random. It was a deliberate attempt to avoid the stigma associated with the latter term (pensions were typically understood as gratuities) and instead to categorize such benefits as an indemnity for loss. By requiring not only medical proof that the disability was connected to service but also that the claim be filed within five years of discharge, the system was designed to limit eligibility as much as possible.[25] Progressives drew inspiration from workmen's compensation laws, then in force in some thirty-six states. Pushing back against martial citizenship, they sought to treat service members as merely another category of workers, one whose employer was the United States and whose industry was simply "extra hazardous."[26]

In a nutshell, the War Risk Insurance Act of 1917 aimed to replace a system associated with corruption, patronage, and runaway spending with one that would be scientific, nonpartisan, and self-liquidating. It sought to diminish the importance of monetary transactions by substituting in-kind services such as medical care, which were presumably harder to abuse. In its effort to achieve economy and efficiency in government through the use of supposedly neutral expert knowledge, the law was a typically Progressive endeavor. Most importantly, it was an effort to implement a new vision of veterans' policy in which former service members were on a par with the rest of the population. It was aimed at undermining martial citizenship and reasserting the ideology of breadwinner liberalism.

The New Cycle of the Veterans' Movement

One reason why this law was able to pass Congress was the disarray in which the veterans' movement found itself. When the Great War broke out in Europe, the GAR was but a shadow of its former self, down from its peak of over 400,000 members to only 170,000.[27] Veterans of the Spanish-American and the

Philippine-American Wars merged into the VFW in 1914, but the new group had only a little over 5,000 members at first.[28] None of the hundreds of smaller organizations that existed played a significant role on the national stage. As the war effort got under way, former service members did not have a voice in the debate about which benefits their future counterparts would receive.

Only a year and a half after the passage of the law that directly affected them did members of the American Expeditionary Force begin to organize in earnest. A few months after the end of the war in November 1918, the 2 million soldiers still present in France started forming their own groups such as the left-wing Private Soldiers and Sailors Legion of the U.S.A. and the more moderate Comrades in Service (the latter had the blessing of President Wilson and General John Pershing).[29] These organizations responded to a growing discontent. Rank-and-file doughboys stationed overseas became more and more impatient as days and then months went by after the armistice, demanding an end to the grueling military discipline and to return home as quickly as possible. They were in the midst of a volatile postwar situation, with revolutionary fever sweeping Europe and an influenza epidemic causing the death of millions. Morale in the American Expeditionary Force was low and radical ideas on the rise.

Planning for the American Legion got under way in January 1919 to quash this mounting unrest and to answer the more mundane search for comradeship among former service members. The man who best captured the early spirit of the group was Theodore Roosevelt, Jr. With a high forehead, a wide and narrow grin, and a typical elite education at Groton and Harvard, Roosevelt inherited from his father, the twenty-sixth president, a thoroughly WASP sense of noblesse oblige and a fascination with war as one of the highest occupations of manhood. He was also an Anglophile who played a leading role in the prewar military preparedness movement: the inspiration for the name "American Legion" came from an eponymous group that he had helped create in 1915 to assist the government in finding volunteers with useful military skills. For Roosevelt, the war offered an opportunity to escape the drudgery of everyday life and to match the heroic deeds of the Civil War generation. He shared with many other leaders of the American Expeditionary Force the sense that their time in Europe had been a great odyssey, whose memory they wanted to keep alive. Like many other Legion founders such as Hamilton Fish, Eric Fisher Wood, George A. White, and William "Wild Bill" Donovan, Roosevelt had a deep aversion to radical ideas, belonged to the northeastern Republican establishment, and enjoyed deep connections with the business community. All of these factors contributed to the Legion's success.[30]

Indeed, the group rose to national prominence remarkably rapidly. After an initial meeting of twenty officers handpicked by Roosevelt in February 1919, the process gradually picked up speed. An initial caucus the following month at the cirque Métropole in Paris set up the basic administrative machinery, while Roosevelt rushed back to the United States to prepare the first stateside meeting in St. Louis in May. Over the following months, the focus shifted to recruiting as many enlisted personnel and officers as possible and to securing support and funds from the business community, the press, and politicians. In a country where anticommunist fever was running high, Legion leaders presented their group as "the greatest bulwark against Bolshevism and anarchy."[31] In their view, white male veterans were the first defenders of "American institutions" against the threat of radicalism.[32] The pitch worked: a year after its first national convention in November 1919, the Legion already boasted a chapter in nearly every county as well as 850,000 members (one-fifth of the eligible population), which made it the largest veterans' group in U.S. history.[33]

The GAR acted as a foil for this new organization. Aware that the Civil War group's close association with the Republican Party had helped taint the pension system, Legion leaders inserted a clause in their constitution forbidding members to officially endorse a political candidate, so as to avoid any accusation of partisanship. They were also very careful not to be seen as a strictly northern group. Though most Legion founders came from the Republican establishment, they included in their ranks several figures from the southern wing of the Democratic Party, such as Bennett Champ Clark of Missouri. They also invited representatives of the Confederate War Veterans to their own events throughout the 1920s.[34] The goal was to establish the Legion as the voice of *all* veterans of the Great War, not just one section of them.

In this effort, Legionnaires faced competition from a range of other veterans' groups. The VFW experienced rapid growth after 1918, with its membership reaching nearly seventy thousand ten years later.[35] Contrary to the Legion, this organization was not limited to veterans of the Great War, though it accepted only those who had served abroad. Overall, VFW members tended to have a more working-class background and the politics of their group to be more populist.[36] The other major veterans' association was the DAVWW, created in 1920 by decorated World War I veteran Robert Marx. Open only to the war-disabled, its membership grew to over forty thousand by 1924. The group focused on issues most relevant to its followers, such as hospitals and vocational training.[37] Each of these three groups had its own constituency whose interests did not always coincide with those of the others, as we will see.

Nevertheless, they also shared similar features. Beyond veterans' affairs, their politics were aligned: they all advocated for the same conservative brand of nationalism and their membership often overlapped. All three also adopted a military-like uniform for official business as a way to stress their distinction from civilians. Not unlike fraternal orders such as the Elks or the Odd Fellows, their meetings involved the performance of carefully scripted rituals for events such as the initiation of new members or funeral services. Moreover, they all had their own women's auxiliary group for female relatives. With two hundred thousand members in 1925, the Legion Auxiliary not only focused on charitable and community work—activities traditionally seen as female—but often played an outsize role in many Legion lobbying campaigns.[38] In this sense, the Big Three continued the tradition of the GAR by acting as both fraternal orders and political pressure groups.

Another feature of the GAR that these organizations shared was its discriminatory attitude toward racial minorities. Not unlike their predecessor, they tended to either exclude black veterans outright or to treat them as second-class members barred from leadership positions.[39] They also refused to advocate for the specific needs of this minority group, remaining largely silent about the violence and discrimination that many African American veterans and their relatives faced.[40] While white veterans had access to medical care, their black counterparts often received inferior treatment if not outright neglect. Only after a prolonged struggle did they manage to open an all-black veterans' hospital in Tuskegee, Alabama (against the opposition of local Legionnaires).[41] The Big Three mostly ignored these problems. The official publications of the Legion tended to portray all World War I veterans as white men and they provided little information about its 3,500 black members. When black characters appeared in the short stories carried by the group's national magazine, it was only "as clowns" or "minstrels in olive drab."[42] Whiteness remained a crucial pillar of the veterans' movement in the interwar years.

The Legion, the VFW, and the DAVWW shared the same dismissive attitude toward women. Contrary to what took place abroad, in the United States women veterans were routinely overlooked and discriminated against (German veterans' groups accepted women and war victims as equals, for instance, while in Great Britain widows often played a more prominent role than veterans in war commemorations).[43] The foremost example of this was the treatment of the 223 women known as "Hello Girls" who worked in the vital and dangerous role of telephone operators for the U.S. military in France. Once the war was over, they were denied veteran status on the ground that they had only been hired as civilian contractors and not active-duty personnel, even though this was never made clear to them at the time.[44] In the context of a postwar backlash against the advances achieved by women in wartime, the claims of the "Hello Girls" went ignored by everyone, including the veterans' movement. Though the Legion and the VFW were open to women in the interwar period, the latter never enjoyed more than a subordinate role.[45] As the Legion's official historian wrote decades later, the character of the group remained "definitely male. Its sprinkling of nurses and yeomanettes and its large Auxiliary of wives, mothers and daughters gave it a feminine touch and added much to its good work, but The Legion was decidedly He-man."[46]

Yet another feature of the GAR that the three leading organizations of the veterans' movement perpetuated in the interwar years was its federalist structure. In the Legion as well as in the VFW and in the DAVWW, local posts were organized into state chapters (known as "departments") which were themselves under the leadership of the national organization.[47] This framework meant that they could exert influence on all three levels of the government at the same time, making them particularly efficient at lobbying. It also meant that power was supposed to flow from the bottom up in a democratic manner: once passed by local posts and approved by their department, official resolutions could be voted upon at the annual national convention and become official policy. In practice, the system was more hierarchical. Not only were individual Legionnaires prohibited from publicly disagreeing with the organization's official positions, for instance, but their national leadership was also relatively insulated from grassroots pressure. The national commander was supposed to be elected every year by the membership, but in reality he was often handpicked by a small number of Legion notables dubbed the "kingmakers." Outside of conventions, the group's daily business was managed by the National Executive Committee, which met three or four times a year in Indianapolis along with a dozen more specialized committees (such as those on Americanism or rehabilitation) whose staff formed a kind of permanent bureaucracy that could act more or less independently. Still, the nature of the Legion and of the Big Three more broadly as mass-based, voluntary groups that were heavily reliant on dues meant that their leaders could never stray too far away from the consensus, lest their members simply vote with their feet and leave.[48]

The majority of veterans interacted with their movement through social activities at the local level. Legionnaires participated in a wide range of youth projects (such as Junior Baseball and Boys' State) as well as programs for the wider community (like disaster relief and vaccination work). These activities varied from place to place: in Illinois for instance, the Legion helped bail veterans out of jail and provided firing squads at funerals.[49] The VFW operated similarly, with its Department of Athletics and Recreation sponsoring softball and marble tournaments.[50] Not all of these activities were of a purely civic nature: some Legion posts took it upon themselves to censor public speakers deemed too radical or to sponsor manuals that put forward a conservative view of U.S. history (the group even published its own history textbook).[51] The appeal of joining a post could also be more self-interested: these centers of social life played a role similar to that of a political machine in many small towns, providing members with access to some of the most prominent community members.[52] The local life of the veterans' movement was thus remarkably autonomous from its national incarnation, a sign of its vitality and deep roots.[53]

There was another way in which the local level played a key role in the veterans' movement. The hundreds of service officers who worked for the Legion, the VFW, and the DAVWW rendered essential services. Their mission was not only to patrol veterans' hospitals and to report any complaints by patients but also to help individuals navigate the system. Empowered to act as veterans' attorneys, these officers were allowed to assist (pro bono) those who wanted to file a disability claim. In the Legion, their activity was managed by the group's National Rehabilitation Committee, whose chairman had a direct phone line to the VA director. The fact that this agency was itself largely a veterans' institution helped make the relationship amicable (by the early 1930s, former service members accounted for two-thirds of its personnel). As one renowned political scientist put it, such "administrative" lobbying may not have been as high profile as its "legislative" counterpart, but it was no less important.[54] This phenomenon demonstrated the lack of any clear boundary between the veterans' movement and the state.

For all that these three groups had in common, there was no denying that the Legion was the most influential. With between ten thousand and twelve thousand local posts throughout the interwar period, it was present in nearly every community across the land and could therefore exert direct influence over most of the nation's representatives in Congress. Though its leaders liked to claim that their group was "a representative cross-section of the population," in reality it was composed largely of white men who worked as small businessmen, professionals, and civil servants—middle-class people with the time and resources to get involved in civic activities. Nowhere was the Legion more influential than in small towns and rural areas. Its center of gravity was in the Northeast and the Midwest, where its three largest departments (New York, Illinois, and Pennsylvania) were located along with its national headquarters (in Indianapolis). The group was weakest in the solidly Democratic South because of its association with the Republican establishment and its exclusion of African

Americans. Overall, its membership fluctuated from a low of 610,000 in 1925 to a high of 1.1 million in 1941, which meant that it represented between 15 and 25 percent of all doughboys.[55] With these numbers, the Legion was a key player not only in veterans' affairs but also in national politics.

No one embodied the power of the new cycle of the veterans' movement better than John Thomas Taylor, the Legion's chief lobbyist in Washington. Involved in the group since its first Paris caucus, Taylor belonged like so many of its leaders to the northeastern wing of the Republican Party. On the cover of *Time* magazine in 1935, he was described as a teetotaler and lover of lobster New-burg who could be seen around the federal capital wearing spats, a snap-brim hat, and a walking stick. With a "stentorian" voice and "steely grey" hair, Taylor was a decorated veteran who had a talent for self-publicity and enjoyed "the biggest reputation of any lobbyist in Washington." His status as the "high priest" of the veterans' lobby stemmed from his thorough knowledge of the legislative process: members of Congress who forgot their own voting record often called him for help. In addition to detailed committee testimonies and the shrewd use of the-atrics, Taylor's signature strategy was to coordinate a "barrage" of petitions and letters from the rank and file to overcome any obstacle. Congress members who blocked passage of an important piece of legislation would sometimes receive over 350,000 telegrams overnight.[56] In an age where interest groups of all kinds were becoming increasingly entrenched in the policy-making process, Taylor and the Legion were among the most important representatives of what some commentators called an "invisible government."[57]

As the new cycle of the veterans' movement was taking shape, more and more doughboys faced the challenge of readjusting to civilian society after their discharge. In the process, they came into contact with the policies introduced by the War Risk Insurance Act for the first time. The chaotic situation that resulted shed an unforgiving light on the Progressive vision for reform, and it paved the way for veterans to reassert their power.

The Unraveling of the Progressive Vision

An average veteran returning home in 1918 or 1919 faced an array of difficul-ties. To begin with, the demobilization process felt excruciatingly slow to the many doughboys who did not want to remain on European soil any longer than necessary. Upon their return home, able-bodied personnel were discharged and summarily sent home with nothing but their uniforms, shoes, coats, sixty dollars, and the cost of a train ticket.[58] Those who tried to get a job faced a labor market already glutted with the millions of defense workers and civil servants who had been dismissed at war's end. The situation grew even worse when the country slipped into a severe recession a few months after the armistice, throwing more than three million Americans and two-fifths of all veterans into unemployment. So many former service members resorted to panhandling that cities issued ordnances restricting the practice.[59] Even the disabled had a hard time obtaining assistance, for federal agencies were overwhelmed by the sudden influx of claimants.

All these problems shared the same root cause. As one historian noted in hindsight, "if 1917 caught us unprepared for war, 1919 surprised us just as unready for peace."[60] Like other Allied powers, the United States had expected Germany and Austria-Hungary to keep fighting for at least another year. Their abrupt collapse in the fall of 1918 forced the country to face the challenge of demobilization with very little preparation. This caused major challenges in several areas, but perhaps nowhere so acutely as in veterans' affairs.[61] Having barely begun to implement the new policies of the War Risk Insurance Act of 1917, the three agencies in charge of its administration now had to deal with the impending return of over 4.5 million service members. The magnitude of the task facing the Bureau of War Risk Insurance was particularly daunting: on their own, the life insurance policies on its books in April 1918 were worth half of the total amount of insurance carried by private U.S. companies.[62] The agency now had to transform this system into one based on voluntary payments as opposed to automatic deductions, while at the same time handling the return of service members, evaluating their disability claims, and making arrangements for medical treatment and rehabilitation— areas in which it had no prior experience and shared responsibility with two other agencies. The abrupt end of the war also meant that not enough hospitals were ready to treat disabled veterans, resulting in a massive application backlog.[63] The initial goal of not allowing military hospitals to discharge patients until they had been entirely "cured" of their disabilities proved unrealistic, as many veterans chafed under strict military discipline and demanded to be released as quickly as possible.[64] The situation only grew more difficult over time.

In these conditions, the Progressive vision of a new system of veterans' benefits premised on the assumption that former service members were not a special group quickly unraveled. These chaotic conditions were a godsend for veterans' groups. The obvious shortcomings of existing policy gave them the chance not only to reassert martial citizenship but also to rally new members to their cause. The failure of government policy was as much, if not more, responsible for the resurgence of the veterans' movement after World War I than anything that the movement itself did.

Its leaders moved quickly to demand change. Their first priority was to increase the maximum monthly disability payment from a paltry thirty dollars to eighty dollars. They reached this goal with a dramatic strategy that would prove effective for many years to come: in 1919, Taylor had the idea of bringing disabled veterans from Walter Reed Hospital to a congressional hearing, using their physical presence and their dramatic stories of mistreatment to compel lawmakers to act.[65] Over the next couple of years, veterans' groups became involved in the campaign to consolidate the administrative structure of veterans' health care and to obtain the construction of new hospitals. While the need for both was widely recognized, there was no agreement on the form that this consolidation should take. Holding on to the Progressive vision, some Republicans pushed for a unified Department of Public Welfare that brought all of the federal government's social programs under the same roof, but the project was doomed by infighting.[66]

This paved the way for the veterans' movement to advance its own alternative. In December 1920, Legionnaire and Republican representative from Massachusetts John Jacob Rogers introduced the first bill to consolidate the three agencies responsible for World War I veterans' benefits into one. This proposal appealed to newly elected president Warren Harding, who had campaigned on a promise to streamline the federal bureaucracy. The next year, he acquiesced to the Legion's request by signing a law creating the Veterans' Bureau (VB), which replaced the Bureau of War Risk Insurance and assumed responsibility for the veteran-related functions of the Federal Board of Vocational Education and the Public Health Service.[67] Great War veterans now had their own separate federal agency, a symbol of their special status that gave them a direct avenue to make claims on the state. The VB immediately assumed gargantuan proportions: in its first year, it spent over $480 million, employed a staff of nearly thirty thousand, and administered over 1.4 million medical examinations in nearly 180 hospitals.[68]

The Progressive vision had not yet disappeared, however. The benefits for World War I veterans remained legally and administratively distinct from those for veterans of earlier wars, which were still under the responsibility of the Bureau of Pensions and the National Home for Disabled Volunteer Soldiers. Moreover, most observers still assumed that the VB would eventually disappear as more and more veterans returned to civilian status.[69]

The exact opposite happened. Under the aggressive leadership of its first director, Charles Forbes, the VB expanded rapidly—so rapidly, in fact, that

Forbes made powerful enemies and eventually landed in prison due to allegations of corruption. He nonetheless managed to secure the agency's future. Within a year of its creation, the VB was managing its own hospitals instead of merely overseeing the care of its beneficiaries in public or private institutions. An entity initially created with the goal of supervising the care of veterans in government hospitals transformed into one with authority over its own veterans' hospital program.[70] This was yet another rollback of the Progressive vision.

The veterans' movement won several more legislative victories that helped reassert martial citizenship. The same law that created the VB also established a presumption of service connection for tuberculosis and neuropsychiatric cases, for instance. World War I veterans no longer had to prove that these impairments had been incurred or aggravated during the conflict, which marked the first breach in the dam established by the War Risk Insurance Act of 1917 to limit future disability claims. In 1924, two landmark pieces of legislation passed that advanced the movement's agenda even further. The first was the World War Adjusted Compensation Act, discussed later in this chapter. The second was the World War Veterans' Act, which not only extended the presumption of service connection to other disabilities but also allowed veterans with non-service-connected conditions to access veterans' hospitals. Though the latter measure attracted little attention at the time, it would have momentous consequences.

That same year, the House of Representatives fulfilled one of the chief goals of the veterans' movement when it created a committee dedicated solely to World War I veterans' issues. By removing veterans' bills from the purview of other committees where they were not necessarily a priority, the creation of this new entity served to speed up their passage. The makeup of the committee on World War Veterans' Legislation provided yet another example of the interpenetration of the veterans' movement and the state: its first chair, Royal Johnson, was a member of both the Legion and the VFW and over half of its twenty-one first members were veterans.[71] This committee represented one more step toward the separation of veterans' benefits from those of civilians.

The 1924 reforms paved the way for the dramatic expansion of veterans' welfare state. Over the next eight years, its cost rose from $650 million to over $830 million, or more than four-fifths of all federal spending on social welfare.[72] The number of veterans in hospitals increased rapidly as well, from almost 25,000 in 1924 to 43,500 in 1932 (of whom almost two-thirds were treated for non-service-connected causes).[73] This growth was reinforced by the passage of a service pension for all permanently disabled veterans of World War I in 1930. Two years later, the number of veterans receiving disability payments had gone from

840,000 to nearly 1.3 million.[74] On a symbolic level, this piece of legislation represented the failure of Progressive efforts to prevent the return of monetary payments based only on military service.

One of the lawmakers instrumental in its passage was John E. Rankin.[75] A World War I veteran and lawyer, Rankin was a "little man with bushy hair and a Hallelujah voice" who was elected to the House of Representatives as a Democrat from Mississippi in 1921.[76] He became the chairman of the Committee on World War Veterans' Legislation ten years later and remained in this position until his defeat in a primary in 1952. Notorious for his rants against Jews, immigrants, and African Americans, Rankin was both a demagogue and one of the House's "ablest parliamentarians."[77] Like many other southern Democrats, he embraced a populist worldview that combined economic progressivism (he coauthored the bill to create the Tennessee Valley Authority) with white supremacy and anti-communism. In this sense, he shared much of the agenda of the veterans' movement, of which he was a key ally. Not only was he on a first-name basis with John Taylor, but he also applauded the Legion's "gallant fight" against left-wing ideas in the interwar period.[78]

In addition to witnessing the passage of a service pension, 1930 was also the year when President Herbert Hoover backed a proposal to merge all veterans' agencies as a way to cut costs and improve efficiency. This resulted in the creation of the VA, which brought together the VB, the Bureau of Pensions, and the National Home for Disabled Volunteer Soldiers. Its director was Frank T. Hines, who had taken charge of the VB after the downfall of Forbes in 1923. Accounting for one-fifth of the federal budget and one-third of federal employees, the new agency was "one of the most important ones in the whole Government," according to Hoover himself.[79] The creation of the VA removed the administrative separation introduced by Progressives between programs for World War I veterans and those for earlier generations. For the first time in U.S. history, all benefits for former service members were under the same roof and clearly separated from social policies for the rest of the population.

By 1932, the programs under Hines' responsibility not only constituted the most important pillar of the U.S. welfare state but they were also among the most generous in the world. While many other former belligerents of the Great War devoted substantial resources to the welfare of their veterans, none of them came even close to matching the cost of U.S. programs.[80] That year, the federal government spent almost as much on veterans' welfare as Great Britain, France, Germany, Italy, and Canada combined.[81] This was all the more remarkable given that the United States had suffered fewer casualties and mobilized fewer soldiers:

"only" 234,000 out of 4.7 million, whereas for instance France had suffered 6.2 million casualties out of an army of 8.4 million. One reason for this spending gap was the more advantageous economic situation of the United States. The fact that it granted benefits even to veterans with disabilities not directly connected to service also played a role. A few countries adopted the same approach, but none went as far.[82]

This is not to say that this issue was not controversial at home. In fact, the interwar period witnessed repeated attempts to limit the growth of U.S. veterans' benefits. These efforts were typically led by the White House, for the more porous institutional structure of the legislative branch made Congress less likely to resist the pressure wielded by mass-based, federalist groups like the Legion or the VFW. From Woodrow Wilson to Franklin Roosevelt, the executive branch pushed back against attempts to extend benefits to veterans with non-service-connected disabilities, on the ground that former service members should not constitute a separate category of the population. In 1923 for instance, president Calvin Coolidge argued that the federal government had no special obligations toward those veterans not disabled in service, since "the fit and able-bodied veterans are offered the opportunities open to every other citizen."[83]

Criticism of veterans' benefits came from other corners of American society as well. Liberal journals like the *New Republic* condemned Legionnaires as "professional patriots," nationalist fanatics who were doing the bidding of big business by engaging in violent actions against pacifists and trade unions.[84] The American Civil Liberties Union called the Legion "the most active agency in intolerance and repression in the United States today," for example.[85] Critics from the right focused on the cost of veterans' benefits, especially after the outbreak of the Great Depression in 1929. With federal revenue rapidly drying up, veterans' programs (the single biggest item of federal spending in 1933) were a prime target for economy-minded groups.[86] Business organizations such as the National Industrial Conference Board openly questioned the idea that "the nation owes a living to every veteran" and that completion of military service "should be regarded as sufficient ground for the creation of a special class of social dependents."[87] Meanwhile, the American Medical Association argued that the extension of medical benefits to non-service-connected veterans would pave the way toward "state medicine."[88] From both the left and the right, skeptics agreed on the need to check what they saw as the corrupting influence of veterans in national politics.

President Franklin D. Roosevelt took office in March 1933 against this background of heated debate. Less than two weeks after being sworn in, he made good on his campaign pledge to balance the federal budget by signing the Economy Act. This law repealed all pieces of legislation concerning World War I and Spanish-American War veterans and gave the president the authority to rewrite them by executive orders. The twelve decrees issued by FDR led to dramatic cuts of $460 million in veterans' programs, most of which targeted non-service-connected benefits. Not only was the 1930 service pension rescinded, but payment rates were also revised downward for everyone and access to veterans' hospitals was tightened. As a result, half a million veterans were removed from the pension rolls and the number of patients who received VA medical care for non-service-connected disabilities went from over one hundred thousand in 1933 to slightly more than forty thousand the next year.[89] This was only the second time in U.S. history that veterans' benefits had been cut by law, and the first that a service pension was repealed.[90]

Though the Economy Act dealt a major blow to martial citizenship, in the long run it only ended up confirming the strength of the veterans' movement. For one thing, the conditions of its passage were exceptional: it took nothing less than the convergence of a severe economic depression, a sizable Democratic majority in both chambers of Congress, and aggressive presidential leadership.[91] Even in such favorable conditions, the White House was forced to backtrack when news emerged of desperate veterans committing suicide after being thrown out of hospitals or being denied their pension. Most of the cuts were rolled back within two years under intense pressure from the Big Three, which convinced Congress to override the president's veto.[92] By 1935, the only major provision of the Economy Act that remained untouched was the rescission of the service pension for World War I veterans.

This brief episode would be remembered for decades. As one historian has noted, the Economy Act left a lasting "heritage of bitterness. . . . Representatives of the veterans' organizations would never forget the traumatic experience of seeing fourteen years of painstaking gains swept aside by the stroke of a pen."[93] We will see in later chapters how the Economy Act remained a powerful symbol in the collective memory of the veterans' movement, used either to warn of the risk of backlash or to spur the rank and file into action against a piece of legislation.

Beyond this fiasco, the record of the Roosevelt administration on veterans' affairs was mixed. New Dealers managed to reverse the trend of rapid expansion that had characterized these programs since the 1920s. By 1941, veterans' spending was still only three-quarters of what it had been in 1933 and pension rolls numbered "only" 850,000 as opposed to 1.3 million.[94] But those numbers were still far from negligible, and growth continued in other sectors. The numbers of patients in veterans' hospitals rose back up quickly after 1934, for instance. Six years later, the VA treated almost 200,000 patients, of whom over 90 percent were there for non-service-connected causes.[95] Veterans were also granted preferential admission terms in many New Deal programs such as the Civilian Conservation Corps.[96] Their groups defeated the proposal of the Brownlow Committee (created by FDR in 1937 to reorganize the executive branch) that the VA be placed under the authority of a new Department of Welfare.[97] In sum, there was no clear break in the forward march of veterans' benefits throughout the interwar period. Despite the steadfast opposition of the White House, their growth never really stopped.

War as Disability: The Campaign for Adjusted Compensation

No other issue illustrated the ability of the veterans' movement to overcome obstacles better than adjusted compensation, or as its detractors liked to call it, the Bonus. Of all the benefits available to former service members in the interwar period, this one attracted by far the most public attention. The idea behind it was simple: former doughboys demanded to be paid a lump sum as a way to compensate for the gap between their low military wages and the higher ones received by civilian workers on the home front. Its implications were nonetheless momentous. With every doughboy eligible for payment, it promised to be the most expensive veterans' program yet.

More broadly, the Bonus represented a paradigm shift in understandings of military service. Because its supporters viewed war itself as a form of disability, they argued that the state should assist all veterans instead of only those who suffered from a mental or physical disability, as had hitherto been the norm.[98] As the national commander of the Legion explained in 1921, adjusted compensation amounted to treating able-bodied veterans as yet "another class of disabled, the *financially* disabled," who deserved to be "cared for" in the same way as their "physically incapacitated buddies."[99] In this sense, the campaign for the Bonus represented an effort to expand the definition of what counted as a disability and therefore the ranks of those who deserved assistance.

This fight was important for another reason. It was the first time that veterans, in their effort to make claims on the federal government, resorted to large-scale protests rather than their usual behind-the-scenes lobbying. After nearly a decade in which the conservative establishment of the Legion had ruled veterans' affairs, the economic downturn that began in the late 1920s paved the way for the rise of the more populist VFW, whose advocacy of immediate Bonus

payment quickly found an echo in the streets. This shift demonstrated the strategic fluidity of the veterans' movement, which was never limited to only one type
of collective action.

The demand for adjusted compensation arose out of widespread feelings
of resentment among veterans of the Great War. Many of them were convinced
that their military service had been unfairly rewarded. Unlike in earlier conflicts, the majority of the 4.7 million American soldiers who served during
World War I were conscripts, compelled by law to accept an average pay of one
dollar per day. The difference between their situation and the inflated wartime
salaries available to many workers on the home front fueled perceptions of
injustice. Almost as soon as the war was over, lawmakers began introducing various forms of bonus plans, ranging from straightforward cash payments to land
settlement programs and farm- or home-loan assistance. These proposals were
not immediately popular with the leadership of the veterans' movement, for
they clashed with the Legion and the DAVWW's desire to put the needs of the
physically disabled first. Yet the overwhelming support of their base overrode
all resistance, so that by the early 1920s the Big Three had endorsed the idea of
a lump-sum payment.[100]

Race and especially class were central to this debate. On the one hand,
some white southerners opposed the Bonus on the ground that an infusion of
cash might allow African American veterans to escape the Jim Crow system of
racial segregation.[101] On the other hand, populist resentment against the fortunes
made by war profiteers was a major driver of veterans' activism on this issue. As
one Legion department commander admitted candidly, "sometimes I think I am
almost bolshevist in my feelings against the vested interests that are opposing
this Adjusted Compensation bill."[102] Indeed, the leading opponents of the Bonus
for much of the 1920s—Secretary of the Treasury Andrew Mellon and the U.S.
Chamber of Commerce—were unabashed defenders of big business and the economically privileged. The Republican-controlled White House was on their side,
with both presidents Warren Harding and Calvin Coolidge vetoing bonus bills.
This campaign showed the limits of liberals' charge that veterans' groups were
puppets of the capitalist class.[103]

As always, Congress proved more responsive to veterans' pressure than the
executive branch. While Harding's veto was sustained, Coolidge's was overridden in 1924.[104] With a federal budget surplus expected at over $300 million that
year, arguments for fiscal prudence had less purchase.[105] "Silent Cal" signed into
law a compromise that postponed full payment more than two decades into
the future. Under its terms, veterans who had served at least sixty days were

to receive adjusted compensation certificates of $1 a day for domestic service and $1.25 for overseas service, payable with interests either in 1945 or at the recipient's death (hence its nickname, the "Tombstone Bonus"). The law was nevertheless a major accomplishment: with an average individual payment of $1,000 and nearly 3.5 million veterans eligible, its total cost was predicted to be over $4 billion.[106] In a decade when the federal government *as a whole* spent between $3.5 and $4 billion annually, this represented a radical expansion of the nation's social policy.[107]

This compromise was enough in a period of relative economic prosperity, but it did not survive the onset of the Great Depression in 1929. With the unemployment rate among World War I veterans over 50 percent higher than for their age group, the pressure for government relief in the form of immediate payment of the Bonus mounted.[108] The chief advocate of this new campaign was Wright Patman, a Democratic congressman from Texas who presented it as a "reflationary" device to increase consumer spending and thereby spur production. Though he was a Legionnaire, Patman failed to convince the more conservative leadership of the group to support his cause: over the next couple of years, the Legion oscillated between endorsement and rejection.[109] By contrast, the VFW embraced the cause wholeheartedly and rejected President Hoover's repeated calls for moderation. Their more confrontational stance proved wildly popular, allowing the group to grow to over 190,000 members in 1932 (twice the level of three years earlier). Throughout the early 1930s, the VFW campaigned for immediate payment through marches, petition drives, and radio programs.[110]

The effort stirred grassroots activism. Early in 1932, a jobless veteran of the Great War named Walter Waters who lived in Portland, Oregon, began to urge his comrades to get on a train and head to Washington, D.C., in order to claim the money that he thought was rightfully theirs. After a few false starts, some three hundred veterans followed him and climbed aboard empty train boxcars. As they hitchhiked their way east with the support of local Legion and VFW posts, their numbers and media coverage slowly grew. Soon, they became known derisively as the "Bonus Expeditionary Force" or simply the "Bonus Army." Remarkably for a period when racial segregation was the norm, the movement was integrated: black and white veterans mixed freely among the protesters. By the time they arrived in the capital in late May and set up camp in the Anacostia flats, their numbers had grown to around twenty thousand. They enjoyed a mixed reception: the local chief of police went out of his way to accommodate them, but military and FBI officials feared that the movement was infiltrated by communist agents and they began to plan for a potential insurrection.[111]

Figure 2. Veterans make claims on the state: a delegation of Bonus
Marchers on the steps of the Library of Congress, ca. 1932. A few African
Americans can be seen within the white crowd, illustrating the movement's
rather liberal attitude on race (for its times). From Jack Douglas, *Veterans
on the March* (New York: Workers Library Publishers, 1934).

It may seem paradoxical that veterans were the only group of Americans to
march on Washington at a time when unemployment was reaching almost 25 percent nationwide and economic hardship was affecting millions of people who did
not have access to the special benefits available to former service members. Yet
this was precisely the point. In contrast to other citizens, veterans had an old and
tangible relationship with the federal government. Over time, their benefits had
forged a group identity that made former service members more likely to mobilize in their defense, in the same way that the creation of Social Security would
later turn the elderly into a powerful political constituency.[112] As the first nationwide protest of veterans and one of the first marches on the federal capital in
the nation's history (Fig. 2), the Bonus Expeditionary Force illustrated the central
role that the federal government had come to play in the lives of former service
members long before its reach was extended to other categories of the population.

Once they had arrived, the marchers began to lobby Congress. Their efforts
seemed to succeed when the House approved the Bonus bill in mid-June, but it
was soundly defeated in the Senate a few days later. Despite this failure, Waters and
most of the marchers refused government offers to pay for their return train tickets

and announced that they would remain in the capital until 1945 if necessary. After weeks of mounting tensions, the police began to evict veterans from some downtown buildings in late July. The situation spiraled out of control and an altercation led to the death of one marcher. Seizing this long-awaited opportunity, Army chief of staff Douglas MacArthur swept in with six hundred men, cavalry, and tanks. He brutally cleared the camps and drove the marchers out of the city with tear gas, a callous approach that provoked an immediate backlash. Images of soldiers with gas masks and bayonets fighting veterans in the streets of the capital against a background of smoldering ruins became instant symbols of Hoover's disregard for the plight of the disadvantaged. The scandal contributed to his defeat at the polls in November against his Democratic opponent, Franklin Delano Roosevelt.

The forceful expulsion of the Bonus Expeditionary Force from the capital did not spell the end of the Bonus as a political issue, however. Smaller groups of marchers continued to arrive in Washington, D.C., every year from 1933 to 1935, but FDR handled their arrival more skillfully. He made sure that they were treated well even while refusing to accede to their demands. When a bill to provide immediate payment passed Congress in 1935, he delivered his veto in person before both chambers—the first time a president took such a step—in order to underscore how important he considered the issue to be. His message directly questioned two of the fundamental premises of martial citizenship. Not only did he stress that rewarding military veterans alone was unfair to the millions of civilians who had directly contributed to the war effort by their work in the defense industry or in agriculture, but he also concurred with his predecessors that the state had an obligation to assist only those veterans who had been disabled in service and the survivors of those who had been killed. "A man who is sick or under some other special disability because he was a soldier should certainly be assisted as such," Roosevelt recognized, "but if a man is suffering from economic need because of the depression, even though he is a veteran, he must be placed on a par with all of the other victims of the depression." He called for welfare benefits to be extended "to all groups and all classes who in an emergency need the helping hand of their Government," rather than merely to "a single group or class."[113]

Roosevelt's dramatic appearance convinced Congress to sustain his veto, but it did not stop the Bonus from gaining traction. Not only did mounting rank-and-file pressure force the conservative Legion to finally endorse immediate payment, but the issue became a rallying cry for some of the most influential voices on the left, such as Catholic priest and radio host Charles Coughlin and Senator Huey Long, Democrat from Louisiana. With public opinion behind them, their combined forces were more than FDR could handle. When a new bill providing for immediate payment passed Congress again in 1936, he could read the writing on the wall. Rather than delivering his veto in person, he sent Congress a perfunctory note referring to his message of the previous year. As expected, he was overridden. Almost twenty years after the armistice, 3.5 million former doughboys finally received their Bonus checks by mail, for a total value of $1.9 billion. Ironically, a measure that FDR had so steadfastly opposed ended up helping his reelection bid in November by injecting some much-needed cash into the economy and by removing the one issue that had helped bring together his critics on the left.[114]

The outcome of this protracted controversy was not entirely positive for the veterans' movement, for its victory cemented within certain segments of society the idea that former service members cared only about their own interests. This was particularly true among elite circles, as illustrated by the rapid growth of the Veterans of Future Wars, a group created in 1936 by isolationist students at Princeton University. Anticipating that their country would soon be drawn into another European war, they demanded immediate payment of a $1,000 bonus to every man of military age while he was still alive to spend the money. What started as a mere college prank was soon met with an unexpectedly enthusiastic response from campuses across the nation, with five hundred posts and fifty thousand members joining within two months. Mocking what they saw as veterans' constant demands for more benefits, students adopted the "itchy palm" greeting, an ironic twist on the fascist salute in which the extended hand was turned upward instead of downward to mimic the expectation of charity (Fig. 3). The group quickly collapsed due to its inability to agree on a common agenda, but not before revealing the cynicism with which many children of the nation's upper class viewed veterans' claims.[115] Nor were they alone, for non-service-connected benefits were far from popular among the general public: in February 1938 for instance, polls found that 56 percent of respondents disapproved of giving a pension to survivors of a veteran who had died from causes not connected to the war.[116] Clearly, the reservoir of hostility that the Economy Act had tapped into in 1933 never ran dry.

However unpopular, the achievements of the veterans' movement would remain largely untouched over the next few years. By the time of the Japanese attack on Pearl Harbor in 1941, veterans' welfare state was still a central pillar of U.S. social policy, its programs more sizable and generous than perhaps anywhere else in the world. Despite the retrenchment that had taken place during the New Deal, the VA continued to be a major force in government. Responsible for the treatment of over 2.4 million patients throughout the interwar period, in 1941 it managed

Figure 3. The Veterans of Future Wars' "itchy palm" salute captured the hostility of some sections of American society toward the veterans' movement in the late 1930s. Lewis J. Gorin, Jr., *Patriotism Prepaid* (Philadelphia: J. B. Lippincott, 1936), 98, Princeton University Archives, Department of Rare Books and Special Collections, Princeton University Library.

over ninety medical facilities, administered $433 million in monetary benefits to 856,000 recipients, and oversaw 613,000 life insurance policies worth a total of $2.5 billion.[117] It was precisely because of its importance that the agency continued to attract attention, with liberals and conservatives alike debating its future.

The resilience of such a colossal and separate welfare state would probably have bewildered Progressives if they could have foreseen this development back in 1918. Their camp had seemed to emerge triumphant from the Great War, having dealt a severe blow to martial citizenship with the passage of the War Risk Insurance Act. Yet their agenda quickly showed its limits. The sudden capitulation of the Central Powers ushered in a chaotic demobilization in which veterans, feeling abandoned by the state, turned to their own groups to defend their shared interests. Drawing inspiration from the time-tested structure and strategy of their Civil War elders, organizations like the Legion, the VFW, and the DAVWW formed the core of a new cycle of the veterans' movement that rose phoenix-like from its own ashes. Congress and the White House proved largely unable to resist the pressure. Step by step, this new generation of former service members not only won back many of the same benefits granted to Union veterans but also obtained new ones. The immediate payment of the Bonus in 1936 was the final nail in the coffin of the Progressive agenda. By recognizing war itself as a disability and by extending compensation to able-bodied and disabled veterans alike, the law marked the triumph of martial citizenship.

The interwar years were not just a conflict between two opposite visions of veterans' place in society, however. There were also areas in which the Progressive agenda overlapped with that of the veterans' movement, as in the case of medical benefits. Introduced in the hope of "curing" former service members of their disabilities, these benefits did not disappear over time but instead assumed an ever-larger role as veterans' hospitals achieved independent status and grew in size. Albeit unwittingly, Progressives were responsible for the creation of one of the most popular veterans' programs. Their successors in the New Deal also contributed indirectly to the growth of veterans' welfare state, this time by vastly expanding the boundaries of social policy as a whole. In a context where the federal government created many new programs for various categories of the population, veterans' legislation became merely "a subset of the general social welfare assistance now available to Americans classified as deserving poor."[118] As more groups benefited from federal assistance, the controversial character of veterans' services diminished. In time, new programs like Social Security would far outgrow benefits for former service members and help draw attention away from them.

That day had not yet arrived in late 1941, when the country joined the Second World War. As lawmakers turned their attention to the problem of creating yet another system of benefits for future veterans of this new conflict, the memory of the divisive fight over the Bonus was foremost in their mind, acting as a foil in the same way that the Civil War pension system had for Progressives over two decades earlier. The drawn-out campaign for adjusted compensation had instilled into elected officials a keen sense of the disruptive and costly impact that millions of disgruntled former service members could have in national politics. To prevent the return of this issue, everyone understood that the government would not only have to start planning early but that it should extend assistance to both able-bodied and disabled veterans. The shadow of the Great War loomed large as yet another cohort of veterans was beginning to emerge.

CHAPTER 2

Rebirth

The Veterans' Movement in World War II

In late November 1941, the debate over veterans' benefits remained as bitterly polarized as it had been throughout the interwar years. This was illustrated by the reaction to the testimony of the Big Three before the U.S. Senate on behalf of two bills that sought to expand non-service-connected benefits and to restore the service pension rescinded by the Economy Act of 1933.[1] The effort of veterans' advocates ran up against fierce opposition from the national press, especially once the total cost of the proposals became clear (estimates ranged from $5 billion to $20 billion).[2] The *New York Times* denounced the bills as "utterly reckless" and the products of the "strong and wily ... veterans' lobby."[3] The most widely circulated magazine of this era, *Reader's Digest*, condemned veterans' "war against the Treasury" and called the bills "a new tentacle from an old octopus," namely the "professional patriots" in "the ex-soldiers' lobby."[4] These blistering attacks echoed public opinion, which disapproved of non-service-connected pensions.[5] The national leadership of the Legion took the situation so seriously that they devoted an entire session of their executive meeting that November to discussing a response.[6]

Though the reputation of the Big Three was far from excellent at the onset of the Second World War, the situation would change dramatically in the span of just four years. By the time of the final Japanese defeat in August 1945, veterans' prestige was replenished. The change was admittedly never complete and negative images lingered. Nevertheless, it is fair to argue that the process of generational transition that began in 1941, with the addition of a new and larger cohort, transformed the leading organizations of the veterans' movement profoundly.

As one Legionnaire put it, these groups experienced "a rebirth in the blood of World War II."[7]

Nowhere were the dynamics of this renaissance more evident than in the Legion, for this group had been created specifically as the voice of a different cohort of former service members (from the Great War). Since the VFW and the DAVWW advocated for the needs of veterans who had either served overseas or were disabled, accepting a new cohort did not entail an essential change to their mission (in fact, the VFW had already gone through a similar metamorphosis when its founding generation of Spanish-American War veterans had welcomed ex-doughboys). Legionnaires faced a different challenge: they had to abandon their founding identity as a "single-generation" group to become a "two-war" organization. Exploring more in details the internal workings of this organization therefore brings the process of intergenerational transition that began within the veterans' movement during this conflict into sharp relief.

Just as the resurgence of the movement in the aftermath of World War I was closely related to the failure of Progressive reform, its revitalization during World War II was inseparable from the policy discussion over which benefits the new generation should receive. The circumstances of this debate were quite different, however. Rather than seeking to limit the state's obligation toward those who served, lawmakers were now inclined to treat veterans generously. This was partly because they sought to avoid a repetition of the same protracted and divisive argument over a Bonus that had animated much of the interwar period. But it was also because they had to reckon with the still-considerable influence of the Big Three, contrary to 1917 when the GAR was all but absent from national politics. World War II was the first time in U.S. history that veterans of a previous war decisively shaped the legislation affecting a new generation. The more generous outcome of this conflict stemmed, finally, from the new balance of power in Congress. Unlike in the First World War when Progressive policies had faced little resistance, this time liberals faced a resurgent conservative coalition of midwestern Republicans and southern Democrats who opposed the continued growth of the New Deal welfare state. Though theirs was never a firm alliance, former service members found support among many conservatives who regarded veterans' programs as a more limited alternative to the broad expansion of civilian welfare championed by FDR.

As a result, veterans of the Second World War were given access not only to all the benefits available to their predecessors but also to brand new ones with the Servicemen's Readjustment Act of 1944, better known as the "GI Bill of

Rights." This law was premised on the same idea as the Bonus, namely that the federal government should help disabled and able-bodied veterans alike readjust to civilian life. The Legion was chiefly responsible for steering this landmark piece of legislation through Congress, taking advantage of the groundswell of public support for the GI citizen-soldier.[8] Framed as a way to both repay the nation's debt toward those who performed the highest sacrifice and to avoid a repetition of the chaos of 1918–19, the GI Bill proved immune to the criticism often wielded against other types of veterans' benefits, even though it was animated by the same ideal of martial citizenship. The passage of this law represented the ultimate defeat of the New Deal's agenda, for Roosevelt had long argued that able-bodied veterans should not receive special treatment.[9] In the same way that Progressives had failed to stop the unraveling of the War Risk Insurance Act in the interwar period, New Dealers proved unable to impose their own policies in wartime.

At the onset of the Second World War, though, martial citizenship remained as disputed as ever. We start here at the beginning of this debate, looking at how veterans' groups reacted to the arrival of a new cohort and how their efforts would in turn help congeal veterans' special status into law.

From Military Preparedness to the War Effort

Just like the nation as a whole, the veterans' movement became gradually involved in World War II long before December 1941. After years of staunch isolationism, the VFW gradually shifted positions as Hitler's threat became more real. By 1940, the group was backing the administration's support for Great Britain.[10] It took the Legion a little longer, but the fall of Poland and then France convinced the group to abandon neutrality.[11] Both organizations fell back on their long tradition of support for military preparedness.

Their collaboration with public officials at all levels of government offered perhaps the clearest example of how the veterans' movement could act in symbiosis with the state. For the Legion, this was a matter of both patriotism and self-interest. When the debate over U.S. intervention began, its leaders sought to capture public attention. In December 1940, they entered in a partnership with the Federal Bureau of Investigation. Sixty thousand Legionnaires ultimately worked with J. Edgar Hoover's G-men over the course of the war, sharing information on political dissidents and potential spies in what was called

the "Contact" program.[12] A handful of Legionnaires visited Great Britain with
FDR's blessing, both to learn about its defense system and as a way to attract
media attention back home.[13] Many of them also held key state-level posts in the
Office of Civilian Defense, the federal agency created to improve the country's
readiness for war.[14]

These early efforts paled in comparison to the renewed energy with which
veterans threw themselves into the conflict once the United States joined the
fray in December 1941. The day after the Japanese attacks in the Pacific, National
Commander Lynn Stambaugh declared that "our 1,130,000 Legion members
know that war calls for united service. They will give that to America."[15] As
one memorandum to Roosevelt noted with satisfaction two years later, Legion
leaders "want to be known as your good right arm. . . . The American Legion
wants you to know that it, as an organization, offers itself for you to command
in the same manner as you command the Army and Navy of our country."[16] The
group continued to play a leading role in civilian defense. Hundreds of thousands of Legionnaires worked as aircraft warden observers, first-aid workers,
volunteer police, and members of ration boards.[17] Likewise, the VFW helped
collect blood and partnered with the Office of Civilian Defense.[18] The veterans'
movement essentially became an extension of the warfare state.

It also served as an intermediary between the armed forces and the public. As
a suggested address prepared by the Legion's National Publicity Division noted,
"In the last war the men of The American Legion were the men behind the guns.
In this war Legionnaires are mostly the men behind the men behind the guns."[19]
Members of the group were indeed present at nearly every stage of a soldier's life,
beginning in high school where they helped implement a program designed to
improve future draftees' physical fitness.[20] Legionnaires were also essential to the
operation of the Selective Service system: in states like Illinois, they represented
more than 75 percent of all draft board members.[21] On the day when draftees
departed to boot camp, it was not uncommon for those who lived in small towns
to walk to the train station led by a Legion color guard and drummer.[22] Once
inside the armed services, soldiers might receive one of the 2 million copies of
the Legion booklet *Fall-In*, which introduced them to military jargon and discipline.[23] They were also likely to encounter material provided by the countless
scrap drives sponsored by the group, not to mention the hundreds of thousands
of personal items sent to overseas units like cigarettes, playing cards, and new
phonograph records. Active-duty soldiers on furlough were welcome in Legion
facilities.[24] Finally, Legion posts often helped maintain the local "Honor Roll"
bearing the names of a city's soldiers.[25] The VFW conducted similar activities,

such as collecting books for service members.[26] In all these ways, the veterans' movement enthusiastically backed the armed forces.

The Two-War Experiment

At the same time as they supported the war effort, Legionnaires began to debate whether to admit in their ranks the future veterans of this new conflict. A clear majority of the rank and file supported the move from early on.[27] Some posts were so eager, in fact, that the national leadership feared that they would "jump the gun . . . and start taking in" the new veterans without waiting for an official decision.[28] Realizing that this was "the most important issue which has confronted The American Legion, from an internal organization standpoint, in its history," Stambaugh enjoined his members to start discussing it in the spring of 1942, ahead of the upcoming national convention in the fall.[29] Over the next few months, compelling arguments were deployed on either side of this debate.

Those who were against opening the group to a new cohort tended to believe that there could be no such thing as a united veteran community and that former service members of different wars did not have enough in common to form a joint organization. Behind the age gap lay a fear that the experiences of the two cohorts were simply too different to allow for common ground (the average Legionnaire was forty-seven years old in 1941, compared to twenty-six for the average U.S. service member in World War II).[30] "The veterans of the present war," one Virginia post argued, "are not of our day and age and are not and will not be able to understand our past and present problems, nor to enter into our comradeship, the disparity in age being too great to overcome."[31] History seemed to prove their point, for never before had a veterans' group opened its ranks to former service members of more than one war without an additional criterion such as location of service, disability, or religion. Whether an organization could manage to be the voice of *all* veterans without prioritizing the needs of one generation over those of another was an open question. As one Legion historian later put it, this was truly a "two-war experiment."[32]

The difference in age was compounded by the fact that the new cohort seemed poised to be several times larger than the old. In 1942, there were already as many people in military service (3.8 million) as there were veterans of the Great War still alive.[33] Whereas the ranks of the former were growing rapidly, those of the latter were on a course of inevitable decline. In this context, some Legionnaires feared becoming a minority within their own group.[34] One high-ranking official wrote that "while I am always open to conviction I still believe that we should hold onto this legion of ours.... [I]f this change is made and the men now in the service take advantage of the opportunity I can readily see where we will be entirely absorbed."[35] A day later, he stressed that the move "would really mean changing our entire American Legion."[36]

Such fears also tapped into broad cultural trends. The concern expressed by some members over whether future veterans would "be dedicated fundamentally and primarily to fostering and maintaining the American way of life" reflected widely shared anxieties about the impact of military service.[37] Even as they celebrated those who served, many Americans suspected that the inherently totalitarian and violent institution of the military would erase recruits' individuality and alleged love for democracy.[38] Moreover, both government officials and a majority of the population expected high unemployment and economic depression to return at the end of the war.[39] In this uncertain context, some worried that veterans' military discipline would make them the favorite targets of demagogues looking to overthrow the system.[40] "Will the veterans of World War II turn into Storm Troopers who will destroy democracy?" Columbia University professor Willard Waller asked provocatively in 1944. "*Unless and until he can be renaturalized into his native land,*" Waller wrote, "*the veteran is a threat to society.*"[41] Beyond politics, expectations of "a postwar crime wave" in which unemployed veterans would be "holding people up, robbing banks, breaking into apartments" were sufficiently common that J. Edgar Hoover felt the need to publicly deny that the Army was "breeding criminals."[42]

Not everyone saw these fears as a reason to refuse admitting the new cohort, however. Some Legion officials considered the risk posed by younger veterans to be one reason why they should be allowed in. After all, one of the motivating factors behind the creation of the group in 1919 had been the effort to prevent the spread of militant ideas among doughboys. As a top official of the group argued in a letter to the *Los Angeles Times* in 1944, "many of us ... are interested in the American Legion as an instrumentality through which to stabilize one large group of its citizenry and mobilize their efforts along constructive lines for the good of the nation and her civilization.... [L]arge percentages of men who come out of a war can either make a country or break it, or promote national and world order, or World War III. The outcome will depend much upon the leadership at this time."[43]

Just like their opponents, those who favored opening the Legion to a new cohort were motivated by both pragmatic and moral incentives. Some emphasized the similarities between the two world wars and the cohorts shaped by them. A North Carolina Legionnaire argued for instance that "the Veterans of all wars have one and the same bond of fellowship 'Service to our country in peace as well as in war.'"[44] Others stressed that about one hundred thousand sons of Legionnaires were already servicemen and that in all likelihood "they would like to belong to the same post as their fathers."[45] The advantages that both generations could derive from this union were also obvious: the new "crop" of veterans could take advantage of the established position of the Legion to avoid having "to go through the same laborious years as did those of [world war] No.1 to bring their newer organization to a peak" and the new generation would allow the Legion to "live for 100 years at least."[46]

Such comments reveal that Legionnaires were acutely aware of their position within the veterans' movement. Since membership was open only to veterans with an honorable discharge, the Legion was at a disadvantage compared to the VFW, whose constitution allowed the recruitment of active-duty soldiers. This led some among the rank and file to fear that "unless The American Legion open our door [*sic*], the men of this war are very likely going to join the other organization [VFW]. If they do, and we close our doors, the other organization is going to be far stronger than we are in the next few years."[47] One Legion official put the challenge in even starker terms when he argued in a speech that "this Legion of ours stands at the crossroads because of history." He added, "We shall either live again, take on a new life and find a period of Legion renaissance through our children, our sons and our neighbors' sons, or we shall gradually fade out as the Grand Army of the Republic did . . . because they had no children to take their place."[48] The memory of previous cycles of the veterans' movement was very much alive. For Legionnaires at midcentury, World War II represented an opportunity to break with the long-standing pattern whereby a veterans' group lived only as long as its founding generation.

Though arguments were presented on either side, the outcome was not really in doubt. After a lively debate at the local level throughout the spring and summer of 1942, an overwhelming majority of departments came out in favor of welcoming the new generation.[49] At the national convention in Kansas City that September, divisions within the leadership were ironed out behind closed doors and the final resolution was adopted unanimously.[50] The bill amending the Legion's congressional charter sailed through both chambers of Congress before being signed by Roosevelt the following month. The Legion was now officially open to honorably discharged U.S. veterans of World War II, whether serving with allied or American forces. The first new members were officially admitted that same day.[51]

Selling the American Legion

This was but the first step. As one journalist put it, the new "formula" of the Legion "will take some selling because war veterans are notoriously diverse in their organizations."[52] The DAVWW was going through a similar process of generational transition, which led its officials to adopt a shorter and less war-specific name, the Disabled American Veterans (DAV).[53] Beyond the "Big Three," there were around two hundred smaller organizations such as the Blinded Veterans' Association, the United Negro and Allied Veterans of America, and the Marine Corps League.[54] As every cohort before them had done, veterans of World War II created their own associations, the most important of which were the centrist American Veterans of World War II, the AMVETS, and the more liberal American Veterans Committee, the AVC.[55] More radical groups also attempted to recruit returning soldiers, from the far-right Protestant War Veterans created by Nazi sympathizer Edward J. Smythe to the Communist Party of the USA.[56]

Facing intense competition for new members, the Legion created a World War II Liaison Committee in November 1942 to coordinate recruitment efforts.[57] As one committee member wrote, local posts were "the hub of the wheel around which the entire program revolves."[58] In a letter to all post commanders, its chairman argued that "it is purely a public relations program" and that "the big, all-important job now is for Posts and individual Legionnaires to keep in contact with the men and women in service from their community by letter or postal card. Let the members of the armed forces from your community hear from you!"[59] The role played by the Legion in the war effort provided a ready-made platform for such efforts. As Wisconsin's *Badger Legionnaire* noted, "War activities have given [the Legion] more extensive publicity this last year than perhaps at any other time. Locally, the recruiting, salvage, war bond, high school victory corps and numerous other projects have earned hundreds of columns of newspaper space."[60] In this as in many other instances, the Legion greatly benefited from its close relationship with the state.

But the Liaison Committee did more than simply recycle preexisting activities. With a $250,000 budget, it considerably expanded recruitment efforts both at home and overseas, for instance by creating public relations offices in London and Paris.[61] Legionnaires were urged to send their copies of the group's magazine to someone in service (Army writer Justin Gray later recalled that the Legion distribution system abroad was sometimes better than that of the Army's own weekly, *Yank*).[62] Soldiers on active duty were likely to come across constant reminders of the Legion's interest, in the form either of one of the clip sheets, sponsored articles, editorials, and cartoons that the group placed in Army or Navy newspapers, or of the one thousand Legion motion picture trailers distributed to movie theaters. Overall, the group distributed more than 21 million pieces of literature to service members throughout the war.[63] The goal of all this activity was to "keep the name of The American Legion before those now in uniform."[64]

A brief look at the activities of the Benjamin A. Fuller Post helps us understand what this recruitment campaign looked like on the ground. A center of civic life in the small town of Pittsburg in the southeastern corner of Kansas, this post welcomed new draftees for a complimentary "army style" dinner a few days before their scheduled departure. Designed to "simulate army chow," the banquet gave draftees and Legionnaires an opportunity to mingle. The centerpiece of the program was a speech by a Legion official about veterans' benefits. Among other services, the post sent a monthly shipment of cigarettes overseas, welcomed members of the armed forces in its own facilities, and prepared wills free of charge. In late 1943, it opened a canteen at the local train station. Under the supervision of the Red Cross, volunteer personnel drawn from the Legion Auxiliary and other women's groups distributed coffee, doughnuts, and cookies to service members. Those traveling through Pittsburg received an announcement card as their train approached the town: on one side was the canteen's menu and on the other the name of the post and the Legion's emblem. "It is hoped," one Legionnaire noted, "that some of these cards will be kept by the recipients and will in the future stimulate a friendly feeling toward The American Legion."[65]

Aside from the ever-popular cookies and doughnuts, the organization also appealed to a sense of shared comradeship. The *American Legion Magazine* proclaimed that "Spiritually, the veterans of the First World War and of the conflict now raging all over the globe are one, for the aggressions that brought us into uniform in 1917–1918 and those which the United Nations are in process of crushing utterly, stem from the same source—Germany."[66] Another way to insist on this comradeship was to emphasize veterans' differences from the rest of the population, which was one of the core dimensions of martial citizenship. In a suggested talk for local speakers, the National Public Relations division presented the Legion as "the most exclusive organization in the nation. . . . No proclamation of President, edict of king or dictator can command admission. . . . The Legion's door opens for veterans only on the presentation of a bit of parchment, worn, torn, and begrimed as it may be, which certifies to an honorable discharge."[67]

In practice, a discharge certificate was not always enough to open the Legion's door. Despite its professed love of freedom and democracy, the group continued to tolerate the outright exclusion of African Americans from most of its southern departments and their de facto segregation in many states north of the Mason-Dixon Line. Black Legionnaires relentlessly denounced this hypocrisy. One of them pointed out that racial segregation was "contrary to the very essence of our Democracy and to the principles for which the last war was fought and for which the present World War is being fought."[68] "We fought side by side with the white men that makes up [*sic*] the Legions of this country," wrote a reverend from Alabama, "and we feel that we are entitled to a post where we can at least meet and enjoy the comradeship of one another."[69] Such complaints fell on deaf ears. Throughout the war, the all-white national leadership of the Legion stuck to its laissez-faire attitude on issues of race, allowing posts and departments to exclude whomever they saw fit.[70]

Women were also treated as second-class members. Though they were not subjected to the same outright exclusion as black veterans, they were often encouraged to join separate posts. By 1944, sixty posts were entirely composed of women, and there were between ten thousand and thirty thousand female Legionnaires in total.[71] As the group's national adjutant admitted frankly, women were kept out of leadership positions because "many of our male members are not in favor of women in the organization."[72] Whenever the Legion did recognize its female members in public, it focused more on their physical appearance than on their accomplishments. In a letter sent to local newspapers around the country encouraging them to write stories about the Legion, for instance, the National Publicity Division suggested that journalists inquire into whether some women had signed up in their area, for "they might be photogenic."[73] Such sexism was hardly exceptional in the Big Three: though the VFW had admitted women in the interwar years, it excluded them from 1944 to the late 1970s.[74]

However incomplete, the ideal of shared comradeship was only one of the ways in which the Legion appealed to World War II veterans. The group also resorted to more self-interested arguments. Membership is "the greatest bargain ever offered the veterans of any war," a suggested talk argued. With "posts in almost every community and whistle stop in the nation," "splendid clubhouses everywhere," leaders "from all walks of life from the President in the White House to the village constable," "unparalleled prestige and influence," and "more than $100,000,000 in physical assets," the Legion offered the kind of power no other veterans' group could match. And it promised to use this clout to defend veterans' interests long after their return home. "Veterans soon become a forgotten generation unless there is somebody who will not forget them," a suggested radio script read. "That somebody is the American Legion."[75]

This expensive recruitment drive had mixed results. The fact that soldiers on active duty could not join placed the Legion at a major handicap compared to its competitors. As columnist Drew Pearson noted in July 1944, though the VFW started the war with only 240,000 members (four times less than the Legion), it "has picked up more than 400,000 new members since [then], while the Legion's gains have been relatively paltry.... Today the VFW magazine has the largest overseas circulation of any non-governmental publication."[76] Unable to vie for members on equal terms, the Legion turned to what had long been its core strength: championing veterans' interests on Capitol Hill.

Martial Citizenship and Public Policy

The policy debate over veterans' benefits during World War II revolved around a familiar question: should veterans be treated like other citizens or as a special group? The balance of power had changed, however. Liberals continued to argue that former service members should be put on an equal footing with the rest of the population, and they continued to face the resistance of the veterans' move- ment with its usual allies in the executive and legislative branches (the VA and Rankin). This time, though, the Big Three enjoyed the support of the resurgent conservative coalition, which had grown more powerful in Congress since the late 1930s.[77] This was not a firm alliance, for many southern Democrats and midwest- ern Republicans were uneasy about a larger federal government and higher levels of welfare spending (especially when not all of its recipients were white men). Still, they proved willing to tolerate the expansion of veterans' benefits when the latter were framed as an alternative to more broad-based New Deal programs for the entire population. As during World War I, the general assumption was that these benefits would only be a temporary readjustment measure. Hardly anyone anticipated the colossal size that they would take in the postwar period.

The first item on what would become the long list of benefits for veterans of World War II was signed into law even before the United States officially entered the fray. The nation's first peacetime conscription law, passed in September 1940, contained a clause giving veterans the right to return to the job that they had occupied before enlisting. Such reemployment rights provoked little debate at the time but they later became a major problem for trade unions.[78]

The debate started in earnest shortly after the Japanese attacks in the Pacific in December 1941. As the country returned to full employment in the wake of the declaration of war, administration officials confronted the new problem of labor shortages. They sought to update and expand the rehabilitation program implemented during World War I as a way to return as many disabled men and women to economic productivity as possible. Though rehabilitation was initially placed under the authority of the Veterans' Bureau, it had reverted to the states in the late 1920s. For FDR and other liberals, the war therefore represented an opportunity to federalize this program and to add one more brick to the larger edifice of the New Deal welfare state. Hoping to override congressional resistance by taking advantage of the broad support for legislation involving service members, the president made clear in the fall of 1942 that he wanted "a single Rehabilitation Service ... for both veterans and civilians."[79] The Federal Security Agency director and committed liberal Paul McNutt produced a plan that placed rehabilitation under the aegis of an agency amenable to the New Deal agenda—his own. Soon, supporters of the administration introduced corresponding bills in Congress.[80]

As hearings got under way, New Dealers ran into strong, if predictable headwinds. All the major actors of the veterans' movement testified against this scheme. The Legion's core objection was that the plan "would treat all disabled alike": by placing former service members under the same umbrella as civilians, it amounted to "denying the veterans the class distinction they have always enjoyed" and thereby violating the core principle of martial citizenship.[81] Using similar language, the DAV argued that war-disabled veterans should "be kept in a class separate and apart ... through the Federal agency, which has been designated by Congress to attend to veterans' matters"—namely, the VA.[82] For its part, the VFW feared that the plan would "destroy the identity of veterans as a group for special consideration."[83] Allies of the movement made themselves heard as well. VA administrator Frank Hines came out against the bill, stressing that the responsibility for veterans' rehabilitation should rest with his own agency.[84] Senator Bennett Champ Clark, a Legion founder and the group's voice in the upper chamber of Congress, argued that "the veterans ought to have special treatment.... [I]t is our view that since these men are treated specially when they are taken from civil life and put into the armed services, they should be treated specially when they come out of the armed services and back to civil life."[85]

This pushback was more than the administration could handle. After the November 1942 midterm elections produced a more conservative Congress in which FDR's opponents had the upper hand, it was not hard for veterans' advocates to score their first major legislative victory of the war. Lawmakers eventually passed two separate rehabilitation bills, one involving former service members (under the responsibility of the VA) and another for civilians.[86] In defeating a plan endorsed by FDR himself, the veterans' movement dealt yet another blow to his vision of a more inclusive social policy that placed civilians on the same level as veterans.

The next legislative skirmish confirmed that progressives were on the defensive. They tried to recover from this defeat by introducing an ambitious postwar plan to expand social insurance, known as the Wagner-Murray-Dingell bill. Directly inspired by the "Beveridge Plan" introduced in Great Britain the year before, the bill called for creating national health insurance as well as maternity and disability benefits, and for federalizing the U.S. Employment Service and unemployment insurance. It was named after three liberal stalwarts: Senator Robert Wagner of New York, who had introduced some of the most iconic pieces of New Deal legislation such as the National Labor Relations Act of 1935, Senator James Murray of Montana, and Representative John Dingell of Michigan. The conservative turn of Congress meant that their plan was dead on arrival, however. Roosevelt knew this and he did not endorse the bill, which remained buried in committee.[87]

Rather than supporting a bold liberal plan that would expand social programs to civilians and veterans alike, in the summer of 1943 the president called on Congress to pass legislation that would apply only to the latter. In a fireside chat otherwise largely focused on the progress of the war, he asked for laws providing for mustering-out pay, educational assistance, unemployment insurance, disabled pensions, and improved health-care services for former service members. Those who listened carefully to his radio address could hear a brief admission that Roosevelt had quietly abandoned his long-standing opposition to treating veterans as a special group. The man who had declared a decade earlier that "no person, because he wore a uniform, must thereafter be placed in a special class of beneficiaries over and above all other citizens" now publicly recognized that "the members of the armed forces have been compelled to make greater economic sacrifice and every other kind of sacrifice than the rest of us, and they are entitled to definite action to help take care of their special problems."[88] This statement fell far short of a ringing endorsement of martial citizenship, but it was nevertheless an unmistakable sign that the president would no longer put up a fight against veterans' legislation. Not only did he understand that the makeup of Congress doomed such efforts to failure, but he also focused most of his attention on the management of the war. After giving two more official messages on the subject a few months later, he left it to legislators and his subordinates to hash out the details.[89]

The president and his liberal allies had not lost all hopes of seizing at least a limited victory, however. In the same way that Roosevelt had initially designed his rehabilitation program to expand the scope of the federal government, he hoped that federal financing of education for GIs could be an "entering wedge" that would bring under his purview a policy field hitherto reserved for individual states. As his assistant Samuel Rosenman later recounted, FDR was aware that "even the most rabid opponent of federal aid to education would not dare raise his voice against federal financial aid for educating GIs." This law could set a precedent that would make it "much easier thereafter to get more and more federal aid for all children in states that could not provide decent educational facilities out of their resources."[90] In order to achieve this goal, control of the program had to be in liberal hands, which is why the plan introduced on behalf of the administration by Senator Elbert Thomas of Utah assigned responsibility for educating and training veterans to the U.S. Office of Education, a part of the Federal Security Agency.[91]

Thomas's proposal was only one of the more than 240 veterans' bills introduced in Congress by late 1943, a sign of the agitation around that issue.[92] Rather than waiting for the administration to act, the VFW had taken the lead in the spring of that year by urging immediate action to help disabled veterans.[93] The Legion tried to seize back the initiative in September, when its new national commander, Warren Atherton, went to Washington, D.C., after his election. There, he captured the headlines by disclosing the results of a survey showing that the compensation claims of over fifteen hundred veterans in thirty-four states had been delayed by red tape for months, forcing them to survive on charity.[94] Calling the situation a "national disgrace," Atherton asserted that the cost of their rehabilitation was "just as much a part of the cost of waging war as is the building of battleships, planes, or tanks, and that is a Federal responsibility." While demanding the immediate passage of a mustering-out pay bill, he appointed a committee to design a larger plan for the readjustment of all World War II veterans.[95] In typical Legion fashion, the team was bipartisan. It was headed by John Stelle, a former Democratic governor of Illinois with ties to the Roosevelt administration, but its key member was Harry Colmery, a Kansas Republican who had been the chairman of the national veterans' committee for the 1940 GOP presidential candidate, Wendell Willkie.[96]

After holding meetings with representatives from industry, agriculture, business, and government in Washington, D.C., Colmery and his committee brought together the main features of the various pieces of legislation then before Congress into a single "omnibus bill."[97] Combining different legislative provisions into one giant bill was an old and notorious tactic meant to ram controversial measures through. Just a few months earlier, the Legion had used the same approach to help pass legislation introducing various changes in veterans' disability and death benefits.[98] This time, the bill not only provided additional funds for veterans' hospitals but also established new educational benefits for college, vocational school, or on-the-job training, as well as a program of guaranteed home, business, and farm loans, employment services, and an unemployment allowance of up to a year—all under the responsibility of the VA. Atherton later recognized that the bill made public by his group in early January 1944 contained nothing new: all of its provisions had antecedents in state or federal law and many had been inspired by similar benefits implemented in Canada.[99]

As the national commander had requested, mustering-out pay came up separately before Congress. The idea of a one-time, lump-sum payment to all service members upon discharge had broad popular and bipartisan appeal (a Gallup poll found almost 90 percent of respondents in favor). Lawmakers on both sides of the aisle saw it as a way to forestall the mounting calls for a new bonus, which promised to be even more expensive than the one passed in 1924.[100] Still, the debate revealed disagreements between the main organizations of the veterans' movement on the issue of which category of veterans should receive the most money. Not surprisingly for a group open only to those who had served abroad, the VFW believed that the "extra hazards and discomforts of foreign service" entitled those veterans to receive more, while the Legion advocated payment on the basis of length of service only.[101] Congress eventually agreed on a compromise that took both length and location of service into account: individuals who served less than sixty days were to receive $100, those who served for over sixty days stateside $200, and those who served overseas $300. The Legion tried to defeat this bill on the ground that service members did not decide where the military sent them, but to no avail.[102] In a small victory for the VFW, the president signed the bill into law in early February 1944.

The differences brought forth by the discussion over mustering-out pay did not disappear overnight. Not long after the law was passed, the VFW, the DAV, and two smaller veterans' groups wrote an open letter in opposition to the Legion's omnibus bill. "Everything that glitters is not gold," their missive began. Calling upon the memory of the interwar period, these organizations argued that the proposed benefits were so generous that they would "jeopardize the entire structure of veteran benefits and provoke" a backlash in the form of "another Economy Act." In their view, Congress should focus on helping disabled instead of able-bodied veterans.[103] Both the DAV and the VFW sought to pass a bonus bill similar to that introduced in the interwar period.[104] This clash reflected policy differences as well as pettier dynamics. From the standpoint of

VFW officials, the Legion's push for an omnibus bill was a last-minute effort to steal the spotlight that should rightfully have been theirs, the "most colossal and ruthless grab for credit and glory in years."[105]

If this campaign was a publicity stunt, it was a very efficient one. Even though other veterans' groups had been pushing for similar measures much earlier, the Legion proved far more successful. Echoing the GAR's collaboration with the *Herald Tribune* in the post–Civil War era, Legionnaires entered into a partnership with the newspaper chain of the rabid anti–New Dealer William Randolph Hearst, who supported their fight against the administration. More broadly, Legion officials simply carried out on a larger scale the same time-tested strategy they had followed throughout the interwar period, using their federalist structure to garner grassroots support behind the omnibus bill. They sent a mimeographed copy to every daily newspaper, resulting in the publication of more than six hundred favorable editorials. Every local post received its own as well, along with instructions about what to do to gather community support. Uniformed Legionnaires were often present in the lobby of local movie theaters, with blank cards ready to be signed by patrons and mailed to their representative. In mid-March, the Legion conducted a national "Sign-Up" day during which it gathered more than 2 million signatures. Meanwhile, the Legion clip sheet service supplied more than eleven hundred Army and Navy publications with full coverage of the bill's progress in Congress.[106]

All this publicity was carefully orchestrated by the national leadership. As posts and departments conducted the campaign at the local and state levels, the members of Stelle's special committee worked around the clock to secure votes on Capitol Hill. They kept a day-by-day tally of the situation in both chambers of Congress on a large wall chart. When the graph indicated that some lawmakers were hesitant, at the end of the day "telegrams would go out to Legion officials in the States, or districts, in which the doubtful votes were found," urging "the local Legion forces to direct a flood of public opinion against the hesitant legislator."[107] A good example of this coordination and of the committee's media savviness was the fact that Atherton presented the 2 million signatures gathered during "Sign-Up" day to Speaker of the House Sam Rayburn on the steps of the Capitol in the presence of several other members of Congress and a "battery of photographers."[108]

This maelstrom of advertising helped obscure the role played by other veterans' groups, but we should be careful not to exaggerate its effects. Polls showed that an overwhelming share of the population was already behind similar measures long before the Legion's campaign even started.[109] It is more accurate to say that rather than creating a political groundswell from scratch, the group simply tapped into the deep reservoir of patriotic support for the white, male citizen-soldier.[110] One way that it did so was by calling its omnibus measure a "bill of rights for G.I. Joe and G.I. Jane" (later shortened to simply the "GI Bill of Rights"), thereby making the connection with service members explicit.[111] By framing their benefits as earned rights rather than "gratuities," the Legion managed to avoid the stigma attached to older forms of veterans' benefits such as pensions, even though its bill was premised on the same principle of treating former service members as a select group.[112] When opponents deployed the familiar charge that the Legion was a "powerful lobby" acting on behalf of a special interest, allies responded that its "energy" was merely "displayed in behalf of the men and women serving our country in this war."[113] The campaign projected an image of the Legion and of the veterans' movement as public-spirited instead of self-interested.

This is not to say that the GI Bill of Rights sailed effortlessly through Congress. The veterans' movement remained divided: the VFW rallied behind the Legion after the bill was amended to include some of its own proposals, but the DAV continued to oppose it, preferring measures that targeted the disabled first.[114] The issue of higher education and training also caused problems. With the support of the education community, liberals were still holding out hope for Senator Elbert Thomas's bill, which placed these benefits under the responsibility of the U.S. Office of Education instead. Yet it soon became clear that the plan was doomed by a lack of support from the administration.[115] To reassure congressional conservatives, Colmery made it clear that the Legion's bill would not expand the New Deal state: vesting all authority within the conservative-minded VA, he wrote, would defeat any attempt by supporters of the president to use these benefits as "entering wedges" in fields where the federal government had traditionally been absent.[116] As one Legion official argued, their omnibus bill was simply "a temporary program of definite duration to meet the special problems of a special group," not a stepping stone meant to advance the social reform agenda of the administration for the entire civilian population in the postwar period.[117] Presented in this limited way, the bill appealed to many conservatives.

There was a rich irony to this situation, of course. Since the VA was in charge of its provisions, the bill *was* expanding the federal government—just not the part of it that liberals favored. New Dealers may have hoped to use demobilization planning to promote their own social policy agenda, but the alternative supported by the veterans' movement and its allies on the right was to expand welfare programs on a selective and (allegedly) temporary basis. Nonetheless, conservatives were still accepting a transfer of authority away from the states and toward the federal government.

Not all of them consented. In the end, the most serious threat that the veterans' movement had to overcome came from perhaps the least likely source: John Rankin, the conservative chairman of the committee to which the GI Bill had been assigned in the House. Though he had been one of the Legion's most steadfast allies throughout the interwar period, Rankin made several objections to the GI Bill. As a fervent anticommunist, he believed that higher education was ripe with "Red school teacher[s]" who would indoctrinate the nation's veterans. As a Southern Democrat and rabid white supremacist, he was concerned that the bill's unemployment benefits would allow African American veterans to escape the Jim Crow system of economic apartheid that forced them to accept low-paying jobs, and he wanted to make sure that job search benefits would remain under the purview of the states. Finally, as a longtime champion of the Bonus, he wanted to include one for World War II veterans in the bill.[118]

Rankin's opposition brought the Legion's campaign within a hair's breadth of defeat. In late May 1944, after the GI Bill had passed the Senate and the House, the Mississippian stalled the deliberations in the conference committee between both chambers, thereby preventing the enactment of the bill. Late in the afternoon on June 9, Stelle's team learned that if they did not bring John S. Gibson, a committee member absent for illness, back to D.C. by 10 AM the next morning to cast his vote, the bill would not pass in that session of Congress.[119]

The Legion immediately began searching for the representative of the Eighth Georgia District. In the process, it made good use of its deep connections within civil society and the state. Calls to southern Georgia were normally delayed by five hours due to wartime restrictions, but the night city editor of the *Atlanta Constitution* used his paper's telephone priority to get the Legion's calls through. To locate Gibson, the group enlisted the help of radio stations in Valdosta and Atlanta, as well as of the Georgia State Police and the *Jacksonville Times-Union*. A phone call to Assistant Secretary of War Robert Patterson obtained a high plane priority and the Hearst press chain convinced Eastern Air Lines to hold its 2:20 AM flight from Jacksonville to D.C. Once Gibson was found around 11 PM in a town 155 miles away from the airport, the Georgia Legion Commander drove him to a nearby Army air base where he switched to a fast car with two chauffeurs. Cruising at 90 miles an hour into the night, the car brought Gibson in time to Jacksonville for his flight. After being greeted by Stelle's entire committee at Washington's National Airport, Gibson delivered his crucial vote on the morning of June 10 to break the stalemate. Had the Legion not been able to mobilize its far-reaching network on such short notice (what Stelle appropriately called "real teamwork"), the GI Bill would have floundered in its final stretch.[120]

It was a tribute to the central role played by the veterans' movement that several top Legion and VFW officials were present in the Oval Office on June 22, 1944, when Roosevelt appended his signature to what was known officially as the Servicemen's Readjustment Act.[121] The signing of the bill attracted remarkably little attention at the time, partly because it coincided with the invasion of Normandy. But this neglect also reflected the fact that few expected the GI bill to have a large impact. Most contemporary observers did not see it as a "historic" law but rather as a temporary measure meant "to facilitate, as quickly as possible, the readjustment of veterans to civilian life"—exactly the message that veterans had used to reassure conservative lawmakers. Only a small fraction of former service members were expected to use its provisions.[122] Neither was it seen as a perfect piece of legislation. From the standpoint of the VFW, the GI Bill presented significant drawbacks: its chief lobbyist complained that the "administrative problems and cost will be terrific" and that it would "penalize the veterans with real service" because it made no difference between soldiers who had been discharged after a short period and those who had served abroad for a long time. He also pointed to a little-noticed clause in the last section of the law, which provided that if an adjusted compensation bill were to be enacted in the future, any benefit received under the GI Bill "shall be charged against and deducted from such compensation."[123] The fact that lawmakers had designed the Servicemen's Readjustment Act as an insurance against another expensive bonus did nothing to please the advocates of the latter. It helps explain why its passage was not universally celebrated.

The GI Bill may not have been recognized as such immediately, but it was nevertheless a landmark in the long history of veterans' welfare state. Not only did it further enshrine into law the idea that the federal government had a duty to help even able-bodied veterans readjust to civilian life, but it was also a major defeat for New Dealers who had hoped to design a comprehensive social policy that would place veterans on a par with the rest of the population—or, failing that, to at least use the bill as an opening wedge for the federal government in a field like education. As a measure for veterans *only*, the GI Bill reinforced the separation of their programs from those for civilians. The fact that responsibility for its administration went to the VA instead of the Federal Security Agency ensured that it would not expand the New Deal state, and that Hines's agency would retain control of old as well as new veterans' programs. The VA's status as the single agency responsible for former service members was further confirmed and entrenched. Finally, this law reflected a broader reorientation of the nation's social policy agenda during World War II, as attempts to expand broad-based policies such as Social Security all failed. The country eventually decided to extend benefits only to a special category of the population: war veterans.[124]

Not all former service members were treated equally, however. The predominance of southern Democrats in Congress ensured that the GI Bill would not challenge racist practices on the local level.[125] In a manner typical of many other pieces of legislation passed during these years, the federal government provided funding but the administration of the law was shared between the VA, individual states, and private institutions. For instance, veterans had to obtain the approval of a bank before the VA could guarantee part of their loan. As most southern banks refused to lend to African Americans, the overwhelming majority of those who lived in this region were unable to take advantage of the provision. The same logic applied to educational benefits. Most schools in the South refused to enroll blacks, forcing them to flock to overcrowded and underfunded all-black institutions. Likewise, those who applied for vocational training were often told to accept low-skilled jobs below their actual qualifications.[126] The Big Three did nothing to prevent this. When faced with Rankin's attempts to torpedo the GI Bill out of fear that it would undermine white supremacy, Atherton did not defend black veterans but instead argued that the Mississippi Democrat underestimated the degree to which "states rights" were embedded into the law. "Control of many of the features of the bill," he assured conservatives, "will still rest with the individual states."[127]

In the same way that the GI Bill reinforced the connection of martial citizenship with whiteness, it discriminated against female veterans. Since women were generally seen as men's dependents who belonged in the private sphere, most people assumed that the 350,000 or so who had served in the military during World War II would return home, find a husband, and become housewives and mothers rather than use their benefits to get an education or start a career. Lawmakers not only expected the recipients of the GI Bill to be mostly male, but they also actively discouraged the possibility of civilian men relying on their veteran wives for a living.[128] Thus a married woman who wanted to use the GI Bill's educational benefits could not claim her husband as a dependent if she wanted to receive an additional allowance (whereas a male veteran could do so for his civilian wife). Veterans' widows were eligible for a GI Bill loan, but not widowers. Beyond the letter of the law, neither the Legion nor the VA actively reached out to women veterans to inform them of their rights and encourage them to apply, as they did for men. The emphasis on the figure of the male citizen-soldier only reinforced the notion that women's contributions were inferior to men's and that their benefits would therefore be unequal. Most women took this for granted: a survey conducted decades later revealed that almost 60 percent of those who had served in World War II did not even know that they were eligible for GI Bill benefits.[129]

Gender-based discrimination was also embedded in the last major piece of veterans' legislation of the war, the Veterans' Preference Act. Signed into law just a few days after the GI Bill in June 1944, this measure generated far less debate, for veterans' preference in civil service had existed since the Civil War.[130] The act was nevertheless an important milestone, as the first time that such advantages were systematically codified into law rather than being enforced by executive orders.[131] The Big Three stood united behind it. The only bone of contention during the hearings concerned the status of veterans' dependents. Charles LaFollette, a liberal Republican and member of the House from Indiana, proposed amendments to equalize the status of male and female spouses of former service members by allowing husbands instead of only wives to benefit from preference. He argued that there was no sense in denying husbands this right solely on the ground that they might be "a bad fellow," since "for us to object to whom a woman might marry is to presuppose that every girl that an ex-serviceman marries is a perfect woman." While the Legion did not address this issue, the VFW testified that these amendments threatened to "reverse the old American idea of a wife being dependent upon her husband, which is the basis for the existing grant of veteran preference to wives and widows of war veterans." The DAV agreed, noting that the amendments risked "[bringing] ridicule upon the entire veterans' preference legislation."[132] LaFollette's proposals were not included in the final version of the law, which served as yet another example of how ideas about male breadwinners and female domesticity were embedded into martial citizenship.

All of the veterans' legislation passed during the war, then, served to enforce an external as well as an internal fault line. The external division was between veterans and civilians: from reemployment rights in 1940 to civil service preference in 1944, these laws all applied to veterans only, extending to this special category of the population a series of benefits from which those who had not served in the military were excluded, regardless of how deserving and dangerous their work on the home front or abroad may have been. The second fault line was within the veteran community itself. Though most of these pieces of legislation were technically gender- and color-blind, in practice they were designed to reflect and reinforce the long-standing view of veterans as white male breadwinners. Former service members who did not fit into this category were never explicitly and completely denied access to their benefits, but they often found such access much more difficult if not impossible. Far from being accidents, these dividing lines were the intentional result of the lobbying of the veterans' movement.

At the same time as these policies were being hashed out, their future recipients were already engaged in a debate of their own about what they would do after the war was over.

From GIs to Veterans

The debate among service members about the veterans' movement was in many ways a mirror image of the discussions that had taken place earlier among Legionnaires about whether they should allow their younger counterparts to join. Both revealed the persistence of strong feelings of generational identity as well as a complex mix of self-interest and altruism. The question of how the new cohort would relate to the older one was never self-evident.

For all the money it spent on trying to recruit new members, the Legion achieved little. With most service members primarily concerned about "getting the job done" so that they could go home, few devoted much thinking to what they would do after the fighting was over. Even when they did, the issue of which veterans' organization to join typically ranked quite low on their list of priorities, far behind finding a job or getting married. As famous war cartoonist Bill Mauldin later wrote, during the war the soldiers' attitude toward veterans' groups "ran pretty well to one feeling: it's better to be a Mister than a Veteran. A few thought it would be nice to have a social club to keep war-made friendships alive; a handful thought the vet should organize for political reasons. But most guys . . . didn't want anything in the way of clubs, uniforms, parades, or conventions—anything that would remind them of what they had been through."[133]

This did not mean that soldiers had no opinion on the question. Many GIs did in fact plan on joining some form of veterans' group after the war. An April 1945 survey of more than thirty-seven hundred soldiers in Europe found that 55 percent would definitely join and that only 3 percent thought such organizations were a bad idea.[134] The letters they sent to Army newspapers such as *Army Times, Stars and Stripes*, and *Yank: The Army Weekly* help us understand their expectations.

In general, most GIs seemed to agree with the feelings expressed by one of them that "we ought to have a vets' organization of our own. We are young and we will make the future. The Legion and VFW just don't have our ideas."[135] *Yank* writer Charles Bolté wrote that when his magazine asked its readers for their thoughts on the topic in early 1945, the mail it received was "two to one in favor of a new organization."[136] Serving as a public relations officer during the war, the Legion's John Thomas Taylor arrived at the same conclusion. In a private letter, he wrote that his daily interactions with service members convinced him that "they are going to get a show of their own started as soon as they can."[137]

There were several reasons for this preference. In some cases, it stemmed from a gut feeling that the failures of the previous generation were somehow responsible for World War II—or as an article in *Stars and Stripes* put it, that "the older group may not have done so well on their plans, or we might not be in this war."[138] More often, it came from a rejection of the conservative politics of the previous cohort. "We will not be led like sheep into the fold of the Legion with its ideas of a quarter-century ago," wrote one private, "We will not be dazzled by brilliant uniforms on dull minds. We are not looking back, but forward. We are fighting for a better world—our world—and we will not be led, we will lead."[139] The Legion's right-wing positions on issues such as labor, immigration, or the New Deal were clearly a problem for at least a few GIs. As a more progressive alternative, some liberal World War II veterans led by Gilbert Harrison and Charles Bolté created the AVC in 1943.[140]

Above all, the fact that many GIs preferred forming their own group reflected a widespread feeling that the current war was fundamentally different from the last. They were hardly the first to think this way: over two decades earlier, the same motivation had been behind the creation of the Legion. "The problems, attitudes, ideas and needs of World War II soldiers are different from those of World War I veterans," wrote a staff sergeant in 1945, "We fight a global war. They fought only in France. We have many times their numbers. We have been longer overseas under conditions which they never faced."[141] Not unlike those Legionnaires who had argued against opening their group to the new cohort, many GIs were concerned that these differences would produce tensions. "Would we not be the junior members of the American Legion or VFW?" asked a sergeant. "Would it be possible for us to bring forth our true thoughts and efforts when the executive positions of our organizations would be held by men of another generation? ... Would they as the officers of our organization work as diligently for soldier benefits for us as they did for themselves?"[142]

Even those GIs who argued in favor of joining preexisting groups did so not out of a belief in shared comradeship and ideals, but because they saw it as the easiest way to secure political influence. As one private asked, "Instead of every World War II vet and his pal initiating a postwar vet outfit why not join an established organization like the American Legion? In this manner World War II vets could solve the problem of quick and efficient unification. . . . A multitude of vet organizations, each trying to gain or initiate their own objectives, will only tend to defeat our common goal of happiness and prosperity."[143] The same argument was made for joining the VFW.[144] It should not surprise us that the men and women who had gone through the privations of the Great Depression and the sacrifices of a total war thought primarily about their own interests. A contemporary survey found that when it came to postwar life, "the soldier was mainly thinking about himself and his family, not about his country or the world," and that he saw veterans' groups as tools not to reform society but to ensure "the protection of veterans' rights and provision of personal help."[145]

The first tangible effects of this debate began to be felt in the winter of 1944–45. As more and more veterans were coming back, Legion posts were encouraged to organize lively homecoming parties with "bands, orchestras, glee clubs, vaudeville acts, community singing of war songs, etc."[146] Of the 2 million soldiers discharged prior to the end of the war, approximately 285,000 had already joined the organization by December 1944.[147] This influx of new blood heralded a radical transformation. "Day by day, all former membership records are being shattered," National Adjutant Donald Glascoff reported in August 1945. "New Posts are being chartered rapidly. . . . Legion Posts generally throughout the country are buying new clubhouses, building new homes, remodeling and expanding existing quarters. Legion full-time staffs, whether they be county council, district, department or national, are being augmented constantly with additions of WWII veterans."[148] The signs of the expected "rebirth" were here (Fig. 4).

The integration of new Legionnaires did not always go smoothly. As Texas Legion leader Alvin Owsley wrote, the problem was that "many of our . . . Posts have become 'old soldier homes' where a lot of old worthless, bald-headed, men sit around, spit on the floor, shoot craps, play dominoes, checkers, poker, put their nickels and dimes in the slot machines and stay about half-drunk and blear-eyed."[149] Interactions between generations at the local level could indeed be difficult. Based on hearsay, one self-proclaimed "Legionnaire of long standing" from Pennsylvania reported that "in many posts there is a sharp cleavage between so called WW1 and WW2 boys. . . . [T]here is a reluctance, in some cases even abhorance [sic], to grant equality of expression, action, and participation

Figure 4. Two World War II veterans and their ten-week-old baby are
sworn into the Edsel B. Ford American Legion Post No. 379 in Ypsilanti,
Michigan (ca. July 1945). Lisle H. Alexander to Jack Cejnar, July 27,
1945, reel 95-1059, American Legion Archives, Indianapolis, Indiana.

in Post direction to the new members. Furthermore, there is a tendency on the
part of the old guard to manipulate to exclude the new boys, while perpetuating
themselves in office, meanwhile referring to the new veterans as inept, irrespon-
sible, radical, etc."[150]

In part because of this sometimes cold reception, but also out of a natural
desire to be among themselves, many new Legionnaires decided to create their
own posts. By July 1944 there were seven of these; a year later, at least twenty-
two.[151] This practice was not new—women and racial minorities had long formed
their own posts as well—but it was greeted with misgivings by some old-time
Legionnaires who feared that World War II veterans would go astray without
their guidance. If young veterans chose to form their own posts, an official from
South Carolina wrote to the national headquarters, "I can easily visualize a Post
made up entirely of young men of this war flying off at an unfortunate tangent

to the main program and principles of our organization and thereby becoming involved and, at the same time involving us, in trouble."[152] As Legion leaders were beginning to realize, even those younger veterans who joined their organization remained attached to their identity as members of a separate generation.

In the last stretch of the war, the Legion undertook one final public relations drive. The effort was led by the Americanism Endowment Fund, a small group created by Owsley in 1943 to promote patriotic values.[153] He hired the New York–based Institute of Public Relations a year later to reshape the Legion's public profile.[154] Over the course of the next eight months, the Institute carried out a wide-ranging promotional campaign whose main goal was, in its own words, to lift the Legion "from the *public acceptance* status of a strictly veterans' service organization into the sphere of an institution of broad national service concerned with the whole fabric of our nation." Sparing no effort, the Institute cooperated with the national commander to help prepare speeches, radio addresses, and press articles, and it printed tens of thousands of booklets and reports to build support for various Legion activities. The Institute reported in June 1945 that the result was "a gradual awakening of greater interest" in the organization. "While some still see the Legion as a 'pressure group,'" the Institute asserted, "they recognize it as a 'pressure group' for a strong united nation . . . rather than for any single element of our population."[155]

There is no doubt that the Legion emerged from the war more popular than it had entered it: as one of its officials reported in 1945, "the newspapers are backing the Legion" and many "with huge circulation" were urging young veterans to join.[156] The Institute erred in claiming credit for this change, however. What really enhanced the group's profile was not this single public relations campaign but rather the decision taken in 1942 to welcome the new generation of veterans. By taking GIs in, the Legion inherited the prestige bestowed on them by wartime patriotism, which helped it shed its more negative prewar image—though never entirely, as we will see in the next chapter.

This "two-war experiment" marked a turning point in the long history of the veterans' movement, as the first time not only that a major group accepted more than one generation of former service members without any additional restriction, but also that one generation decisively influenced the shape of the benefits available to another. The irony here is that former service members of both world wars decided to join forces not because they were no longer attached to their identity as members of a different cohort, but precisely because they realized it was in the best interest of their own generation to do so. The outcome of the war seemed to prove them right, for the evolution of veterans' policy during World War II followed a course that was much more favorable to former service members than that during the Great War. Rather than treating them as merely one category of the population among others, a series of major laws recognized and even expanded their special status. In this sense, the Second World War marked the triumph of martial citizenship and contributed to entrenching the division between veterans and civilians further into the structure of the state.

Amid this atmosphere of rapid change came news of Japan's defeat in August 1945. The end of hostilities meant the beginning of the Legion's real effort, for most service members were going to bé discharged and therefore eligible for membership. The new national commander, Edward Scheiberling, recognized this when he wrote a telegram on the day after the second atomic bomb was dropped on Nagasaki and before the surrender of Japan had been announced, urging "immediate initiation of department and post membership promotion plans, so when cessation comes, world wide membership contacts will be started at once."[157] Scheiberling knew only too well that the success of his group in the postwar period was far from assured. The VFW had built up a substantial lead— six hundred thousand new members had joined since the beginning of the war, compared with the Legion's four hundred thousand—and it seemed bent on further progress.[158] The AVC and the AMVETS were also asserting their position as influential voices for the new generation. At stake in the upcoming scramble for new members was nothing less than the leadership of the veterans' movement.

CHAPTER 3

Clash

Intergenerational Transition and the Postwar Housing Crisis

As the first enlisted man to receive the congressional Medal of Honor in World War II, Charles Kelly found the media attention lavished upon him and his family difficult to bear. "This hero business is more strenuous than army life in Italy," he admitted to a newspaper in the spring of 1944. At twenty-three, "Commando" Kelly was often described by a press not afraid of ethnic stereotyping as a "fighting Irishman." After being awarded the medal for almost single-handedly defending an ammunition storehouse against German attacks during an entire night in an Italian town south of Naples, he returned home to tour the country in support of the war effort around the same time as the GI Bill was signed into law. Thrust under the spotlights, Kelly compared his situation to being "like a monkey in a cage."[1]

One of the many pictures of his tour drew the nation's attention more than others (Fig. 5). It showed his mother on the doorstep of their family's home in Pittsburgh's "Deutschtown" neighborhood, a working-class area originally developed by German immigrants. The press found the living conditions there particularly shocking. One journalist described the Kellys' home as "two rooms and an attic on the second floor of a ramshackle frame building in a setting of converted barns, junk yards and dangling fire escapes," with "no electricity, no hot running water, no inside toilet facilities." To their dismay, Americans learned that "Hero Kelly" lived in what one newspaper called "a typical slum building."[2] Widespread assumptions of soldiers' deservedness were clashing with the reality of the substandard housing that many of their families lived in. "Will anyone," the *Times* demanded, "dare say that [this house] is good enough for the Kellys?"[3]

THE PRIVATE HOME OF A NATIONAL HERO

Press Association photo

Figure 5. Charles Kelly's mother Irene Kelly (left, holding a newspaper) is seen here with her neighbors on the steps of her home in Pittsburgh. The headline drew attention to the contrast between Charles's heroic status and the poor quality of his living accommodations. *Public Housing* 10, no. 4 (April 1944): 15.

While everyone agreed that service members deserved better, there was no consensus as to how they should be rewarded. Some argued that the state should step in. Journalist I. F. Stone asked in the left-wing *PM* "whether in the future America ought not to do better for its heroes." Pittsburgh's mayor agreed and he proposed that the family stay in an "expensive suite in a downtown hotel" during Charles's visit. Not to be outdone, the city's Public Housing Authority presented his mother with a permanent new apartment in a nearby project. She turned both offers down, refusing to move until the "hullabaloo" of war had subsided. Other voices seized on her reaction to push back against what they saw as a threat to private industry. Some papers reprinted a syndicated editorial castigating advocates of public housing as "misguided social uplifters who adopt the New Deal formula of regeneration at no matter what cost of dissatisfaction." Georgia's *Pittston Gazette* lauded the mother's "pride" and condemned the housing authority for its humiliating offer, presenting its own position as "not a defense of poor housing, but a protest against the unconscious snobbery of a lot of professional do-gooders."[4]

The squabble over the Kellys' accommodations was an early example of how the return of World War II veterans would give new momentum to the long-simmering debate over public housing that dated back to the Great Depression. Due to the economic downturn of the 1930s and then to wartime restrictions, the country's housing supply was woefully inadequate in 1945. This problem became particularly urgent with the sudden return of millions of veterans, as policymakers feared unrest on an even larger scale than after the Great War. The solution embraced by the Truman administration as well as by many young veterans was the expansion of public housing. Obtaining the approval of the legislative branch proved exceedingly difficult, however.

What set this debate apart from the one that had unfolded during the war years is that veterans' interests were now colliding directly with those of a powerful industry bent on resisting state intervention: private housing. Real estate, home finance, and construction groups formed one of the most powerful lobbies in Congress with long-standing connections to the GOP. These trade associations rejected public housing as an unwarranted intrusion of the federal government, even as they favored less obtrusive measures such as federal mortgage guaranties and slum clearance subsidies. Against them stood an ad hoc coalition made up mostly of liberals but also of some conservatives, which defended public housing as the most expeditious solution to an enduring national problem, and for whom the return of millions of veterans represented an opportunity to finally overcome the opposition that had long stalled their program.

As public housing came to the fore in national politics, it also acted as a catalyst for the process of intergenerational transition within the veterans' movement. After V-J Day, the steady trickle of new members who had already joined during the war became a flood. The membership of the Legion, VFW, and DAV reached a historic peak in 1946, at respectively 3.3 million, 1.5 million, and 105,000.[5] Only in the first of these groups, however, did the arrival of World War II veterans cause a major upheaval. This was in part because neither the VFW nor the DAV had been founded to defend the interests of a specific cohort, which meant that they could welcome a new one without any fundamental change. But it was also the result of the Legion's conservative leadership, which opposed public housing whereas the more populist VFW quickly embraced this issue. Since the needs of disabled veterans came first for the DAV, housing took a back seat to other priorities such as the reform of VA hospitals. Only in the Legion, then, did housing become controversial and intimately intertwined with the already contentious process of generational change. The fight over public housing within this group was also a fight for control between the old and the new cohorts.

This internal debate ended in 1948 with a victory for proponents of public housing when the Legion reversed its long-standing opposition to this program. In a sense, this move was remarkably counterintuitive: one of the most powerful forces for conservatism in the United States now stood behind a key plank of President Harry Truman's liberal Fair Deal. This was in part the result of the large influx of World War II members, which helped erode the reactionary grip of the old guard. More broadly, it was only the latest example of the Legion's long record of support for expanding welfare benefits and sacrificing fiscal austerity when it came to issues that benefited former service members. Even while they professed to oppose big government, the white men who accounted for the overwhelming majority of the membership of the Big Three had long been fighting for special access to government services in the name of martial citizenship. Seen from this perspective, the surprise reversal of the Legion on public housing was no surprise at all.

To understand how the Legion changed its stance on public housing, this chapter opens where the previous one left off. The intergenerational tensions already palpable within the group at the end of the war only increased with time. Rather than a seamless amalgamation of two cohorts, the aftermath of VJ Day witnessed a tumultuous fight for power. At stake in this conflict were both new benefits and the broader question of whether there could be such a thing as a cross-generational veterans' group.

The "Problem" of World War II Veterans

Despite all the laws passed by Congress, the transition to peacetime remained difficult for many GIs. More than a million of them came home every month from October to December 1945.[6] Even then, many found that the pace of demobilization was not fast enough. Their frustration produced small-scale mutinies in military bases across the globe, from Manila to Calcutta to Paris.[7] Once at home, they were often disappointed. Years of service abroad had led

many GIs to paint for themselves a glamorous picture of civilian life. They
became easy targets for swindlers eager to sell them fanciful business ventures.[8]
More broadly, it was difficult to transition from the comradeship of military life
to what one veteran called the "civilian world of competition, money profits,
the black market, and what often seems . . . like a niggardly scramble for purely
personal gain."[9] A survey found that more than 40 percent of discharged soldiers felt that the war had changed their life for the worse, leaving them "more
nervous," "irritable," and "short-tempered," not to mention the widespread cases
of alcohol and gambling addiction.[10]

These issues fueled a lively debate on the "veteran problem." At the end
of World War II, Americans harbored what one historian has called a "sharply
divided consciousness that both honored the veteran and feared his potential
to disrupt society," as captured by the title of psychologist Alanson Edgerton's
book, *Readjustment or Revolution?* (1946).[11] His was only one of the many publications on the topic in the aftermath of the war. As Charles Bolté noted, this literature often reproduced old stereotypes of the veteran as either "a simple-witted
boy whose only thought is coming home to Mom and blueberry pie, a trained
killer who will stalk the land with a tommy-gun shooting up labor leaders and
war profiteers, a mental case whose aberrations will upset the tidy households
and offices of America for a generation, a bitter and cynical man who will ruth-
lessly seize the reins of political power for selfish ends, a starry-eyed idealist who
will fashion a perfect world single-handed, or a hopeless incompetent who will
flounder when released from army discipline and become a charge upon the
community."[12] However hackneyed, these tropes reflected very real anxieties
over the political impact of this new cohort. One journalist wrote that "postwar
America's most precious prize" was "the mind of the veteran."[13] Yet not all former
service members were of the same mind, which was unavoidable for a cohort of
16 million. As we saw in the previous chapter, veterans' groups ran the gamut
from the communist left to the liberal center and the far right.[14]

The American Legion was eager to maintain its leadership within this
movement. Encouraged by their early success—six hundred thousand new veterans had joined by November 1945—Legion leaders set their sights even higher,
hoping to reach 5 or 6 million members in the near future.[15] They spared no
expenses, more than quadrupling their public relations budget to over $300,000
in 1945–46.[16] The money was spent on countless movie trailers, posters, window display cards, stickers, clip sheets, and pamphlets.[17] In all this whirlwind
of publicity, Legionnaires strove to change their image as a group dominated
by an old establishment of conservative "kingmakers." They hammered on the

message that the new generation would soon have a decisive influence within the organization, simply by virtue of its larger size.[18] One suggested address asserted for instance that "we expect you younger Legionnaire to become members of the team. Our democratic processes within the Legion assure you early control. Every member has an equal voice and an equal vote. The majority controls. It is as simple as that."[19]

The reality was more complicated, for not every member was treated equally. In describing women, for instance, Legion publications continued to stress first and foremost their physical appearance. Female members brought "a new element of glamor and beauty" into the Legion, as one pamphlet describing the "new strength" of the group argued. Describing one of them, it noted that she was a "former Harry Conover model in New York" before adding that "her likeness still adorns the Marine recruiting posters."[20] More broadly, the Legion made no efforts to address the specific needs of its female members, leading one of them to complain that the group was "'missing the boat' by not making an all-out effort to obtain the membership of the woman veteran." She added, "There are thousands of them who know nothing of the Legion, who have never been approached to join."[21] The same disinterest applied to veterans of color, not a single one of whom appeared in that same pamphlet. The colorful covers of the *American Legion Magazine*, one of the nation's most widely circulated periodicals, almost never featured a black person throughout the 1940s and 1950s.[22]

Even among white male veterans, the passing of the baton from one cohort to the next was far from seamless. Though younger Legionnaires soon outnumbered their elders by a ratio of two to one, leadership positions remained firmly in the hands of the World War I cohort, which made only token efforts to bring in new faces. Two former GIs, Fred LaBoon and H. Dudley Swim, were for instance appointed national vice-commanders in 1945 while Paul Griffith, a veteran of both world wars or "retread," was elected national commander the following year.[23] Though they had all served in World War II, these three men hardly represented a break with the past: LaBoon had spent his childhood in Legion programs, while Swim was a rabid anti–New Dealer and a former treasurer of the America First Committee.[24] As for Griffith, his election was likely the result of a deal struck years earlier between kingmakers to give the job to someone from Pennsylvania, one of the Legion's most populous departments. The vice president of an East Coast electric corporation and the owner of dairy and public relations businesses, Griffith belonged to the same elite that had long monopolized top Legion positions and he intended the transition between the two generations to take place very slowly. "I am for the World War II boys one hundred per cent," he wrote. "But I am of the opinion that it would be very unwise to turn an organization as large and as great and as influential as The American Legion over to men who know nothing about its program."[25]

The American Legion College was created in 1946 to ensure that this would not happen. A two-week long course of study for a small group of promising World War II Legionnaires, the college sought to familiarize them with all aspects of the group's activities. This educational program was described as "a complete American Legion course of indoctrination."[26] The idea was not only to fast-track the promotion of future group leaders—as other groups like the DAV were also doing—but to make sure that they would be imbued with the Legion's conservative values.[27] Indeed, the course sought to increase "knowledge and appreciation on the part of the future leaders of The American Legion for our American way of life and our Constitutional form of government."[28] As one knowledgeable critic put it, the college represented "self-perpetuation in power with a vengeance."[29]

The very existence of this "indoctrination" program was an admission that the gap between both cohorts was not as negligible as Legion publications made it out to be. Over the next few years, no debate illustrated this divide as well as that over housing.

The Politics of the Postwar Housing Shortage

The immediate aftermath of the Second World War witnessed a global housing crisis. In the United States as elsewhere, the roots of the problem went back more than a decade. The Great Depression had caused housing construction to enter a long slump. Even after the war effort revitalized the economy, most building resources like lumber or steel were strictly reserved for military production. The only housing construction allowed during World War II was for defense workers, millions of whom flocked from the countryside to urban centers in search of work in war industries. Those who already lived in cities were prohibited from building new homes. As a result, municipalities filled up quickly.[30] When peace finally arrived, millions of veterans returned home with limited savings and incomes to find that affordable housing was in extremely limited supply. The rapid postwar rise in birth rates made the shortage even worse. In September 1945, only two thousand vacancies could be found in New York City's 2.2 million dwellings.[31] Nationwide, the official appraisal of the total number of homes needed in 1946 only to answer short-term needs was 2.7 million.[32]

The crisis affected veterans and nonveterans alike: approximately two-fifths of all respondents to a survey in early 1946 said they were either doubling up with friends or family or actively looking for a different place to live.[33] Still, former service members faced particularly dire conditions. As early as September 1945, when only about 2.5 million of them had been discharged, an official survey from the National Housing Agency (NHA), the entity in charge of coordinating all federal housing policy, noted that their situation was "bad" and only getting worse. Slightly over half of all veterans lived in units lacking one or more standard facilities like a private shower or central heating, a quarter of married veterans were doubling up with in-laws or friends, and only a little more than 10 percent of all veterans were homeowners.[34] The nature of the problem varied from region to region: the Northeast and the urban centers of the Midwest lacked affordable apartments to rent; southern housing was cheaper but often of poor quality; in the West, most veterans sought to buy but prices were often too high. In general, about a third of all former service members wished they could move out of their current dwellings.[35]

This shortage was a particularly bitter pill to swallow for those who had just returned from service. "Home is probably the most precious thing in the world to a man who endured war," Navy veteran Franklin D. Roosevelt, Jr., wrote. "There is hardly a man who didn't spend hours remembering his home, how it used to look, or how it was going to look when he and his wife got a place and bought their furniture."[36] Disappointment was compounded by disbelief among those who remembered the engineering feats pulled off by their country in wartime. As another veteran explained, "To me, and to hundreds of thousands of other ex-GIs who watched the Army and Navy build whole cities all over the world almost literally overnight, the housing shortage at home seemed incredible. We couldn't believe that the United States, having put up a roof for the GI on Guam, couldn't put one up for the GI in Ephrate [sic], Pennsylvania."[37] Many veterans who had been promised better treatment saw the housing shortage as a direct affront.

We saw earlier how former doughboys were among the first groups to organize mass protests during the Great Depression. It should come as no surprise, then, that veterans were once again quick to mobilize in response to the housing crisis—especially in big cities and through left-leaning groups. In California, they dramatized their plight by organizing a motorcade to the state capitol dubbed the "Veterans' Housing Caravan."[38] In the fall of 1945, thousands of former service members gathered at a rally sponsored by the AVC in New York City to elect a Veterans' Housing Committee led by Franklin D. Roosevelt, Jr., who consulted with federal housing officials in Washington, D.C.[39] The following year, some veterans carried out a dramatic "sit-down" in the New York Senate Chamber in Albany to ask that a special session of the legislature be convened to solve the problem.[40] Knowing that the situation required more than piecemeal action, both the AMVETS and the VFW urged President Truman to tackle this "acute national crisis."[41]

The situation within the federal government was hardly less confusing than at the local level, however. Policymakers who had spent the war expecting the return of widespread unemployment were not prepared to handle a housing shortage. As a result, the administration made a major mistake when it removed all wartime price controls on housing materials one month after VJ Day. Rather than stimulate construction, this decision only caused prices to soar, forcing Truman to backtrack in December 1945 and reinstate controls. But the government's disarray stemmed also from internal debates as to whose needs should be addressed first—veterans' or the general population's. For instance, New Deal officials within the NHA wanted to provide shelter to as many Americans as possible by resuming the public housing program interrupted by the war. Echoing FDR's earlier opposition to martial citizenship, the NHA director rejected special housing programs for veterans on the ground that they would merely "obstruct or complicate" more comprehensive plans for the entire population.[42]

However sympathetic Truman may have been to such views, he had to contend with the pressure of veterans' groups. Their outcry led him to take a series of decisions that recognized the more urgent needs of this category of the population, such as speeding up the release of surplus war housing and building supplies, or granting veterans preference on the sale of homes built with certain materials.[43] He also appointed the liberal Democrat Wilson W. Wyatt to the new position of housing expediter, with the mission to coordinate policy in this field. The ex-mayor of Louisville, Kentucky, faced a nearly impossible task: after the administration had wasted precious time with counterproductive measures, demand for an immediate solution was reaching a fever pitch just as the country as a whole was turning against restrictive wartime controls. Wyatt had to find a quick answer to a problem that had dogged the country for over a decade, and he had to do so in an increasingly hostile environment.

He announced his solution, the Veterans' Emergency Housing Program (VEHP), in February 1946. Premised on the continuation and expansion of wartime emergency controls, the plan included other measures such as the prevention of all new and nonveteran's housing construction, government loans to manufacturers of prefabricated houses, and the expedited release of surplus war housing. Wyatt hoped to create nearly five times more homes in 1946 than in 1945, and even more in 1947. Yet his bold plan immediately ran into fierce opposition in Congress, where the conservative coalition of southern Democrats and midwestern Republicans allied with the private housing lobby delayed its passage for months.[44]

While Wyatt focused on the needs of veterans, the administration sought a long-term solution for the general population. It was embodied by the Taft-Ellender-Wagner bill, or T-E-W, named after its three Senate sponsors: Robert Taft of Ohio, the leader of the conservative wing of the GOP; Allen Ellender of Louisiana, a populist southern Democrat; and Robert F. Wagner of New York, the champion of the urban liberal wing of the Democratic Party. Inspired by the housing reform movement of the Progressive era, the bill had been in gestation in Congress for a long time and its exact content varied from one year to the next. Its essential provisions included a declaration of national policy making it the government's role to provide decent housing to its citizens, funding for housing research, loans to farmers for home improvements, federal aid to slum clearance and urban redevelopment, and, last but not least, the construction of several hundred thousand public housing units over a decade.

The names of the three cosponsors of the bill spoke volumes about the extraordinary character of postwar housing politics. How could a liberal Democrat like Wagner find himself in coalition with Taft, someone described by a colleague as "the patron saint of the ultra-conservatives," and with Ellender, a staunch white supremacist?[45] Wagner had long sought to improve the living conditions of the working class in big cities like New York. Having cosponsored the 1937 Wagner-Steagall Act that expanded the reach of the federal government in public housing, he was the Senate's foremost authority on the issue. Ellender came to the problem from a similar angle but with a different starting point: like many southern Democrats who supported the early New Deal, he sought the assistance of the federal government to alleviate the slum conditions endemic in many southern cities. Taft's support was more surprising. Though a vocal critic of the New Deal, his own visits to the slums in his hometown of Cincinnati convinced him of the need for action. He recognized that government had to step in if private industry could not satisfy the demands of low-income groups, and he believed that decent housing was key to preserving the unity of the family.[46] Behind these three men stood a range of liberal interest groups coordinated by the National Public Housing Conference, such as the National Association of Housing Officials, the U.S. Conference of Mayors, social workers, the AFL-CIO, religious groups, women's groups like the League of Women Voters, and civil rights groups like the NAACP.[47] Though public housing appealed to some conservatives, it remained primarily a liberal cause.

Not unlike the GI Bill, public housing was premised on a division of power between the federal government, which provided the funds, and local authorities, which both approved new projects and decided their location. Also not unlike the GI Bill, this framework was designed to avoid challenging discriminatory practices on the ground. Not only were most public housing projects racially segregated, but they were often built in lower-income urban areas instead of the more attractive land of the suburbs, which were typically reserved for white families. Gender-based discrimination was rampant as well, since public housing managers tended to select applicants based on their idea of a two-parent, male-breadwinner family. The applications of single persons and single parents were generally rejected, while apartments were regularly inspected to ensure that wives maintained "good housekeeping habits." In other words, public housing was yet another "affirmative action program" in which the federal government provided assistance to some but not all categories of white, working-class Americans.[48] It was also a typical example of the driving force behind much of the New Deal welfare state, namely breadwinner liberalism.

Public Housing and the Veterans' Movement

The veterans' movement came late to this debate, and it did not speak with one voice. While the VFW and the AMVETS were quick to demand national action, the Legion reacted more slowly.

Accustomed to working hand in hand with the state, Legion leaders were ill prepared for an emergency that government officials either ignored or misunderstood. Even when mail began to pour in to demand immediate action, the national commander remained largely unmoved and he promised only that local posts would cooperate with whatever action the government would take.[49] Throughout 1945, the only thing that the Legion did on the issue of housing was to push for a revision of the home loan provision of the GI Bill.[50] Still dominated by the World War I generation, its leadership failed to grasp that a clear majority of the veteran population was convinced that industry alone would not solve the shortage and that government had to step in.[51] Four grassroots groups of Legionnaires mobilized to move their organization in a different direction.

Ironically enough, the first one stemmed from a sworn enemy of the Legion, the Communist Party of the U.S.A. (CPUSA). Like the rest of the country, the

CPUSA expected returning World War II veterans to have a major influence in national politics. In an attempt to win over this powerful section of the population, communist leaders envisioned a bold postwar program in which labor unions and veterans' organizations would work together to provide leadership to ex-GIs, uniting to form a "powerful progressive movement" around issues such as public housing, price control, or racial democracy.[52] The official party journal, *Political Affairs*, argued that this movement would come together only if unions urged their members to join the two leading veterans' groups (the VFW and the Legion) in order to fight "the reactionary policies of [their] present leadership."[53] Communist veteran Justin Gray explained that "if enough World War II guys like ourselves got into the Legion, we could remake it in our own image. . . . [B]y staying out, we were handing the Legion over to the reactionaries by default."[54] In short, he and others like him were hoping to take the group over from within.

This was easier said than done. After meeting with the party functionary in charge of veterans' affairs, a small group of about half a dozen former correspondents of the army newspapers *Yank* and *Stars and Stripes* joined with other left-leaning veterans working in the radio and entertainment industry to form the Duncan-Paris Post No. 1422 in New York City in early 1946. Its commander was Marion Hargrove, author of the best-selling *See Here, Private Hargrove* (1942).[55] With the support of more than three hundred other posts in New York, Duncan-Paris launched a citywide campaign entitled "Operation Housing" in support of Wyatt's VEHP. It featured several high-profile events over the course of the next three months, including one where a veteran spent four days in the show window of Ludwig Baumann's famous department store chatting with celebrities like actress Lucille Ball. The climax was a rally held in mid-May at the Sixty-ninth Regiment Armory, where three thousand World War II veterans met New York Governor Thomas Dewey and stars such as Gene Kelly.[56] The operation was so successful at drawing media coverage—it was on the front page of the *Times*—that Duncan-Paris soon came under accusations of being a communist front and its charter was suspended a few months later.[57] Having realized that their secretive tactics were no match for the Legion, the CPUSA moved on.[58] It focused instead on infiltrating the AVC, a smaller group whose more liberal politics made it a softer target.[59]

The efforts of the CPUSA went in the same direction as those of a second group of dissidents, the National Conference of Union Labor Legionnaires. Created in 1938 by two posts in Chicago and Los Angeles, the purpose of the Conference was to give a voice to Legionnaires who were also union members and who disapproved of the group's long history of antilabor activity. More broadly, it aimed to be the "connecting link" between the Legion and labor unions.[60] Its leaders consistently denied any connection with the Communist Party, but their goals were very similar. Both tried to "steer [the Legion] away from fascism" and to "convert [it] into a liberal, progressive force."[61] Initially small, the Conference's ranks swelled with the arrival of World War II veterans: in May 1946, it claimed to have 138 posts made up entirely of union members with a total membership of fifty thousand.[62] Its agenda focused of course on labor issues, but the Conference also pushed the Legion to take a more aggressive position on the housing shortage. In 1946, it adopted a resolution asking for immediate passage of T-E-W.[63]

The Conference faced stiff opposition. Not only were its posts routinely refused a charter, but the Legion leadership created a special subcommittee to smear the group with red-baiting accusations.[64] The Conference was also handicapped by a lack of support from labor unions: the AFL, the CIO, and the Railroad Brotherhood all turned a deaf ear to its increasingly desperate calls for help. The Conference newsletter complained in October 1945 that "organized labor has been busy resisting all appeals ... for substantial financial support.... By failing to support us officially, [it] has made it impossible for us to organize more effectively on a national scale. We wonder when Labor will start looking at the Legion!"[65] Most labor leaders refused to get involved in the internal affairs of a group with such a long history of hostility to their cause, however. They also feared that supporting the Conference would only result in creating a competitor.[66] With no aid forthcoming from both within and without, the Conference was hamstrung by a lack of funds and it eventually dissolved in the late 1940s.[67]

Black Legionnaires were yet another insurgent group. With 1 million African Americans serving during World War II, the number of black Legionnaires increased substantially after 1945. "Colored posts" went from three hundred in 1944 to more than nine hundred in 1950.[68] Many of these new members mobilized forcefully in defense of their rights, for instance by sponsoring resolutions calling for the abolition of racial segregation within the group.[69] But resistance was equally fierce. When some thirty black veterans of both world wars picketed outside a Legion convention hall in 1946 to demand "open membership in all American Legion posts, North and South ... on the basis of equality of sacrifice—not race or color," they were beaten up and dispersed by white Legionnaires.[70] Still, the group was forced to change its overall attitude. After the war, southern departments gradually abandoned their policy of racial exclusion in favor of segregation.[71] This was a small improvement, but an improvement nonetheless.

Housing was a key issue for black veterans. Often poorer than their white counterparts, they tended to rely more on public housing and price controls. In large cities such as Chicago or New York, black veterans played a central role in protest movements targeting racial segregation in several areas, including housing.[72] Black Legionnaires drew attention to this problem: the commander of a black Legion post in Chicago's South Side, for instance, expressed "keen disappointment at the existing [housing] conditions" in his neighborhood. Black veterans, he argued, "feel discontented because on returning home, they could find no adequate housing" due to "restrictive covenants and obdurate owners who want to sell at exorbitant prices or who refuse to sell to colored citizens."[73] Yet Legion leaders continued to ignore the needs of their members of color. In the summer of 1946, for instance, the group was conspicuously missing from the list of attendees to a conference held by the American Council on Race Relations to find ways to tackle the discrimination embedded in GI Bill benefits.[74] As a columnist in the *Pittsburgh Courier* noted, this silence had dramatic consequences. "Housing is almost the special and peculiar need of Negroes wherever you find them," he wrote. "By opposing liberal housing programs, the Legion places its seal of approval on every Negro slum ghetto in the United States."[75]

Pressure for action on the housing issue came from one last source: college campuses. As a *New York Times* survey reported in early 1946, many colleges and universities were "turning away thousands of discharged war veterans because of insufficient housing, overcrowded classrooms and lack of instructional staff." Of all these problems, housing was the "most serious."[76] Those veterans who managed to enroll often lived in ad-hoc accommodations ranging from gyms filled with rows of bunk beds (for singles) to hastily built trailer parks (for married couples).[77] On many campuses, veterans responded to the crisis by organizing. The first "campus post" of the Legion was created in October 1944 at the University of Oklahoma; by December 1945, there were approximately thirty nationwide.[78] The range of their activities varied from school to school, but they typically included emergency loan funds, counsel to university administrators on veterans' issues, sports teams, and so on. Housing figured prominently on their agenda.[79]

While Legion leaders dismissed the complaints of the first three groups, veteran students presented an altogether different challenge. The national leadership saw this mostly white and male population as the ideal future Legionnaires: as one official wrote, they would likely go on to become "leaders of thought in their own communities" and thus "will be of tremendous help to the Legion if they are properly indoctrinated in the work of the Legion now."[80]

Their complaints therefore found a more receptive audience. In December 1945, National Commander John Stelle invited representatives from six college posts to meet with him in Indianapolis. Coming from schools such as Indiana University and Michigan State College, all the delegates reported facing an "immediate and critical housing shortage." They adopted a resolution calling for President Truman to use his wartime emergency powers and for Legion departments to take immediate action.[81] The National Executive Committee approved the resolution unanimously, but failed to act on it.[82]

Deep internal divisions lay behind this confusing course of action. On the one hand, Legion leaders were well aware that grassroots pressure was reaching a fever pitch. A Legion employee in charge of reporting legislative developments recognized in early 1946 that "housing is the hottest issue of the day" and that "if we do not meet the issue face to face we will lose immeasurable ground."[83] On the other hand, many of the World War I veterans who dominated the group's leadership remained steadfastly opposed to direct government intervention in this field. Unable to stake out a clear position, the Legion was stuck in limbo. When Stelle issued a public release in support of the VEHP, for instance, he was immediately rebuked by three congressmen from the conservative wing of the GOP, all of them World War I Legionnaires and adamantly opposed to Wyatt's program.[84] After Stelle withdrew the release, the only action that the Legion dared to take through the summer of 1946 was to join Wyatt's Veterans Advisory Council, a consultative body with little power.[85]

Months of pent-up frustration were on full display at the annual convention in September–October of that year. Only about twenty-five thousand members showed up in San Francisco, less than had attended in 1939. World War II veterans represented no more than one-fifth of convention delegates, even though they accounted for over two-thirds of all Legionnaires.[86] Such poor attendance was in part the result of the precarious economic situation of many recently discharged GIs, few of whom could afford to make the trip. But it also reflected widespread dissatisfaction with the leadership.[87] Reporters noted a "rumble of discontent" among younger veterans, who resented the hand-picking of Paul Griffith by the kingmakers for the position of national commander.[88] In an attempt to push the Legion to endorse the T-E-W bill, nearly one hundred World War II Legionnaires spontaneously assembled in a "rump caucus" to demand "a more vigorous attack" of the "vital housing problem."[89] Legion leaders responded by packing the meeting with their own men.[90] They succeeded: even though a few departments had previously endorsed T-E-W, the convention went on record against it. Delegates voted instead to refer the question to a new National Housing Committee

(NHC).[91] Before the caucus dissolved, it issued a reassuring statement that "there were no schisms or dissidence," and that "the welding of the partnership of World War I and World War II veterans had made great progress."[92]

The truth was quite the opposite. The fact that the seven members of the new NHC were all World War II veterans was the only concession made by Paul Griffith when he appointed them in early October. All of them embraced the old guard's conservative line. The chairman, Richard Cadwallader, was a former Army engineer and a Harvard law graduate from Baton Rouge, Louisiana, who made no mysteries of his feelings toward the government's role in the economy. "I am a Southerner," he declared, "I am a Confederate. And, I am a States Rights man. I believe that John C. Calhoun was right. And, we talk about Damn Yankees, and of course, we don't like [the] federal government anyway."[93] Nearly all other committee members were reported to have personal ties to the real estate and construction business.[94]

Still, the NHC did not remain idle. Its members toured different sections of the country to gather information on the crisis.[95] Their work culminated in a housing conference in early November in Washington, D.C., at which nearly every group of national stature testified, ranging from churches to labor unions to banks to real estate. The NHC released its report a few days later in a great fanfare of public relations, following the same template used by the Legion in 1943 when it had seized media attention by publishing a report on disabled veterans to kick off its campaign for the GI Bill.[96] Here as well, the group played on widespread fears that veterans would be a disruptive force if their problems were not addressed. In a radio broadcast, for instance, Griffith announced in threatening undertones that "there is a new army present in America today," which "has been mobilized from tents, from shanties, from trailers, from crowded homes throughout the nation. It is the army of homeless war veterans."[97] As it had done before, the Legion hoped to use this report to catch up on its competitors and claim a leadership position in a debate to which it had come rather late.[98]

There was one key difference, of course. Whereas in 1943–44 the group had demanded more government intervention, this time it was pushing for less. As a draft of a press release made clear, "members of the committee did not believe . . . that ample housing could be granted by writing a national law, or issuing a federal edict." It continued, "The American Legion plan was aimed at brushing aside those controls and impediments which were throttling the housing program" and at stimulating "our system of free enterprise and competition." The NHC report blasted federal agencies for their "incompetence and red tape" as well as for having taken so long to recognize the emergency of the situation. Explicitly rejecting T-E-W, the report advocated instead for the abolition of the NHA and the Office of Housing Expediter, for an immediate increase in rent control levels, and for the Federal Housing Administration to guarantee home loans in full.[99] In other words, the Legion was staking out a position diametrically opposed to that of other major veterans' groups such as the AMVETS, the AVC, and the VFW, which all supported Wyatt's VEHP and T-E-W.[100] The veterans' movement was once again divided.

By the time the Legion report was released in late 1946, Wyatt's program was running into headwinds. The liberal Kentucky Democrat was still far from his self-proclaimed goal of 1.2 million house starts for the year and discontent was brewing across the country. Strikes in the lumber, steel, railroad, and coal industries had caused shortages in essential building materials while the prefabrication industry was able to produce far fewer assembly-line homes than Wyatt had hoped. But the crushing blow to his program came with the landslide Republican victory in the November 1946 midterm elections, which seemed to demonstrate the unpopularity of wartime controls (the GOP had campaigned on the slogan "Had enough?"). Truman lifted almost all of them a few days later, in what amounted to a death warrant for the VEHP. Wyatt was forced to resign the following month.[101] With his emphasis on veterans gone, the federal government returned to focusing on public housing programs for the entire population, leaving the needs of former service members largely in the hands of private builders.[102]

Legion leaders were pleased with this turn of events. President Truman did not abolish the NHA and the Office of Housing Expediter, but the two new administrators he appointed to replace Wyatt at the head of these agencies immediately announced that they would adopt a more passive stance.[103] They both met with Griffith, who agreed that their policy declarations met the "final objectives" of the Legion's housing program by scaling down the government's involvement in housing.[104] Meanwhile, T-E-W made barely any progress: though it had passed the Senate by a voice vote, it was bottled up in the House Banking and Currency Committee. Its chairman, the conservative Michigan Republican Jesse Wolcott, was "a long-time friend of the private housing groups." After the Republican victory in November, the bill stood almost no chance of passing the next session of Congress.[105]

With 1946 drawing to a close, Legion leaders seemed to have made up for their initial failure to grasp the importance of the housing crisis. By creating the National Housing Committee, they had channeled the grassroots insurgency within their group into an outlet for their own conservative agenda. Even though the Legion stood virtually alone in the veterans' movement with its opposition to public housing, Wyatt's resignation seemed to validate its stance. But these were only short-term victories, which did nothing to solve the continuing problem of the housing shortage.

The Legion and the Real Estate Lobby

The fact that the Legion came out against Wyatt's VEHP and the T-E-W proved to many observers that the group was "playing hand-in-glove" with the "powerful real estate lobby." In the months following the San Francisco convention, the charge that the Legion's kingmakers had silenced younger veterans in order to advance their own antigovernment agenda became increasingly common. For instance, the nationally syndicated *Washington Post* columnist Drew Pearson never missed a chance to attack the Legion for "sabotaging" Wyatt's program.[106] Another influential detractor was the World War II veteran and noted cartoonist Bill Mauldin. "Youth has no voice in the Legion," he charged, for it "is a political machine in the hands of a comparative few," whose policies "are made at the top and not by the votes of its individual members."[107] From the standpoint of the AVC's national housing chairman, Roosevelt, Jr., opposition to T-E-W amounted to nothing less than a "surrender by the Legion hierarchy to the vested housing interests."[108] These attacks worried Legion officials, who knew that they were repeated in local newspapers "throughout the country."[109]

Given the predominance of these critics, it is worth pausing to discuss the nature of the "real estate lobby" that they so often attacked. The term was a shorthand for a wide-ranging coalition of trade associations, the most prominent of which included the National Association of Real Estate Boards, the National Association of Home Builders, and the United States Savings and Loan League. Together, they formed one of the most powerful lobbying blocs on Capitol Hill. Their zealous opposition to the VEHP and T-E-W stemmed from the fact that they represented a uniquely decentralized sector. Unlike other major industries like steel or oil, housing was still dominated by small companies operating primarily on a local scale. Much more so than their big business counterparts, such groups tended to see themselves as embodying "the true spirit of the free enterprise system" and to fiercely oppose state intervention (though they were careful to distinguish between unobtrusive public programs such as FHA-insured mortgages, which had played an essential role in making the industry stable and profitable, and more direct ones such as public housing, which they rejected).[110]

The arguments of the real estate lobby echoed larger postwar trends. In the context of the early Cold War, congressional conservatives and real estate advocates embraced an exceptionalist narrative that rejected the "socialist" housing policies of France or the United Kingdom as fundamentally un-American. They saw public housing as an opening wedge for the expansion of the federal government that would in time lead to total state control of the economy. In response to the arguments of reformers that decent public housing would cure most social ills, they asserted that it would encourage idleness and create a class of citizens who relied on the state for a living. The real estate lobby pushed for a model in which private builders had sway and the role of the federal government in encouraging construction and guaranteeing mortgages was obscured from the public.[111] Their embrace of the language of "free enterprise" tied into a larger postwar campaign led by right-wing business groups such as the National Association of Manufacturers to reassert the political power of business against the labor movement and the New Deal state.[112]

The national leadership of the Legion adopted a similar anticommunist and probusiness rhetoric. Paul Griffith criticized public housing as "a potential trend of socialization," which he thought "dangerous to the democratic principles of free enterprise."[113] Cadwallader felt similarly. In his remarks at a National Association of Home Builders convention, he argued that with the war over, "we've got to get back to a system of free enterprise and a condition where the law of supply and demand operates."[114] He added, "I think that when we are talking decontrol we have to go the whole way. Sure, we have to get rid of federal legislation. We have to get rid of federal administration. We have to get rid of all these central props that have been built up that artificially interfere with this free competitive system."[115] The other members of the Legion's National Housing Committee were of the same mind.[116]

While Legion leaders embraced probusiness views, the charge that the group "was stooging for real estate people" was an overstatement.[117] Legionnaires always had their own reasons for opposing T-E-W, chief among them the fact that it failed to give veterans priority. None of the titles of that bill were specifically aimed at former service members, a major problem for a group that believed in martial citizenship. Legion leaders wanted the government to solve veterans' issues first before dealing with problems affecting the entire population. They also feared that the bill's slum clearance provision would make the situation worse by evicting many of the veterans who were forced to live in "submarginal property" for lack of a better option.[118] Finally, they were concerned that an "economy-minded" Congress would be tempted to fund public housing "by depriving veterans of some of their other hard-won benefits."[119]

For the Legion as well as the VFW, the ideal counterweight to government intervention was not just private enterprise but local community action. "The only way we are ever going to be able to lick the problem of prices, of housing," Cadwallader argued, "is to get back to a realization that the local community is the basis of democracy."[120] For him, the "bedrock principles" of the Legion's housing policy should combine "private ownership and operation, private financing and local community control and management without government subsidy."[121] The VFW likewise called on local community leaders to take the initiative rather than leaving homeless veterans "to the mercies of greedy speculators."[122]

Both groups took steps to turn their community-centered perspective into action. Early in 1947, the Legion released a pamphlet entitled *Operation Housing* with details on six "community action plans" that had been "found successful in widely separated areas" in the hopes that they could inspire others.[123] The introduction to the pamphlet emphasized the need for veterans to tackle this problem themselves: "You are the only one who can do the job. . . . Your government can help but it cannot and should not be expected to provide these individual homes. That is not 'the American way.'"[124] These local projects were popular, though it is impossible to estimate their total number (Legion officials themselves admitted that they had "no idea as to how many actually exist").[125] In Larchmont, New York, for instance, fifty veterans started a venture in cooperative building and financing in early 1946. With help from GI Bill loans, they each saved approximately $2,000 by using the same plan for all houses. Completed nine months later, the project received the affectionate nickname of "Foxhole Acres."[126] The AVC and the AMVETS sponsored similar cooperative efforts, while the VFW had its own affordable housing projects.[127] Clearly, community-based campaigns found an echo in the veterans' movement at large.

The Mixed Success of Public Housing

However popular, these piecemeal initiatives were not enough for the 2.8 million families doubled up and the additional half a million still living in temporary housing, trailers, and rooming houses in the spring of 1947.[128] In January of that year, more than half of all Americans saw housing as the most important topic for the new Republican Congress to deal with.[129] Many Legionnaires continued to support public housing despite their leaders' opposition.[130] Yet the situation was still deadlocked, with T-E-W bottled up in the House.[131]

Things were slowly beginning to change, however. In 1947, Truman sought to merge the NHA and other federal housing agencies into a single entity, the Housing and Home Finance Agency, as part of his larger drive to streamline and modernize the federal government. The Legion opposed the plan on the grounds that it would not only mark the government's intention to remain involved in housing but would also give the administrator of this new and larger agency substantial power.[132] The group attempted to sink the bill with its time-tested "barrage" strategy, but to no avail: it passed Congress.[133] As one Legionnaire noted with apprehension, "senators representing states in which the American Legion is reputedly strong, voted loudly and firmly" in favor of the measure.[134] This defeat was a clear sign that the organization's uncompromising position was less and less tenable. The same official commented that "this action foretells a bad situation for the [housing] program at our National Convention" later that year.[135]

The twenty-ninth national convention of the Legion opened in late August 1947 in New York City. As expected, public housing was a major bone of contention. An attendee later observed that T-E-W provoked three days of "intense and at time, acrimonious" debate in committee as well as two hours of discussion on the floor. No consensus was reached.[136] According to one journalist, "No brass knuckles were used, as far as I know, nor was anyone slugged with a dead cat, but every other tool of controversy was brought into play.... When the chips were down on the Convention floor, feeling was still running so high that Commander Griffith had to declare everybody out of order at one point."[137] Seven departments submitted resolutions in favor of T-E-W, but a final roll call vote gave a landslide victory to its opponents by almost four to one. The vote provoked the same wave of negative reactions in the press as the year before.[138]

The outcome of the convention was more complex, however. Delegates rejected T-E-W but they elected a national commander who was a champion of public housing, James F. O'Neil of New Hampshire.[139] A "retread" like his predecessor Griffith, O'Neil was a former journalist and Manchester police chief.[140] The fact that he was rumored to be the kingmakers' choice suggests that the national leadership had seen the handwriting on the wall and decided that it was time for them to change course.[141] This new direction was made clear when Cadwallader resigned and O'Neil replaced him at the head of the NHC with Walter E. Alessandroni. A self-described "good Republican," Alessandroni was a typical representative of the GOP's moderate wing. He had served as the executive secretary to the mayor of Philadelphia from 1940 to 1947 and was then appointed director of the city's housing authority.[142] As one observer noted, his "big-city" background was key, for "Alessandroni automatically thinks in terms of Philadelphia and the *problems* of 2,000,000 people all bunked together, while Cadwallader instinctively remembers Baton Rouge and its 38,000 people."[143]

This change of leadership sent ripples through the group. Drew Pearson called it an "American Legion Rebellion," arguing that Cadwallader had been ousted by O'Neil "under pressure from disgruntled World War II veterans" because of his support for the real estate lobby.[144] Though it is difficult to ascertain the exact reason behind Cadwallader's dismissal, its consequences were clear. Over the next few months, Alessandroni inched the group toward a new position on public housing. In internal communications, he emphasized repeatedly "that the Legion could do a great deal for the cause of housing for the veteran if we spent less time following the negative policy of condemning public housing and expend more effort in advancing a program of our own."[145] The demise in December 1947 of the "king of the kingmakers," William H. Doyle, played into Alessandroni's hands. Doyle's behind-the-scenes presence had kept the conservative clique more or less united; with him gone, its hold over the Legion's power structure weakened.[146]

As 1948 began, T-E-W remained the primary topic of debate. After Wolcott had buried it in committee the previous year, Truman decided to make housing reform in general and the passage of the comprehensive housing bill in particular a key topic of his reelection campaign. His strategy was simple. Since the bill was popular but unlikely to pass a Republican Congress, he hoped that forcing a negative vote would allow him to portray the GOP as a party sold to "special interests" and thus to sway voters at the polls in November.[147] Pressure was clearly building in his favor: in early spring, five major veterans' organizations including the AVC, the VFW, the DAV, the Jewish War Veterans, and the Catholic War Veterans organized a Veterans' Housing Conference in Washington, D.C., to mobilize congressional support behind T-E-W. The event was a success, bringing fifteen hundred veterans to the capital and resulting in plans for more mass meetings in other cities.[148]

What finally convinced the Legion to join the rest of the veterans' movement was the introduction by the first-term Republican senator from Vermont, Ralph Flanders, of a series of amendments to T-E-W, one of which gave preference to veterans in applications for public housing.[149] Flanders was acting on behalf of party leaders, who assigned him to introduce these changes after he led a seven-month long joint congressional investigation of housing conditions across the country.[150] His amendments built on the model of veterans' preference that existed for new single-family dwellings and rental housing as well as for public housing at the local level.[151] They helped nudge the Legion closer to supporting the bill. In early April 1948, the NHC decided that while the proposal was by no means perfect, "it certainly presented an improvement over the old TEW bill . . . and was worthy of our support."[152] The National Executive Committee officially endorsed T-E-W a few weeks later.[153]

This decision amounted to the reversal of what had been official Legion policy for the past three years. After having charged repeatedly that public hous-ing was tantamount to communism, the Legion now found this measure to be "entirely a proper and democratic way of accomplishing our objectives."[154] The move was the result of months of patient behind-the-scenes maneuvering by Alessandroni and O'Neil. In a report to the National Executive Committee, Alessandroni reportedly emphasized "how the tide is running against the Legion because of their indifference to this piece of legislation."[155] O'Neil hinted at the same reasoning when he publicly admitted that "I don't think we can ever stand in very good grace before anybody if we are willing to accept federal subsidies for ourselves and indicate we want them denied to anybody else."[156] It had taken several months, but the change of guard introduced at the New York convention had finally borne its fruits.

Even with the backing of the Legion, the comprehensive housing bill made little headway in Congress at first. Reintroduced in April 1948, it passed the Sen-ate but died once again in Wolcott's committee. The bill experienced the same fate during the special August session called by Truman, which gave the presi-dent the example he needed to press his case with voters against the GOP. After his surprise reelection in November, Truman made the bill a central plank of his "Fair Deal" address in January 1949. The Senate passed T-E-W again, and for the first time in four years it got out of committee in the House and reached the floor for a vote. With help from the young Democratic representative from Texas Olin E. Teague (about whom we will hear more in the following chapters), the Legion managed to defeat efforts by Republicans to limit veterans' preference to a certain time window after discharge.[157] The group then announced that it would join other major veterans' organizations and throw "its full weight behind the . . . bill."[158] After more debate, the House passed it and the president signed it in July. It was the only piece of his Fair Deal agenda that would be turned into law.

In its final form, the Housing Act of 1949 gave veterans and their family a permanent priority in applications for public housing as well as in govern-ment loans for the building of homes on farms.[159] Legion news services hailed it as "the greatest American Legion legislative accomplishment in the present

Congress."[160] This was an exaggeration, of course: in practice, the group had rallied late to the cause, and it had merely added its strength to that of other veterans' organizations that supported T-E-W for much longer. Yet the veterans' movement undeniably played a key role in tipping the balance in the bill's favor. The pro-T-E-W *Journal of Housing* later recognized that "had it not been for this tremendously effective veterans support, we would all have been in a bad way."[161]

In the long run, the legacy of the Housing Act of 1949 was ambiguous. Though it authorized the construction of 810,000 public housing units over the next six years, the continued efforts of the real estate lobby at the local level meant that the actual number of units built was much lower. Barely two years after its passage, public housing advocates were already complaining that their program had lost so much steam as to be "a vanishing vision." Over the next eleven years, Congress only funded some 322,000 units.[162] Not only were fewer projects built than planned, but the share of veterans' or service members' families in public housing also decreased over time.[163] The 1944 GI Bill and the relative economic prosperity of the postwar years combined to allow increasing numbers of veterans to become homeowners instead of renters. Simply put, the Housing Act of 1949 both failed to produce as many public housing units as expected and proved less useful for white working-class veterans and their families than predicted.

The law also directly hurt the interests of veterans of color. The rejection of an amendment barring racial discrimination meant that public housing projects would continue to be segregated.[164] More broadly, one of the provisions of the Housing Act concerned urban "redevelopment," also known as "urban renewal." Under this title, the federal government provided funds to cities seeking to raze and then rebuild "slum" neighborhoods with the help of private enterprise. Over the course of the 1950s and early 1960s, the program earned a notorious track record as many of the "slums" slated for rebuilding were African American communities. Abuses were so common that the program became known as "negro removal": inhabitants typically had little input in the decisions and they were given few affordable relocation options.[165] By throwing its weight behind the act that set urban redevelopment into motion, the veterans' movement dealt a severe blow to the already precarious economic situation of former service members of color living in urban areas.

These developments were still years in the future when T-E-W was signed into law in 1949. The measure did not end the housing crisis overnight: an investigation published by *Collier's* that year found that 1.5 million mostly middle-class veterans were still living in "unbearable conditions" in the reconverted war housing that was supposed to have been only a temporary shelter.[166] Signs of improvement were nevertheless beginning to appear. Nearly 3.5 million housing units had been built between 1946 and 1949, and 1950 would be a record year with an all-time high of almost 1.4 million. Housing was no longer a burning national concern.[167] By 1950, the situation had improved so much that the NHC recommended its own dissolution.[168]

The year 1949 marked the end not just of the most contentious phase of the public housing debate. It also brought to a close the process of generational transition that had begun within the veterans' movement during World War II. In August, the VFW elected men who had served only during this war (as opposed to "retreads") to its top three offices, including the highest, commander-in-chief.[169] The Legion did the same a week later when delegates chose George Craig as their new national commander. With this decision, the *Times* noted that "the nation's two largest veterans' groups are now in the hands of soldiers of the last war."[170] The DAV had taken a similar step three years earlier.[171] This transition allowed the Big Three to expand their already considerable influence. For instance, in 1950 the Legion moved into a new and larger national headquarters in Indianapolis, an imposing $2.5 million limestone structure paid for by the state of Indiana. A few weeks later, it laid the cornerstone of a new building for its legislative branch on D.C.'s K Street, not far from the White House.[172]

This transition process was closely intertwined with the debate over public housing, as illustrated by Craig's career. A lawyer and veteran of Patton's Third Army, Craig had made a name for himself by protesting antiveteran discrimination in a federal housing project in his home state of Indiana.[173] His election marked the failure of the campaign begun four years earlier by the old guard of World War I Legionnaires to make sure that their group would continue to oppose government intervention in housing. This unpopular stance became less and less tenable as time went by, given the Legion's position in a highly competitive movement where members could always decide to join other groups with more aggressive politics. The kingmakers were forced to concede ground to public housing advocates, until by 1948 their initial position had been entirely overturned and the new generation had effectively seized control. In the end, housing did serve as the torch that welded the partnership between the two generations.

This was a truly remarkable development. Never before in the history of the U.S. veterans' movement had most members of a new generation chosen to join already established groups instead of their own. Contrary to what had taken place after the Civil War, the Spanish-American War, and World War I, veterans of World War II flocked not to newly established organizations representing their own cohort such as the AMVETS or the AVC but rather, in their overwhelming majority, to the Legion or the VFW. In the midst of a difficult transition to civilian life, most of them realized that these two groups offered a surer and easier route to influence. World War II was the first war that consolidated instead of upsetting the balance of power within the veterans' movement.

This is not to say that the outlook was entirely positive for the Legion in the late 1940s. In 1941, more than a quarter of all World War I veterans had been Legionnaires; eight years later, with an eligible population of 18.9 million, the Legion's share had dropped to 16 percent.[174] After a peak at 3.3 million in 1946, the group's membership declined to around 2.7 million in the early 1950s, far from the 5 million mark that Legion leaders had set as their goal back in 1945. This drop had major consequences: Legion finances were in the red from 1947 to 1949, leading O'Neil to sound the alarm.[175] In an article entitled "We Spread Ourselves Too Thin," the national commander argued that his group was trying to do too much, at the risk of forgetting its core mission of defending martial citizenship.[176] Though O'Neil did not mention it by name, the recent creation of the economy-minded Hoover Commission indicated that veterans' benefits were once again coming under threat.

CHAPTER 4

Generations United

The Fight over the First Hoover Commission

On May 2, 1950, newsreel and television cameras filmed a new group of self-proclaimed revolutionaries gather on the steps of Independence Hall in Philadelphia. The president of Temple University, Robert L. Johnson, was there with several other speakers to launch the National Reorganization Crusade, whose goal was to "reach citizens everywhere with the message of federal efficiency and economy." He was relaying the proposals of the Commission on Organization of the Executive Branch of Government chaired by former president Herbert Hoover, better known as the First Hoover Commission. Created a few years earlier, the commission had issued a series of recommendations that it was now trying to push through Congress. The Crusade was an effort to generate grassroots support for these measures.[1]

The main attraction of the day in Philadelphia was the Cracker Barrel Caravan, a road show that would go on to visit seventy-seven communities in the Midwest, Northeast, and Mid-Atlantic over the next few months. The Caravan revolved around a red-white-and-blue trailer carrying a thirty-foot-long imitation of an old-fashioned country store fitted out with grocery-stocked shelves and an actual cracker barrel serving as rostrum. Used as a symbol of a simpler past when town-hall meetings were the source of sound decision making, the setting sought to offer a contrast to the current condition of the federal government. Actors brought the issue of government reorganization alive at each stop (Fig. 6), while local speakers gave short speeches expressing the viewpoints of a "typical" housewife, World War II veteran, and college student. Throughout the performances, basket-toting volunteers crisscrossed the audience to hand out literature and gather signatures. Over three months, the Caravan distributed

Figure 6. The Cracker Barrel Caravan in action, 1951. At the top, a picture of
a "typical meeting" with speakers waiting for their turn on the stage provided
by the trailer-turned-country-store. Note the joint portraits of Truman and
Hoover on the right, illustrating the Hoover Commission's effort to achieve
bipartisanship. At bottom, a close-up of two actors dramatizing the stakes of
the Hoover Report in front of radio microphones, with Uncle Sam tied in
actual red tape and an actress playing the Report, and a barrel in the foreground.
Citizens Committee for the Hoover Report, "Impact! Of the Cracker Barrel
Caravan," n.d. (ca. July 1951), box 32, folder: Charles B. Coates, 1950, Records
of the First Hoover Commission, Herbert Hoover Presidential Library.

ninety thousand pamphlets and thousands of petitions, thanks to the financial
backing of some of the world's largest corporations such as General Foods, Esso
Standard Oil, and Ford Motor.[2]

It was hardly a coincidence that among the many viewpoints offered at every
stop of the Caravan was that of a "typical" GI, for veterans' benefits occupied a

central place in the Hoover Report (the collective title of the nineteen reports published by the commission). Their already vast and separate welfare state had massively expanded both during and after World War II. From $637 million in 1940, the expenditures of the VA skyrocketed to $6.9 billion in 1949, more than any other single item of federal spending save the military.[3] This rapid growth brought its share of scandals: by the late 1940s, the agency was the target of several congressional investigations. Around the same time as the Hoover Report was released, the country's most widely circulated magazine, the *Reader's Digest*, called the VA "a national disgrace."[4] National Commander O'Neil reacted by sounding the alarm in the *American Legion Magazine*. He realized that the "honeymoon for veterans" was over.[5] Only a few years into the postwar period, the broad wartime support for their benefits was already evaporating.

The commission's proposals represented the first systematic effort to cut back on veterans' benefits since the 1930s. In addition to the backing of big business, the Crusade had bipartisan support.[6] Liberals followed in the footsteps of Franklin Delano Roosevelt in opposing privileged treatment for a segment of the population based only on military service and in seeing veterans' benefits as an obstacle to the growth of a more universal welfare state. The *New York Times*, for instance, argued that it was "the duty of the citizen to defend his country" and that "he should expect no special reward for carrying [it] out."[7] For their part, conservatives not only rejected the idea of a welfare state but they also worried that centralized state planning and mounting government spending would pave the way for a totalitarian regime—a very real concern in the context of the early Cold War. As the *American Legion Magazine* put it, though the "welfare staters" and the "ultra-conservative[s]" "[hated] each others' [*sic*] guts," they each had "their own reason for wanting to strip the veterans' program."[8] Contrary to World War II, when conservatives had supported the expansion of veterans' benefits as a more limited alternative to the Progressive agenda, or to the postwar debate over public housing, when former service members had joined forces with a mostly liberal coalition, this time veterans were defending their interests against both sides of the aisle. It shows how they were never tied to one camp or another for very long.

The countercampaign of the veterans' movement proved remarkably successful. Despite the commission's positive record overall—more than 70 percent of its recommendations were implemented—none of its major proposals on veterans' affairs were translated into law.[9] This outcome was largely the product of veterans' mobilization. Unlike in the debate described in the previous chapter, this time organizations such as the VFW, the DAV, the AMVETS, and the

Legion presented a united front. Hoover's lieutenants saw the latter group as their chief obstacle. And for good reason: now that they faced a common enemy, the two generations of Legionnaires were able to overcome their divisions and turn their association into a powerhouse that the Hoover Commission could not match. In this sense, the campaign marked the climax of the veterans' movement in the postwar period.

It did not achieve victory on its own, however. As always, veterans' groups forged alliances with other actors. Some were long-standing allies, such as the VA administrator and the head of the House Committee on Veterans' Affairs. Others were more opportunistic, like civil service employees' unions and the American Medical Association (AMA). They also benefited from favorable circumstances such as the outbreak of the Korean War in 1950, which made policymakers less inclined to consider major reforms. More fundamentally, the structure of the debate itself was in veterans' favor: trying to pass new laws, as the Hoover Commission was doing, was always more difficult than simply defending the status quo, especially when these laws seemed to be taking benefits away from people. While veterans were defending programs that they cared deeply about, popular support for specific aspects of government reform—as opposed to the idea itself—was never really forthcoming. Finally, Hoover and his followers were hamstrung by their own flawed strategy: not only did they refuse to engage in the same kind of forceful pressure tactics that veterans excelled at, but they also drew most of their support from a rather elite segment of the population.

Still, the outcome of this battle was far from preordained. The press as well as most experts sided with the commission, and the larger political climate was favorable to advocates of economy. Wartime enthusiasm for the figure of the GI citizen-soldier had been replaced by concerns over the runaway growth of the federal government. The military buildup and anticommunist fever of the early Cold War placed advocates of welfare programs on the defensive. This was reflected by the increasingly frequent use of the term "welfare state" in public discussions, which was introduced in the late 1940s by opponents of the New Deal along with other "scare words" like "collectivism" and "statism," as a way to evoke fears of a European-style "centralized government undertaking more and more functions and on which citizens must come to depend increasingly for their well-being."[10] As a central part of these new "functions," veterans' benefits attracted more than their share of criticism.

The controversy over the First Hoover Commission suggests a broader lesson about the role of interest groups and policy feedback in the formation of political identity. In their countermobilization campaign, veterans' groups had to convince World War II veterans that their interests were at risk. This was not an obvious realization: GIs who faced their own readjustment problems and who took their benefits for granted were unlikely to respond to the threat of the commission as seriously as their elders who had lived through the bitter interwar period. Legion officials sought to overcome this problem by tapping into the collective memory of the movement: they recalled the example of the Economy Act and other such episodes in order to throw the stakes of this debate into stark relief. The debate over the First Hoover Commission therefore shows how veterans' programs contributed to creating and strengthening the sense of a shared political identity among former service members. Public policy shaped the veterans' movement as much as it was itself shaped by it.

This chapter tells the middle part of our story, the culmination of the efforts made in previous years to bring the old and the new cohort of former service members together. It can be read as a story of triumph, one in which generational divisions seemed to disappear and the "two-war experiment" finally came to fruition. Contrary to the debate over public housing in which the Legion had tried hard to sway public opinion, this time the group largely turned inward, focusing on lobbying Congress and on mobilizing its own members. But this story also stands as an example of the fragility of the gains of the veterans' movement, which were already coming under sustained criticism only a few years after the end of the war. Either way, we should note that this outcome was never determined only in the halls of power.[11] As in previous chapters, the veterans' movement combined rank-and-file activism with the expertise of its national leadership and the support of allies both within and outside the state. The constant back-and-forth between the local and the national is once again at the center of our narrative.

The First Hoover Commission and Veterans' Welfare State

In order to understand why the push for government reorganization came to the fore in the late 1940s and early 1950s, we need to remember the scale of the growth experienced by the U.S. state over the previous couple of decades. A few figures are enough to illustrate this point. With 1.6 million men and women, the military in 1949 was more than four times larger than its prewar peak. Federal debt per capita reached $1,700 that same year, a more than tenfold increase from 1929. Annual federal expenditures skyrocketed from nearly $3 to $39 billion in the same period and the number of civil service employees almost quadrupled to over 2 million.[12] Put simply, veterans of World War II came home to a very different state, one that was both larger and farther reaching.

Most of this growth had taken place in a rapid and disorderly fashion under the presidency of Franklin Delano Roosevelt. As his successor, Harry Truman, recognized, "President Roosevelt often said he was no administrator. He was a man of visions and ideas, and he preferred to delegate administration to others."[13] FDR had tried to reorganize the executive branch in 1937 by appointing a committee chaired by the University of Chicago political scientist Louis Brownlow. The group issued a series of proposals to strengthen the authority of the president, but most of them were ignored by Congress in a context of mounting opposition to Roosevelt's agenda due to the Supreme Court–packing scandal. The notorious "alphabet soup" of administrative agencies only grew longer over the next few years. By 1949, the president had authority over between seventy-four and eighty-nine different staff offices, departments, regulatory agencies, boards, and commissions, whose functions often overlapped.[14] Administrative entities had become what the Brownlow Committee called a "fourth branch" of government, with their own margin of action.[15] The debate over the scope of what one historian has called the "administrative state" was a major part of interwar politics.[16]

World War II imposed a temporary halt on such discussions, but they returned to the fore in the postwar period. President Truman had firsthand experience of reorganization efforts dating back to the 1920s when he was involved in county reform as a Missouri judge. During the war, he made a name for himself as chairman of the Special Committee Investigating National Defense, which revealed numerous examples of corruption and red tape. He was at heart a fiscal conservative who believed in the virtue of balanced budgets.[17] Reorganization was a natural choice for the theme of his first message to Congress in May 1945, in which he asked for and obtained the right to submit plans that would go into effect unless Congress vetoed them within sixty days. Yet his efforts on this front were stymied during his first two years in office by the same congressional coalition of conservative midwestern Republicans and southern Democrats responsible for blocking T-E-W. Bent on rolling back the New Deal, conservatives opposed the president's attempts to streamline its structure.[18] Economy nonetheless remained a major concern for Truman, who had to find a balance between the constant pressure for a military buildup and his own desire to preserve civilian programs.[19]

Ironically, the same politicians responsible for this stalemate would provide the key to unlock it. After the GOP won the 1946 midterms, many observers were confident that Truman would lose the upcoming presidential election as well. Acting on this widespread assumption, Republicans created the Commission on Organization of the Executive Branch of the Government in July 1947. They wanted this blue-ribbon group to lay out a blueprint for scaling back government that the next Republican administration would find ready to use upon taking office. The appointment as chairman of Herbert Hoover, the ex-president turned champion of the GOP's right wing, made it clear that the commission's goal was the liquidation of the New Deal state. Hoover was then just emerging from over a decade in the political wilderness after his defeat by FDR in 1932. His opposition to the New Deal was so deep-seated that, after their first meeting, Truman found him "to the right of Louis the Fourteenth. . . . [H]e doesn't understand what's happened in the world since McKinley" (the twenty-fifth president of the United States, in office from 1897 to 1901).[20]

Hoover embraced his mission wholeheartedly and controlled the group's early work. His task was made easier by the fact that even though the commission was nominally bipartisan—the twelve appointees were evenly split between Republicans and Democrats—it was de facto dominated by like-minded conservatives. Only three of the commissioners were reliably liberal: Dean Acheson (who was appointed secretary of state by Truman while on the Commission), former administrative assistant to Roosevelt James Rowe, and University of Michigan political scientist James J. Pollock, a liberal Republican. Aside from Acheson and Rowe, the other four Democrats were either conservative southerners (Representative Carter Manasco of Alabama and Senator James McClellan of Arkansas) or detached from the commission's deliberations (the former ambassador to Great Britain Joseph P. Kennedy allowed Hoover to use his vote by proxy and the secretary of defense James V. Forrestal was handicapped by declining health). In addition to Hoover and Pollock, the four Republican appointees were Vermont senator George D. Aiken, Representative Clarence Brown of Ohio, paper magnate George Mead, and Civil Service Commission member Arthur Flemming, all of whom had unimpeachable conservative credentials.[21]

Truman's upset victory at the polls in November 1948 dealt a major blow to Hoover's plans. Facing the prospect of another Democratic administration and Congress, the former president struck a deal with the current one to salvage his work. Hoover agreed that his commission would no longer try to challenge some of the basic functions of government, but simply find ways to "make it work better."[22] By turning a commission initially designed to do away with his legacy into an instrument to solidify it, Truman seized the chance to claim bipartisan authority for his own reorganization plans. As his budget director wrote him after the election, "there is now a possibility of getting the last Republican

President to urge you to accept an implementation of and organization for executive responsibility that the Republican Party has historically denied to Presidents.... This could serve to establish a fundamental advance in the nature of the Presidency and its relations with the Congress."[23]

The commission eventually submitted nineteen reports over the first half of 1949, each covering a specific part of the executive branch.[24] The reports' goal was to streamline the tangle of agencies and departments that this branch had become by applying three basic management principles. First, they called for the establishment of a centralized and uninterrupted chain of command flowing from the president through heads of departments down to the field level and vice versa, so that ultimate responsibility and accountability would always lay at the top. Second, the reports sought to eliminate functional overlaps between agencies, with the goal of consolidating them into a third of their present number. Lastly, the commission wanted to expand the staff assigned to the president and to the members of his cabinet so as to allow for better supervision.[25] From these broad principles stemmed no less than 273 specific recommendations, some narrowly technical and others more substantial. They included for instance the unification of the military under a civilian secretary of defense and the decentralization of personnel recruitment and management away from the Civil Service Commission.

Veterans' benefits loomed large in the Hoover Report. This was hardly a surprise, for as described in Chapter 2, they had expanded massively during World War II. At the outbreak of the conflict, the main functions of the VA were still the same as those assigned to its predecessor, the VB, in 1921: life insurance, pensions, and medical benefits. The Second World War witnessed the creation of new programs and the expansion of old ones. From nearly 4 million in 1940, the clientele of the VA jumped to 19 million in 1949. Following the passage of the 1944 GI Bill, the agency provided millions of new veterans with services it had never handled before: education benefits; business, home, and farm loan guaranties; and unemployment compensation. With 129 hospitals and a daily average patient load of 107,000, the VA hospital system was now the single largest in the nation. 2.3 million veterans received disability compensation, pension, or retirement pay, up from merely 600,000 in 1940.[26] With 200,000 employees, the VA was the third largest government entity behind the military and the Post Office.[27] This mind-boggling expansion was best summarized by Canadian government official Robert England, who wrote that the VA had become in just a few years "bank, benefactor, hospital, custodian, life insurance company, educational endowment, guardian of orphans, medical adviser, vocational counselor, welfare agency, protective and benevolent association,

property appraiser, loan guarantor and broker, compensation board, old age
shelter and burial society, to nineteen million adults who under its auspices go
to school, seek and find jobs, purchase farms and businesses, buy houses, are ill
in veterans' hospitals, and buried in national cemeteries. Even the flag to drape
the casket comes from the V.A."[28]

All this growth was not without pains. Despite the repeated assurances of
VA director Frank T. Hines, his agency proved woefully unprepared to handle
the increase in workload that came with the demobilization. Hines's ingrained
conservatism and the highly centralized structure of the VA were compounded by
wartime restrictions on doctors and construction materials.[29] Damning exposés
of the situation began to appear with increasing frequency in the press in early
1945, leading to calls for a congressional investigation. For instance, journalist
Albert Deutsch called the VA a "vast dehumanized bureaucracy, enmeshed in
mountains of red tape, ingrown with entrenched mediocrity, undemocratically
operated under autocratic control centered in Washington, prescribing medieval
medicine to its sick and disabled wards, highly susceptible to political pressures,
rigidly resistant to proposed reforms."[30] At a news conference in May, Truman
conceded that this "mess" would have to be "modernized."[31] More than two
decades after the end of World War I, veterans' benefits were once again engulfed
in a postwar crisis.

Truman reacted by accepting Hines's resignation and replacing him with
four-star general Omar N. Bradley, a square-jawed hero of World War II. The
president hoped that Bradley's popularity and his experience managing over one
million service members in Europe would make him the right person for the job
of reforming the VA's sprawling structure. During his two years in office, Bradley implemented a series of reforms that overhauled the agency. In an attempt
to loosen its top-down hierarchy, he created thirteen branch offices, each with
operational authority over several states. Striving to improve the quality of VA
medical personnel, he formed a new Department of Medicine and Surgery
exempted from civil service rules. He also fought with Congress to end the
patronage politics that plagued VA hospitals, pushing to affiliate them with top
medical schools on university campuses.[32]

Bradley was unable to solve all of the VA's problems before his planned
departure in December 1947, however. Despite his best efforts, the agency's reputation would remain tarnished. "There was simply too much to do and not
enough time," he later admitted.[33] The sudden demobilization of millions of
veterans had created an insuperable increase in workload. Nearly four hundred

thousand disability claims were submitted every month after the end of the conflict, while requests for conversion of wartime life insurance into peacetime policies accounted for 6.5 million letters in Bradley's first six months in office—in his own words, "the most mind-boggling mail logjam I have ever seen."[34] The administration of the GI Bill posed another set of issues. As we will see in a later chapter, its various titles were rife with scandals. All these factors contributed to a sense that the VA and veterans' affairs more broadly were in a state of crisis, which gave reform advocates an opening. As one of Hoover's lieutenants remarked in 1951, "there is no more vulnerable agency in government today than the VA."[35]

Taking advantage of this window of opportunity, the First Hoover Commission made three sets of recommendations concerning veterans' affairs. The first one stemmed from its emphasis on eliminating functional overlaps. Most importantly, it called for the consolidation of the federal government's medical activities into a new United Medical Administration (UMA) that would include not only VA hospitals but also military facilities and the Public Health Service.[36] This radical proposal would take away from the VA its largest and most prestigious division, for the Department of Medicine and Surgery had been the only unqualified success of Bradley's tenure.[37] Thanks to the alliance forged with medical schools and the AMA, by the time of his departure observers asserted that veterans' health care had become "second to none!"[38] The commission also recommended the transfer of the GI Bill home loan guaranty program from the VA to the Housing and Home Finance Agency, and of hospital construction to the Department of the Interior.[39] The VA itself was to be streamlined in order to give more control to its administrator.[40] In sum, the agency stood to lose some of its core functions and to see its administrative structure overhauled.

The second category of recommendations for veterans' affairs reflected the commission's effort to strengthen the authority of agency leaders and to improve the quality of their administrative staff. Here, Hoover took aim at a benefit that attracted little public attention but was very popular among veterans: civil service preference. Former service members had enjoyed a steadily expanding range of advantages in this field for generations.[41] By the 1940s, not only did they receive five additional points on entrance exams (ten if they had a service-connected disability), but certain positions such as guard or elevator operator were reserved for them. Minimum educational, height, age, and weight requirements were waived. Veterans were also the last to be fired and the first to be reemployed.[42] As a result, a growing share of the civil service workforce was made up of former service members: they accounted for nearly three-fifths of all civilian employees of the federal government in 1951, compared to only 15 percent six years earlier.[43]

The Hoover Commission did not see this as a positive development. Its members viewed veterans' preference as an obstacle to the establishment of a merit-based civil service system, for it made it harder to hire and promote the best candidates and to fire incompetent workers. Hoover called for the Civil Service Commission to relinquish some of its control over the recruiting and examining process and to give the heads of departments and agencies more leeway. He also recommended ending the absolute preference enjoyed by veterans in reduction-of-force procedures. Finally, instead of giving former service members a straightforward point bonus, all applicants for a given position were to be grouped in categories such as "outstanding" or "qualified," and able-bodied veterans were to be considered ahead of nonveterans only within those categories. The commission also recommended carrying out a nationwide recruiting campaign over the next few years to help place veterans in government positions, but this was clearly an effort to sweeten the pill of what amounted overall to a blistering attack on veterans' preference.[44]

The third major set of recommendations of the Hoover Report on veterans' affairs concerned life insurance. It was a major part of the VA's work, for the agency was in charge of the millions of policies that veterans of both world wars had contracted during their service and maintained after discharge, which represented a total value of over $41 billion (about a quarter of all life insurance in the country). The VA was the single most important entity in this field, with a business whose size far exceeded that of any private life insurance company.[45] Hoover recommended that these activities be incorporated as a Veterans' Life Insurance Corporation within the agency, so as to allow more "economical and efficient performance."[46] His emphasis on copying the methods of the private sector was a leftover from the initial, more conservative approach of the commission. A firm believer in the idea that the government should draw inspiration from the world of business, Hoover appointed to his staff the heads of some of the nation's largest private insurance companies, such as Prudential or Penn Mutual.[47] Little wonder, then, that these men recommended the same practices they followed in their own corporate careers.

Taken as a whole, these three sets of proposals—the creation of the UMA, the reform of veterans' preference, and the reorganization of life insurance—entailed a dramatic restructuring of veterans' welfare state. Hoover's recommendations represented a direct blow to martial citizenship and to the veterans' movement that defended it.

Administrative Reform Against Martial Citizenship

A seasoned stateman, Hoover knew that his recommendations would not sail effortlessly through Congress. The normal course for his commission would have been to disband after it submitted its last report in June 1949. Instead, he took the additional step of creating the Citizens' Committee for the Hoover Report (CCHR), a group whose mission was to organize a public relations campaign in support of the commission's proposals.[48] Hoover maintained close ties with the committee but delegated its day-to-day operations to Robert L. Johnson, who as we saw earlier was the president of Temple University and a former vice president of *Time* magazine. Its director of public relations was Charles B. Coates, an executive at General Foods, and its research director was Robert L. L. McCormick, a banker and Harvard Business School graduate.[49]

The CCHR received wide support from corporate sources. With $390,000 budgeted for its first year, the group had affiliates in thirty-seven states. It sponsored television shows, published various pamphlets and newsletters such as *Washington Watchdog*, and provided thousands of newspapers as well as hundreds of companies nationwide with favorable material.[50] The Cracker Barrel Caravan was only one example of how the CCHR strove to create a broad constituency in support of its reform agenda. Arguably, never before had the rather dry subject of government reorganization received so much publicity.

Three messages were at the core of this public relations campaign. First, the CCHR claimed that it defended the public good against special interests. Coates said that his organization represented a "national civic cause" that was nonpartisan and above politics.[51] Some of the posters on display during the National Reorganization Crusade carried both Truman and Hoover's portraits, with the inscription: "President and former President Agree. Enlist Now."[52] Second, the CCHR argued that government reform was essential to preserving national security and global leadership in the ongoing Cold War. "Every dollar, every scrap of material, every bit of human effort we waste is a gift to the enemies of freedom," declared a CCHR pamphlet issued after the outbreak of the Korean War.[53] Last, the group exploited anxieties over the rapid expansion of the federal government by asserting that its growth not only would whittle away at American families' purchasing power but also risked turning the country into the kind of system it was up against. "Free peoples all through history have yielded their freedom when bureaucracy overwhelms them economically," Johnson said, "This is not necessarily because of any plot or plan. . . . [W]e can drift into slavery if we fail to swim against the tide."[54] At a time when politicians of all stripes were focused on the threat of communism, the message of economy in government was particularly appealing.

This helps explain why the proposals of the commission found bipartisan support. As political scientists Charles Aikin and Louis W. Koenig wrote in October 1949, "it has become something of a mode to favor the Hoover reports, just as one opposes sin."[55] The first National Reorganization Conference organized by the CCHR in December 1949 illustrated this point. Not only did Truman send a message of support, but the list of speakers included the Democratic governor of Illinois Adlai E. Stevenson, secretary of labor Maurice J. Tobin, Lewis Hines of the AFL and Stanley Ruttenberg of the CIO, Republican senator from Wisconsin Joseph McCarthy, and the women's division of the Democratic National Committee.[56] Business-friendly groups such as the Junior Chamber of Commerce and the U.S. Chamber of Commerce were among the CCHR's most fervent allies, but the liberal American Veterans' Committee, led by the owner of the *New Republic*, Michael Straight, also endorsed the Hoover Report.[57]

Broad support could be found among the national press and the larger public as well. The conservative *Chicago Tribune* praised the commission's "great intelligence and drive," while the *Wall Street Journal* lauded its "fine service in showing us what a cancer bureaucracy has become." More centrist publications joined in, with the *Washington Post* calling the report "the most thorough job in history in a study of this Government" and James MacGregor Burns writing in the *New York Times* that the commission's "excursion into the Dark Continent of the national bureaucracy" had shown that "our super-Government . . . has become a fixed part of the 'American way of life.'"[58] Many Americans approved. In September 1950, the White House mailroom counted no less than 45,600 newspaper poll clippings and petitions in support of the commission.[59] The academic community welcomed the report too, with the *American Political Science Review* devoting a symposium to what it called "the most monumental product of government research in American history."[60]

Yet the same political scientists who had compared endorsing the reports to opposing sin also noted that "just as many of us deplore sins we have never experienced, so, unfortunately, many who exalt the Hoover reports actually have never read them."[61] Indeed, a poll found that 69 percent of respondents either did not know about the reports or did not understand them well. The survey also showed a class bias, with the percentage of respondents informed about the report ranging from two-thirds among the college educated to less than one-fifth among those who had only graduated from grade school.[62] The other problem was that even though a large majority of Americans supported the goal of economy in government, they did not necessarily agree on how to achieve it. For instance, the U.S. Chamber of Commerce and the National Association of Manufacturers both heartily endorsed the idea of cutting costs but they opposed a reorganization plan that would have abolished the office of general counsel of the National Labor Relations Board. The *Reader's Digest* mocked this approach as the "We're for economy, but—" school of thought.[63]

If the general approach of the First Hoover Commission elicited broad support, this was also true of Hoover's proposals on veterans' affairs more specifically. Expert opinion was particularly enthusiastic here. Think tanks such as the Public Affairs Institute, for instance, welcomed as "both sound and obvious" the transfer of VA hospitals to an integrated medical administration, on the basis that "veterans are first and foremost citizens and . . . their needs should be considered in the same way as the needs of other human beings."[64] The conservative Brookings Institution likewise called for the revision of veterans' preference in civil service, comparing these advantages to "a handful of sand in a gear box," which "fouled and stalled the whole delicate machinery that had been set up to find, measure, and secure merit."[65]

Major national newspapers concurred. The *Washington Post* declared that it "would not be entirely unfortunate from the point of view of the public interest" if veterans' preference was dropped altogether and the *New York Times* argued that the Hoover Commission was "not going nearly far enough."[66] Writing in the former, Ysabel and Robert Rennie saw the commission as a chance to "reconsider most seriously that bright political line dividing the veteran from the citizen." They argued that "functionally," the centralization of so many different jobs into one agency was "absurd." The recommendations of the Hoover Commission to put these functions back "where they belong" made sense, for veterans should be treated just like any other citizens.[67] These comments make clear that the debate over the Hoover Report's recommendations for veterans' affairs was never just about technical matters of administrative efficiency. Its proposals represented yet another effort to push back against martial citizenship and to integrate veterans' programs within a more inclusive social policy framework.

The arguments advanced by Hoover's supporters were familiar. On the one hand, liberals saw the growing size and cost of veterans' benefits as a threat to more universal welfare programs. They thought that giving more to a specific group of the population entailed giving less to everyone else. In a message to Congress, Truman said for instance that instead of providing special benefits to veterans without service-connected disabilities, "our objective should be to make our social security system more comprehensive in coverage and more adequate, so that it will provide the basic protection needed by all citizens."[68] On the other hand, right-wing figures such as the columnist George Sokolsky opposed the expansion of the federal government in general. "Profligacy is a misery no matter who practices it," he wrote, "and a profligate government becomes a menace to its citizens."[69] The conservative Tax Foundation joined in, criticizing the separate status of the VA hospital system as "socialized medicine for a favored group."[70]

Despite the elitist bent of this bipartisan coalition, the leading organizations of the veterans' movement saw it as a grave menace. The VFW considered the commission's proposals to be a "serious threat to [the] future welfare of all veterans," while for the Legion they represented a "real crisis for all war veterans."[71] The DAV was of the same opinion.[72]

The fact that such comments came from groups that stood at the peak of their power makes them all the more meaningful. At a time when the study of interest group politics was becoming the dominant focus of U.S. political science, its most prominent practitioners recognized that "organizations representing war veterans have always been among the strongest of pressure groups."[73] Among these associations, the primacy of the Legion was clear. V. O. Key, Jr., one of the nation's leading political scientists, wrote for instance that "the Legion leaves nothing to chance. Its Washington lobby is one of the most able."[74] In his landmark work *The Governmental Process* (1951), David Truman made the same judgment.[75] Dayton McKean wrote likewise that the Legion was "commonly regarded by Washington newspapermen as the most powerful pressure group of any sort."[76] In the late 1940s, the public image of this organization remained broadly positive as well, enjoying "widespread and varied respect" in a Roper survey.[77]

Though the veterans' movement projected an image of power and prestige, it struggled to adapt to the massive influx of World War II veterans. The DAV was facing serious financial problems, as most of its expenses were covered not by membership dues but by fund-raising, which was not easily scalable.[78] The Legion confronted a similar challenge. The number of disability claims filed with the VA nearly quadrupled from over six hundred thousand in 1940 to 2.3 million in 1948, but the Legion's national rehabilitation staff only increased from 40 to 71.[79] Its national commander admitted frankly that "yes, today, nationally, though we have grown our task has grown more—*and we no longer measure up to it.*"[80] On top of this, the relative decline in membership after 1946 meant that the balance sheet of the group was in the red for three consecutive years.[81] One Legion official admitted in 1949 that "we have been forced to dig into our reserve and restricted funds to meet budget requirements. We approach the bottom of the barrel."[82] The group was forced to increase its national dues for the first time and to earmark the additional revenue for rehabilitation efforts. The threat of the Hoover Commission featured centrally in its effort to convince members to approve the increase.[83]

The response of the veterans' movement to the Hoover Report was twofold. First, the Big Three denied that the report would produce the economy and efficiency that it promised. The DAV compared the dismemberment of the VA "to an abandonment of the atomic age for a return to the bow and arrow era" and the VFW saw it as "turning the wheels of progress back thirty years."[84] Legionnaires concurred, arguing that the dispersal of veterans' programs into several agencies would entail not only the duplication of veterans' records but also a tax increase. A suggested script for local speakers compared these proposals to telling General Motors that "you may retain your administrative functions, but you will have to divorce yourself from the other operations of your corporation. Ford will take over your production. Engineering will go to Studebaker. Your distribution will be conducted by Chrysler. And your sales can be handled by Kaiser-Fraser."[85] Veterans would no longer be able to rely on a "one-stop" service and "conceivably might have to visit four or five different Federal agencies."[86]

But the clash between the veterans' movement and the Hoover Commission went deeper than technical disagreements about the best way to achieve efficiency. At its core, it was about competing visions of citizenship. The VFW argued for example that the "traditional American policy" of "special consideration for veterans" was threatened by the commission's claim "that it is no longer feasible, and practical, to set [this group] apart from the rest of the population."[87] The Legion advanced similar arguments, noting that veterans' benefits were the product of a moral contract with the government, "a sacred obligation of the nation."[88] Their programs were not "welfare"—understood as charity for the undeserving poor— but earned rights. From this standpoint, the idea of taking away some of the VA's functions appeared dangerous not just because it would fail to cut costs but more importantly because it would "divorce all veterans from their identity as veterans" and thus "tear down what [the Legion] has worked a lifetime to build."[89]

The paramount goal of the veterans' movement was indeed to defend martial citizenship by keeping veterans' programs separate from social policies for the rest of the population. "It is particularly alarming," wrote a top Legion official, "to have the veterans' benefit programs classified as welfare programs. We resist that idea whenever it is possible to do so.... The American Legion has consistently held to the position that the cost of caring for the disabled veteran is as much a part of the cost of war as are the cash moneys laid on the barrel head to pay for the ships and guns and tanks and planes.... [S]uch Federal veterans benefits are a direct cost of war. They have no relation to the Oscar Ewing type of welfare state cost" (a reference to the man in charge of the Federal Security Agency, which was responsible for some of the most emblematic New Deal welfare programs like Social Security).[90] Another Legionnaire recognized that "we don't want the veteran taken out of the class ... in which he has been placed throughout the history of this beloved nation of ours, and placed in the position where he has to be hospitalized and cared for by an all developing, overlapping Federal Agency designed to do things for people."[91]

These arguments were hardly new; we saw similar claims in previous chapters. But the late 1940s presented novel challenges. While Legion officials were reasonably confident that the older generation of veterans would respond to this new menace because they had already witnessed similar criticism in the past, the reaction of the younger cohort was less certain. To make sure that freshly discharged GIs would not remain on the sidelines, Legion leaders tried to convince them of the urgency of the threat by drawing comparisons with the interwar period. As its assistant director of public relations wrote in a private letter, the Legion self-consciously tapped into the collective memory of the veterans' movement. "Obviously we can't cite any recent condition as example of what we are trying to prevent from happening again," he noted. "The World War II veteran received everything on a gold platter. If we are going to dramatize the consequences of the proposed dismemberment of the VA we must go back into history and drag out and dust off the tragic lessons of the past."[92]

Among these "tragic lessons," none were more useful than those learned from the "infamous, callous, and cold-blooded" Economy Act of 1933, whose deep cuts in veterans' benefits had been such a shock to veterans' advocates.[93] The memory of the act served the Legion's purposes in more ways than one. Not only had it been a traumatic experience for many veterans, but it also offered an example of a successful countermobilization, since most of its provisions had eventually been rescinded. It was a model both of what the younger generation should fear and of what it could achieve. The Legion made this connection explicit when it appointed Edward Hayes at the head of the committee charged with responding to the Hoover Report. As national commander in 1933–34, Hayes had devoted most of his term to rolling back the cuts of the Economy Act.

A speech he gave before heads of departments in early 1950 illustrates how the Legion used memory in its effort to mobilize younger veterans. "You World War II fellows," he declared, "have the responsibility now of being told by some of us 'grey hairs,' if you will – what you've got to do before the fact." He added, "Don't let it be said that you didn't have the intestinal fortitude" to "take the action which would preclude a recurrence of what we saw." As a result of the Economy Act, his own generation "saw suicides because men were taken out of hospitals. . . . Don't let that happen to you World War II fellows," he continued. "Keep in mind that they [who supported the National Economy Act in 1933] . . . had propagandized just as these people [of the Hoover Commission] have been propagandizing . . . , and they had our general public almost ready to believe that anyone who wore the uniform of World War I was not only willing but anxious to destroy the structure of the economy of the government to which he had offered his life." In conclusion, Hayes enjoined younger Legionnaires to "go into your communities and stop this movement. . . . Let's don't let them pass it this time [*sic*] so that we won't have the suicides."[94] This was only one of the many speeches in which the Legion helped transmit the collective memory of the veterans' movement from one generation to the next.

The group drew on other historical examples as well. The irony of Hoover demanding the partial dismantlement of the same agency he had helped create did not go unnoticed. As the head of the Legion argued, "President Hoover ordered the organization of the VA in 1929 because the system now recommended by the ex-President's advisors then existed and was wasteful, inefficient and subject to political meddling."[95] The VFW noted the same paradox.[96] At the local level, some Legionnaires went even further: one Chicago post called the former president "the greatest enemy of the ex-service man," referring to the brutal expulsion of Bonus marchers from the federal capital in 1932.[97] In all these ways, the strategic deployment of the past played a key role in the countermobilization of the veterans' movement (Fig. 7).

Such claims were purposefully overblown. Far from being "forgotten," veterans could rely on their own advocates as well as on strong allies. In addition to the Legion, the VFW, the AMVETS, and the DAV all pushed back against most of Hoover's recommendations.[98] The leaders of the Big Three actively coordinated their response, holding several meetings in which they agreed to "bury our differences" in order to fight "this great anti-veteran propaganda machine."[99] They also had important supporters within the federal government. Not surprisingly, Bradley's successor at the head of the VA, Carl R. Gray, Jr., saw the commission's proposals as a threat to his administrative turf. In a letter to Congress, he argued that nearly all of the recommendations of the Hoover Report were "in basic conflict with the traditional policy of the Government to accord to veterans as a class, special consideration through one agency responsible for administering the various benefit programs."[100] Over on Capitol Hill, John Rankin also stood ready to assist. Thanks to the Legislative Reorganization Act of 1946, the

Figure 7. Veterans' advocates drew explicit comparisons
between the post–World War II period and earlier phases of
veterans' history, arguing that they were witnessing "the same
old story": in the aftermath of war, public opinion tended
to quickly shift from "undying gratitude" to concerns over
"economy," often to the detriment of the needs of disabled
veterans. *American Legion Magazine*, July 1949, 31.

Mississippi Democrat was now the chair of the House Committee on Veterans'
Affairs, with power over all veterans' legislation instead of only that for former
service members from the Great War.[101]

Public opinion was more ambiguous, however. When a Gallup poll conducted in February 1950 asked respondents their thoughts on the reform of
veterans' affairs put forward by the Hoover Commission, a plurality sided with

veterans (44 percent) but the percentage of those who supported the commission was not very far behind (34 percent), with a sizable minority still undecided (23 percent).[102] As Americans were being asked to decide between two visions of the government's role toward veterans, the situation remained fluid.

The Fight over Veterans' Welfare State

Though the veterans' movement was clearly at loggerheads with the Hoover Commission, their antagonism did not burst into the open immediately. Veterans' affairs ranked low on the list of CCHR priorities in 1949.[103] Only after Congress adjourned at the end of the year did the group enter into top-level negotiations with the Legion, which CCHR officials recognized as the leader of the veterans' movement. Hoover's delegates hoped a deal could be made to avert a head-on conflict.[104] McCormick knew that it would not be easy, but he also thought that neither camp would benefit from "an open battle": it "would put our organization in the position of being against the veteran," he wrote, "and it would put their organization in the light of being opponents of progress and reforms."[105] Coates shared his optimism. After several meetings, he thought in mid-January 1950 that "the peace pipe [had] been smoked."[106]

This was a serious miscalculation. While CCHR officials held out hope of an agreement, the Legion was only buying time for an all-out attack. As negotiations were still running, Craig organized a meeting at the national headquarters in Indianapolis to "discuss and formulate plans to defeat the Hoover Commission Report and the legislation that has been introduced as result of such recommendations."[107] The Hoover Commission, he stressed, would be their "NUMBER ONE legislative problem" in the near future.[108] When the meeting opened in early January 1950, Legion officials presented "Operation Survival," a nationwide public relations campaign that delegates were to launch upon returning to their individual states.[109] The goal was to sway public opinion and to lobby Congress ahead of the National Rehabilitation Conference held by the group the following month in D.C., when officials would meet with their congressional representatives.[110] The official launch of the campaign came a week later, when the national commander testified at a highly publicized hearing of Rankin's committee and then met with President Truman.[111]

Aware that success depended largely on their rank and file's response, Legion officials went on the attack. The bellicose tone of the *Badger Legionnaire,* the official monthly of the Wisconsin department, was typical. An article headlined

"Legion Declares Private War" asserted that Craig had sounded a "call to arms" and outlined a "mobilization plan" that relied heavily on local participation. Post commanders were to act as "combat company commanders" leading the "over-all post offensive."[112] The material distributed at the January meeting was described as a "full supply of ammunition."[113] Not mincing words, the *Badger Legionnaire* went on to proclaim that the Hoover Commission was responsible for a "ruthless campaign to sell the veteran down the river," and that the report was "another knife in the backs" of veterans. "The time for silk gloves is past," it concluded, "Now is the time to take off the gloves . . . use brass knucks [*sic*] if necessary . . . and keep swinging until we have kept faith with our less fortunate veterans!"[114] The Legion's *News Service* also published a cartoon portraying Hoover as insensitive to the plight of disabled veterans.[115] Feeling that this direct attack on a former president went too far, Legion officials tried to withdraw it from the mails, but it was too late.[116]

This aggressive strategy backfired. As Coates commented cheerfully, the cartoon and the warlike language of Operation Survival "brought the newspapers and Members of Congress down around [the Legion's] ears like a swarm of hornets."[117] At a hearing on the UMA in late March 1950, Craig was castigated by a wide range of congressmen, from the Georgia Democrat and proud segregationist Henderson Lanham, who called the Legion propaganda "very unwise" and "very unfair," to the African American and liberal Democrat from Chicago William L. Dawson, who advised Craig that "sending threatening letters . . . raises an antagonism."[118] The pushback in Congress was nothing compared to the almost uniformly negative reaction of the national press. The *Washington Post* and the *New York Times* dismissed the Legion's charges as "plain tommyrot" and "the height of absurdity," while the *Washington Times-Herald* called the Hoover cartoon the "dirtiest kind of dirty pool."[119] Clearly, veterans' popularity had limits.

The press not only disapproved of the Legion's strategy but it also rejected the idea of martial citizenship itself. For Long Island's *Newsday*, the view that veterans belonged to a privileged class of citizens and that their benefits should therefore remain separate was nothing more than a self-interested position underpinned by "the idea of perpetrating [the Legion's] own power to manipulate the VA."[120] "In the long run," the *Post* agreed, "the real enemy of the veteran may prove to be the leader who wants to keep him out of the main stream of American life, who wants to isolate him and make him a member not of the whole community but of a manipulable special interest group."[121] The *Times* also called on the Legion to stop "acting as though the veterans of this nation are and want to be a specially privileged class set apart from the rest of the population."[122]

Editorial comment was so vitriolic that one Legion official feared his group might "lose a great deal of the prestige we have gained during the past years."[123]

As a new session of Congress began in 1950, four different bills embodied the recommendations of the Hoover Commission on veterans' affairs. Two of them—to reorganize the VA and to create a Veterans' Insurance Corporation—fell under the jurisdiction of Rankin's committee, and he buried them without a hearing for the whole year. In the meantime, the bill to reform federal personnel management went before the House and Senate Committees on Post Office and Civil Service. In his testimony against it, a Legion official argued that the bill would "result in destruction of veterans' preference and encourage the return of the patronage and spoils system."[124] But it was the UMA that the Legion saw as the most serious threat. As Craig argued, "the medical and hospital program of the VA is the key point in that organization. . . . Take that out of the VA, and the remaining structure is greatly weakened."[125]

Since the UMA debate took place within the broader context of the fight over national health insurance, it is worth stepping back for a moment to understand the dynamics at play here.[126] In January 1949, Truman had proposed the creation of a Department of Welfare to replace the Federal Security Agency. The powerful and conservative doctors' lobby, the AMA, opposed this move on the grounds that it would have elevated to cabinet rank those officials who were among the staunchest advocates of national health insurance, which the AMA condemned as "socialized medicine." Southern Democrats were also against it because of Ewing's support for civil rights. As a result, the Senate voted the plan down. The Hoover Commission tried to sidestep this controversy by transferring health activities not to the Federal Security Agency but to the United Medical Administration and by recommending the creation of a new Department of Welfare with authority only over education and social security.[127] This compromise displeased both sides. The AMA believed health activities should be incorporated into a cabinet-level Department of Health, while Ewing declared himself "unalterably opposed" to the transfer of the Public Health Service away from his agency.[128] Each for their own reasons, the agency and the AMA joined the veterans' movement in opposing the UMA.

The real strength of the Legion lay beyond Capitol Hill, however. Long before the first hearings had even been held, the response from the rank and file exceeded all expectations. Less than two weeks after the January meeting, more than half of all departments in the continental United States reported having taken action.[129] In Texas, the twenty-one district commanders met and agreed to poll their own congressmen and to plan meetings in all 758 posts in the state.[130]

In Ohio, the department adjutant reported an "enthusiastic," "emergency state-wide meeting," "with perhaps 700 to 800 present," of which "about 70 per cent" were World War II veterans."[131] In Washington State, model petitions were sent to individual posts, veterans applying for disability claims received flyers, department officials crisscrossed the state to give speeches, and a speaker's bureau was set up.[132] A pro-Hoover group in northern California reported to the CCHR that "a vigorous attack is being made by the American Legion" in the region, adding that "we are encountering it everywhere."[133] Finally, Alabama sent a petition with twenty thousand names to Washington, D.C., and local newspapers featured large anti-Hoover Report ads at no cost.[134]

The results did not take long to materialize. Though the *Army Times Newsletter* did not support the Legion's campaign, it had to admit only a month after its launch that the drive "already can be labeled an unqualified success," with "members of Congress . . . jumping through Legion-held hoops like well-trained animals."[135] Many departments reported that their congressional delegation was "on record squarely behind our program."[136] By February, influential legislators on both sides of the aisle, such as former chairwoman of the House Committee on Veterans' Affairs Edith Nourse Rogers, a Republican from Massachusetts, and House Majority Leader and Massachusetts Democrat John W. McCormack, had come out against the recommendations of the Hoover Report on veterans' affairs.[137] In a letter to the president, both Democratic senators from Oklahoma expressed the position of their state's entire congressional delegation in terms that could have been the Legion's own. "We believe," they wrote, "that in order to provide a special service for a segment of our people, a special agency must be provided for its administration. . . . [T]here remains uppermost in our minds the necessity for a continuous program of benefits for our war veterans above and beyond those provided for the whole of our citizenry."[138] In the House, Texas Democrat Olin Teague agreed "100%" with the Legion.[139] Noting this widespread support, one Legionnaire wrote that while his group was "definitely losing [the fight] in the press," "we may win [it] in Congress."[140]

The CCHR was reluctantly coming to the same conclusion. Informed of the Legion's massive countercampaign, an alarmed McCormick wrote to Coates that "if we wait too long before we do our work, we will be completely stopped."[141] In February, they both recognized that the Legion had been "giving us a very bad time" and that the CCHR should respond at once if it wanted to prevent Legionnaires from "trying to rope and hogtie all the Congressmen in advance."[142] It was clear to them that, more than any other group in the veterans' movement, the Legion would be the "apparently insuperable obstacle" in their path.[143] McCormick thought that the ideology of martial citizenship was only a fig leaf that concealed Legionnaires' more self-interested motives. As he wrote to Hoover, "it all comes down to one fundamental. *They do not want anything removed from the Veterans' Administration because it is their private preserve and they are able to exercise leverage when it is separate.*"[144]

CCHR officials recognized the urgency of the situation but refused to adopt the same kind of aggressive tactics. They genuinely believed that the Hoover Report was above politics and that its defense should be grounded mainly in the austere exposition of facts, as opposed to what they saw as the Legion's "strictly emotional appeal."[145] CCHR speakers were urged to "avoid rip-snorting words such as 'slash,' 'abolish,' 'taxeater,' 'bureaucrat,' 'living at the public teat,'" and to strive "above all, [for] exactitude."[146] "We do not intend to engage in any shirt-waving," McCormick made clear in a private letter; "that's not our specialty."[147] This high-minded approach failed to overcome the opposition in Congress. As McCormick acknowledged, none of their four bills on veterans' affairs had made any substantial progress in 1950.[148]

The following year did little to improve the situation. Robert Johnson had hoped that the election of a new Legion chief in October 1950—Erle Cocke, Jr., of Georgia—would be enough to "brush aside a great many of the irritations of the past."[149] Yet negotiations broke down again after two meetings, with the positions of both groups still "irreconcilable."[150] In light of the hostile reaction of the larger public to Operation Survival, Cocke decided to avoid any overt publicity of his group's position, which he knew would only add grist to the CCHR's mill. He chose to focus instead on what the Legion did best: lobbying legislators behind the scenes by flooding their offices with mail from constituents back home.[151] As one top Legionnaire put it, "it is pretty much our policy this year to oppose these things in the Committees of Congress rather than in the press of the nation."[152] The Legion continued to rely on Rankin to bury the bills to reform the VA and create a Veterans' Insurance Corporation. The Mississippian refused to even invite the CCHR to testify at hearings, a decision interpreted by Johnson as "*exactly as though a court of law were to announce that it would hear only witnesses for the defense.*"[153]

CCHR officials knew that they stood little chance of making progress as long as the veterans' movement was united against the report. This is why they formed the Independent Veterans' Committee in August 1951, a group whose mission was to "demonstrate to Congress and the public that the established veterans' organizations are not the sole spokesman for the nation's veterans in this issue," and more specifically to free Congress "of its fear of the Legion" in order to get action on the reform of the VA.[154] The editor of the *San Francisco Chronicle*, Paul Smith, a decorated veteran of the Pacific, was its chairman, and its founding members included such prestigious names as Hollywood actor Douglas Fairbanks and Generals Lucius Clay and A. C. Wedemeyer.[155] In truth, the committee was merely a figurehead. Handpicked by Coates and McCormick, its members were there only to give speeches while the CCHR handled all the staff work behind the scenes.[156] The committee was what would later be known as an "astroturf" group: a staged grassroots campaign which, as the Legion fully realized, had "no other purpose than to lend the name 'veterans' to the support of the Hoover proposals."[157]

Even with this manufactured ally, the CCHR made few advances in 1951. Rankin was as unyielding as ever, preventing any discussion of the bills to reform the VA and to create a Veterans' Insurance Corporation. The bill to create a UMA was replaced by one to create a Department of Health, but nobody was willing to seriously consider such sweeping reforms in the emergency situation created by the Korean War.[158] The only minor victory for the CCHR was on the bill to reform civil service, which the Senate passed one day before adjourning.[159] By the end of the year, the CCHR estimated that slightly more than half of all the commission's recommendations had been implemented and that $5.5 billion could still be saved with the remaining proposals.[160] It decided to focus for the next year on six bills "of primary importance," those "in areas where the greatest savings can be made." Of these six, three had to do with veterans' affairs: federal personnel management, the Department of Health, and the reorganization of the VA.[161] The CCHR opted to continue operating until May 1952 in order to make a final push for these bills, after which it would suspend its activities to avoid taking sides in the upcoming presidential campaign.[162]

Meanwhile, the Legion was charting its final offensive. Aware that their foe would soon disband, Legion officials decided to embark on one last push in order "to get these fellows on the defensive."[163] Though it was called "Operation Victory," the new campaign essentially replicated the approach of Operation Survival. The head lobbyist of the Legion, John Thomas Taylor, asked members to "literally flood" Congress with letters and petitions, while national officials met with their representatives in person at several events during the spring.[164] Since the press and to a lesser extent the public remained relatively hostile, Taylor again directed his campaign inward, seeking to mobilize members rather than to sway collective opinion.

Confident that he had the upper hand, Taylor sought to score a clear-cut victory. He took advantage of the ties forged with Rankin over more than two decades of close collaboration to convince the Mississippian to finally allow hearings on the bills to reorganize the VA and to create a Veterans' Insurance Corporation, so that they could be defeated once and for all in the open.[165] When the hearings took place in the spring, it was clear that Taylor's strategy had worked, for the CCHR faced a skeptical committee. Rankin argued that the reorganization of the VA along functional lines, with each core service under the responsibility of one deputy, would take power away from the administrator and thus make the agency less subservient to congressional authority.[166] Olin Teague also opposed the reorganization.[167] In the end, Rankin suspended action on both bills until the results of a management survey of the VA was made public in September. This decision amounted to a defeat for the CCHR, since it meant that Congress would adjourn in July without any decision on the matter.[168]

Outside of Rankin's committee, the other two bills of consequence—on federal personnel management and the Department of Health—met a similar fate. Backed once again by the DAV, the AMVETS, and the VFW, as well as by a coalition of federal employee unions, the Legion repeated the same familiar arguments against the reform of civil service.[169] Taylor was confident that the House Committee on Post Office and Civil Service felt "well disposed toward us at the moment" and he was correct: the bill was not reported out before the end of the session.[170] Likewise, the bill to create a Department of Health never got out of committee.[171]

The suspension of the CCHR's activities and the adjournment of Congress in July 1952 brought the Legion's campaign to a successful conclusion. As the Independent Veterans' Committee recognized, "in nearly three years little real progress toward better organization and management had been made."[172] By contrast, the Legion could boast of having had "a good legislative year," not least because "not a single one of the bills advocated by the CCHR and opposed by The American Legion was enacted into law."[173] In recognition of Taylor's work, the Legion passed a resolution praising his "magnificent accomplishment of Operation Victory."[174] For a total cost of less than $30,000, the campaign had lived up to its name.[175]

The success of this operation was the product of more than just Taylor's lobbying skills, however. More broadly, it reflected what the veterans' movement could achieve when the World War I and World War II cohorts came together. By drawing on the memory of the interwar period, Legion officials turned these two generations, which were just emerging from several years of bitter infighting over public housing, into a united force with considerable political clout. The defeat of the First Hoover Commission showed the potential strength of the "two-war experiment."

If we take a step back and place this episode in the longer trajectory of veterans' policy, we can see that the success of Operation Victory was also facilitated by the centralization of all veterans' programs into one agency, the VA, in 1930. The creation of a single entity with responsibility over benefits for all generations of former service members, as opposed to separate bureaus for each cohort (as was previously the case), meant that an attack on this agency was a threat to the entire veteran population instead of just to a specific age group. The VA thus became a common denominator between veterans of all ages; its existence gave them something to rally behind even when they otherwise felt no immediate connection with other cohorts. The feedback effect was clear: policy was both the result and the driving force of the veterans' movement.

Path dependence was similarly crucial. It is indeed remarkable that the First Hoover Commission failed to take advantage of the postwar scandals affecting veterans' affairs, whereas the veterans' movement had used a similar window of opportunity to reassert martial citizenship in the aftermath of the Great War. The different outcomes resulted from the fact not only that the Big Three could rely on the support of powerful allies within the state and of a strong grassroots base but also that they had a credible claim to be defending the status quo. Lawmakers largely accepted the argument that veterans' advocates were fighting to preserve the established practice of treating former service members as a separate and privileged group of the population, as opposed to the new course proposed by the Hoover Report. Since it is always harder to change things than to stay put, the task of the Big Three was made easier by the fact that martial citizenship had become the new normal in the mid-twentieth century. In other words, the success of Operation Victory was greatly facilitated by the previous achievements of the veterans' movement.

This episode marked the peak of the movement in the postwar period, but other threats were already emerging just as Taylor was planning his final push. With the outbreak of the Korean War, the country was forced to discuss once again which benefits to grant a new generation of veterans. And the issue of government reorganization did not fade away. Both major parties endorsed it in their platforms for the 1952 presidential election.[176] The Legion took note of these developments, commenting that same year that "the present status of the veterans medical and hospital program is in a rather fluid situation."[177] The larger conflict over martial citizenship was far from over.

PART II

Eclipse

CHAPTER 5

A House Divided

Anticommunism and Its Discontents

Tradition required every national commander of the American Legion to open his one-year term with a big homecoming celebration. The first World War II veteran to assume this position made no exception. After his election in the summer of 1949, George Craig received what the group's own journalists called a "royal welcome" in his hometown of Brazil, Indiana. On November 3, this otherwise sleepy municipality of nine thousand was gripped by "a carnival atmosphere" when more than thirty thousand Legionnaires and their guests showed up. With the afternoon designated as a holiday by the mayor, businesses and schools were closed and tents were planted on two downtown streets with "enough food and drink for a good sized army." The climax of the festivities was a six-mile, two-hour-long parade featuring floats, more than forty bands, thirty-five hundred marchers, and the "impressively thunderous" flyover of four jet fighter planes and three B-29 bombers. At the reviewing stand were representatives from forty-six Legion departments as well as the governor of Indiana (who had proclaimed a state-wide "George N. Craig Day") and the city's mayor and U.S. senator Homer Capehart.[1]

The joyous spirit of the afternoon's celebrations jarred with the more anxious tone of the evening's speeches. Before a packed high school gymnasium, the governor, Craig, and other high-ranking Legionnaires gave lectures about the precarious state of world affairs, which were broadcast nationwide by famous radio tenor Morton Downey. The atmosphere was tense: Craig's family had received death threats that forced state police to guard his four-month-old daughter at home. In his speech, the commander declared that his priority was to resist the progress of domestic communism and "to eliminate the enemy termites in our midst." He added, "There is no room in the United States today for both the American Legion and communism, and the Legion does not intend to move out."[2]

Craig's homecoming captured two important dimensions of the veterans' movement in the late 1940s. The first was its renewed popularity and prestige. The arrival of a new cohort had not only generated good will among the larger public but had also greatly enlarged and rejuvenated the ranks of the Big Three. The presence in Brazil of top government officials, fighter planes, and large crowds all attested to how deeply groups like the Legion were interwoven into the fabric of American life in the postwar years. This was true not just in conservative midwestern states like Indiana but in the country as a whole. An extensive survey conducted shortly after the war found that over three-fourths of respondents thought "well" of Craig's organization.[3] Many observers of public affairs ranked the Legion as one of the most important groups in national politics, equal in status and influence to other heavyweights such as the Chamber of Commerce, the American Federation of Labor (AFL), and the Congress of Industrial Organizations (CIO).[4]

Second, the topic chosen by Craig on the evening of his homecoming revealed the return of anticommunism to the center of veterans' agenda. This was an old issue: the fight against "radical" ideals had been a central part of the Legion, the VFW, and the DAV's mission throughout the interwar period. Yet such concerns had been relegated to the background during World War II and its immediate aftermath. It was only at the end of the 1940s, with the country in the grip of the Second Red Scare, that the struggle against "subversive" influences returned to the top of the Big Three's priority list. Veterans' issues were no longer the movement's sole preoccupation, though they never went away (just as Craig was delivering his Brazil speech, his organization was preparing its response to the Hoover Report). More liberal groups such as the AVC took a less hard-line stance, but they never represented more than a small minority of former service members.[5]

A sustained look at the inner workings of the Legion shows that anticommunism played a more complex role within the movement than previously understood. Indeed, the issue created a profound schism between moderate and radical conservatives. In the former camp were those, like the former national commander Ray Murphy of Iowa, who argued that the Legion should continue to focus primarily on veterans' benefits. Their answer to the communist menace was to encourage the spread of patriotic values through "positive" educational and community-level programs such as high school oratorical contests on the Constitution or Junior Baseball. On the other side were advocates of a more "negative" approach like Craig or Karl Baarslag, whom we will introduce later in this chapter. They not only wanted their group to make the fight against communism its top priority, but they also pushed for more top-down countersubversive programs that directly addressed the communist threat. These two factions vied with each other to determine whether martial citizenship would remain at the center of the Legion's agenda or be replaced by anticommunism.

No obvious winner emerged. Rather than a clear-cut victory, this confrontation produced two paradoxical outcomes.

The first is that the Legion played a central role in the anticommunist crusade despite the fact that the more "negative" approach enjoyed the support of only a minority of its leadership and rank and file. While most Legionnaires supported "positive" educational programs, they resisted focusing all their efforts on the fight against the "Red" menace and they rejected more controversial methods that ran the risk of damaging their respectable image as well as their ability to lobby for veterans' benefits. Their disinterest also stemmed from the fact that many members lived in rural areas where communist activity was only a distant concern, and that younger veterans tended to care about this problem less than their elders. Anticommunism would remain a central part of the Legion's creed, but the group never adopted the kind of single-minded focus on countersubversive activities that some of its leaders advocated for.

The second paradox is that far from cementing the group's leadership in national politics, anticommunism only wound up pushing the Legion to the margins. This was because the Second Red Scare provided an opening to a vocal minority of far-right activists who embraced a hard-line stance. Since the national leadership of the organization was reluctant to crack down on a faction with whom they disagreed more about methods than goals, these activists managed in 1955 to have the group endorse a conspiracy theory against "world government" that rejected U.S. participation in the United Nations (UN) and its affiliates. This move backfired, costing the organization much of its credit and authority. Though the Legion would remain an essential voice in veterans' affairs and a major pillar of social life in thousands of communities across the country for decades to come, by the late 1950s it had lost its central place in national politics.

At one level, this chapter is therefore the story of how, as one Legionnaire put it, in a decentralized institution like his own "organized minorities radically devoted to a 'cause' can often prevail" against a more "sober" majority.[6] This episode also marks an inflection point in the larger narrative of this book. In contrast with previous chapters that traced the way in which the veterans' movement restored its public profile after the low point of the late 1930s, this chapter and the ones that follow chronicle its gradual, albeit incomplete, marginalization.

The picture of the Second Red Scare presented here is different in several respects from the one we are familiar with. First of all, it undermines the conventional view that U.S. senator Joseph McCarthy was central to the anticommunist hysteria that swept the nation during these years. The demagogue from Wisconsin plays a secondary role in our story, reminding us that he was only the symptom and not the cause of a much larger phenomenon. More importantly, the fact that many officials and a majority of the rank and file of the Legion proved reluctant to embrace countersubversive activities shows that the Second Red Scare was primarily, as one scholar has suggested, a top-down "battle waged by a relatively small and often elite group of anticommunists" rather than a mass movement.[7] This is not to deny the dramatic impact that these militants had on the course of postwar politics, but only to stress how much a zealous minority can achieve when the majority remains silent.

Second, the chapter highlights not just the successes but also the costs of hard-line anticommunism. Much of the existing scholarship on the Second Red Scare has focused on the witch-hunting that was so widespread during this period, depicting its devastating consequences for thousands of ordinary Americans as well as for the gay and lesbian community and former New Dealers.[8] We know much less about the degree to which anticommunism ended up being a liability for those who defended its more aggressive version. The example of the Legion shows how uncompromising adherence to this ideology could lead to a diminished political standing, especially after public opinion began to turn against it in the mid-1950s. In short, anticommunism did not always work in U.S. politics.

Finally, this chapter provides a useful corrective to the main thrust of recent works on the rise of the conservative movement. Over the past couple of decades, historians have tended to move away from an earlier portrayal of right-wing activists as irrational actors who resisted progress, striving instead to take their ideas and actions seriously.[9] There is no need to resuscitate the condescending psychological explanations advanced by a previous generation of scholars, but what happened within the Legion during the Second Red Scare shows that we should not dismiss the role of paranoia as a motivation for at least a minority of far-right activists. The anti-UN conspiracy theory that they deployed reflected the resilience of an isolationist mind-set in the midst of an internationalist age. It suggests that we need to see such ideas not as aberrations but as recurrent and integral features of U.S. politics.

As Craig was making his speech in the Brazil high school gymnasium, these developments lay far beyond the horizon. His own leadership of the Legion represented the success of the "partnership" between the World War I and the World War II generations that had done so much to restore the influence of the veterans' movement. In his mind, the onset of a new anticommunist crusade promised only to reinforce this trend, by offering the group an opportunity to cement its position at the center of American life.

At the Heart of the Second Red Scare

Historian Ellen Schrecker has described the Federal Bureau of Investigation as the "bureaucratic heart of the McCarthy era," which is to say the nucleus of the state apparatus behind most of the anticommunist campaigns of the postwar years.[10] By comparison, the Legion was in many ways the "civic heart" of the Second Red Scare. With posts in nearly every community across the country, the veterans' group was the indispensable counterpart to the FBI in civil society. In the same way that the *National Review* brought together the different strands of the conservative intellectual tradition in the mid-1950s, the Legion served as a rallying point for an earlier wave of right-wing activists.[11] Few other organizations contributed as decisively to the resurgence of anticommunism.

This ideology ran deep in the Legion's blood. One of the main motivations for its creation back in 1919 had been to help contain the spread of radical ideas among disaffected doughboys in France. Throughout the interwar period, the Legion was at the center of the anticommunist movement. Its members lobbied on behalf of various bills ranging from antisedition to anti-immigration. Under the leadership of the rabid anticommunist Homer Chaillaux, who chaired the Legion's National Americanism Commission from 1934 until his death in 1946, the group played a key role in the establishment of the Dies Committee in the late 1930s.[12] The Legion also tried to block public lectures or textbooks, films, and plays that it deemed subversive. Its members clashed with left-wing labor groups in the streets, participating in violent confrontations against the Industrial Workers of the World in the early 1920s and against the CIO in the mid- to late-1930s. Finally, the Legion maintained friendly ties with other right-wing groups like the Daughters of the American Revolution.[13]

Though most Legionnaires approved of the need to fight communism, they did not all agree on how to do so. Activists like Chaillaux wanted the Legion to focus almost single-mindedly on the fight against radicalism, but other leaders feared that his extreme positions would only squander their political capital and reputation (as for instance when Chaillaux attacked FDR's secretary of labor, Frances Perkins, for refusing to deport labor leader Harry Bridges). In the view of this more moderate faction, Legionnaires should devote their attention first and foremost to the fight for veterans' benefits and especially to the needs of the disabled. Among these voices were National Commanders Ray Murphy of Iowa (1935–36) and Harry Colmery of Kansas (1936–37), who both attempted to rein in Chaillaux's excesses. Upon his election, Colmery promised Legion delegates to stop his group's tendency "to stick our nose into other people's business instead of keeping within the confines of the Legion's program."[14]

After a lull during World War II, concerns about radicalism returned to the forefront of national politics in the postwar period. In response to a historic wave of strikes in 1946, the U.S. Chamber of Commerce exploited growing fears of disorder in a nationwide public relations campaign aimed at rolling back the gains of the labor movement and of New Deal liberalism. Republicans joined in, accusing Democratic policies of bearing a "made-in-Moscow label."[15] Such red-baiting tactics were key to their victory in the midterm elections that same year. Making good on its campaign promises, the GOP not only passed the anti-labor Taft-Hartley Act but it also increased funding for the House Un-American Activities Committee, which made headlines by investigating the movie industry. Meanwhile, the notion that communist spies represented a threat gained popular credence with the discovery of a Soviet spy ring in Canada. Hoping to placate his increasingly loud chorus of critics on the right, President Truman implemented a loyalty program for government employees in March 1947. That same month, he vowed to contain communist influence worldwide in a landmark speech before Congress. The Cold War had begun in earnest.

The Legion greeted these developments with a sense of vindication. "We have seen a decided change in the nation's thinking on un-American activities and influence," John Thomas Taylor declared triumphantly in 1947. "For many years we have been called Red-baiters and warmongers, but finally the entire country seems to be aroused to dangers recognized by the Legion long ago."[16] In response to the change in climate, the group increased funding for its Americanism program in 1946.[17] That fall, Legion leaders appointed Karl Baarslag at the head of a subcommittee of the National Americanism Commission charged with overseeing "Un-American Activities."[18]

In his mid-forties, Baarslag was a rising star within the circles of anticommunist experts. Initially sympathetic to the Russian revolution and to Bolshevism, he claimed to have changed his mind after the notorious massacre of rebellious sailors at Kronstadt in 1921, which started his lifelong interest in "former Communists and Communist defectors."[19] During the interwar period, he worked on ships "as a seaman, oiler, radio operator, and sometimes as a mate, deck officer." He cut his teeth fighting the communist infiltration of his commercial telegraphers union in the 1930s. After Pearl Harbor, he joined the antisubversive branch of the Office of Naval Intelligence.[20]

Once hired by the Legion, Baarslag rapidly got to work. He enlarged Chaillaux's index card system, which contained information on individuals and organizations with potentially subversive affiliations.[21] He also began distributing the newsletter *Firing Line*, which kept track of recent developments in the fight against communism.[22] Finally, his subcommittee published a number of anticommunist pamphlets of its own.[23]

The message at the core of all these publications was simple. It boiled down to the belief, as a Legion official testified, that communism was "not an idea ... a club ... [or] a political party," but rather "an organized international conspiracy." American communists were not "debaters arguing about ideas" but "coldly scheming revolutionists and betrayers" who received their orders directly from Moscow.[24] The point of arguing that communism was not an idea, of course, was to exclude it from the protection of the First Amendment to the U.S. Constitution and thus to be able to censure and arrest its supporters. This message was neither new nor unique to the Legion: outlawing the Communist Party of the USA had ranked high on the agenda of many other right-wing groups since well before World War II. It was also just a first step, for Legion officials saw the CPUSA as the tip of a much larger iceberg. They believed that most communist influence was exercised in secret and behind front organizations.[25] This is why Baarslag created so many new index cards to keep track of communist sympathizers and why the Legion so enthusiastically supported the Internal Security Act of 1950, which required all members of the CPUSA to register with the government.[26]

The other two members of the Big Three shared essentially the same positions. The VFW supported legislation to outlaw the CPUSA on the ground that it was "a domestic branch of a criminal conspiracy to conquer all free peoples."[27] Not to be outdone, the DAV adopted resolutions supporting the death penalty in "extreme cases of traitorous activity" and the confinement of known communists in "security camps."[28] The major actors of the veterans' movement shared the same conservative views.

Trying to outlaw the CPUSA was only one goal of the anticommunist crusade. In practice, the campaign also pushed back against New Deal liberalism and the Truman administration. Legion discourse grew increasingly partisan in the late 1940s, especially on foreign affairs. After the "loss" of China and the test of the Soviet atomic bomb in 1949, the group went on record declaring its "clear lack of confidence" in the State Department.[29] A few years later, it "forcefully demand[ed]" the immediate dismissal of Secretary of State Dean Acheson.[30] The criticism extended to domestic policy. In an address to the AFL, Craig decried the relief measures implemented by Truman and his predecessor. He condemned the idea of the "Welfare State" and the "growing disposition on one part of more and more of our people to surrender their rights and freedoms, bit by bit, in return for government guarantees of their present and future security."[31] The *Legion Magazine* featured so many attacks on the legacy of the New Deal that one reader complained that it was "printed only for Republicans and Dixie-crats."[32] Truman himself admitted privately that he considered Legion leaders to be nothing more than "fascists."[33]

Though anticommunism was hardly a new issue for the group, its postwar incarnation was different in two ways. First, the Legion largely avoided physical violence, notwithstanding a few isolated episodes.[34] Second, its major targets were no longer labor unions and immigrants, but the two realms in which the left still enjoyed an edge after 1945, namely culture and education. Artists, writers, publishers, journalists, and foundations, as well as teachers and professors all came in for criticism.[35] Schools were a topic of particular concern, for Legion officials had long seen them as places where "communists are being mass-produced" and "young minds are being softened for the red virus" (Fig. 8).[36] The postwar expansion of higher education only heightened these concerns.

Both words and actions show how the Legion was the "civic heart" of the vast anticommunist network. A major instrument of the group's influence was the financial support that it extended to right-wing activists by publishing their work in the *Legion Magazine*, then one of the nation's most circulated periodicals.[37] The list of its authors read like a *Who's Who* of the early days of the conservative movement, including former "fellow travelers" such as J. B. Matthews ("Mr. Anticommunist") and Louis F. Budenz, conservative writers and journalists like George Sokolsky and William F. Buckley, Jr., and right-wing radio broadcaster Fulton Lewis, Jr.[38] Their work also appeared in the anticommunist newsletters that Baarslag encouraged Legionnaires to subscribe to, such as *Counterattack* or *Plain Talk*.[39] His subcommittee doubled as a lecturing agency, maintaining a list of recommended speakers for anyone interested in scheduling a talk on communism.[40] Finally, the Legion regularly hired these experts itself.[41] Before Clarence Manion went on to create his own radio show and play a crucial role in

Figure 8. College professors were often suspected of spreading radical ideals during the Second Red Scare. The terms written on the blackboard and on the spine of the books in the background ("imperialism," "Lenin," "Marx," "Revolt," "Moscow," "Asia") paint a picture of the constellation of right-wing fears during this period. *American Legion Magazine*, November 1951.

the formation of the conservative movement, for example, he was an advisor to the Legion's National Americanism Commission.[42] The group distributed thousands of copies of his anti–New Deal tract *The Key to Peace* (1951).[43]

Beyond individual activists, the Legion maintained close ties with right-wing organizations. It helped the American Bar Association in its effort to purge the legal profession of left-wing members, for instance.[44] The Legion worked with the FBI as well. Not only was the Contact program resumed during the Korean War, but both groups also shared personal connections, as illustrated by Lee R. Pennington's career. A World War I Legionnaire, Pennington started working for the FBI in 1929 and became its liaison with the Legion's Americanism Commission a decade later.[45] He attended so many meetings over the next several years that he reportedly joked that he "really ought to be on the Legion payroll."[46] After his retirement from the FBI in 1953, he was appointed director of that same commission.[47] The Legion also supported all congressional committees investigating communism, including the House Un-American Activities Committee, which it urged Congress to make permanent throughout World War II.[48] When Rankin succeeded in doing so in 1945, some congressmen admitted that the Legion's support had been decisive.[49]

Legionnaires helped promote anticommunism on the international stage, too. Like many other conservatives, they saw their struggle against radical ideas at home as part of the global Cold War.[50] In 1949, the group launched the "Tide of Toys" operation, whose goal was to collect and send toys to children of European countries ravaged by war in order to win hearts and minds. It quickly gained traction nationwide, receiving the support of some of the highest-profile celebrities of the day such as Kate Smith and Amos 'n' Andy.[51] On the Old Continent, the campaign was touted by the State Department, the Voice of America, and the pope. Over the course of six months, the Legion sent over 3 million toys to fourteen Western European countries.[52] After the end of the Korean War, the group also joined the Wooden Church Crusade, a nondenominational project launched by a German aristocrat who sought to rebuild West German churches destroyed by the war. His idea was to "ring the Iron Curtain with a circle of churches" and to "build a wall of faith as our great shield against Communism." With the support of the West German and U.S. governments, the program aimed to raise enough money to build forty-nine wooden churches, one for each of the forty-eight states and D.C.[53] The Legion paid for three of them.[54]

These examples demonstrate the depth and breadth of the Legion's partnership with the federal government. The group was but one of the many private organizations mobilized by the U.S. government throughout the Cold War.[55] Their collaboration was so close that some outside observers saw the group as yet another extension of the state, not fundamentally different from the police or the armed forces.[56] At the same time, their relationship could be manipulative. During the debate over universal military training in the late 1940s and early 1950s, for instance, Army officers used the Legion as their unofficial mouthpiece in order to avoid charges of militarism that they feared would arise if they advocated for the program themselves (it was never adopted).[57] The gap between the goals of both sides was even starker in the case of the Back to God program launched by the Legion in 1952 to fight the threat of communism by encouraging a religious revival. President Dwight D. Eisenhower participated in annual telecasts, but he used the project to buttress the legitimacy of the federal government instead of undermining it, as Legionnaires had hoped.[58]

All these examples illustrate the role of the Legion as the heart of the anticommunist movement in civil society. Beneath the surface, however, the group was in a state of turmoil.

The Limits of Anticommunism

The public façade of leadership projected by the Legion belied the division that reigned within its own ranks. As it turned out, neither its leadership nor its rank and file showed the same interest in countersubversive activities as they had in the campaign for the GI Bill or against the First Hoover Commission. Throughout the 1940s and early 1950s, successive efforts to launch such "negative" programs all foundered.

The first attempt was during World War II, when an influential member of the National Association of Manufacturers sought to raise money to expand the Legion's perpetually cash-starved Americanism program.[59] The result was the Americanism Endowment Fund, created in early 1945 and chaired by Alvin Owsley of Texas. A lawyer and former national commander in the 1920s, Owsley was a southern Democrat who had actively supported the New Deal early on but later turned against it.[60] He wanted to use the fund in order to launch an ambitious public relations campaign that would both defend conservative ideas and enhance the Legion's public image.[61] The *Indianapolis Star* reported that the fund's "primary object ... will be to slap down all radical 'isms' in the United States and to keep the dreamers and ideologists at a safe distance."[62] Owsley hoped to raise $50 million.[63]

His idea never came to pass. It faced immediate opposition from top Legion officials, who resisted the prospect of adding yet another fund-raising campaign on top of those already undertaken in support of the war effort. Many were also concerned that the "super-patriotism" of this campaign would put off returning veterans tired of military parades. Moreover, they doubted that local posts would relinquish control of their Americanism programs to the national organization.

Many of the largest departments asked Owsley not to collect funds in their state, with the result that he was limited to his home state of Texas.[64] He had raised merely $65,000 by October 1948, far less than what the Legion had spent to promote the program. The fund was soon discontinued.[65]

Around the same time as the Americanism Endowment Fund collapsed, Baarslag began to organize the "Seminar on Counter-subversive Activities" in Washington, D.C. During a four-day meeting in November 1947, eighty hand-picked Legionnaires gathered to hear lectures by noted anticommunist experts such as Chairman J. Parnell Thomas of the House Un-American Activities Committee, ex-communist journalist Howard Rushmore, and founder of the CPUSA Benjamin Gitlow. Topics ranged from the history of the Russian Revolution to communist influence on American religious organizations.[66] Similar in its structure to the Legion College held a year earlier for World War II veterans, this seminar sought to teach a select group of members "the facts and 'know how' of detecting and exposing Communists" with the expectation that they would then go home and establish follow-up seminars at the state and local level, thereby spreading interest in subversive activities as widely as possible.[67] "With 17,000 Posts," National Commander James O'Neil argued that "the Legion should have at least 17,000 fairly well trained and qualified specialists on subversive activities."[68]

The program fell far short of this ambitious goal. As Legion officials admitted half a year after the first seminar, "the response in the various Departments to date has been disappointing." They complained, "Few have conducted seminars, and few have utilized the knowledge gained by the Legionnaire who attended the [national] Legion seminar."[69] Only seventeen of the Legion's fifty-nine departments held their own seminars by October 1948.[70] A month later, the head of the National Americanism Commission admitted that his staff was "rather discouraged" by these poor results.[71] Some posts did follow suit, such as Indianapolis's Broad Ripple Post No. 312, which held its "Hoosier Counter-subversive Seminar" with McCarthy's aide Roy Cohn as guest speaker in 1954.[72] Yet it was obvious to the national leadership that the program had for the most part failed to disseminate anticommunist "information and materials down to a post level."[73]

This fiasco prompted a new approach. Instead of focusing on their own members, Legion officials decided to look outward and to form what Baarslag called "a grand coalition of all big national organizations opposed to the further spread of Communism in the United States."[74] Shortly after being elected national commander, Craig invited several groups to an "All-American Conference to Combat Communism" in New York in January 1950.[75] The list of

sixty-six organizations that sent delegates to this first meeting had a clear conservative bent, including groups such as the American Heritage Foundation,
the U.S. Chamber of Commerce, the National Association of Manufacturers,
and the Daughters of the American Revolution. The VFW and the DAV also
attended, along with smaller veterans' groups, labor unions like the CIO and
the AFL, and fraternal orders. The roster of speakers included prominent anticommunist advocates like South Dakota senator Karl E. Mundt, chairman of the
California Committee on Un-American Activities Jack B. Tenney, and famous
Catholic radio host Msgr. Fulton J. Sheen.[76]

Upon calling the meeting to order, Craig declared that the conference had
three goals: "to form a united front against communism," to "devise ways and
means of strengthening government agencies in the restraint and abolition of
communist activities," and to "try to find some medium to coordinate activities
of all these organizations."[77] He later announced that he hoped to raise $5 mil-
lion in order to "saturate the airlanes [sic], the television, the periodicals, and the
editorials with the program of Americanism; something that we have looked
forward to having an opportunity to do in The American Legion these many
years which we have been prohibited from doing because of the cost involved."[78]

Not unlike the Americanism Endowment Fund and the seminars, the conference yielded disappointing results. Its fundamental problem was that moderate and conservative groups were never able to unite behind a common agenda.
For almost two years, both sides disagreed over whether to focus on "positive"
grassroots programs like Know Your America Week or on more "negative" coun-
terespionage tactics.[79] Moderates in the American Jewish Committee and the
National Education Association were afraid that the conference would turn into
"an active vigilante organization designed to 'police' the activities of American
citizens in the fields of religion, education, and politics," and they wanted it to
focus solely on educational activities.[80] Infighting reduced the group to little
more than a speechmaking outlet. Months after Craig's ambitious announcement, staff members complained that "his promises of raising funds have not
consummated" and "so far the results are NIL."[81] With only a paltry $4,000 in
its treasury by September 1952, the group was a hollow shell.[82] As Baarslag later
reported, forty of the initial sixty-six organizations "quietly dropped out" within
a few years. By the time the conference was dissolved in 1974, the Legion and
"most of its early and ardent supporters" were no longer on board.[83]

Even smaller programs such as the Memorial Book Plan, launched by
Baarslag on Memorial Day in 1952, failed to stimulate grassroots interest.[84] The
goal here was to encourage posts to donate anticommunist books to their local

libraries, with each volume bearing a "memorial bookplate" honoring a soldier from that same community who died in Korea.[85] In Baarslag's mind, this campaign promised not only to be affordable but also to "offset [the] dearth of books on anticommunism in our public, school, and college libraries."[86] Yet even a project that demanded so little time and effort collapsed. As Baarslag later recognized, "Pennsylvania and a couple of other states showed some temporary interest" but overall the program "simply fizzled out at the local level."[87] Only 850 books had been purchased nationwide by May 1953, when the goal had been for the Legion's seventeen thousand posts to buy one or two tomes each.[88] The disinterest of the rank and file was clear. Though the plan continued to run for the next few years, it had failed to deliver.[89]

More limited attempts to interest posts in countersubversive materials met with the same disappointing fate. For instance, the newsletter *Firing Line* never captured a large readership within the Legion. Its monthly distribution was still limited to two thousand four years after its launch in 1947, not much higher than the initial five hundred.[90] As Baarslag noted, the majority of subscribers were not even Legionnaires but rather "the heads of state troopers, police chiefs, and various security and intelligence agencies and firms."[91] Likewise, an attempt to distribute booklets extolling the virtues of capitalism and free enterprise produced only disappointing results.[92] Despite all the efforts of Baarslag and other like-minded activists, countersubversive activities never found an audience within the Legion.

There are two ways to explain these repeated failures. One is to focus on the divisions that plagued the national leadership, the other on the disinterest of the rank and file. Let us explore each of these in turn.

If we adopt a top-down perspective first, one problem becomes immediately clear. As had been the case throughout the interwar period, the kind of "negative" anticommunist activities favored by Baarslag remained low on the agenda of the Legion leadership throughout the postwar period. This was illustrated by their share of the group's budget: from 1945 to 1960, the organization spent on average over five times more on the defense of veterans' benefits than on its Americanism program.[93] And Baarslag's subcommittee received only a small fraction of these funds: its budget for 1952 was approximately $3,000, for example.[94]

This neglect was the result of the continuing turf war between those who advocated for a more aggressive focus on countering the threat of communism and those who championed a more indirect emphasis on local patriotic projects. The fault lines were the same as during the interwar period. "Positive" activities, as one Legion official put it in 1948, were "concerned with the fostering and perpetuating of the ideals, customs, and institutions which constitute our American way of life," whereas "protective" or "negative" ones focused exclusively on countering potential threats to these ideals.[95] As it had done in the interwar period, the Legion leadership continued to allot the lion's share of funding to "positive" Americanism programs well into the postwar years.

Baarslag and the other members of his subcommittee on "Un-American Activities" did all they could to improve their subaltern status. They scored a small victory in November 1950 when they were upgraded to a committee, whose chairman was the champion of public housing, Walter Alessandroni.[96] Yet they were still under the umbrella of the Americanism Commission, for Legion leaders refused to make the committee fully independent—a decision that was reportedly a "tremendous disappointment" to Baarslag.[97] The result was an absurd situation, which one Legionnaire described in a statement worth quoting at length:

> You have set up a Committee on Un-American Activities and have given it no tools with which to work. We have no budget at all. We have no paid officials to whom we may turn for information and assistance. In fact, to do a job at all, we must go to the National Staff and beg for a few dollars of the already small allotment belonging to the Americanism Commission . . . Fighting Communists and Communist Infiltration is a specialized business and should be placed in a category by itself. It should not be just a part of our Americanism Commission. We are convinced that a separate Commission to deal directly with Communism should be a part of our permanent organization. . . . As presently constituted, the Committee on Un-American Activities cannot effectively function. We cannot continue to be responsible to two masters. We must be free to outline an effective program and free to use money for its implementation.[98]

His plea fell on deaf ears, as illustrated by the budget for that same year. In 1953, the Legion spent $14,000 on a single "positive" activity like high school oratorical contests but only $2,500 on Baarslag's committee—even less than the previous year.[99]

There was more to this than bureaucratic turf wars, however. The fact that Americanism officials were protective of their "positive" programs may explain why they restricted funding for countersubversive activities, but not why the rest of the Legion hierarchy was on their side. To understand their reaction, we need to keep in mind the nature of the group as a voluntary organization whose budget was heavily dependent on membership dues. This meant that the Legion had to be very protective of its image: negative publicity could drive members away, with immediate consequences on their bottom line and their ability to lobby lawmakers.[100] While all Legion officials embraced anticommunism, they were therefore reluctant to adopt methods that stepped outside the boundaries of what they saw as respectable behavior. This is why the group never endorsed the controversial Joseph McCarthy, for instance, even though it shared many of his positions and regularly went on record supporting congressional committees investigating communism.[101] This fear of scandal also explains why all of the Legion's national publications were vetted internally to avoid "libelous matters."[102]

In response to this defensive mind-set, Baarslag and other like-minded activists promised that the fight against "Reds" would bring great benefits to the Legion if only the group embraced it wholeheartedly. Alessandroni argued for instance that the creation and expansion of the New Deal welfare state had diminished the need for separate veterans' programs, since there were now "provisions made for all kinds of people who get themselves in trouble." The cause of veterans' benefits may still be as great "in our hearts" as it used to be, "but practically it isn't." According to him, the slow decrease in membership experienced by the group after 1946 was only the first sign of a long-term decline. The only way to avoid such a fate, he argued, was for the Legion to reinvent itself by adopting instead "some great and enthusiastic cause like the fighting of Communism," which would "inculcate a sense of fervor in our membership." He added, "We need some of the zeal and some of the enthusiasm" associated with this crusade, "and we can transfer it . . . to this great army of veterans who haven't joined our ranks yet."[103] Put simply, Alessandroni wanted the Legion to abandon the defense of martial citizenship and embrace the fight against communism as its core mission instead.

His argument proved unconvincing. Baarslag continued to be "subjected to subtle, but increasing pressure on the contents of what I was writing in the *Firing Line*." He was often told that his work might alienate potential members and he began to hear complaints from his colleagues "about the danger of costly litigation" and "the allegation that 'red-baiting' was now passé." This "growing but intangible sentiment on the part of at least a small fraction of the Legion's brass," compounded by his repeated failures to mobilize the Legion's rank and file, led him to reach "a point of almost total discouragement." Unhappy with his Legion salary, he was convinced that he could make more by working on Capitol Hill. The situation came to a head in March 1953, when Baarslag was denied the authorization to reprint in *Firing Line* the names on a *Daily Worker* petition demanding amnesty for communist leaders jailed under the Smith Act. After a

Legion lawyer asked him if every name had been cleared individually, Baarslag protested that the request was "preposterous." He refused to accept a stricter censorship of his newsletter and was fired.[104]

Baarslag's departure was a clear sign that advocates of a "positive" Americanism focused on educational programs had the upper hand over those who pushed for a more "negative" approach. The events that followed only confirmed this trend. After Baarslag was hired as McCarthy's research director, the Legion's Un-American Activities Committee fell into a stasis.[105] It was returned to its original subcommittee status a few months later.[106] Following the appointment of Lee R. Pennington to the head of the National Americanism Commission, the job of writing the *Firing Line* was reportedly outsourced to an FBI official.[107] For the rest of the decade, the subcommittee did little more than publishing this newsletter, answering mail, and writing reports that went largely unread. In 1955, the national commander made it clear that his group's "interest in Americanism is not essentially national. It is local, stemming from a post's pride and solicitude in its own community. . . . Nationally, we have neither the personnel nor the authority to function as an investigative agency. That is the role of the FBI."[108] The writing on the wall was clear: Baarslag and Alessandroni's hopes that the crusade against communism could become the Legion's first priority had been squashed.

Important as the events that unfolded within the national leadership may be, they provide only part of the answer to the question of why the group never embraced a more forceful version of anticommunism. For if the debate over public housing had showed anything, it was that rank-and-file Legionnaires could force their leaders to change views if they mobilized in large enough numbers over a long period of time. The same phenomenon could have happened here. What we need to understand, then, is not just why Legion leaders did not support Alessandroni's committee but also why ordinary members showed a similar disinterest.

A number of secondary sources confirm this point. Studies of the Second Red Scare in four midwestern states all found to varying degrees that "the interest of the [Legion] national office in the anticommunist crusade was not reciprocated at state and local levels" and that "genuinely grass-roots responses" were "few" and "sporadic."[109] Reports produced in the early 1950s by the American Civil Liberties Union and the National Education Association, an organization representing half a million school teachers, reached the same conclusions. As regular targets of Legion attacks, these two groups would have had an incentive to exaggerate their enemy's anticommunist activity in order to tar its reputation, but they did exactly the opposite. In a National Education Association survey of over a hundred elementary- and secondary-school teachers across the country, only one respondent mentioned that a Legion post was "actively trying to limit academic freedom."[110] Likewise, American Civil Liberties Union leaders asked state affiliates to report on the Legion's interference with civil liberties in their area, hoping to use the responses in a scathing report. They received only three replies, of which just one mentioned that the Legion was active.[111] These materials confirm what internal documents have already told us, namely that the Legion never managed to create the kind of nationwide enthusiasm for counter-subversive activities that some of its leaders had called for.

Two factors help explain such apathy at the grassroots. First, the fact that communist activity tended to be concentrated in large cities meant that it was only a distant concern to the majority of Legion posts located in small towns. In the late 1930s, as much as 40 percent of the membership of the CPUSA was in New York City.[112] A Legion historian noted by contrast that "American Legion membership always throve in the smaller cities and the towns and rural sections of the US more abundantly than in the large centers of population."[113] The result was a gap that was well known to Legion officials. Responding to J. B. Matthews's request that he circulate copies of an anticommunist newsletter within the group, Baarslag wrote that "many of these posts of course would be poor prospects, particularly those in the agricultural and far west States," and he suggested focusing instead on those in the "densely populated and other commy-infested cities."[114] Despite all the talk about the immediate danger of communist subversion, most rank-and-file Legionnaires in large swaths of the country simply did not feel directly concerned by this issue.

The second factor that helps explain the lack of grassroots response was the generational transition that took place within the veterans' movement after 1941. As a group, veterans of World War II tended to be less supportive of anticommunism than their elders from the Great War. Baarslag noted "a subtle and indefinable air or odor of anti-anticommunism by mainly the younger World War II Legionnaires rapidly coming to the fore and out-numbering and steadily displacing the older World War I veterans."[115] Two contemporary surveys confirm his observation. In *Communism, Conformity, and Civil Liberties* (1955), social scientist Samuel A. Stouffer interviewed fifteen hundred local community leaders in small to midsized municipalities across the country, including the commander of each city's largest Legion post. He found that "World War II veterans are significantly more likely to be tolerant [of radicals and nonconformists] than World War I veterans" by a ratio of 43 percent to 24 percent, a difference he attributed to the fact that the former group was "much better educated."[116] An internal poll conducted by the Legion also found that nearly 85 percent of members from World War I rated the group's activity on the "communist question" as either "excellent" or "good," compared to only slightly more than 70 percent of their World War II counterparts.[117] It should come as no surprise that many of the men and women who had experienced a war in which Soviet Russia was their ally and who had grown up under the more progressive climate of the New Deal would attach less importance to the threat of communism than their elders (especially since some of the latter had fought the Bolsheviks as part of the Allied military expedition to Russia in 1918–20). Whether this gap was the result of differences in educational levels or in life experiences is impossible to determine, but it was nonetheless significant.

Division within the leadership and disinterest among the rank and file were the two main reasons why the Legion failed to adopt the kind of "negative" methods that some of its leaders had hoped. To be sure, Legionnaires were far from passive in this field. At the same time as they rejected Baarslag and Alessandroni's emphasis on countersubversive tactics, they played a key role in helping spread anticommunism at the local level through a range of educational programs. Besides, those who had dreamed that the fight against "Reds" would replace the defense of martial citizenship as the core mission of the Legion proved prescient in at least one respect. This ideology did generate "zeal" and "enthusiasm" among a small group of Legionnaires, as we will see now.

From the Mainstream to the Margins

A vocal minority of far-right activists made their voices heard during the Second Red Scare. Taking advantage of the decentralized structure of the Legion and of the anticommunist fever that gripped the country, they pushed the group to adopt a conspiracy theory about the UN and its affiliate the United Nations Educational, Scientific and Cultural Organization (UNESCO). In the process, they dealt a major blow to the prestige of the Legion.

The roots of this episode date back to the end of World War II, when UNESCO was created with the mission to promote mutual understanding between peoples. In the early postwar years, its activities ranged from carrying out research about education programs to surveying international library facilities. The project that set it on a collision course with U.S. conservatives was an effort to revise school textbooks in order to purge them of "traces of nationalist bias." The campaign was immediately controversial, with right-wing newspapers like the *Chicago Daily Tribune* calling it "antipatriotic and tantamount to propaganda."[118] In October 1951, freelance writer and activist Florence Fowler Lyons accused the Los Angeles school superintendent of using UNESCO teaching manuals to impose the ideology of "world government" on children. Lyons and her conservative women's groups saw these textbooks as a threat to national sovereignty, pointing to their alleged advocacy of "world-mindedness" and racial mixing. Her campaign received extensive media coverage and McCarthy himself flew to Los Angeles to meet her. Overwhelmed, the Los Angeles Board of Education withdrew all UNESCO material from its schools.[119]

The Legion was initially at odds with Lyons. At the end of World War II, the group endorsed the idea of a muscular UN that would maintain world peace with its own military force.[120] But things changed after the outbreak of the Cold War. As fears grew that Moscow and its allies would use the international organization to disseminate their ideas, the Legion turned against the UN. In 1952, the *Legion Magazine* published an article by J. B. Matthews that reproduced some of Lyons's accusations.[121] The charges became official policy the next year when the National Executive Committee passed a resolution deploring "the use of material furnished by the UNESCO" in public schools and calling upon all educational institutions to "cease and desist from" using such documents.[122] The Legion was not the only major veterans' group to take such a position: in 1952, the VFW passed a resolution endorsing the UN but condemning UNESCO textbooks as "a subversive effort to destroy the faith and loyalty of the youth of America in the sovereign right of the American people to remain free and independent."[123]

The Legion entrusted one of its committees, chaired by Ray Murphy, with the task of investigating the issue.[124] A Democrat and an insurance lawyer, the Iowan had been one of the most important voices of moderation within the Legion during the interwar period, when as national commander he had pushed back against Chaillaux's more militant brand of anticommunism. Having attended the Dumbarton Oaks and San Francisco conferences as the Legion's consultant, Murphy was an expert in international affairs.[125] He was no liberal, however. Not only did he join the American Bar Association's Committee on the Study of Communist Tactics—a group formed mainly to attack the left-wing National Lawyers Guild—but he was on record opposing "world government" and supporting the Bricker amendment, a piece of legislation then under discussion in Congress that aimed to restrict the scope of foreign treaties.[126] His appointment illustrates that the debate within the Legion over UNESCO was not between centrists and conservatives, but rather between conservatives and the far right. Both camps agreed on the need to fight communism aggressively; they differed only on how to do so.

By the time Murphy began his investigation, the growing opposition to UNESCO on the right had become a matter of serious concern for the federal government. Officials feared that this controversy would undermine public support for an organization that they hoped to use as a vehicle for the worldwide dissemination of information favorable to their side of the Cold War.[127] Knowing how much influence the Legion wielded in national politics, they did all they could to keep it on their side. The State Department gave Murphy's committee full access to all its files on the topic in an effort "to have the Legion reverse past stands and uphold UNESCO."[128]

After extensive research and interviews with public officials, the committee submitted its first report in May 1954. It found charges that UNESCO was subversive, was atheistic, or advocated for "world government" to have "no basis in fact."[129] The report provided a comprehensive rebuttal of the attacks levied by Matthews and Lyons against the international organization. Nevertheless, the document was not officially endorsed by the Legion. Instead, the group adopted more resolutions censuring UNESCO.[130] This confusing situation was similar to the one in which the group had found itself early in the housing debate, when the appointment of officials who supported public housing like Alessandroni and O'Neil had contradicted the official stance of the Legion. Here as well, Murphy's position was at odds with that of the group he was supposed to represent. This discrepancy reflected the confusion that reigned once again within the organization's bureaucracy.

The turmoil did not prevent hard-line anticommunists from lashing out at Murphy. After being alerted by Lyons, the head of the Florida department, Joe Jenkins, complained about "this whitewashing report."[131] Far-right groups such as the antisemitic American Flag Committee publicized the document in an attempt to alert Legionnaires.[132] The situation came to a head at the next meeting of the National Executive Committee in May 1955. In two diametrically opposed reports, the Murphy Committee repeated its earlier finding that the charges against UNESCO were "utterly without foundations" and the National Americanism Commission asserted that UNESCO "has consistently endeavored to bring about a climate of international mindedness in the US and a subsequent decay in patriotism, national pride and national sovereignty."[133] These two contradictory documents show that the group was profoundly divided, with neither faction having the upper hand. As the *Christian Century* asked, "Which Legion Is the Real Legion?"[134]

No one seemed to know the answer. Legion leaders cautiously avoided taking sides, preferring to wait until the national convention later that year in Miami to see which camp would have the most delegates. Shortly before the gathering, Murphy's pro-UNESCO report was leaked to the press, probably in an attempt to build public support in the moderates' favor.[135] The enthusiastic reaction demonstrated how the Legion remained an important player in national politics. As the *Atlantic* later reported, "words of respect and hope came not only from the Legion's friends but from some of its severest critics of the past."[136] The *Washington Post and Times Herald* welcomed the report as "a factual, documented, eyes-open study by a group of Americans whose patriotic credentials give them full credence."[137] Even *Life*, usually not a close follower of veterans' affairs, saluted the findings of the "ultrarespectable" Murphy committee as "encouraging signs that the Legion is mending its ways."[138] President Eisenhower himself praised the report as "analytic, factual, honest and fair." In a phone call to secretary of state John F. Dulles, he called it "the most sensible analytical job he has heard of" on UNESCO. The two men debated whether to endorse the report officially, but they eventually decided against taking sides in a battle whose outcome was far from certain.[139]

At the same time as the mainstream press and the administration were celebrating the Murphy report, far-right elements within and outside the Legion continued their propaganda campaign against it. The intensity of this fight left the authors of the report "deeply disturbed."[140] The right-wing paper *Free Men Speak*, for instance, asked readers to let Legion officials know of their opposition to the report.[141] Merwin K. Hart and his antisemitic National Economic Council denounced the report as "completely unconvincing" and called on the Legion to reject it.[142] Conservative midwestern Republicans even attacked the group on the floor of the House.[143]

Internal pressure was equally high. In Los Angeles, the California department formed a special committee to denounce the report as "slanted."[144] A local Legion official wrote to his superiors that "never has there been evidenced more intense indignation over any previous action of our national leaders" and he warned that the adoption of the Murphy report would be "disastrous."[145] In the *Florida Legionnaire*, Jenkins cautioned readers against the "peril" lying in UNESCO.[146] The "anti-subversive chairman" of the Washington State department not only compared the Murphy report to Karl Marx's *Communist Manifesto*, he also charged UNESCO with attempting "to create an Intellectual Dictatorship to control the minds of men throughout the world, by means of devious methods."[147] The cover of a report by a Texas Legion committee illustrated the stark, binary terms in which far-right activists saw the situation (Fig. 9).

The pro-UNESCO camp did not respond to this propaganda campaign. While the National Americanism Commission distributed anti-UNESCO

Figure 9. This cover of a 1955 anti-UNESCO report shows how far-right activists within the Legion understood the stakes of the debate. While the Murphy committee allegedly advocated "World Government" as embodied by the "Genocide Convention" and the "Covenant on Human Rights," the American Legion defended "National Sovereignty" encapsulated by the "Bill of Rights" and the "U.S. Constitution." Box 541, folder 5, J. B. Matthews Papers, David Rubenstein Library, Duke University.

material to Legionnaires throughout the country, the Murphy report was never widely circulated.[148] As a result, far-right voices enjoyed influence on a scale disproportionate to their actual numbers.

The bitterness of this debate can be measured by looking at the private correspondence of some of the Legionnaires involved in this controversy. Jenkins for instance treated Murphy as a misguided child who "sure need[s] educating about UNESCO" and whose committee was but a puppet of the State Department.[149] Murphy responded that his critics relied mostly on "emotion and garbled information" and that their arguments "range from the scurrilous to the ridiculous, and have been hastily put together under a false front of alleged documentation that is in essence odorously fraudulent."[150] William G. McKinley, a member of the Murphy committee, echoed such feelings in a strongly worded letter. "In the colloquialism of our Post riot rooms," he wrote, Jenkins's charges "could be reduced to a vulgarism pertaining to a certain equine excretion having value in agriculture, but in the vernacular connoting the sum total of nothing." In his view, the "power and prestige" of the Legion had been "exploited" by "fanatics."[151]

Such harsh rhetoric shows the extent of the divide between the conservative and the far-right factions within the Legion. We should nonetheless keep in mind that this debate never spurred the participation of large numbers of Legionnaires. As an outsider observed, the controversy around UNESCO "is an issue within the old guard" of the Legion. Moderate Legion leaders like Murphy "are no less anticommunist than anybody else," he wrote, "but to them it seems that the Legion's future is being endangered by the increasing commitment to extreme 'nationalism,' isolationism, possibly even to racism and Catholic bigotry" (Murphy was Catholic). "While the Legion rank-and-file understand little about the situation and care much less," he concluded, "the ruling 'machine' is badly worried."[152]

With both sides at each other's throat, the thirty-seventh national convention of the Legion opened in Miami on October 10, 1955. National Commander Seaborn Collins launched the festivities with a plea for moderation. In his opening speech, he claimed that the Legion's name was "too often ... tied to causes which may be perfectly good in themselves, but which do not merit our sanction as a veterans' organization" and which resulted in "a loss of prestige and impact for our major programs." "To speak out or act without carefully considering the facts," he warned, "is to invite public distrust and indifference."[153] Though everyone could read between the lines, the fact that Collins did not explicitly mention UNESCO showed once again how the national leadership was careful not to take sides.

His call for caution fell flat. When the joint committee tasked with drafting a final resolution on UNESCO met, the hard-liners had the upper hand. According to Murphy, the far-right faction had lobbied to make sure that the committee was "heavily weighted with known opponents of UNESCO" and to limit the distribution of his report to delegates. The exchanges that took place during the seven-hour long committee debate illustrated how the case against the international organization was driven by racism and isolationism. For instance, one committee member argued against UNESCO on the grounds that it was connected to research proving that "white and black blood types were the same" and another argued the UN should simply be "tossed into the sea." Moderates were outnumbered and easily defeated. The final resolution reaffirmed the Legion's opposition to UNESCO, urged Congress to immediately investigate the group, and called for the U.S. National Commission for UNESCO to be disbanded. When the resolution came to the floor of the convention, it was put to a vote without debate and adopted with only the delegation from Murphy's home state of Iowa going on record against it.[154]

The vote provoked a torrent of criticism in the press. Murphy commented that it brought a "tremendous volume of critical editorials and articles," which "did the Legion a great deal of harm."[155] *Newsday* argued for instance that the Legion had "acted completely irresponsibly" on UNESCO.[156] *Life* declared the Legion "disgraced," and quoted Collins's opening statement to say that "if men who fought two wars to defend democracy cannot win it for themselves, they will deserve nothing but 'public distrust and indifference.'"[157] For the *New York Times*, the Legion's stance on UNESCO was "a prize example of sophomoric xenophobia."[158] The *Nation* found it "reckless."[159] But the blowback went further than just the national press. A Legion review found no less than 240 editorials written across the country in reaction to the vote in Miami, with more than half negative.[160]

This episode marked a turning point. The victory of the hard-liners on UNESCO cost the group much of the prestige and popularity it had gained from its decision to welcome World War II veterans several years earlier. Legionnaires continued to oppose the international organization in the following years, but few observers took them seriously anymore.[161] A congressional subcommittee dismissed their charges after extended hearings, finding that they had "no credible evidence" and were often entirely invented.[162] Perhaps the most telling measure of how far the Legion's reputation had fallen was the change in how the American Civil Liberties Union reacted to the regular demands made by every Legion convention after 1952 that it be investigated. These attacks had been a

major problem when the veterans' group was still a force to be reckoned with in
the early 1950s. By the second half of the decade, however, an assistant director of
the organization admitted that the national office "pretty much ignores [Legion
charges] now," since they received "less and less press notice" and were therefore
no longer a threat.[163] "More and more people," he added, "are getting to realize
that the Legion's activity are [sic] pretty much a farce."[164]

The Miami fiasco did not mark the end of the Legion's involvement in the
crusade against "Reds." As the group drifted further and further to the right
over the next few years, its anticommunism found a new outlet in the fight
against racial integration. This was best illustrated by the growing importance of
the rhetoric of states' rights, which the Legion adopted to denounce the liberal
Supreme Court of Chief Justice Earl Warren after it issued a string of decisions
in 1956–57 that undid much of the legal apparatus behind the Red Scare.[165] The
group used identical language to attack the civil rights movement. At the same
time as the Legion demanded an investigation of the National Association for
the Advancement of Colored People, it for example deplored "the continued
usurption [sic] of States Rights by the federal government, specifically in those
matters so clearly spelled out by our founding fathers and in the Bill of Rights
and the Constitution," which "will eventually result in a socialistic or dictatorial
form of government."[166] The Legion was far from the only organization whose
anticommunism translated into an opposition to racial integration: throughout the South, segregationists routinely denounced civil rights activists as communist "agitators."[167]

Beyond their rhetoric of states' rights, Legion leaders made a series of racist
statements—including one in which Collins commented that he did not "regard
Negroes as his equal"—which made clear that their position was motivated by
more than just a strict interpretation of the Constitution.[168] A number of southern white Legionnaires resisted the cause of civil rights, too. The commander
of the Georgia Legion endorsed an amendment to the Virginia state Constitution that sought to enforce school segregation despite the *Brown* decision.[169] In
Jackson, Mississippi, the charter of the all-black William Walker Post 214 was
canceled after it denounced two other posts for cosponsoring a meeting with a
White Citizens' Council, the middle-class counterpart to the Ku Klux Klan. The
Walker post had ties to the civil rights movement (its service officer was NAACP
field secretary Medgar Evers) and it had tried to register black citizens to vote.[170]
Finally, many Legionnaires criticized President Eisenhower's decision to use the
National Guard to force the integration of Central High School in Little Rock,
Arkansas, in the fall of 1957. The Arkansas Legion gave the Americanism Award

to Governor Orval Faubus for opposing the move.[171] That a defender of segregation could be honored for his "Americanism" captured the extent to which anticommunism had become an instrument to defend white supremacy.

This is not what the men who had started the Legion down this path had intended. In the early postwar years, Legion officials like Owsley, Baarslag, Alessandroni, and Craig had embraced the countersubversive legacy of Chaillaux in an attempt to cement their group's newly acquired prestige. By claiming the leadership of the anticommunist movement, they hoped both to secure lasting influence and to infuse their group with a renewed sense of mission. Things went astray almost immediately. Not only did a majority of their colleagues in the leadership refuse to turn the group away from its long-standing focus on veterans' benefits, but most of the rank and file simply never cared enough about countersubversive methods to devote a significant amount of their time and resources to them. While the Legion played a central role in the anticommunist crusade of the late 1940s and early 1950s, the more radical or "negative" approach advocated by the likes of Baarslag largely failed to find an audience. Instead of enhancing the group's profile, they empowered a vocal minority of far-right activists who took advantage of the indecision of the national leadership to push a conspiracy theory about UNESCO. By refusing to abandon the hard-line version of an ideology that by the mid-1950s had lost its grip on the country as a whole, the Legion squandered much of its credibility. In the long run, anticommunism proved to be not an asset but a liability for the veterans' movement.

Another area where the Second Red Scare had unanticipated effects was in the relationship with the U.S. state. Legion leaders had initially hoped, with good reason, that their position at the forefront of the anticommunist crusade would help them cement their long-standing partnership with government officials. This is what happened in the early years of the Cold War, as the group actively participated in various state-sponsored efforts to fight communism both at home and abroad. Yet the relationship was always transactional; it thrived only as long as both state actors and Legionnaires stood to gain something from it. When the Legion began to attack not only "Red" leaders but also their alleged sympathizers in the Truman administration, the collaboration broke down. It was brought back to life after Eisenhower entered office with the Back to God program, but by then the Legion's reputation was increasingly tarred by the controversy over UNESCO, which put it at odds with the government. Having lost its bipartisan and respectable status, the group was no longer such an attractive partner for the state. As we will see in the next chapters, its relationship with the

Eisenhower administration only grew more distant and adversarial throughout the rest of the 1950s.

In all these ways, the Second Red Scare represented a turning point for the Legion. After its influence reached a peak in the aftermath of World War II, the anticommunist crusade marked the beginning of an eclipse. It was far from absolute: the Legion lost its central position in national politics but it remained a major actor in the field of veterans' affairs as well as a prominent presence in local community life. Something crucial did change in these years, though. Longtime critics of the group were not the only ones to think, as the *Nation* did, that the Legion was "dying as an important social force."[172] One of its own officials noted in the late 1950s that "we [Legionnaires] are slipping our anchor which has held us in the forefront of the American scene for the last forty years."[173] Anticommunism contributed greatly to this slippage.

CHAPTER 6

Consolidation and Backlash

The Korean War in the Shadow of World War II

On the morning of January 13, 1951, a federal grand jury in New York City indicted nearly two hundred World War II veterans on charges of defrauding the VA of almost a quarter million dollars. According to the chief assistant U.S. attorney for the district, this was "the largest [indictment] of its kind ever handed up in U.S. District Court and one of the largest in any Federal court in the country." The accusation was simple. In an effort to take advantage of the educational benefits provided under Title II of the GI Bill, Ora Grow and his wife, Dassie, had enrolled a large number of former service members in the "Grow System School of Beauty Culture" located near Times Square without holding any actual classes. Another assistant U.S. attorney asserted that 90 percent of the indicted veterans "never knew where the school was." This so-called silent student scheme allowed both sides to reap a handsome profit. Individual veterans received from the government a subsistence allowance averaging $1,000 a year while the school received $300 in tuition and $30 in supplies for each "student," in addition to kickbacks. Oversight was so weak that it took more than two years before the FBI uncovered the fraud. The Grows were ultimately found guilty and sentenced to several years of imprisonment with thousands of dollars in fines. Of the 198 veterans, 165 pleaded guilty.[1]

The Grow School scam involved an unusually large number of participants, but similar examples of GI Bill fraud were not rare in those years. In the second half of the 1940s, accusations of corruption and mismanagement tainted nearly all of the various provisions of the law.[2] Neither was it the first time that such problems beset veterans' politics. Those who remembered the scandals that had ensnared the Civil War pension system in the late nineteenth century or the Veterans' Bureau in the early 1920s must have felt a sense of déjà vu. The aftermath of World War II witnessed only the latest manifestation of an enduring pattern in the history of veterans' welfare state, whereby the multiplication of postwar scandals provided critics with a political opening. The Grow School case and many others like it helped convince the public that the benefits granted veterans of the Second World War were excessively generous and that they needed to be reined in.

As this debate was raging at home, North Korean troops attacked the U.S.-backed Republic of Korea in late June 1950, igniting the first large-scale military confrontation of the Cold War. President Truman responded a few days later by sending troops. With GIs fighting on distant shores yet again, the question of what benefits they would receive upon returning home arose once more. Lawmakers had to decide whether the new readjustment benefits created in the previous war with the 1944 GI Bill constituted a valuable precedent that should be extended, or a failed experiment that should not be repeated. Over the next two years, Congress, the White House, and the veterans' movement debated the issue vigorously. They eventually reached a compromise, whereby Korean War veterans received their own GI Bill but with lower payments, less freedom of choice, and stiffer penalties than the original law. In this sense, the war on the east Asian peninsula witnessed both the consolidation of martial citizenship and a backlash against it.

The diminished standing of the veterans' movement contributed to this outcome. Its major organizations were never united on the issue. While the American Legion supported a straightforward extension of the 1944 GI Bill, the VFW backed a more limited approach and the DAV focused its attention on the disabled. As a result, Legionnaires could not present themselves as the authoritative voice of all veterans. Their strident criticism of the management of the conflict by the Truman administration further undermined their partnership with the state. We saw in the previous chapter how the Second Red Scare led the Big Three to embrace hard-line anticommunist positions. In the process, they joined a chorus of right-wing critics who pushed the president to escalate the war against North Korea and its ally, "Red" China. This decision cost these groups their mainstream and nonpartisan status as well as the access and influence that came with it. The lack of a close and mutually beneficial relationship with state actors made the task of the veterans' movement considerably more difficult.

Broader trends in postwar America exacerbated these developments, such as the improved economic situation of the country. By the early 1950s, fears of an economic depression had receded and lawmakers expected the economy to be able to absorb the smaller number of Korean War veterans (they were 5.7 million, or three times less than the previous cohort) without as much assistance from the state. The lack of public support for the conflict in east Asia also played a role. Policymakers refused to even acknowledge the new engagement as a "war": Truman called it a mere "police action" and Congress never officially declared hostilities. The public largely lost interest once the conflict turned into a drawn-out stalemate, and the kind of popular groundswell on which the veterans' movement had capitalized to enact the GI Bill in 1944 never materialized. Finally, the rise of an influential new figure within the House Veterans' Affairs Committee, the most important clearinghouse for all veterans' legislation in Congress, helps explain the less generous provisions of the 1952 GI Bill. As the career of the committee's long-time chairman, John E. Rankin, drew to a close (he lost his bid for reelection in 1952), power gradually shifted to Olin "Tiger" Teague, a younger southern Democrat and a decorated veteran of World War II from Texas. Though he had initially been a firm ally of the veterans' movement after his election in 1946, Teague grew more independent as he accumulated seniority and expertise. During the Korean War, he became an eloquent and steadfast critic of the excesses of martial citizenship. With the economy booming, the public largely apathetic, and Congress no longer so subservient, the veterans' movement was on the defensive.

One last reason behind this outcome was the changing nature of warfare at the dawn of the Cold War. Whereas World War II had produced a clear victory after only a few years of mobilization, U.S. policymakers saw the armed struggle in Korea as merely the opening act of their larger confrontation with the Soviet Union, which they expected to last for the foreseeable future. This new kind of ideological war of attrition led to the long-term mobilization of public and private resources on an unprecedented scale, in a process that scholars have called the rise of the "national-security state." Everyone expected the country to remain on a warlike footing long after Korea, with a peacetime draft and military spending at an all-time high. Some critics feared that this massive and permanent expansion of federal power would create a "garrison state" that stifled liberties at home in the urge to defend them abroad; others were more concerned about making this new commitment financially sustainable in the long run and called for cuts in nonmilitary spending.[3] Veterans' benefits were among the programs that they targeted.

This suggests a larger lesson about the national-security state. Historians have often argued that benefits for former service members were one of the many types of defense-related programs that thrived under this new state-building regime.[4] Yet the impact of the Cold War on veterans' welfare state was far from uniformly positive. The return of the peacetime draft in 1948 meant that the veteran population would increase steadily year after year rather than diminishing naturally over time. This led many observers to question the financial wisdom of extending generous benefits to a growing share of the population, especially when disabilities had not been incurred during service. As Democratic presidential candidate Adlai Stevenson asked in 1952, "we are rapidly becoming a nation of veterans. If we were all to claim a special reward for our service, beyond that to which specific disability or sacrifice has created a just claim, who would be left to pay?"[5] The ideology of breadwinner liberalism reared its head once again, with policymakers like Teague raising concerns about veterans' benefits amounting to a "dole" that would turn men into wards of the state rather than self-reliant heads of households. This context led to renewed efforts to rein in the veterans' programs inherited from the previous war, even though their most central features were perpetuated. Hence the ambivalent nature of the 1952 GI Bill. The law constituted both a victory for the veterans' movement, in the sense that it ensured that the readjustment benefits created during World War II would become the norm for future generations, and a defeat in that its provisions were markedly less generous than what some of its advocates had called for. The rise of the national-security state was a mixed blessing for martial citizenship.

This development helped push the veterans' movement away from its position at the center of American politics. The many scandals related to the GI Bill in the second half of the 1940s proved that not all former service members deserved to be placed on a pedestal, and by extension that it was not necessarily a good idea to place so much power into the hands of a single agency, the VA. At the same time, the process that began in the previous chapter continued. Driven by their commitment to anticommunism, the Big Three adopted an increasingly partisan posture that cost them their prestige and mainstream status. In all these ways, the Korean War had long-lasting effects on both the veterans' movement and veterans' welfare state.

Expansion, Scandals, and Reform

By the time the Grow School scam was exposed in 1951, news of GI Bill fraud had become so widespread as to be almost banal. One congressman remarked that "it has become a national pastime to milk Uncle Sam" under the 1944 law.[6] All of its provisions witnessed abuses, beginning with the one providing weekly unemployment allowances of twenty dollars for a maximum of fifty-two weeks.

On paper, eligible veterans were required to be looking for work and were forbidden from refusing a job offer deemed "suitable" to their qualifications.[7] In practice, state unemployment boards were overwhelmed by the massive numbers of returning veterans and found it nearly impossible to maintain rigorous standards. Criticism mounted quickly. In 1947, the right-wing *Chicago Tribune* called on Congress to abolish this "dole," which "encourages young men in habits of dependency when they ought to be acquiring habits of industry, self-support, and self-respect."[8] Though fraud seems to have been limited, the program soon became known derisively as the "52–20 club" or "rocking-chair money."[9]

Concerns about abuses in another section of the law, which provided veterans with government-guaranteed loans to buy a home, business, or farm, were more warranted. As we saw in an earlier chapter, the postwar housing shortage proved a godsend for swindlers of all stripes, who were able to exploit veterans' desperate desire to find shelter for themselves and their families. The problem proved difficult to solve. As late as 1952, the VA issued a warning to veterans that "many [mortgage] offers that sound like heaven-sent opportunities are actually the work of shysters and gyp artists."[10]

The section of the law providing educational and on-the-job training benefits sparked by far the most controversy, however. Employers often abused it by recruiting veterans who were already proficient in their trade and deducting the GI Bill living allowance from their wage, thereby turning the program into a de facto labor subsidy.[11] Educational institutions were also quick to recognize an opportunity for easy profit. Barely a year after the passage of the bill, the *New York Times* deplored the "immediate and pressing" problem "that fake colleges and fly-by-night vocational schools are springing up on a nation-wide scale to mulct war veterans."[12] The number of for-profit institutions grew by 300 percent between 1944 and 1949.[13] Such "schools" routinely charged veterans inflated rates for tuition and supplies, falsified cost data and attendance records, billed the government for unenrolled students, attempted to bribe VA officials, and offered courses in such "frivolous" fields as cocktail mixing.[14] The extent of the abuse was such that one journalist called this part of the GI Bill "the greatest boondoggle of all time."[15]

It was widely understood that the root cause of these problems lay in the design of the law itself.[16] Even if the GI Bill was entirely paid for by the federal government, its administration was in the hands of state agencies and local institutions. This mixed local-state-federal structure had been designed to overcome the opposition of southern Democrats and conservative Republicans to any straightforward expansion of federal authority. The result was a patchwork of oversight. Some states were able to handle the sudden return of millions of former service members but others lacked the funds, experience, or political initiative. For instance, the Pennsylvania Department of Public Instruction had only two or three poorly qualified inspectors, whom schools routinely bribed with trips to Atlantic City in return for a speedy approval.[17] The fact that federal control had been reduced to a minimum to satisfy congressional conservatives was one major reason behind the explosion of GI Bill fraud.

As this problem became clear, pressure mounted for Congress to act. After the VA shut down a private school in the federal capital, eight hundred of its veteran students marched on the House Office Building in January 1948. Ohio Republican Homer A. Ramey responded by forming a subcommittee to investigate.[18] He reached the same conclusions as many journalists, namely that fraud stemmed principally from "the extremely limited power of the VA to maintain forcibly anything like a decent standard among the thousands of schools offering training to veterans."[19] In response, Congress passed a series of amendments that enhanced federal oversight and limited benefits, for instance by giving state approval agencies additional funds or by barring veterans from enrolling in courses deemed "avocational and recreational," such as dancing or photography. These measures sought to eliminate fly-by-night schools interested only in robbing gullible veterans of their GI Bill benefits.[20]

The Servicemen Readjustment Act of 1944 was not the only source of controversy in postwar veterans' politics. The old specter of service pensions, the source of so much division in the post–Civil War and interwar periods, reared its head once again. In 1949, the Legion and the VFW came together to urge that pension rates be revised upward.[21] Endorsing their proposals, Rankin went further and introduced a general pension bill to give veterans of both world wars aged sixty-five and older monthly payments of $90 regardless of need or disability, and $120 to all those so disabled as to require an attendant.[22] With 19 million potential recipients, the bill's estimated impact was colossal. According to VA administrator Carl Gray, Jr., it would cost a minimum of $1.8 billion in its first year—a quarter of the VA's budget—and upward of $100 billion over the next fifty.[23] Not surprisingly, the proposal ran into fierce opposition in the House and from the Truman administration.[24] Most members of Congress feared coming out against a measure supported by the two largest veterans' groups, however.[25] When the bill finally came to a roll call vote on the floor of the House in late March 1949, opponents managed to send it back to committee by a margin of only one vote. Rankin later drafted a watered-down compromise, which passed the House but died in the Senate.[26]

The idea of a bonus for World War II veterans was also making headway.[27] Soon after the end of the war, an unlikely coalition of groups including the VFW, the AMVETS, the CPUSA, and trade unions like the United Auto Workers began pressing for an "adjusted compensation" bill similar to the one granted veterans of the Great War in 1924. In their view, such a measure was needed out of fairness to the millions of older World War II veterans who had had no use for the GI Bill because they already had a job and a home before enlisting.[28] With sixteen states having already passed a bonus by early 1949, most observers assumed that it was only a matter of time before the federal government would follow suit.[29] Service pensions threatened to cripple the federal budget, but the perspective of a bonus was equally, if not more sinister: the total cost of one proposal was estimated at $67.5 billion, more than all federal spending for 1949.[30] Rankin threw his support behind this measure, which the *New York Times* called "the most fantastic of all post-war veterans bills."[31] For the next several months, rumors that his committee was about to approve a bonus bill were enough to make headlines, even though the bill was never reported to the floor.[32]

Public views on veterans' benefits were ambivalent during this period. A slight majority of respondents to a 1947 Gallup poll (53 percent) agreed that "veterans' benefits are adequate at present," indicating that they saw no need for new programs.[33] The picture was equally mixed for specific benefits. Only 48 percent of respondents to another survey that same year supported the idea of a federal bonus, while 52 percent approved without qualifications of a bill providing $90 pensions to all veterans of World War I and II when they reached 65.[34] These results suggest that the general public remained broadly supportive of benefits for former service members, but that it was not willing to write them a blank check either.

The national press was more critical. Major newspapers continued to make the same argument advanced by critics of martial citizenship for decades, namely that military veterans should not be treated as a special group on the sole basis of their service. Most columnists rejected the idea of establishing "war veterans as a specially favored class in the American community."[35] The *New York Times* argued that demanding a bonus or a pension amounted to saying "that service in the armed forces in wartime is not a simple duty of citizenship but an action that merits a special handout from the state." "It is the duty of the citizen to defend his country," it went on, and "he should expect no special reward for carrying out his duty. . . . Nothing is too good for the veteran who suffered disability in line of duty; but veterans are not and should not form a privileged class apart from other citizens."[36] *Collier's* agreed, stating plainly that it "does not believe that our millions of veterans should be set apart as a separate class and treated like mercenaries."[37] The *Christian Science Monitor* likewise condemned the "grab philosophy" of "professional veterans."[38]

The postwar context gave new urgency to these old arguments. In the late 1940s, the federal government spent more on veterans' benefits than on any other welfare program, from social insurance to public aid to education and housing.[39] More importantly, the return of the peacetime draft in 1948 meant that the population of former service members would continue to grow in the future. Even before the outbreak of war in Korea, a study from the Brookings Institution noted that "if we maintain a standing army of 1.5 million men and continue the draft, there will be an annual increment of about 400,000 new veterans," which would produce "an increase in veterans' families to an estimated 62.5 million persons by 1957."[40] Truman himself recognized that "before many years, nearly all the population may be veterans or the dependents of veterans. This means a profound change in the social and economic import of Government programs which affect veterans."[41] Since his primary goal was to expand civilian welfare programs, he and other liberals opposed granting special benefits to a group that would soon constitute nearly half of the total population.[42]

In a Cold War environment where pressures to cut nonmilitary spending were growing ever more urgent, veterans' programs were increasingly vulnerable. In the span of just a few years, the enthusiastic desire of a grateful nation to reward those who fought on its behalf during World War II had turned into intense criticism of their benefits, which occupied a central position in the postwar welfare state. It was against this background that war broke out in east Asia.

Behind the Troops, Against the Administration

On June 25, 1950, the North Korean military crossed the thirty-eighth parallel into South Korea. Within days, the civil war between the Soviet-backed North and the U.S.-backed South escalated into global warfare. Backed by the UN Security Council, the United States led a coalition of twenty-one countries to defend the South.

Despite the anticommunist fever grasping the nation, the new conflict soon became unpopular. This was in part the result of decisions made at the top: since the United States was acting under the umbrella of the UN, Congress never passed a formal declaration of war. In a press conference four days after the outbreak of hostilities, President Truman insisted that "we are not at war" and that U.S. involvement should be seen as merely "a police action under the United

Nations" to rescue a country "unlawfully attacked by a bunch of bandits."[43] The consequences of this official denial were far-reaching. Many Americans reasoned that if both the executive and the legislative branches claimed that the country was not at war, then why should *they* pay attention? Especially after the conflict turned into a stalemate in mid-1951, press coverage grew limited, prompting one Navy sailor on leave to complain upon reading his hometown newspaper that "Korea just didn't seem to exist."[44] A year after the war had begun, only 44 percent of respondents to a Gallup poll thought the country had done the right thing by intervening; a few months later, 56 percent agreed that the conflict was "utterly useless."[45] Complaints of widespread "public apathy" became a familiar refrain.[46]

With the population seemingly uninterested, the veterans' movement assumed once more the mission of assisting the U.S. government. The VFW issued a pledge of support for Truman's decision to enter the war.[47] A few days after conflict started in Korea, Legion commander George Craig called for a special meeting of all forty-nine continental departments "to discuss plans for immediate mobilization." The session ended with the adoption of various policy goals that the group would pursue in wartime, including universal military service, a strong civil defense, and "protection from sabotage by termite subversives." Craig pledged in a televised speech on CBS that Legionnaires "stand ready to perform what tasks the Government may assign to us."[48] The group soon resumed its secret Contact program with the FBI.

The federalist structure of veterans' organizations helped them perform the role of middleman between the state and the general public. Local posts, state departments, and the national organization all took initiatives to support the war effort, sometimes in coordination with each other but more often on their own. Two Legion national commanders visited Korea in person to express support for the troops.[49] Hundreds of posts either cooperated with blood donor banks such as the Red Cross or established their own.[50] In Minot, North Dakota, a post took part in the relief of Korean civilians by collecting some twenty-five thousand pounds of clothes and $1,000 in cash, which were shipped free of charge by railroad companies and Navy ships.[51] Other veterans' groups carried out similar activities. For instance, DAV posts in Seattle sold decorative Christmas stickers to support hospital and rehabilitation work.[52]

Veterans' organizations also endeavored to raise troop morale. In November 1950, the Legion reinstated its "morale-building team" for war amputees, which was composed of amputees "who have succeeded in rehabilitating themselves."[53] The team visited several military and VA hospitals during the war and also met with the president and the surgeons general of the Army, Navy, and Air Force.[54]

The DAV likewise sponsored a benefit show at the Madison Square Garden in New York City for all paraplegics.[55] The Legion later launched a program to support "public ceremonies for the presentation of Certificates of Honor and Appreciation" to returning veterans.[56] In Chicago, these certificates (called "Scrolls of Honor") were written in solemn gothic script and signed by the mayor, the Illinois Legion commander, and an Army colonel.[57] By the end of the war, at least twenty departments and "hundreds of communities" had adopted the program.[58]

The most successful project of this kind was "Hometown, U.S.A.," a tape exchange program that connected active-duty personnel with their families. The idea was simple: anyone with a relative serving overseas could go to their local Legion post and record a short message on tape as well as make a request to play a certain musical tune (Fig. 10). Provided at a discount rate by a private company, the tapes were then turned over to the Department of Defense and shipped overseas. Upon receipt, soldiers could either listen to their greeting privately or forward it to an Armed Forces radio station for broadcast, and then use the tape to record their own voice message and send their tune request back to their folks at home.[59] The formula proved astoundingly popular. By mid-1953, the program received an average of two hundred requests per day, with over two thousand radio stations signing on across the country.[60]

By helping the state, veterans' groups were helping themselves. As in World War II, the Legion never lost track of the fact that active-duty service members were potential recruits. One internal memorandum on "Hometown, U.S.A." noted that the program "spotlights the American Legion in the community very effectively. By so doing, it cannot help but stimulate membership. . . . Each of these men participating in 'Hometown USA' is . . . being subtly made to think very seriously about joining our organization upon discharge."[61] The wartime partnership with the state was an all-around public relations boon. As the Legion found, encouraging local communities to provide certificates of honor "furnished the [group] with many columns of favorable press publicity."[62] Both patriotism and self-interest were behind the partnership of the government and the veterans' movement.

Nonetheless, the relationship of the Big Three with the Truman administration quickly deteriorated. The VFW, DAV, and the Legion had initially supported the decision to fight North Korea, but they grew critical after the intervention of Chinese troops in October 1950. Their leaders sent the president a scathing joint letter in early December, arguing that his decision not to escalate the conflict by attacking China directly was potentially treasonous. "No one

Figure 10. A Legionnaire helps a mother and her baby record a message
to be sent overseas as part of the Legion's "Hometown USA" program
in Flint, Michigan, ca. 1953. *Hometown USA, Project Scrapbook*,
1953, oversize volume 3, American Legion, Dept. of Michigan
Records, Bentley Historical Library, University of Michigan.

knows how many GIs have died because of imposed limitations which have pre-
vented them from fighting on equal terms with the Communist aggressors," they
wrote. Accusing Truman of "appeasement," the letter urged him to authorize the
bombing of "vital military targets" across the Manchurian border and to give the
supreme commander of UN forces, General Douglas MacArthur, "full authority
to employ such means as may be necessary to save our troops from disaster."[63]
The following year, the Legion called for the U.S. government to help Chiang
Kai-Shek's Nationalist forces invade the Chinese mainland from Taiwan.[64] In
short, the Big Three wanted to turn a limited conflict into a regional conflagra-
tion aimed at the destruction of Asian communism.

The growing alienation between these organizations and the Democratic
administration came to a head in April 1951, when Truman dismissed MacArthur
out of concern for his increasing insubordination. The decision shocked many
Americans, for whom the five-star general remained a war hero. Veterans' leaders
sided with him. Upon returning from a visit to Korea, Cocke declared that
MacArthur was forced to fight "with both hands tied behind his back" and that

he should be allowed to bomb enemy positions in Manchuria.[65] Truman reacted to this explicit attack on the administration by abruptly canceling a meeting with the Legion commander.[66] When MacArthur's relief was made official the day after, Cocke commented that it was a "dark . . . hour."[67] Many Legionnaires seem to have felt the same way, given the hundreds of phone calls, letters, and telegrams received by the group's national office in the days after MacArthur's relief, almost all of which were sharply critical of the president.[68] The VFW was of the same mind: in late April, it cosponsored a massive "Loyalty Day parade" in New York City to show its support for MacArthur, who was in attendance.[69]

By coming to the general's defense, the Big Three were taking sides in the highly partisan debate over U.S. foreign policy. Ever since the "loss" of China in 1949, the politics of the Cold War and of national security had grown increasingly polarized, with right-wing Republicans and southern Democrats often charging Truman with being "soft" on communism.[70] Led by Ohio senator Robert Taft, the so-called conservative coalition took advantage of its growing influence in Congress to levy a constant barrage of attacks on the administration.[71] Though the Legion was careful never to endorse any politician explicitly, there was very little daylight in practice between the positions of its leadership and those of Taft. After Cocke observed in May 1951 that "this is the first time in American history that we have gone into a war afraid that we might make our enemy mad," the Democratic mayor of St. Louis boycotted a luncheon at which the national commander was scheduled to speak.[72] A Roper survey conducted in the spring of 1952 found that 26 percent of respondents identified the leaders of the Legion and the VFW as Republican-leaning, and only 11 percent as Democratic.[73]

Cocke seemed little concerned by this development. Embracing the red-baiting language of the Red Scare, he condemned "our present-day Benedict Arnolds" in the administration, who "by their confused thinking and acting . . . serve as the communists' best friends."[74] In a private letter, he argued that the government's "definition of victory in the Far East" was virtually "synonymous" to "that of the Communists."[75] His successors at the helm of the Legion followed in his footsteps. In 1952, the group adopted a resolution calling for Truman to abandon "political control" and to give the military complete authority in the conduct of the war.[76] In a speech to the AFL, National Commander Lewis Gough argued that the UN should authorize the use of atomic weapons if necessary—a position he repeated several times over the next months.[77] With such statements, the Legion and the veterans' movement more broadly were moving further and further to the right, losing not only their bipartisan image but also the kind of top-level access to government officials that they had enjoyed during

World War II. This shift had crucial consequences on their ability to influence the debate over which benefits the new cohort of veterans should receive.

The Debate over Korean War Veterans' Benefits

At the dawn of the conflict on the east Asian peninsula, GIs were in a peculiar situation. Due to the absence of an official declaration of war by Congress, those who served after June 27, 1950, the date of U.S. entry into the war, were initially treated as peacetime, not wartime, veterans. This status gave them access to less generous benefits. The fact that much of veterans' legislation was war-specific (it covered only former service members who had served during a given time period) also meant that this new conflict was not yet covered. As of August 1950, most Korean War veterans did not have access to vocational rehabilitation, GI Bill benefits, mustering-out pay, and homestead preference. Neither could they extend their National Service Life Insurance after separation. Access to VA hospitals was restricted to those who had suffered service-connected disabilities.[78] Lawmakers therefore had to decide whether the benefits already available to previous cohorts would be extended to the new one.

This process began on the same day that the United States joined the war, when Rankin introduced legislation to extend GI Bill benefits.[79] In mid-July, he sent a letter to all veterans' groups asking for their input.[80] At an emergency meeting, Craig announced that the Legion would suspend its push for new pension or bonus legislation and give priority to the war effort. "It is a case today of powder or pensions," he proclaimed, "bullets or bonuses!" His group would focus instead on making more benefits available to veterans of the current conflict.[81]

Momentum built rapidly in favor of the blanket extension of all benefits available to World War II veterans. In early July, a bill was introduced in the Senate to do just that.[82] The DAV and the VFW supported this effort.[83] When Cocke met with Truman later in the year, he reported that the president agreed that "GI benefits for the veterans of Korea would be most in order."[84] By early September, over a dozen bills were already under discussion in Congress to extend GI Bill benefits to Korean War veterans.[85] Following the strategy that had worked so well six years earlier, the Legion tried to consolidate all these different initiatives into a single omnibus bill, which Rankin introduced on its behalf. Not only did the measure recognize Korean War veterans as wartime veterans, but it also gave them access to VA hospital care, vocational rehabilitation, and GI Bill readjustment benefits.[86]

Had the 1944 GI Bill not been the source of so much controversy, lawmakers would probably have voted then and there to extend it to veterans of the ongoing conflict. Yet the continuing flow of negative press coverage led many to question the wisdom of such a move. Just a few months before the outbreak of the war, Truman had raised concerns that the number of veteran students enrolled in trade and vocational schools under the 1944 law was not declining as expected but was instead growing fast.[87] At his behest, the Bureau of the Budget and the VA conducted a joint investigation that confirmed his fears. As Truman put it, the agencies found that "the recent rapid increase . . . has included training of less than acceptable quality." He added, "Such failure is costly to the veteran, to his family, and to the Nation."[88] The report found that it was more profitable for a veteran in some low-wage areas to enroll in classes under the bill, regardless of their quality, than to be employed. The allowance had become "an end in itself" rather than a way for veterans to acquire new skills in preparation for a career.[89]

Washington was thus already in the midst of a heated debate about the most important piece of veterans' legislation passed during the previous world war when hostilities broke out in Korea. In August 1950, the House voted unanimously to create a select committee to further investigate the GI Bill.[90] Its chairman was Texas Democrat Olin E. Teague, a junior member of Rankin's Veterans' Affairs Committee.

Raised in a relatively poor family in rural Oklahoma and Arkansas, Teague had earned his nickname of "Tiger" for the resolve and tenacity he showed on his high school football team. After working his way through the Agricultural and Mechanical College of Texas (now Texas A&M), he joined the National Guard and reported for active duty as an officer in the fall of 1940, at the age of thirty. Severely injured while fighting in Europe, he received multiple medals. After his return home, he was elected to the House from the Sixth District of Texas in 1946.[91] His political profile was not altogether different from Rankin's: as southern Democrats, they both opposed most of Truman's liberal Fair Deal platform and were reliable allies of the veterans' movement.

The key difference was that Rankin supported lavish measures such as service pensions and the bonus, whereas his younger colleague believed that there should be limits to the state's generosity. Teague was concerned not only about the taxes required to maintain generous welfare programs for millions of veterans but also about the sense of entitlement that he felt these policies would foster among their recipients. "I think one of the sins of the GI Bill of Rights," he wrote to a fellow Texan, "is that it taught our young men to expect something for nothing. You just don't get something for nothing. You pay for it one way or the other."[92] As a decorated veteran with a service-connected injury, he could voice such criticism without suffering the political consequences. The fact that he hailed from a safe district in the one-party South also meant that he could accumulate seniority without having to fear challengers. The Legion attempted to tag him as "antiveteran" after his opposition to Rankin's 1949 pension bill, but he was reelected anyway.[93] The creation of his select committee in the summer of 1950 forestalled the passage of an immediate extension of the GI Bill, as Congress decided to wait for its final report.

Two other major developments took place before the close of the year. First, the Legion voted to open its ranks to Korean War veterans. Contrary to the animated debate that had taken place during World War II, this time the process barely raised any eyebrows. Since the idea of opening the group to more than a single generation of former service members had already been approved eight years earlier, Legionnaires seem to have readily accepted that Korean War veterans would come in too, as suggested by the fact that officials began working to extend benefits to this new generation immediately after the war broke out. The national organization quickly received a "good many Post resolutions" urging their acceptance.[94] When the thirty-second national convention convened in mid-October, delegates voted to accept the new cohort without debate.[95] Congress approved the change to the group's charter and the president signed it into law in late December.[96] In effect, the Legion was now a "three-war experiment."

On the very same day, Truman also signed a bill granting vocational rehabilitation benefits to all disabled veterans of the current conflict.[97] The fact that the law had passed Congress without a single dissenting voice was not a surprise, for the urge to streamline veterans' benefits focused first and foremost on programs for able-bodied veterans like the GI Bill or the Bonus. The notion that the state owed something to those who had been injured while fighting on its behalf was never really in question. Truman himself recognized the nation's "long-run obligation" in this field.[98]

At the dawn of the new year, then, the outlook for the veterans' movement was mixed. On the one hand, the strength of its major organizations would soon be buoyed by the arrival of millions of new members. On the other hand, the political climate seemed increasingly hostile to demands for generous benefits. The ongoing fight over the proposals of the First Hoover Commission only reinforced this trend. The Legion's Operation Survival had provoked a serious public backlash in 1950, which prompted top officials to keep a low profile in their push for a new GI Bill. In early September, the group introduced its omnibus bill without a press release, out of fear that journalists would "blast" the Legion for demanding more benefits instead of prioritizing the war effort.[99] The first results of Teague's investigation, which came out in December, compounded this problem. He found so much evidence of corruption and waste that Congress extended his committee's mission beyond GI Bill educational benefits to include loan guaranties as well.[100]

The Legion reintroduced its omnibus bill in the new session of Congress in January 1951.[101] When Cocke presented his group's agenda before the House Veterans' Affairs Committee, he insisted that the nation's obligation to Korean War veterans was "every bit as compelling and just" as that toward veterans of previous conflicts and that they should receive comparable pension, compensation, hospitalization, and GI Bill benefits.[102] All the other major veterans' groups—the VFW, the DAV, and the AMVETS—likewise endorsed the extension of most veterans' benefits to Korean War veterans on an equal basis.[103] After several months of negotiations, the president signed into law the Servicemen's Indemnity and Insurance Act in late April, which provided every active-duty soldier who served after June 27, 1950, with an automatic $10,000 life insurance policy.[104]

Congress soon moved one step further. In early May 1951, the story of David R. Arellano, Jr., a twenty-one-year-old ex-Marine who had served in Korea, made the headlines nationwide. Arellano tried to get treatment for a throat cancer contracted after discharge at a VA hospital in Tucson, Arizona, only to find out that as a "peacetime" veteran he was ineligible to receive hospital care for a non-service-connected disability. "We at the veterans' hospital are completely sympathetic with the plight of these men," declared the frustrated hospital manager. "Under the present status we are not at war in Korea so these men are not eligible for treatment. If it isn't a war, I'd like to know what the hell it is."[105] Arellano was not the first former service member to find himself in this situation, but his case captured unprecedented attention thanks to the advocacy of veterans' groups.[106] The morning after his story broke, Erle Cocke sent telegrams to all members of Congress urging action on the Legion bills introduced in January.[107] Truman himself wrote to congressional leaders soon afterward and they reacted with uncharacteristic speed. In less than two hours, both chambers passed a joint resolution providing equal compensation, pension, hospitalization, and medical and domiciliary care, as well as burial benefits, for veterans of the Korean War. The president signed it into law just two days after Arellano's story had surfaced.[108] The benefits for Korean War and World War II veterans were now almost equal; only the extension of the GI Bill remained to be decided.

In arguing for equal benefits, veterans' groups were echoing the sentiments of many GIs in Korea who felt that there was no substantial difference between their war and the last one. After reading in the *Stars and Stripes* that the GI Bill had not been extended yet, three sergeants stationed in Korea sent a letter to Ohio senator Robert Taft. "They may call this a police action," they wrote, "but men are losing there lives [*sic*] the same as in the last war. We are fighting here for freedom of the peoples, the same as in World War II. Why are we any different from the 'GI' of the last war?"[109] The father of two sons serving in Korea wrote likewise that "surely the men undergoing suffering, privation and danger in our present war are just as much entitled to consideration as those of World War II."[110] These arguments clearly had an impact: by mid-1951, around fifty bills to extend some form of GI Bill benefits to the new generation were under consideration.[111]

And yet progress remained excruciatingly slow, for the administration was convinced that the law should be revised instead of simply extended. In a testimony before the Senate, an official from the Bureau of the Budget, the White House's clearinghouse for policy, offered several reasons for this more cautious approach. He argued that the nation was entering "a long period of partial mobilization" that would lead to the steady growth of the veteran population and consequently of the cost of their benefits. He also pointed to the expansion of New Deal welfare programs as another reason why Congress should not be as generous toward veterans as it had been at the end of World War II. Moreover, he noted that prior distinctions "between wartime and peacetime service" were no longer applicable in the context of the Cold War, in which the United States would likely have to fight similar undeclared wars in the future. This made it "impossible to continue to make either a logical or an equitable distinction between a veteran who is drafted . . . for fighting service in Korea . . . and a veteran who may be drafted . . . after the conclusion of the Korean campaign." The Bureau of the Budget was concerned that an extension of GI Bill benefits to veterans of the current conflict would almost inevitably mean their extension "to all members of the Armed Forces during the entire future period of the use of the draft," which would be financially ruinous.[112] As the same official later noted, the new law under consideration was "not a one-shot effort to meet conditions expected to result from very rapid demobilization at the end of an all-out war," as the 1944 GI Bill had been. "Rather, it is likely to be a semipermanent part of our Federal system of benefit programs." Congress should therefore take the time to devise a more sustainable solution.[113] Teague concurred. When asked whether he planned to present his report to Congress before the end of the year, he replied that he refused "to rush it," for he intended to draft a law that would "cover all servicemen in the future," not just the current generation.[114]

As 1951 drew to a close, it became clear that Teague would use his investigation as a platform to advocate for an overhaul of the original bill. He had previously supported a blanket extension of all GI Bill benefits, but the evidence of widespread corruption and waste unearthed by his committee changed his mind.[115] Throughout the spring and summer of 1951, he carried out additional hearings across the country. Altogether, the more than eleven hundred pages of testimonies that he collected presented a damning indictment of the failures of the 1944 GI Bill. As Teague commented, "We do find ... wherever we have gone ... that every group involved ... has done everything possible to get every dollar possible out of the Federal Government."[116] In November 1951, he announced that he would fight for "drastic changes" in the law. "It was a wonderful dream," he said of the educational and training provisions of the original GI Bill, "but it just hasn't worked."[117]

When the Teague report was finally made public in mid-February 1952, it found fault with nearly all aspects of the GI Bill's educational benefits.[118] The root of the problem, in its view, lay in the lack of efficient supervision. Not only were many state approval agencies underfunded, but VA procedures were "cumbersome, lengthy, and in many instances, ineffective," while its regulations were often "arbitrary, ill-advised, ambiguous, and tending to have retroactive effect." "There [was] no doubt," the report admitted, "that hundreds of millions of dollars have been frittered away on worthless training." For-profit vocational and trade schools also came in for criticism, as they often charged excessively high rates, falsified attendance records, and offered expensive but mediocre "night schools" or extension courses. Finally, the report condemned the "minority of veteran trainees who have intentionally and willfully exploited the program and misused their entitlement," noting that "there have been literally thousands of cases where the veterans' acts and intent were highly questionable."[119] In sum, everyone from the administrators of the law to its recipients received their share of the blame.

Building upon these findings, the select committee made a few major recommendations. Most importantly, it called for "an entirely new act, rather than amendment to existing law." This new measure would follow a different approach to educational benefits. Under the 1944 GI Bill, the government had to write three separate checks to two recipients: the school received one for tuition and one for supplies, and the veteran student received one for living allowances. Teague's report recommended lumping all three checks into one and sending it straight to the veteran. Dubbed "direct payment," this new method was meant to shift the burden of supervision from the administrator of the aid—the VA—to its recipient. Making individual veterans responsible for spending their government checks as they saw fit would give them an incentive to seek reputable institutions. "Undoubtedly those students who have a stake in their own education," the report argued, "will most zealously guard against unwise use of the allowance."[120] Akin to a "scholarship grant between the veteran and the federal government," this method had the additional benefit of diminishing the VA's workload by eliminating the need for its staff to interact with schools directly.[121] In the same spirit of eliminating abuses, the report recommended that payments be made less generous, so that veterans would have to make "a small contribution on [their] own part to insure [their] interest in the program primarily for education, rather than money."[122] Lastly, the report called for new safeguards to combat fraud, such as protections against conflicts of interest in the VA.[123] All these proposals aimed to rein in the excesses of the original law.

Teague's report received wide press coverage. The details of various scams and frauds that it contained provided plenty of material for journalists in search of sensational headlines. One newspaper editor wrote that "these hearings were better reading than *Gone with the Wind*."[124] But the press also approved of Teague's recommendations. For the *Los Angeles Times*, the waste of hundreds of millions of dollars illustrated "the rule that nobody is very careful with somebody else's money."[125] The economy-minded *Saturday Evening Post* commented that the passage of the 1944 GI Bill had been "the signal for a mass ganging up on the public till by dishonest institutions, with the connivance, unfortunately, of some veterans who didn't seem to mind looting the Treasury of the country which they risked their lives to defend."[126] The *Herald Tribune* approved especially of the direct-payment method, which "will eliminate a great deal of bureaucratic machinery, will go a long way toward preventing the money-gouging and boondoggling evils that developed under the old law, and will tend to make each veteran who receives the benefits more personally diligent in insisting that he gets his money's worth of government education."[127] Most major press outlets seemed to favor Teague's approach.

The veterans' movement was more divided. The VFW and the AMVETS backed the Texan. In their view, the extension of the GI Bill to a new cohort of former service members was already a victory, even if its provisions were less lavish. By providing readjustment benefits to another generation of veterans, the new law would consolidate this recent addition to veterans' welfare state. Both organizations demanded only minor changes, such as higher payments for educational benefits. As for the DAV, it had already achieved its major objective when rehabilitation and training programs had been extended to Korean veterans. The organization was not closely involved in the negotiation of the new GI

Bill: since its benefits overwhelmingly went to able-bodied veterans, they were not of direct interest to its constituents.[128]

The Legion was the only veterans' group to oppose Teague's recommendations. The organization criticized the idea of granting Korean veterans less generous benefits than their elders, fearing that this would exacerbate class divisions by "favoring the privileged and eliminating the underprivileged [veteran] with equal or greater ability."[129] More fundamentally, the Legion viewed Teague's report as a blow to the ideal of martial citizenship that it held so dear. By providing evidence that veterans were partly to blame for the fraud that had plagued the 1944 bill, the Democrat was undermining the idea that former service members were a select and morally superior group. In addition, his report directly attacked the legitimacy of the institution that best embodied this ideal: the VA. Not only did the investigation prove beyond doubt that the agency had made its share of errors in the administration of the GI Bill, it also recommended a number of curbs on its authority, such as making its decisions open to judicial review. This was anathema to the Legion, which considered any move to share the VA's authority with another entity as an attack on the principle that veterans should be treated separately. These two reasons—the direct criticism of veterans and the push to curb the VA's power—help explain why the organization opposed Teague.

It soon became clear that the political momentum was not in the Legion's favor, however. Legionnaires tried to argue that the veterans who had participated in abuses should not be held responsible, but this position was untenable after so many scandals had come to light.[130] Teague's report noted that "the contention that all veteran trainees are without fault in all instances . . . is a hallucination and a failure to face facts."[131] Likewise, the Legion defended the VA by arguing that the root of the problem lay in its having to share oversight of educational benefits with state approval agencies. As one Legion official argued, the solution lay not in curtailing VA power but rather in expanding it by "vesting final authority in the Administrator of Veterans' Affairs."[132] The problem was that this view ran against the inclinations of the conservative coalition that dominated Congress in the early 1950s and whose members opposed giving the federal government more power over education, traditionally the preserve of individual states. Especially after President Truman announced his support for civil rights, Rankin came to view "the Federal Government . . . [as] waging a cold war" against white southerners, and he proclaimed that he was "strongly in favor of retaining the State's rights so far as the government of our schools are [sic] concerned without Federal interference."[133] Since martial citizenship was closely connected to federal authority, such an expansion was politically unpalatable at this time.

When the debate over a new GI Bill for Korean veterans finally started in earnest, Legionnaires stood almost alone in their support for the blanket extension of existing readjustment benefits. Theirs was one of three major bills under consideration in Congress, along with the one endorsed by the Truman administration and the one drafted by Teague.[134] The latter two had much in common. Both proposed an entirely new law that provided only education and training benefits, with less generous payments. A memorandum circulated by the Bureau of the Budget noted that the consensus within the administration was in favor of smaller benefits, for "the veteran should have a financial stake of his own in the training." The memo also explained why neither the loan guaranties nor the readjustment allowances provided by the 1944 GI Bill were included in this new version. "The circumstances surrounding the discharge of future veterans," it noted, "will be very different from those under which World War II veterans were discharged": "the number released at any one time will be much less," and "housing needs are less acute" than they were seven years earlier. Improved economic prospects not only made readjustment allowances "unnecessary," but the latter risked diverting veterans from the workforce.[135] The major difference between Teague's and the administration's bills was the introduction of direct payment. Government officials were open to adopting the Texan's method, however.[136]

Support for the Legion's bill came only from a few private universities and colleges such as Stanford, New York University, and Boston University. Afraid that smaller government checks for veteran students would cause them to flock to more affordable institutions, the heads of these elite schools joined an organization led by F. D. Fagg, Jr., the president of the University of Southern California, to back the Legion.[137] Their position was not consensual. Most higher education advocacy groups, including the National Education Association, the American Council on Education, and the Association of Land Grant Colleges, came out in support of Teague.[138] With their support, the Texan refused to back down. Arguing that direct payment was "the heart" of his bill, Teague asserted that Fagg was merely trying "to provide extra Federal aid to a favored group of private schools" and that his own goal was to help students, not educators.[139] With both the Legion and Fagg's group on the defensive, Teague's bill passed the House easily in early June 1952, by a roll call vote of 361 to 1.[140]

It is worth pausing here for a moment to consider why the Legion never really tried to stop Teague. Despite evidence that many veterans seemed to disapprove of direct payment, the group did not undertake the kind of large-scale lobbying campaign that it had launched years earlier to ensure passage of the original GI Bill.[141] This was in part because much of its energy was already invested in the effort to defeat the recommendations of the First Hoover Commission. But this reluctance also spoke to Legion leaders' realization that their position at the bargaining table was weak. Having come into open conflict with the Truman administration over the conduct of the war, they could expect no favors from government officials. Teague's bill was by no means perfect, but Legion officials felt that they could not come out openly against a measure that still accomplished many of their goals. As an internal bulletin admitted, "even though [the Teague Bill] is not as liberal as the [1944 GI Bill], it would be of immense value to the new veterans who will seek higher education. There are features in the bill, as well as omissions to which we object but we believe, in fairness to the 800,000 Korean emergency service personnel already discharged, that a bill should be enacted in this Congress. Otherwise another year will go by without such beneficial legislation."[142] Given the hostile political climate and the fact that time was running against them, Legion leaders decided not to block Teague's bill in the House.

The other chamber proved more receptive to their arguments. When the Senate Committee on Labor and Public Welfare began holding hearings, Teague's support for direct payment and lower benefits came in for sustained criticism. The liberal Democratic senator from Rhode Island John Pastore pushed the Texan hard on whether "there is going to be an inclination to shop for a cheaper school." Pastore said, "We do not want to end up with State-supported and municipal-supported institutions being identified as the veterans schools as against private institutions." He was not the only one to have such concerns, as illustrated by the growing size of Fagg's group, which now claimed support from 429 private institutions, including Brown, Georgetown, Columbia, and the University of Chicago.[143] After deliberations, the Senate committee approved the restoration of tuition payment to schools.[144] Seeing that the upper chamber was less hostile to its views than the House, the Legion wrote to every senator to request the return of readjustment allowances as well.[145] Its prayers were answered when Michigan Republican Homer Ferguson introduced an amendment to that effect (though allowances were neither as generous nor as long as the original version).[146]

Teague's approach to educational benefits prevailed in the end. After the Senate passed its version of the bill, a conference committee met to reach a compromise. The final draft restored direct payment and passed both Houses of Congress almost unanimously. Truman signed it into law in mid-July 1952.[147]

The Veterans Readjustment Assistance Act, as it was known officially, struck a balance between the generous vision of martial citizenship that animated the 1944 GI Bill and Teague's thriftier approach. While the eligibility, loan guaranty, and job counseling provisions remained essentially identical, the changes made to the other clauses of the law betrayed a clear effort to limit the state's responsibility. The notion that the government should help veterans readjust to civilian life was still its cornerstone, but it came with significant safeguards and less generous assistance. Instead of readjustment allowances of $20 per week for a maximum of fifty-two weeks, the Korean War GI Bill provided its recipients with $26 for up to twenty-six weeks.[148] Most importantly, educational and training benefits were overhauled, with the maximum period of entitlement reduced from forty-eight to thirty-six months. Under Teague's direct-payment method, Korean War veterans were entitled to receive only between $100 and $160 a month (depending on their marital situation), as opposed to $500 or more for tuition per year and between $75 and $120 in living allowance per month for their World War II counterparts. Their freedom to choose classes was also limited: they were barred not only from taking stand-alone courses that the VA considered "avocational or recreational"—such as bartending—but also from changing their course of study more than once and from enrolling in schools that had been in operation for less than two years or with more than 85 percent of veteran students (the assumption being that such institutions were more likely to be fraudulent). Finally, maximum penalties for misuse were raised from a $50 fine and a six-month imprisonment to a $5,000 fine and three years in jail.[149] In all these ways, the new law marked a departure from 1944.

One area where the Korean War GI Bill only reinforced the legacy of its predecessor was in its attitude toward veterans who were either women or members of racial minorities. Both the 1944 and the 1952 laws did not allow female veterans to claim dependent benefits for their male spouses, even as male veterans could do so for their wives. The 1952 law also retained the same reliance on local institutions, which were free to discriminate against applicants. It even went further: by restricting enrollment to schools with no more than 85 percent of veterans, Teague's measure threatened to inflict additional harm on African American veterans, especially those living in the South. Due to the relative poverty of the black community in this region and the more limited range of educational institutions available to them under Jim Crow, black veterans were more likely than their white counterparts to be the overwhelming majority in any school where they enrolled. The two black members of the House, Adam C. Powell and William L. Dawson (both Democrats, respectively from New York and Illinois), voted only "present" when their chamber passed the bill in order to highlight the discriminatory potential of this provision.[150] Yet Teague was as committed as any southern Democrat to defending white supremacy, and he ignored their complaints. When the issue was raised in the Senate hearings, he asserted that "not too many" black schools only had veteran students, even as he admitted that his select committee had never done any research on the specific situation of the South. Senator Lister Hill of Alabama told the Texan that "your committee may have been thinking too much of States like Pennsylvania, which are much more advanced in the matter of vocational schools than a State like my State and your State." Teague nonetheless insisted that he could not "see that there is any way [this restriction] has any greater effect on a colored private school than it has on any other private school."[151] With the major veterans' organizations remaining silent, this issue never really gained traction.

The lack of research on this topic makes it difficult to determine whether Powell and Dawson's fears actually materialized. Only slightly more than two-fifths of Korean War veterans took advantage of their GI Bill training and education benefits (compared to about half of their World War II counterparts), but Teague's more restrictive approach was not the only potential reason behind this lower percentage. Not only was the economic climate of the early 1950s prosperous enough to allow many veterans to find jobs relatively easily upon their return, but nearly one million of those who fought in Korea had also served in World War II, entitling them to use the original GI Bill instead.[152] The introduction of direct payment did have some of the consequences that its critics had predicted, for two-thirds of Korean veterans ended up attending public universities.[153] There is little evidence that this had negative repercussions on their career paths in the long run, however. A 1970 study found that black, white, and Mexican American veterans of the Korean War not only earned substantially more than their nonveteran counterparts but also slightly more than their peers from World War II.[154]

Still, there is no denying that the provisions of the 1952 GI Bill marked a step back from the more liberal vision of martial citizenship embodied by its predecessor. It showed that the influence of the veterans' movement, and in particular of its leader, the American Legion, had limits. By moving further and further to the right during the war, major veterans' groups lost the kind of privileged access to state actors that they had enjoyed for years, with all the opportunities for behind-the-scenes lobbying that it entailed. The Legion also found that mobilizing its troops on behalf of a new law was considerably more difficult than merely defending existing programs, as it had done with success against the First Hoover Commission.

Wartime dynamics only explain so much. More broadly, this setback also represented a reaction against the perceived excesses of the legislation enacted during the Second World War. In the eyes of many critics, the 1944 GI Bill had given veterans so many benefits with so little oversight that it created the perfect conditions for widespread misuse and corruption. Advocates of a more parsimonious approach, both in Congress and in the press, seized upon the scandals surrounding this law to oppose its blanket extension and to push instead for a more economical bill that gave recipients less leeway. Taking advantage of the change in political climate and of the weakened state of the veterans' movement, Teague replaced Rankin as the new leader in Congress on these issues—one who had veterans' interests in mind but who was not afraid to push back against their demands if he deemed them excessive.

The rise of the Texan to power suggests another reason why martial citizenship was on the defensive in the early 1950s. Most contemporary observers assumed that the political influence of veterans would grow in tandem with their share of the general population. The opposite was in fact true. Compared to 1944, veterans in 1952 accounted for a much higher share not only of the total population but of Congress itself—58 percent of its members, as opposed to 39 percent—and yet the Korean GI Bill passed that year provided less lavish benefits than its World War II predecessor.[155] The reason behind this counterintuitive development was simple. The Legion found it far easier to push for more generous veterans' benefits when the ranks of Congress were dominated by people who had not served and were receptive to the idea that they owed a moral debt to those who did. Such sentimental or patriotic appeals lost much of their strength when veterans themselves occupied positions of power. Not only were they more likely to be critical of a system that they were intimately familiar with, but they were also harder to pressure. It was much more difficult to argue that a disabled and decorated veteran like Teague did not have the interests of his fellow ex-GIs at heart than it had been for someone like Herbert Hoover who had never served in the military, for instance. As the United States became a "nation of veterans," then, martial citizenship became an increasingly difficult sell.

The changing situation of veterans' benefits was also the result of the larger geopolitical outlook. Policymakers reasoned that Korea would not be the last limited and undeclared conflict of the Cold War, and they sought to make the long-term financial burden of future veterans' benefits as sustainable as possible. In a context where nearly everyone expected U.S. defense spending to remain high for the foreseeable future, lawmakers had an additional incentive to find economies. Contrary to what we often think, the rise of the "national-security state" had a mixed impact on veterans' welfare state. As Adlai Stevenson put it in his speech before the Legion in 1952, if the country were to become "a nation of veterans," then their benefits would have to be scaled back.

Just as the Korean War was drawing to an end, Legion leaders were yet again warning of a "dismal outlook for the fiscal affairs of the VA."[156] Committed to reducing taxes and spending, the new Eisenhower administration announced in the spring of 1953 that it planned to cut hundreds of millions of dollars from the VA budget in the next fiscal year, a move that Legion national commander Lewis Gough described as a "blow below the belt" for Korean veterans.[157] Speaking before the national convention, Gough commented on the revival of "anti-veteran sentiment": "Those who choose to decry the system of veterans' benefits have been quite vociferous and extensively publicized during the past year," he argued. "The road ahead may be rough."[158] The veterans' movement would have to remain vigilant throughout the 1950s.

CHAPTER 7

Generations Apart

The Problem of Economic Security
for Aging Veterans

The letters kept pouring in. At the turn of the 1950s, the American Legion was receiving anxious missives from Great War veterans "almost every day now."[1] All expressed the same problem. Among the nearly 3.3 million members of this cohort still alive, many felt excluded from the decade's so-called affluent society.[2] Unable to find work due to old age or disability, they often had to survive on their meager veterans' pension, a situation that one message compared to "starvation."[3] Those over sixty-five and single could only claim a monthly maximum of seventy-five dollars, which placed them below the poverty line.[4] Adding to their misery was the feeling that their country no longer cared. "Have the ill, aged and disabled veterans of WWI," one wife asked, "been betrayed by their own comrades, in the Legion, Congress, the Press, and other positions of influence?"[5] They also resented the treatment of younger cohorts. "Everything is done for the War Veterans of World War II," one letter noted, "but the Veterans of World War I are forgotten and have to fight for everything we get and the other veterans get everything on a silver platter."[6] In all these messages, the same leitmotiv came back time and again: "The veterans of World War I are forgotten men."[7] This image dated back to the not-so-distant Great Depression, when it had served as a popular catchall to describe those in dire economic straits and more specifically poor former doughboys.[8] It resurfaced in the 1950s to highlight their continuing plight.

Such complaints should have found a sympathetic ear in the Legion. After all, the group had been created in 1919 precisely to defend the interests of Great War veterans. It was a measure of the profound changes having taken place in the intervening years that the opposite happened, however. After the Korean War,

World War I veterans pushed for the restoration of the service pension that they had obtained in 1930 and that FDR had rescinded with the Economy Act three years later. But the Legion and the VFW rejected the idea that this cohort should receive payments based only on age and they pushed for more limited changes instead. Feeling marginalized, many doughboys dropped out and formed their own, new World War I–only organization, known as the Veterans of World War I of the USA, or "Wonnies." Throughout the 1950s and well into the 1960s, this association was almost single-mindedly devoted to lobbying for a Great War service pension.

The Wonnies were newcomers, but their arrival was only the latest manifestation of a well-established trend in the long history of the veterans' movement, whose strength had always been intimately connected to the fight for benefits. In the 1880s and 1890s, GAR ranks swelled just as the group was pushing for service pensions; in the 1930s, the campaign for a Bonus led many veterans to leave the conservative Legion for the more populist VFW. The same dynamic was at play in the postwar period. As the more timid approach of these two groups caused them to lose some of their most dedicated members, the process of decline already outlined in previous chapters only intensified.

This episode speaks to the narrative arc of the book in another way, for the exodus of so many older Legionnaires was directly related to the decision taken back in 1942 to open the organization to veterans of more than one war. This move had had positive consequences in the short term: it helped not only to improve the Legion's public image but also to bring different cohorts of former service members together against common threats like the First Hoover Commission. Yet in the long run, the far higher numbers of younger service members from World War II and Korea who joined the Legion meant that World War I veterans lost control of their own organization. Precisely as those who voted against the "two-war experiment" in 1942 had feared, younger veterans proved unwilling to support their elders when the latter began pushing for benefits that affected mostly themselves. Different generations did not necessarily see eye to eye on everything.

Not only was the veterans' movement internally divided, but the general public was also skeptical about the push for service pensions. As the *New York Herald Tribune* noted in 1953, an ever-growing share of the population saw former service members no longer as "conquering heroes" but rather as "tax burdens."[9] Many of the arguments advanced on either side of the controversy over non-service-connected benefits in the 1950s echoed those put forward at the height of the Civil War pension debate or of the Great Depression. The idea that

the United States was becoming a "nation of veterans" continued to dominate
public discourse as well, with the attendant fear that the country could no longer
afford paying for their benefits. In addition, the growth of New Deal welfare
programs made veterans' claims to separate treatment even harder to accept. Special benefits for this category of the population no longer seemed so necessary
now that alternative options were available. The existence of a parallel welfare
state for veterans seemed an outdated relic of the past. For all these reasons, public support for a service pension was far from overwhelming.

The fact that veterans' programs drew criticism well into the mid- and late
1950s suggests that the rise of the "national-security state" continued to be more
controversial than we often realize. By the time Eisenhower entered office in
1953, scholars tend to agree that a bipartisan consensus existed on the necessity of a new state-building regime characterized by high military spending and
frequent interventions abroad.[10] Yet the issue of what to do with the growing
population of veterans produced by the peacetime draft and by "hot" conflicts
such as the Korean War was hotly debated by liberals and conservatives alike
long after "Ike" came into office. Southern Democrats like Teague as well as
many moderate Republicans opposed the kind of blanket payments based only
on age that a service pension entailed; they insisted instead on taking recipients'
income into account. The veterans' movement resisted this emphasis on need,
fearing that it would strip pensions of their "traditional dignity" and turn them
into "charity."[11] Many former doughboys thought that their pensions should be
granted as a right, without any means testing. The fact that they were forced to
strike a compromise shows that support for this new state-building regime was
hardly unlimited.

Despite these new challenges, veterans remained a force to be reckoned
with. While their groups failed to enact new and more liberal legislation, they
were still able to beat back attempts to curtail existing benefits. The asymme-
try of veterans' politics continued to play in their favor: whereas former service
members cared deeply about their own programs, few politicians were willing
to be branded as "antiveteran" (Teague was an exception, thanks to his medals and disability). It was therefore not a coincidence that the efforts to downsize their programs were led mostly by unelected groups, the most important
of which were the Second Hoover Commission, the AMA, and the President's
Commission on Veterans' Pensions. More commonly known after the name of
its chairman, Omar Bradley, the last of these was a blue-ribbon committee created by Eisenhower in 1955 with the mission of crafting, for the first time in U.S.
history, a comprehensive and long-term philosophy to guide the development of

veterans' policy. The prestige and expertise of its members were not enough to overcome the opposition of the veterans' movement, however.[12]

In sum, this chapter concludes our narrative by showing the unanticipated consequences of the new cycle of the veterans' movement that had begun over a decade earlier with the outbreak of the Second World War. Former service members had undeniably achieved a measure of success: by the turn of the 1960s, martial citizenship was deeply entrenched in the structure of the state. Few critics challenged the separate existence of the VA anymore. But the movement that had helped make this happen was itself on the decline, with its major organizations increasingly divided and no longer at the center of national politics. To elucidate this paradox, we need to start when the guns fell silent on the east Asian peninsula.

The Politics of Non-Service-Connected Benefits

Veterans' spending was on the rise after the Korean War, climbing slowly but steadily from $5 billion in 1953 to over $6.2 billion in 1960. Contrary to the immediate aftermath of World War II, this growth was not fueled by GI Bill–style readjustment benefits, which were now shrinking rapidly as most GIs had settled back into civilian life. Two other types of programs were behind the increase. Payments for disability or death were the most important: they accounted for roughly half of the VA budget during this time period (technically speaking, such disbursements were called "compensation" if they were connected to military service and "pension" if not).[13] Medical and hospital benefits came next, representing between 12 and 16 percent of total spending.[14] Though these benefits were open to all veterans, those who sought treatment for non-service-related impairments had to sign a form certifying that they were unable to pay for private care. By law, the VA was prohibited from challenging the veracity of what was known as the "pauper's oath."[15]

Not only was the increase in both categories driven primarily by non-service-connected recipients, but most of these beneficiaries were World War I veterans.[16] Doughboys were overrepresented among signatories of the "pauper's oath" and they also accounted for the overwhelming majority of those on the pension rolls.[17] The rise in veterans' spending after 1953 was therefore mostly the result of growing numbers of older veterans of the Great War and their dependents taking advantage of VA health care and pensions to cover disabilities incurred outside of service.

This trend reflected the situation of the elderly population in the midcentury United States, which was improving but still precarious. Even though private health insurance plans expanded considerably in the postwar period, they generally failed to address the specific needs of retired persons.[18] As for public support systems, they only came into their own in the early 1950s. After its creation in 1935, Old-Age and Survivors' Insurance (OASI, the official name of Social Security after 1939) was mired in endless partisan controversy. Initially designed merely to complement public assistance programs, its payments and coverage remained limited well into the 1940s. The legitimacy of OASI was secured only when Eisenhower endorsed it in his inaugural State of the Union address, thereby dispelling fears that Republicans would seek to dismantle a program hitherto run only by Democrats. Over the next couple of decades, Congress regularly expanded coverage and raised benefits.[19] More than a third of all persons aged sixty-five and over were still living under the poverty level in 1959, however.[20] In these conditions, it was not surprising that those among the elderly who had access to alternative sources of assistance, such as veterans' benefits, made use of them in growing numbers.

However incomplete, the emergence of a national welfare state was changing the terms of the debate over veterans' benefits. Previously, the absence of a strong public safety net had helped former service members argue that they needed their own separate system. Veterans' programs "could be thought of as half a loaf," as one social scientist later noted, since "a kind of social security for some veterans was better than no social security for anyone." But this argument carried less weight in the midcentury, for "now it looked more like a whole loaf for most people and a loaf and a half for the veteran."[21] By the middle of the 1950s, a growing public-private welfare state was indeed offering to the general population many of the same kinds of benefits already available to former service members. Almost two-thirds of Americans enjoyed hospital and surgical benefits, for instance.[22] Increasing numbers of employers began offering their own health insurance plans.[23] Workmen's compensation laws, which served the same purpose as veterans' compensation, were in effect in virtually every state by the late 1940s.[24] Finally, OASI fulfilled the same role as veterans' pensions. Many former service members were able to draw on both systems at the same time.[25]

This situation provided new ammunition to reform advocates. With the veteran population at an all-time high of over 22 million in the second half of the 1950s, the existence of a separate and parallel system of benefits seemed to make little financial and political sense. The progressive think tank Twentieth Century Fund warned that a failure to integrate veterans' pensions with Social Security would result in a "profligate waste of social resources."[26] The conservative

Brookings Institution likewise contended that "except . . . when the disablement is the result of service, the claim of veterans to special treatment over and above the claim of ordinary citizens is emotional, often specious, in its nature."[27] Many other experts agreed that non-service-connected benefits needed to be reined in.[28]

The national press echoed these views. The *New York Times* asserted for instance that "veterans who have suffered no injury or illness as a result of their military life are not a class apart, nor should they be treated as such. . . . [V]eterans are citizens—and taxpayers, too."[29] The Republican-leaning *Saturday Evening Post*, one of the most widely circulated middle-class magazines of the era, argued that the debt owed veterans "must . . . be controlled by how much we can afford to pay," and that the time was fast approaching "when the mounting cost of veterans' benefits will impose an impossible strain on the budget."[30] Conservative voices like the *Chicago Tribune* considered free medical care for all veterans to be "a long step toward socialized medicine" that would ultimately "bankrupt the country."[31] Some local papers shared the same opinion: in Mattoon, Illinois, the *Daily Journal-Gazette* argued that the very principle of pensions "borders on the ridiculous": "It is time the veteran stopped deluding himself that he is the savior of this nation," the paper argued. "He only did what he was supposed to do, and what he did was pre-ordained by a [draft] number in a capsule. . . . The veteran is no more, and no less, than a citizen whose duty it is to protect this country in one fashion or another."[32]

The larger public seemed to have no appetite for lavish spending on veterans' benefits either. In a 1952 poll, less than half of respondents agreed that the next administration should "do more" for veterans.[33] Another survey conducted a year later reported that only 45 percent of Americans thought that the government should give a war veteran "free care and treatment at a veterans' hospital" for injuries unrelated to service.[34] Former service members were themselves divided on the issue: almost two-thirds thought that they deserved favored treatment whenever possible, but pensions and medical care for the non-service-connected ranked among their least favorite benefits.[35]

The attitude of the executive branch on this topic changed little with the arrival of Dwight D. Eisenhower in the White House in 1953. Although Ike was a veteran, he agreed with his predecessors that the state should support only the war-disabled and the survivors of those killed in service. For him, non-service-connected needs should be met not with special benefits but instead with "adequate job opportunities" and equal access to "the broad social-security programs that is [*sic*] provided for nonveterans."[36] As president, Eisenhower focused on enlarging the scope of the programs available to the general population rather than to this specific group. Throughout the 1950s, his administration supported a series of amendments to OASI to expand coverage and increase payments.[37] In the face of constant demands to increase military spending, Ike also sought to balance the budget by finding economies in other areas.[38] For all these reasons, he opposed the growth of non-service-connected veterans' programs. As he remarked in a meeting, "it was a sin and a shame that a veteran may get a larger income with pension simply for 90 days service than the working man gets through social security."[39]

In this hostile environment, the veterans' movement defended its accomplishments on several levels. As always, its advocates argued that former service members were a special category of the population entitled to certain advantages. In the words of one Legion official, "we believe that military service is extraordinary service which transcends the normal duties of citizenship and, consequently, entitles veterans with honorable service to special consideration." Pensions as well as other veterans' benefits, he argued, "were a matter of right and not a gratuity."[40] The VFW agreed that veterans' benefits were "part of the cost of war" rather than ordinary welfare programs.[41] Beyond the defense of martial citizenship, veterans' leaders pointed out that service connection was often hard to establish given the frequent holes in service records and the delays in the adjudication of claims, which meant that many veterans who otherwise deserved this status had either been denied it or were waiting for it to be granted. Since a large number of former service members being treated for non-service-connected disabilities in VA hospitals had other service-connected impairments or were receiving treatment for chronic conditions like tuberculosis or mental problems, Legion officials also argued that they would need care anyway.[42] Better to do so in specialized veterans' hospitals, they claimed, than in local institutions where the equipment and the expertise to deal with such cases were often lacking.

This debate took on added urgency when Congress created the Second Hoover Commission in July 1953. Tasked with finding ways to cut federal spending, the group published its reports two years later.[43] Like many other critics, the commission found that "the greatest of all problems in the administration of medical care for veterans are the non-service-connected cases." Not only did it call for VA hospitals to be given the authority to verify pauper's oaths, but it also argued that the veterans who signed them should be liable to reimburse the cost of their treatment in the future.[44] The commission recommended a number of other reforms that would have dramatically downsized veterans' welfare state.[45] Conservative organs like the *Wall Street Journal* as well as a broad segment of the mainstream and liberal press supported its proposals.[46]

As the First Hoover Commission had learned to its detriment a few years earlier, however, public support was not a guarantee of success. Almost every major stakeholder in veterans' affairs rejected its recommendations, including the Big Three; the VA administrator, Harvey Higley; and Olin Teague (who was now Chairman of the House Veterans' Affairs Committee, after the 1954 midterm elections restored Democratic control of the House).[47] Eisenhower considered Hoover's views of the limited role of government to be "a trifle on the moth-eaten side" and he was reticent to expend political capital on their behalf.[48] As a result, the Second Hoover Commission captured less public attention than the First and it achieved little.[49]

The AMA represented a more serious threat. In the early 1950s, the powerful advocacy group for professional doctors was at the peak of its influence, having just defeated Truman's push for national health insurance.[50] Major veterans' groups like the Legion had been its allies in this fight.[51] But their coalition was purely circumstantial, for the AMA had long opposed the extension of medical services to veterans without service-connected disabilities.[52] After Truman left office in 1953, veterans and doctors no longer had a common enemy and their truce broke down.[53] The AMA began to criticize the idea that all non-service-connected patients except tuberculosis and neuropsychiatric cases should have access to care, on the ground that the growth of VA hospitals produced "a wasteful duplication of hospital facilities and an unwarranted dispersion of health personnel."[54] An article published in the official AMA journal made the point in more overtly political terms, calling the VA medical program "a Trojan horse of ominous dimensions" that, if left unchecked, could nudge the entire population into "socialized medicine and socialism" (Fig. 11).[55]

The AMA immediately embarked on a state-by-state lobbying campaign, reprising the same strategy that had proved so successful against Truman.[56] Taking a leaf from the First Hoover Commission, the AMA even formed its own front group whose members were both veterans and doctors, the National Medical Veterans Society, so as to give its cause added legitimacy.[57] The campaign received support in the press. The *Reader's Digest* for instance ran an article calling the VA pauper's oath "one of the most scintillating frauds ever perpetrated on the American people."[58] Long Island's *Newsday* cheered the attacks, arguing that "simply because a man has been in uniform is no reason why he should be pampered and cajoled for the rest of his days."[59] The Big Three reacted indignantly, with the DAV and the VFW calling the AMA "a bunch of reactionary old dodos."[60] All traces of a coalition between the doctors' lobby and the veterans' movement were gone; they were now at loggerheads.

Guarding the Gate

Figure 11. VA medical benefits were seen by some doctors as the back door for "socialized medicine." In this cartoon, Congress is shown failing to notice the threat of "free medical care available indiscriminately to 18½ million veterans." *Medical Economics*, September 1952, p. 68.

It soon became obvious that the AMA could not win this fight, for a number of reasons. As a physician said in one of its meetings, "if the doctors do not know that the American people have a special regard for veterans, the Congress does know it."[61] Indeed, Representative George Long of Louisiana noted in a hearing that the effort to eliminate non-service-connected medical benefits was quixotic. "The Congress is dead-bent on treatment," the southern Democrat remarked. "There is no use in you and I arguing that question."[62] The AMA was also out of step with other representatives of the medical profession. The partnership created after World War II between medical schools and the VA had proven so successful that their interests had become deeply intertwined. The umbrella association of medical schools argued that they needed "the non-service-connected patient in the veterans' hospital in order to make a balanced program which is any good for teaching."[63] Finally, the AMA simply failed to back up its charges of widespread abuse of the pauper's oath with facts.[64] Its lobbying campaign obtained only one concession: a new VA hospital form requiring patients to give more detailed information about their income and assets. Even this was largely a toothless measure, however, for the agency was still prohibited from denying hospitalization to any veteran signing the pauper's oath.[65]

The Bradley Commission and the War Veterans Security Bill

By the mid-1950s, repeated attempts to curb non-service-connected benefits had all reached the same impasse. After the defeat of the AMA, public attention shifted from medical benefits to payments for non-service-connected disability and death, better known as veterans' pensions.

There was no consensus on this topic within the veterans' movement. Well aware of the unpopularity of service pensions, veterans' leaders feared that the passage of such legislation could trigger a political backlash similar to the Economy Act of 1933.[66] Both the Legion and the VFW had lobbied for World War I service pensions in 1949, but it had taken intense rank-and-file pressure to convince the leadership, and the campaign was suspended after the outbreak of the Korean War. Though the pause was officially to focus on the war effort, veterans' leaders were glad to sidestep this divisive issue.[67] Once the hostilities on the Korean peninsula were over, the Legion did not reendorse the measure.

The fear of a public backlash was not the only reason why service pensions were so toxic; they also fueled intergenerational tensions. Since World War I veterans stood to benefit from these age-based payments much more than their younger counterparts, doughboys supported them in far higher numbers.[68] Many former service members of the Great War thought that it was only fair for their cohort to be granted the same service pension as Civil War and Spanish-American War veterans. "Why is it," as one of them wrote, "that, of all American wars of the past, the soldiers of World War 1 are the only ones to be denied a pension? . . . Unless it is intended that WW 1 veterans go down in history as the only American soldiers to be discriminated against in the matter of pensions, the Legion ought to take some action soon."[69] They also resented the GI Bill benefits received by younger cohorts. One Legionnaire wrote that "it seems everything, and I mean *EVERYTHING* under the sun has been done for WW2 veterans, but the WW1 boys have had, and, still are taking it in the neck [*sic*] when anything is proposed for them."[70] World War I veterans were "apparently . . . the forgotten men," another agreed, for "World War Two and the Korean Conflict veterans have been given every consideration."[71] Many among the older generation felt that the Legion and the VFW were ignoring their complaints.

The creation of the Veterans of World War I of the USA in 1949 was the direct result of this feeling of neglect. As a group open only to former service members of the Great War, it was dedicated to passing a service pension for them.[72] Reprising a familiar theme, its newsletter was titled *The Forgotten Men*.[73] An observer of veterans' affairs remarked that the group was mostly "made up of those who feel that the Legion and the VFW waited too long, and did too little, to close in on the pension objective."[74] Even though the ranks of the Wonnies were initially rather small, the emergence of this new group showed that the arrival of the World War II and Korean War cohorts had not had only positive consequences. Speakers at the group's first national convention argued that the domination of younger veterans in the Big Three meant that "veterans of the earlier war need a separate organization to represent their interests."[75]

Against this background of simmering dissent, Legionnaires continued to push only for minor improvements to the current pension program. It was the passage of a Legion-supported bill providing for moderate cost-of-living increases in pension rates that led Eisenhower to take action.[76] Committed as he was to cutting spending across the board, the president saw veterans' pensions as a logical target.[77] He agreed to sign the bill in August 1954, but only after pointing out the many "inequities and anomalies" that existed in the pension program as a whole and in particular the fact that it duplicated Social Security payments. This was for him evidence of the need "to examine the entire structure, scope and philosophy of our veterans benefit laws in relation to each other and to other government programs."[78] A few months later, he signed an executive order establishing a Commission on Veterans' Pensions, which he hoped would give him political cover by endowing his push to cut veterans' spending with the mantle of expertise.[79]

While many expert groups had investigated veterans' affairs before, this commission was the first to focus exclusively on the topic and to enjoy such a high public profile. Truman had sought to set up such a group as far back as 1945, but he was stopped by "political pressures."[80] Eisenhower chose as its chairman Omar Bradley, the five-star general and former administrator of the VA. The other six commissioners included the former head of the Office of Strategic Services, William J. Donovan; former VA medical director Paul R. Hawley; the president of Standard Oil Co. of California, Theodore S. Petersen; the assistant campaign director for the Republican National Committee, Clarence Adamy; Morgan State College president Martin D. Jenkins; and the vice chairman of Mutual Benefit Life Insurance, John S. Thompson. None of them were from within the VA bureaucracy, a further sign that Eisenhower was serious about reforming the system. To assist in their work, the commissioners had over fifty employees and consultants.[81]

Over the next year and a half, they conducted a thorough review of veterans' programs. The only area excluded from their purview was medical benefits: having just witnessed the AMA's debacle, the White House felt that this field was "quite controversial" and that "to bite that off too in addition to all the other things would cause too much trouble."[82] Even within this reduced perimeter, the task at hand was enormous: the commission eventually produced seventeen volumes totaling over forty-two hundred pages.[83] It was by far the most ambitious and in-depth study of veterans' welfare state to date.

As its report made clear, the commission sought to "modernize" the structure of veterans' benefits, especially the "old backward-looking pension philosophy," by bringing it in line with the "fundamental changes in our society" that had happened since World War II.[84] In so doing, the group echoed many themes familiar to observers of veterans' affairs. Its report noted for instance that "we are rapidly becoming a Nation of veterans" and that the peacetime draft would only accelerate this change.[85]

But the commission also brought fresh arguments to the debate. It stressed for example the different nature of military service in the Cold War: military and civilian pay were now comparable, the greater specialization of military training made it easier to transfer to private industry jobs, and peacetime mortality rates were lower. Since service was less of a handicap, the commissioners reasoned that the need for the state to help veterans readjust to civilian life was not as acute.[86]

In fact, their report found that "the economic condition of veterans as a group is better than that of nonveterans" in their respective age cohorts. Former service members tended to have higher incomes, to be overrepresented in professional and technical occupations, and to be better educated than their peers.[87] This was another reason why readjustment benefits should be reduced.

The commission also made a more general observation on the impact of atomic warfare on veterans' affairs. It had been relatively easy in previous wars to distinguish between "wartime serviceman and civilian noncombatant" since almost all of the fighting had taken place overseas; this would no longer be true in the atomic age. "In the event of an all-out thermonuclear war," the commission noted, "every city, every industrial center, may become a target. Battlegrounds will then have no valid geographical connotation. All occupations will be military; every citizen will be on a potential battleline.... Atomic warfare ... could make of every citizen a combat veteran."[88] All these trends pointed to the same conclusion: it made less and less sense to grant former service members special treatment.

Building on these findings, the commission recommended that "military service in time of war or peace should be treated as discharging an obligation of citizenship and not of itself as a basis for future Government benefits." Those disabled in service should be cared for, but the idea that "anyone who has served in the Armed Forces in wartime ... has a right to special privileges from the Government for the rest of his life, and thereafter for his survivor," was "clearly outmoded."[89] In other words, the commission directly challenged the ideal of martial citizenship.

From this general proposal flowed a long list of more specific ones. Most importantly, the commission suggested that non-service-connected benefits such as pensions "should be minimized and gradually eliminated." Recognizing that this was unlikely to happen immediately, the group recommended that pensions should in the near future "be limited to a minimum level and retained only as a reserve line of honorable protection for veterans whose means are shown to be inadequate and who fail to qualify for basic protection under the general OASI system."[90] To coordinate pensions and Social Security more efficiently, the commission suggested eliminating loopholes and making pensions more reflective of need.[91] It also proposed that most veterans discharged without a service-connected disability should only have access to GI Bill–style readjustment benefits and that civil service preference should be provided only for a limited time after discharge (as opposed to for life).[92] Many of these ideas had circulated in policy circles for years, but the Bradley Commission was the first to bring them under a coherent framework.

As important as what the report said was what it left unsaid. The fact that the commission made no recommendations as to the status of the VA itself showed how entrenched this agency had become. Throughout the interwar period and into the early 1950s, liberals and conservatives alike had tried repeatedly to transfer some of the VA's functions to an all-encompassing welfare agency. Yet the Bradley Commission left the veterans' agency largely untouched, for its members realized that such a move was now beyond the pale. In preliminary meetings, officials from the Bureau of the Budget had emphasized to Bradley and his colleagues that their mission should be to present the facts "in a salable condition," which meant that they would have to "concede that the whole structure of veterans' benefits cannot be dismantled."[93] This decision did not make headlines, but it spoke volumes about the ability of public policy to change politics over time. As years went by, the separate design of martial citizenship was growing more and more ensconced within the state.

The submission of the commission's final report to Eisenhower on April 22, 1956, received enthusiastic coverage. This was unsurprising, for its conclusions echoed what many newspapers had been advocating for years. After extensively quoting from the report, for instance, the *Christian Science Monitor* simply added "Hear! Hear!"[94] *Time* magazine applauded the commission for showing that "the old arguments for gifts to nondisabled veterans are outdated, if not phony, today."[95] The *Washington Post and Times Herald* likewise argued that despite the "self-serving protests from professional veterans," the proposals of the reports made "enormous good sense," for "socially, economically and morally it would be wrong to regard veterans as a privileged class apart from the general population."[96] Observers agreed that the proposal to eliminate veterans' pensions was the most significant.

The veterans' movement reacted less positively. All of the major veterans' groups opposed the report, except for the small and liberal American Veterans Committee.[97] The DAV argued that things would "border on the catastrophic" for many veterans if Congress adopted these recommendations.[98] The VFW saw the report as a "brush-off" that reflected a "backward philosophy."[99] Even the typically moderate AMVETS opposed the idea that veterans were not a "select group" entitled to special benefits.[100] The Legion agreed that Bradley's report was "dangerous because, by stealth cloaked in compliments, it exalts the welfare state and denies to the veteran a special dignity because of service to country."[101]

The Bradley report came out just as the Legion was launching its own pension campaign. Within the group, rank-and-file pressure to endorse a service pension for all veterans above the age of sixty had continued unabated: a resolution to that effect was defeated at the 1955 national convention.[102] The conclave called instead for a broad revision of disability pensions, by increasing payment levels, raising income limitations, and making every veteran over sixty-five automatically eligible.[103] Legion officials described it as "a compromise measure designed to placate those who raised a clamor for a 'General Pension Law.'"[104] They hoped to take advantage of the fact that 1956 was a presidential election year, in which the additional media coverage tended to make members of Congress even more reluctant to vote against veterans' interests than usual.

Legion leaders considered their plan to be a compromise, but they knew that the public would not necessarily see it that way. The stigma that remained attached to the term "pension" prompted one Legion official to advise a fellow member to "stay away as far as you can" from the word.[105] This explains why they chose to present their measure not as a straightforward pension bill but rather as an effort to extend to poor and older veterans the same economic security that the New Deal had made available to other categories of the population. In a deliberate nod to the 1935 Social Security Act, they called their plan the War Veterans Security Bill. To make the reference even more explicit, public relations material argued that the bill provided "a measure of freedom from want," a direct quote from Franklin Delano Roosevelt's Four Freedoms speech.[106] There was a rich irony in this choice of terms: not only had the Legion been a vocal critic of New Deal welfare programs, but Roosevelt had generally opposed granting special benefits to veterans. The fact that Legion leaders borrowed his language to introduce a pension bill spoke volumes about how the latter had become difficult to sell politically.

Legionnaires threw all their weight behind this bill, which they introduced in Congress in early January 1956. It was to be their "greatest legislative campaign since the days of [the] GI Bill in 1944," according to a press release.[107] The reference was not incidental; it was an attempt to overcome the intergenerational divisions that pensions often exacerbated. By comparing the new measure to the original GI Bill, Legion officials were hoping that younger members would support it as a way to repay their debt to the older generation. The head of the group for instance asked all Legionnaires "and especially ALL WORLD WAR II and Korea veterans" to support the new bill. "The veterans of World War I had no GI Bill of Rights," he wrote, "no housing benefits, no educational benefits, no unemployment benefits, no mustering-out pay worthy of the name. Yet they procured all of those advantages and more for us younger veterans. . . . Now we . . . are put to the test of proving that our understanding of the needs of our older comrades is as great as their understanding of our needs was . . . in short, the test of proving that we were worthy of the GI Bill of Rights."[108] The committee in charge of this new campaign was also modeled after the one that had steered the GI Bill over a decade earlier.[109] Both were chaired by the same Legion notable, John Stelle of Illinois.[110]

But 1956 was not 1944. Despite all its careful preparations, the Legion found it impossible to recapture the momentum behind the GI Bill. For one thing, the veterans' movement as a whole did not rally behind the proposal: the VFW pushed for a more generous pension increase for World War I veterans who had served overseas, the Wonnies lobbied for $100 per month at age sixty with "no strings attached," and the DAV rejected all pension plans on the grounds that they would divert public resources away from the war-disabled.[111] Even long-standing allies like the VA balked, judging the Legion's proposal too expensive.[112] Most importantly, the chairman of the House Committee on Veterans' Affairs, who had the most power over the fate of veterans' legislation, remained skeptical.

Olin Teague was ambivalent about non-service-connected benefits. Even though he believed in the core tenet of martial citizenship, namely that "veterans are in a separate class all to themselves," he argued that there should be limits to this status. "Just because a man put on a uniform," he wrote, did not mean "that he should wear a halo around his head the rest of his life."[113] This explains why he voted against Rankin's service pension bill in 1949.[114] As a fiscal conservative and a southern Democrat, Teague feared that welfare programs were financially unsustainable and that they encouraged idleness among their recipients (he opposed expanding Social Security or creating national health insurance).[115] Though he disagreed with the proposals of the Bradley Commission, he was therefore sympathetic to its goal of cutting expenditures, which he hoped to achieve through his own methods.[116] In his view, veterans' legislation should give "first consideration ... to the disabled and to the widows and orphans of men who were killed in service" before those whose disability or death was incurred after discharge. As a World War II veteran, he was also critical of his elders' claims of neglect. "There is considerable talk about World War I veterans being forgotten men," he wrote, "but one out of every three [of them] today are receiving either pension or compensation."[117] Finally, he feared that the lavish service pension bill proposed by the Wonnies would provoke a backlash and he opposed the more moderate proposal of the Legion on the ground that it still included many recipients who were not really in need.[118] As in the previous debate over the Korean GI Bill, Teague proved to be both an ally and a thorn in the side of the veterans' movement.

It was in his committee that the War Veterans Security Bill and the proposals of the Bradley Commission collided. Teague was determined to bottle up the Legion bill, for he knew that it would be difficult for his colleagues to go on record against it on the floor of the House. He did all he could to block it after the hearings concluded in early March.[119] When the Bradley Commission released its report the next month, he seized the opportunity and announced that more hearings were needed. This was a transparent effort to gain time in order to prevent passage of the War Veterans Security Bill before Congress would adjourn in July.[120] Teague was acting largely on his own: under the pressure of the Legion, a majority of the twenty-four members of his committee supported the bill.[121]

As the Texan stalled, negative editorials piled on (Fig. 12). One after the other, national and local papers alike denounced the War Veterans Security Bill, calling it "financial suicide" and "special-interest legislation" pushed by "professional veterans."[122] The most provocative of these columns was published by the *Chicago Tribune*, which called on the "Greedy Legion" to stop pushing for increases in the already "staggering costs of veterans' benefits," noting that otherwise "it may become necessary for patriotic veterans to form a new organization with one objective: Stop the American Legion from Wrecking America."[123] Coming from a paper that had long been an ally of the Legion in the fight against communism, the attack put the group on notice that its reserve of support was eroding fast.

The hearings on the Bradley report opened in a charged atmosphere. At stake were not just the merits of the commission's findings but more broadly the question of whether a parallel welfare state for veterans should continue to exist. During his testimony, Bradley noted that the findings of his report "almost completely and 100 percent oppose[d]" the Legion bill, since the latter provided for a liberalization instead of a reduction of veterans' pensions.[124] In response, Legion, VFW, and DAV witnesses attacked the report for denying that former service members were entitled to "special status."[125] On the question of whether Social Security should replace veterans' pensions, Legion officials pointed out that the former system was still far from covering all types of employment and that its payments were not as generous. "To accept a dovetailing of these two programs," an internal Legion document noted, "would reduce the permanently and totally disabled veteran to the status of a pauper."[126] Legionnaires also contended that the two systems were different by nature. Social Security was a contractual relationship in which the federal government sent payments to an individual after a certain age on the basis of past earnings, whereas veterans' pensions were "based upon the performance of duty in defense of one's country in times of war." In their view, former service members were entitled to both.[127]

While the hearing was taking place on Capitol Hill, veterans all around the country got involved. According to one Legion official, the members of Teague's

"Mind You, We're Against All That Socialistic Stuff—"

Figure 12. This cartoon was one of the many that mocked
the alleged hypocrisy of well-off veterans criticizing the
welfare state ("all that socialistic stuff") while at the same
time demanding "special benefits" for themselves and
their relatives. *Washington Post*, April 26, 1956. Credit:
A 1956 Cartoon, © The Herb Block Foundation.

committee received so much mail on the issue of pensions that many "abandoned
personal answers and were sending out form letters in reply."[128] Another Legionnaire noted that their letter-writing drive was "developing rapidly into an effective
campaign."[129] No less than 217 members of Congress had come out in support of
the bill by late May, with some having received "thousands of personal letters."[130]

In their correspondence, veterans emphatically rejected the proposals of
the Bradley Commission. One Legionnaire from Fresno, California, called the

proposal to merge pensions and Social Security "a plain betrayal of the proud heroic stalwart American Veteran," adding that "you know and I know, that even with the little Social Security and Pensions now permitted a person *can not live decently* [sic], *if he has any dependents*."[131] The elite background of the commissioners also came in for criticism. "All who sat on the Com[mission] are in the $100,000 class who enjoy fabulous pensions and lucrative jobs," one elderly World War I Legionnaire argued. "I think the panel is too high brow and as for Bradley he never cared too much for the buck rear rank private."[132] But perhaps the most creative complaint came from Bert Van Dyke in Tunkhannock, Pennsylvania, who borrowed liberally from Ernie Ford's 1947 country hit "Sixteen Tons" about life as a coal miner to write "Pensioner's Plaint," his own musical take on the plight of a poor retired doughboy: "Each year a year older and what will I get? / Just a kick in the pants and deeper in debt? / Old soldiers don't die . . . or so they say— / Hell, they cain't afford to on an old vet's pay!"[133]

This outpouring of support did not stop Teague from blocking passage of the War Veterans Security Bill. After the hearings ended, he rejected a motion to vote immediately and instead flew out of town for a week. Only after the Legion intensified its pressure (to the point that Teague himself received over two thousand letters per day) did his committee overrule him and force a vote in early June, which they won. But it was too late. By postponing the vote for so long, Teague ensured that it would take a "miracle" for the bill to make it through Congress before the July recess.[134] Even the overwhelming margin of 365 votes to 51 by which the House passed the bill in late June was misleading.[135] Many representatives who voted in favor anticipated that the bill would either die in the Senate or be vetoed by the president, thereby allowing them to shirk responsibility for its demise.[136] They were soon proven right. The powerful chairman of the Senate Finance Committee, Virginia Democrat Harry Byrd, was in no hurry. Dismissing repeated pleas to move quickly, he requested the input of several federal agencies before making any decision.[137] He had yet to receive all of their reports when Congress went home for the year, effectively killing the War Veterans Security Bill.[138] Once again, it was a financially conservative southern Democrat who had blocked the Legion's plans.

This legislative fight left a mark. Legion officials attempted to exact revenge against Teague by organizing a write-in campaign in his home state and by portraying him as an "enemy of the veteran," but they failed to find anyone willing to run against him.[139] As a decorated and disabled former service member, the Texan could easily shrug off such attacks. In the end, he played a key role in defeating the War Veterans Security Bill: though he had the support of the VA, the White House, and the press, and he also benefited from divisions within the veterans' movement, it was he who took responsibility for delaying action long enough. This episode resembled what had occurred during the Korean War, when Teague had blocked the effort to extend the original GI Bill, but with one major difference. This time, Legionnaires had actively pushed for a measure that they hoped would be their "greatest" achievement since 1944. The fact that they were unable to obtain the passage of a bill they cared so much about shows that the influence of the veterans' movement was on the wane.

The Veterans' Pension Act of 1959

The problem of economic security for veterans of World War I continued to rank high on the agenda after 1956, as more and more of them joined the pension rolls. Slightly over a sixth of all the members of this cohort still alive that year were receiving a pension; four years later, they were almost a third. During the same period, the annual cost of those payments swelled from $680 million to over $1 billion, more than the entire VA medical program.[140] The pressure on veterans' groups to pass a service pension bill increased accordingly. At the national convention of the Legion in September 1956, seven departments submitted resolutions to that effect, though without success.[141] The leadership had no appetite for another confrontation with Teague.[142] Early in 1957, the group reintroduced a bill almost identical to the one that had passed the House the previous year, but the Texan simply ignored it.[143]

In the meantime, the Eisenhower administration grappled with the problem of what to do with the Bradley report. Throughout the first half of 1957, the White House struggled to find a way to build consensus behind the group's recommendations despite the opposition of Teague and of the veterans' movement. Their hand was forced by the launch of two Sputnik satellites in the fall. Eisenhower reacted to this new military and technological threat from the Soviets with a major televised address in which he announced cuts in nondefense spending. Since the development of an efficient missile program and of satellite projects would require "a very considerable [dollar] figure," he noted that there would be "tough choices" as to where the budget axe should fall and that "pressure groups will wail in anguish."[144] The administration later explained that it sought to cut veterans' pensions by proposing their merger with Social Security.[145]

Eisenhower's plans ran into headwinds almost immediately, for his fellow Republicans were worried about more than just Moscow. Starting in mid-1957, a sharp domestic recession sent unemployment to new heights.[146] When the GOP registered losses at the state and local levels in November of that year, many party leaders blamed the Soviets *and* the economic downturn. Top administration officials recognized the need to mitigate cuts in nondefense spending lest the recession would worsen.[147] Eisenhower's announcement was also met with the expected volley of criticism from the veterans' movement. The Wonnies sent hundreds of form letters to the White House.[148] One Legion official testified that these plans amounted to "nothing more than what I would call a cold war on veterans" and he threatened that his group would "start a cold war back." Teague assured him that his committee as well as Congress more broadly were on their side.[149] Having regained control of both chambers in the 1954 midterms, Democrats were not going to support a Republican attack on veterans' benefits. On the defensive, GOP lawmakers persuaded Eisenhower "not to pick a fight with the tough veterans lobby in this election year," and instead to "put off the controversy until next year."[150] Unable to sway Capitol Hill, the White House was forced into a "quiet but clear-cut retreat."[151]

The situation within the veterans' movement was equally deadlocked. On the one hand, the pressure for a service pension kept mounting, as illustrated by the ever-growing ranks of the Wonnies. Their membership skyrocketed from around "4,000 or 5,000 members" in 1953 to nearly 140,000 in 1959, with members in all fifty states as well as D.C., the Philippines, France, and Ireland.[152] The group obtained a federal charter in 1958.[153] On the other hand, major organizations such as the Legion continued to resist grassroots pressure and to support more moderate proposals.[154] Still, Legionnaires saw the rise of this new competitor with concern. The Wonnies never accounted for more than a small fraction of their own membership, but Legion officials worried that their vocal advocacy for service pensions would create "an atmosphere of fear in the minds of some Members of Congress," which could lead them to deny "all liberalizations in this field," no matter how moderate.[155]

With the situation seemingly at an impasse, Eisenhower opted for a compromise in January 1959. He accepted the principle that pensions should continue to exist but tried to make them more reflective of need.[156] The bill proposed by the administration accomplished this goal in two ways. First, it introduced a so-called sliding scale mechanism, whereby poorer veterans would receive more money and those better off less. Second, it included more sources of income in the calculation of whether a veteran fell under the required income ceiling, including Social Security.[157] Both measures aimed at reducing long-term costs, even if they were a far cry from the broader overhaul of veterans' benefits prescribed by the Bradley Commission. The *Wall Street Journal* welcomed the bill as "a step in the right direction, but a small one," which illustrated "the political reluctance to tangle with veterans' groups."[158] The bill even contained a grandfather clause allowing those already on the pension rolls to remain under the current system if they so desired.[159] The notes from an interagency meeting in late 1958 explained the reasons for this retreat from the commission's goals. Among the three major obstacles outlined by those in attendance, "Veterans group opposition" came first, then the risk that "Democrats would label us anti-veteran and without heart," and lastly the sheer "difficulty of enactment."[160] Even though the veterans' movement was internally divided and unable to impose its own proposals, its opponents still refused to fight on its own turf.

The introduction of the administration's bill opened the floodgates of pension proposals that Teague had kept so tightly shut after 1956. Even before Eisenhower announced his new plan, the Wonnies were already gearing up for another service pension drive.[161] The Legion also introduced a series of measures that were nearly identical to its War Veterans Security Bill, with the addition of a clause to liberalize access to pensions for widows of World War II and Korean War veterans (probably in an effort to make it more palatable to the younger cohorts).[162] When hearings began in the House, both the Wonnies and the Legion rejected the administration's bill and pushed for their own.[163] Legion officials agreed with the principle of a sliding scale, but they insisted that payments should remain high enough that pensions would not turn into "a 'welfare' type program" stripped of "their traditional honorable status."[164] Teague's committee responded by including the major proposals of both the Legion and the administration into a single omnibus bill.[165] Far from achieving Eisenhower's goal of economy, the measure excluded Social Security from the sources of external income counted toward determining pension eligibility and it included the clause to liberalize access for World War II and Korean War widows, which wiped out the other savings in the bill and produced instead an expected increase in spending of $10 billion.[166] Concluding that the bill presented more advantages than problems, the Legion endorsed it.[167] The VFW did not, seeing it as an "example of the infiltration of the Bradley Pension Commission philosophy."[168] After a short debate, the House passed it in mid-June.[169]

Opposition mounted quickly. The national press denounced Teague for having "played stooge to the more selfish elements of the veterans' lobby" and it called on the Senate to tighten the bill.[170] The administration also opposed the proposal, on the grounds that it was "too costly" and that it departed "significantly" from the president's original bill.[171] The Senate Finance Committee approved a significantly scaled-down version, but the Democratic senator from Oklahoma and long-standing ally of the Legion Robert Kerr managed to erase the cuts during the floor debate.[172] In the end, the bill approved by the Senate was essentially the same as that passed by the House.[173] Eisenhower signed it into law with great reluctance: he knew that Congress would probably have overridden his veto and he feared that, if provoked, lawmakers could pass an even more expensive measure the next year (which coincided with another presidential election).[174]

Officially called the Veterans' Pension Act of 1959, the law bore only the slightest resemblance to the sweeping reforms outlined by the Bradley Commission three years earlier. To be sure, it introduced new restrictions based on need: the sliding scale meant that many veterans with incomes near the ceiling would see their payments decrease significantly and the inclusion of a spouse's income and of net worth in the calculation of income ceilings would make some recipients ineligible. However, the grandfather clause allowed all those already receiving a pension to remain under the previous system while many veterans at the bottom of the income ladder saw the size of their checks grow. On top of this, the law added over two hundred thousand widows of World War II and Korean War veterans to the rolls.[175] The fact that the Legion called the act an "impressive accomplishment" was in itself a measure of the difference between the Bradley report, which it had steadfastly opposed, and the final product.[176]

Administration officials may have thought that the Veterans' Pension Act was going too far, but many Great War veterans were of the opinion that it did go not nearly far enough. As more and more of them were joining the pension rolls (they were 1 million by 1963, over two-fifths of those of that cohort still alive), they continued to push for a more generous measure.[177] Some argued that the higher income ceilings were still too low.[178] Others rejected the new emphasis on need; they found that the sliding scale perverted the honorable nature of veterans' pensions, for it meant that "a veteran must be a pauper, or close to it, to receive any pension whatever," which made it "a dole instead of a pension."[179] But the most common grievance was simply that the act fell short of a service pension, which many ex-doughboys continued to feel they deserved as a matter of right and not depending on their income. The view that they were the "forgotten men of our country," who had failed to receive pensions as generous as their predecessors when they "fought just as hard and deserve the same as [Civil War and Spanish American War veterans] received," was widespread.[180]

The ever-expanding membership of the Wonnies attested to this fact. By 1962, the group boasted 215,000 members as well as a full-time staff in D.C. and officials in every state save Hawaii.[181] It persisted in its push for a $100 service pension, but its efforts were consistently defeated by Teague (in 1961, he noted that he never supported such legislation and "I don't think I ever will").[182]

The veterans who joined the Wonnies continued to come mostly from the Legion and the VFW, whose leadership clung to their refusal to endorse a service pension. Feeling betrayed and marginalized, many older members decided to stop paying their dues and leave. Their exodus was reflected in the slow decline of Legion membership, which went from 2.8 million in 1953 to 2.5 million in 1964.[183] Its leaders were aware that "the feeling that older veterans are unwanted by our organization ... was growing throughout the country," because they felt "[let] down."[184] The passage of the Veterans' Pension Act only amplified this phenomenon. In its wake, many older Legionnaires decided to leave.[185] One former post commander compared the situation to "rats leaving a sinking ship" and a member of forty years reported that "I have joined the Veterans of World War I of the USA and a lot of my buddies have dropped their membership in the Legion."[186]

The disappointment felt by many former doughboys after the passage of this act did not stem merely from their support for a service pension. It also reflected their resentment that the group they had created four decades earlier and to which they were still deeply attached no longer stood up for their own interests. "Why has the Legion completely bypassed the WW1 veterans?" asked one of them in 1960. "After all, we organized the Legion in the first place."[187] Feelings of bitterness toward the younger generations of Legionnaires now at the group's helm abounded. "My personal opinion," one member wrote, "is that World War II Veterans have taken control over the Legion, they like the public, have forgotten the first war and those who fought in it."[188] Having played a central role in the passage of generous benefits for their younger counterparts, many older Legionnaires viewed the latter's lack of support for a service pension as a failure to repay their debt. "The WW2 veteran has gained from the leadership of the World War One veteran," a lifelong Legionnaire wrote. "Why does he not help us now that we need help from his strength."[189] Feeling that the "two-war experiment" had turned into a hostile takeover, many doughboys turned to the Wonnies in an attempt to recreate what the Legion had been before 1942, namely a World War I–only group.

The consequences of their emigration rippled through the veterans' movement. As older veterans tended to be the most active members, their exit from the Legion and the VFW had major consequences. Legion leaders began to notice that their rank and file were increasingly harder to mobilize on behalf of veterans' legislation, which negatively impacted their effectiveness as a lobby.[190]

"Considering the apathy of our membership," one Legionnaire wrote in 1964, "the time is long past when we can browbeat Congress into submission."[191]

With Teague holding firm, World War I veterans never obtained the service pension they had been pushing for throughout the 1950s and early 1960s. Congress did not pass another major piece of legislation on the topic until 1964.[192] The issue had lost most of its urgency by then: death was thinning the ranks of the World War I generation at an accelerated rate, causing the pension rolls to shrink rapidly.[193] One can only imagine the mixed feelings with which this development must have been greeted among Legion leaders, allowing them to finally move past a problem that had long poisoned the relationship between younger and older members while at the same time leading to the disappearance of some of their most devoted and active comrades.

The problem of economic security for aging veterans of World War I had been at the center of veterans' politics from the 1950s to the early 1960s. The question of whether this cohort should have access to non-service-connected benefits proved deeply divisive: a vocal minority pushed for a service pension but the national leadership of the veterans' movement preferred to steer clear of this controversial move. Feeling betrayed and marginalized, large numbers of older veterans reacted by leaving the major organizations and forming their own group, the Wonnies. Such intergenerational division further weakened a movement that was already reeling from the blowback against anticommunism and the 1944 GI Bill. Veterans' groups could still block the agendas of the Second Hoover Commission, the AMA, and the Bradley Commission, but they were no longer in a position to implement their own, as illustrated by the defeat of the War Veterans Security Bill and of the Wonnies' service pension proposals. The Legion managed to shape the Veterans' Pension Act of 1959, but only because both Teague and the administration already supported some of its provisions.

The outcome of this debate speaks to the larger transformation described in this book. After deciding in 1942 to open their group to more than one generation of former service members, Legion leaders had strived to create an organization that, for the first time in U.S. history, could legitimately claim to be the voice of all veterans, as opposed to those from a specific war (as with the AMVETS, for instance), or based on the location of service (VFW), or on ethnicity (Jewish War Vets or Catholic War Vets), or on disability (DAV). This move enhanced the group's influence in the short term but it had unanticipated consequences in the long run. One reason why World War I veterans failed to obtain the return of their service pension in the postwar period is indeed that after 1942, they no longer had a powerful interest group exclusively devoted to defending their own interests. Had the Legion decided to keep its ranks closed, it is difficult to imagine that its leaders could have resisted the pressure from their rank and file for so long. The decision of many ex-doughboys to drop out and join a generation-specific group like the Wonnies was therefore revealing. This move was a disavowal not just of the strategy of their leadership in the fight over pensions but also of the broader rationale that had underpinned the expansion of the Legion for the past two decades. Instead of believing that all veterans were stronger together, they embraced the view that their own generation had to be independent in order for its voice to be heard. This was a challenge to the core of the veterans' movement.

There was a larger paradox at play. While the veterans' movement emerged divided from this debate, martial citizenship remained as entrenched as ever. A social policy expert later noted that the result of the fight over non-service-connected benefits was an "uneasy truce."[194] On the one hand, the kind of service pensions based only on age that the Wonnies had pushed for and that every previous generation of former service members had obtained failed to pass; eligibility was now tied to need, as opposed to being a right. This was a first in the long history of veterans' policy as well as a not-insignificant victory for reform advocates. On the other hand, the separate status of veterans' benefits was left untouched. The growth of public-private welfare programs for the general population should in theory have obviated the need for a parallel structure of benefits that fulfilled many of the same functions but only for a specific category of citizens. This view was commonsense among both experts and the national press throughout the 1940s and 1950s. Yet veterans' programs did not wither away. They became less prominent in social policy debates as the cost of Social Security and public assistance ballooned in the 1960s, but they nonetheless continued to chart their separate path. This was a potent illustration of the difficulty of changing the path-dependent course of public policies that had been embedded in the structure of the state for so long.

Epilogue

The Legacies of Martial Citizenship

The struggles of World War I veterans to obtain a service pension receded to the background just as the Vietnam War was taking center stage in national politics. As the first soldiers of this conflict began to return home in the 1960s, they struggled to readjust to civilian life, facing problems such as high unemployment or drug addiction. At the bequest of the political reformer Ralph Nader, the young scholar Paul Starr set out to investigate their situation. The result was *The Discarded Army* (1974), a deeply researched report on the inner workings of the federal agency responsible for veterans' programs, the VA. Its findings would have been disheartening to those critics who had tried to downsize veterans' programs ever since the First World War, for Starr revealed the failure of their efforts in the long run. Despite its low public profile, in the mid-1970s the VA was still the third largest federal entity in terms of expenditures and the second in terms of employees. More importantly, the agency remained in charge of a vast array of benefits accessible only to a specific category of the population, which is why Starr concluded that "the VA represents the most highly elaborated form the welfare state has reached in America."[1]

This statement may seem surprising to us. After all, *The Discarded Army* was written toward the end of an era that had witnessed a sweeping expansion of welfare programs available to the general population. Under the umbrella of President Lyndon Johnson's "Great Society," liberals had achieved several landmark victories in education, employment, housing, and old-age insurance. The government launched a series of antipoverty programs and the old struggle for national health-care insurance finally reached fruition with the passage of Medicare and Medicaid in the mid-1960s. A few years later, Johnson's successor, Richard Nixon, went even further, taking steps to expand federal authority in the realms of environmental protection and workplace safety. Meanwhile, veterans' benefits stagnated. The most significant piece of legislation in this field during the same period was the 1966 GI Bill, which provided former service members who had enlisted after 1955—the cutoff date for enrollment under the 1952 GI Bill—with relatively meager educational benefits.[2] In this context, Starr's observation that the VA represented the culmination of the U.S. welfare state seems counterintuitive.

His findings are an important reminder of something that his contemporaries understood but that we have largely forgotten today, however. Despite the segregated status of the VA and the claims of veterans' advocates that their programs should not be seen as "welfare," veterans' benefits have always been part and parcel of the U.S. welfare state. By arguing that the VA was its "most highly elaborated form," Starr recognized the basic fact that former service members continued to have access to a wider and more diverse range of welfare programs than any other category of the population. In other words, he acknowledged the success of martial citizenship. *The Discarded Army* shows that veterans' benefits remained firmly embedded in the structure of the state despite the decline of the veterans' movement that had begun in the 1950s. How can we explain this paradox?

The roots of this phenomenon go back much further than the period on which this book focuses, for veterans' benefits predated the birth of the United States. Their institutionalization into federal law was the result of a century-long process of policy sedimentation whereby each new kind of benefit was incrementally layered on top of another, from pensions and land grants in the antebellum period to homes for the elderly poor and civil service preference after the Civil War. The interwar years witnessed the addition of medical care and rehabilitation benefits, while the introduction of the Bonus signaled a new willingness to address the needs of able-bodied veterans. By the time that the United States joined the Second World War, the administration of all these benefits was already separated and centralized into the hands of the VA, itself a distant heir to the Pension Bureau created back in 1815. Together, these preexisting policies and state actors formed a foundation that greatly facilitated the task of veterans' advocates after 1940.

In the same way that public policy was shaped by the legacy of the past, so was the veterans' movement influenced by the example of the GAR. Not only did all the major veterans' organizations of the twentieth century, such as the American Legion, the DAV, and the VFW, replicate the GAR's dual nature as both a pressure group with lobbyists in Washington, D.C., and a fraternal order with deep roots in local communities across the country. They also learned from it the importance of steering clear of partisan affiliations. By refusing to tie their fate to a political party in the same way that the GAR had done with the GOP, veterans' groups were able to exert influence regardless of which camp was in power after 1918. Beyond the late nineteenth century, the interwar period also left a mark on the collective memory of the movement. Traumatic events such as the 1932 Bonus March or the 1933 Economy Act served as powerful reminders of what might happen if the state turned against those who had served on its behalf. Veterans' leaders used these memories strategically in the years to come, either as a way to prod their rank and file into action (as they did in response to several different commissions from Hoover's to Bradley's) or instead to tamper grassroots enthusiasm (for instance when they pushed back against service pensions in the 1950s). In all these ways, the veterans' movement at the midcentury was shaped by the experience of previous cycles.

The crisis that opened a new page in this long history came with the sudden Japanese attack on Pearl Harbor in December 1941. In its aftermath, the United States joined the Second World War and drafted millions of service members who later became veterans. Spurred by this massive influx of new members, the leading organizations of the movement were able to shed some (albeit never all) of their negative reputation as self-interested lobbies acquired in the interwar period. The Big Three were at the center of national politics for a brief moment in the aftermath of the war, enjoying prestige and influence well beyond their own area of expertise, as illustrated by the debate over public housing or communism. The years after 1945 were in many ways unique in the history of the veterans' movement, not only because former service members accounted for a larger share of the total population than ever before (over 12 percent in the 1950s) but also because it was the first time that veterans from so many different wars coexisted with each other, and that some of them took the unprecedented step of joining a group (the Legion) open to all with no restriction of ethnicity, disability, location of service, or otherwise.[3] Their large numbers and political cohesion helped veterans obtain new kinds of benefits—such as those provided by the 1944 GI Bill—but also defend them against attacks from liberals like President Truman and conservative groups like the American Medical Association.

The event that launched the veterans' movement on this upward trajectory may have come in an instant, but the movement's subsequent decline was a long, drawn-out process. The same factors that contributed to its undoing had paved the way to its success. First, the triumph of martial citizenship embodied by the passage of the original GI Bill gave rise to widespread fraud and corruption, which provoked a backlash and helped make veterans' legislation more restrictive. Second, the brand of hard-line anticommunism that had brought the Big Three to the center of national politics during the Second Red Scare grew increasingly unpopular after the mid-1950s. By refusing to change their views, these groups lost much of their prestige and influence. Finally, the intergenerational relations that had done so much to strengthen the movement in its fight against the First Hoover Commission turned sour in the debate over service pensions. The outcome of this last campaign suggests that the interests of younger veterans remained fundamentally at odds with those of their elders. By the end of the decade, the movement was clearly on the defensive.

Though former service members often portrayed themselves as an exceptional group, the Big Three were far from the only voluntary, federalist, and mass-membership organizations to experience such a decline in the midcentury. The Freemasons, the Odd Fellows, and the AFL-CIO, to cite only a few, faced very similar difficulties. Slowly but surely, all of these associations lost members and influence and were replaced by professionally managed, top-down advocacy groups with limited roots at the local level. This shift was the result of broad societal changes, including the phasing out of formal racial segregation and the increasing participation of women in the workforce.[4] Organizations like the Legion, the VFW, and the DAV, in which women and veterans of color played only subordinate roles when they were not outright excluded, came to seem increasingly old-fashioned and out of step with younger Americans.

Nevertheless, we should be careful not to exaggerate the extent of their decline. While the veterans' movement no longer occupied center stage in national politics by the end of the 1950s, it continued to play an important role both at the local level and within the field of veterans' affairs for many decades thereafter. The various social activities sponsored by the Legion—ranging from Boys Nation to high school oratorical contests to Junior Baseball leagues—continued to thrive and local posts remained important centers of community life. Veterans' advocates may have ceded the initiative to Congress and the White House, but they retained the ability to block any major efforts to downsize their programs, thanks less to their own strength than to the imbalanced nature of veterans' politics. Whereas most politicians were reluctant to be publicly branded as "antiveteran," former service members cared passionately about their benefits. As late as the mid-1980s, for instance, Treasury officials were forced to abandon a plan to remove the tax-free status of veterans' disability payments after the multiamputee DAV commander Chad Colley threatened to run a full-page advertisement in major newspapers featuring a photo of himself in a wheelchair under bold letters reading "WHAT'S SO SPECIAL ABOUT DISABLED VETERANS?

That's what a top Treasury official said to Chad Colley."[5] The menace of action was enough to get the desired result. Far from disappearing, then, the veterans' movement simply went into an eclipse. Year after year, it slowly lost its relevance to national politics and came to focus only on subjects that were of direct interest to its own members.

The irony is that this eclipse was a symptom not of the failure of martial citizenship but rather of its success. Indeed, one of the reasons why the veterans' movement gradually abandoned center stage in American life after the midcentury was because the benefits it had defended for so long were no longer as controversial as they once had been. By the turn of the 1960s, veterans' programs had been so successfully institutionalized as to become a routine part of social policy that hardly generated ardent debate anymore. The separation between policies for former service members and those for civilians had survived the repeated assaults of Progressives, New Dealers, and conservatives; after the defeat of the First Hoover Commission, policymakers no longer seriously challenged the idea that all welfare programs for veterans should be concentrated into the hands of a separate agency. The division between veterans and civilians was now embedded in the structure not only of the executive but also of the legislative branch, as authority over all veterans' legislation was placed into the hands of a single and separate House committee in 1946 (the Senate followed suit in 1970). Martial citizenship became so basic an element of public policy that it was rarely even remarked upon. Rather than being seen for what it was, namely the contingent result of decades of bitter political clashes, it would increasingly be taken for granted and viewed instead as the natural result of a long-standing cultural tradition. In these conditions, the veterans' movement no longer needed to be so vocal and controversial, and it could step off the stage—or at least recede to the background—knowing that its central mission had been accomplished.

History never ends, however. Just as the roots of veterans' benefits date back much earlier than 1940, so did the debate about them continue to unfold after 1960. The escalation of U.S. involvement in Vietnam set into motion yet another cycle of the veterans' movement, as millions of former service members began to return from Southeast Asia.

The most striking feature of this new cycle was how it exacerbated the intergenerational frictions that were already palpable in the 1950s. Whatever disagreements previously existed within the veterans' movement over the issue of pensions had remained largely invisible to outsiders. The Vietnam War caused these conflicts not only to shift focus but also to spill into the public sphere.

The tension between the World War II veterans who dominated the movement and their younger counterparts from Vietnam had multiple sources. One of them was political, reflecting their disagreements over the ongoing conflict in Southeast Asia. Groups like the Legion and the VFW as well as policymakers like Olin Teague supported the war effort as necessary to stop the advance of international communism, but the small yet vocal minority of their younger counterparts who organized into the Vietnam Veterans Against the War were steadfast critics. The organization denounced the war crimes committed against the Vietnamese people and it condemned the larger conflict as imperialistic. Political differences were aggravated by more personal factors, for older veterans tended to look at the new cohort, which struggled to readjust to civilian life in the difficult economic context of the late 1960s and early 1970s, as "losers, druggies, and misfits."[6] Those sentiments may not have been voiced by national leaders, but they were unmistakable at the grassroots. During an antiwar protest in New Jersey in 1970, for instance, Vietnam Veterans Against the War marchers encountered counterdemonstrators from a local VFW post, whose chaplain argued they were "blinded by none other than Satan, anti-Christ, anti-God, anti-America." Among the VFW group, one World War II veteran commented that "I don't blame those fellows for not being proud. We won our war. These fellows didn't, and from the looks of it, they couldn't win."[7] Such intergenerational animosity was not a new feature in the history of the veterans' movement, but never before had it been so intense and so public.

Beyond the political and the personal, the clash between younger and older cohorts also revolved around the issue of benefits. The core problem here was that Vietnam War veterans returned home at the same time as the much larger group of former service members from World War II was beginning to require chronic care for old age. As a result, younger veterans who required a specific type of treatment for their war-connected problems—both physical and mental—confronted a VA that was focused on the very different needs of the previous generation. In the early 1970s, nearly half of the agency's budget was devoted to non-service-connected benefits for elderly veterans and only 12 to 15 percent went to Vietnam War veterans.[8] This problem was exacerbated by the fact that the older cohort occupied positions of power in the veterans' movement and Congress. World War II veterans could stymie any efforts to change the status quo, in a manner similar to how the "old guard" of World War I Legionnaires had blocked their own efforts to endorse public housing after 1945. For instance, the Legion and the VFW steadfastly opposed the campaign of Vietnam War veterans to establish mental health programs outside the VA. Only at the end of the 1970s, when the grip of the older generation over the levers of power began to loosen, were these new programs implemented.[9] Once again, the veterans' movement did not represent all its members equally and certain voices spoke louder than others.

These divisions were significant but not permanent. Just as the fight over service pensions had gradually lost its urgency as ever-larger numbers of World War I veterans passed away in the early 1960s, the tensions between Vietnam War veterans and their elders eased over time. The major veterans' organizations began to advocate more openly on behalf of the younger generation in the 1980s, as they realized that their survival depended on bringing in new members. For example, the Legion, the VFW, and the AMVETS all supported the construction of a memorial for Vietnam War veterans on the Mall in Washington, D.C., even when many conservatives opposed its unconventional design.[10] Later in the decade, the Legion also played an important role in the resolution of the controversy over the effects of Agent Orange by conducting its own scientific study, which backed up the claims of a connection between the defoliant and various kinds of health problems such as birth defects and cancers.[11]

As important as these intergenerational conflicts were within the veteran community, they were no longer central to larger arguments about the U.S. welfare state. Unlike the period from the late nineteenth century to the mid-twentieth, when debates over veterans' benefits had featured centrally within the broader social policy discussion, after the 1950s they became relatively marginal. This was not just because martial citizenship was now firmly embedded into law. There was a more pragmatic reason: though veterans' spending continued to rise from one year to the next, it represented a steadily shrinking slice of total government outlays. From a high of over three-fifths of all federal expenditures on social welfare in 1948–50, the share devoted to veterans' benefits declined to slightly over one-fifth in 1960, then one-tenth in 1970, and finally one-twentieth in 1990.[12] As the cost of other programs like Social Security, education, and public assistance skyrocketed, fears that veterans' benefits would constitute an obstacle to the expansion of the civilian welfare state lost their relevance. The needs of former service members no longer occupied center stage in debates about the welfare state, replaced as they were by concerns over the growing importance of racial minorities among its recipients. This was not necessarily a negative development from the standpoint of the veterans' movement, for less public attention also meant less criticism.

Aside from the rapid growth of general welfare programs, another factor that helped move veterans' benefits out of the limelight was the fact that this field witnessed relatively few significant policy innovations in the last quarter of the twentieth century. With the exception of psychological counseling centers in 1979, no major new programs were added to the list of those already under the authority of the VA during these years. Congress did pass new versions of the GI Bill in 1966, 1984, and 2008, but the purpose of these pieces of legislation was merely to reactivate and update the readjustment benefits already introduced in 1944. In the absence of any major and controversial departure from existing policy, veterans' benefits remained a somewhat routine and low-profile matter.

Neither did the position of both major parties on this issue change significantly. Regardless of their partisan affiliation, many of the occupants of the White House after 1960 held essentially the same position on veterans' benefits. From John F. Kennedy to Gerald Ford, Democratic and Republican presidents alike embraced views that would have been familiar to their predecessors going back to the 1920s. They all agreed that military service was a duty not a privilege, and that veterans should not be treated as a special group of citizens. Rather than expanding programs for this specific category of the population, they focused on those available to all Americans. In their view, the first concern of the state should be to help those soldiers who had been disabled in service or the survivors of those who had been killed, and only secondly (if at all) should the federal government endorse responsibility for the welfare of the rest.[13] The position of the White House would have no more influence on the course of veterans' benefits after 1960 than it had had in previous decades, however. Presidents continued to lose when their views came into open conflict with those of the veterans' movement, as for instance in 1974 when Ford's veto of a bill to increase benefits was easily overridden by Congress.[14] The fact that martial citizenship grew regardless of the executive branch's steadfast opposition shows the limits of understanding U.S. state building as simply a struggle between Democrats and Republicans or liberals and conservatives. Some issues transcended this divide.

The discrimination faced by women and veterans of color in their access to benefits was another feature of veterans' politics that persisted long after 1960. Upon their return home, most African American veterans of the Vietnam War faced a particularly difficult readjustment process: their median income was considerably lower and their unemployment rate significantly higher than those of their white counterparts. It was therefore far more difficult for them to take advantage of the meager educational benefits afforded by the 1966 GI Bill, which meant that fewer were able to complete college. The special needs of female veterans were likewise ignored, as most lawmakers continued to design veterans' legislation with only their male counterparts in mind. The fact that women were often responsible for raising children, for instance, meant that many could not complete their education before their benefits expired.[15] And their experience was virtually invisible in society more broadly. Only in the 1970s did Congress grant several groups of women veterans, such as the Women Airforce Service Pilots of World War II or the "Hello Girls" switchboard operators of World War I, access to the benefits they had hitherto been denied (a move opposed by groups like the Legion).[16] The connection between white manhood and martial citizenship proved remarkably resilient.

At the same time as veterans' benefits remained relatively unchanged, those available to active-duty service members expanded considerably. With the end of the draft in 1973, the military changed its approach to recruitment. It began to expand the range of social services available to its members, creating new programs such as free or low-cost health care, housing, child care, and tax breaks, all of it in an effort to attract volunteers.[17] These changes marked less a new departure than a return to what had been the norm prior to the first installment of the draft during the Civil War. Social services had always served multiple purposes for the military, one of them being to reward soldiers for their service and another to ensure a steady stream of manpower.[18] The more striking development of the late twentieth and early twenty-first centuries, then, lay in the fact that the overall importance of veterans' programs diminished just as benefits for active-duty service members expanded (today, the latter account for at least a third of the defense budget).[19] Even as many civilian welfare programs fell victim to the climate of austerity that came to the fore from the 1970s onward, the military welfare state never stopped growing. In this sense, martial citizenship remained as central a part of public policy as it had ever been.

The year 1973 did mark a break in the relationship of the American public with the military and veterans, however. The advent of the "All-Volunteer Force" led to a steady decrease in the share of the population with direct experience of military service, to the point where it has now become a cliché to remark that only "1 percent" of the population serves. Even though this figure underestimates the total number of persons in contact with the military by leaving out relatives, veterans, and civilian contractors, the situation is nonetheless dramatically different from the mid-twentieth century, when fears that the United States would soon become "a nation of veterans" were pervasive. These concerns have been reversed in the early twenty-first century. Most observers now fear that the country has become what we might call a "nation of civilians," in which the needs of veterans and of the military are increasingly foreign to the overwhelming majority of the population. Complaints about a widening "civilian-military gap" have become commonplace.[20]

It is another irony of history that this gap coexists with a broad public support for veterans' benefits. While former service members are routinely portrayed in popular culture as either broken individuals or patriotic heroes, one trope that has virtually disappeared is the view of them as tax burdens. Critics of veterans' benefits still exist, but they are far rarer and their opinions no longer as mainstream as in the period that this book focused on.[21] Most Americans today tend to regard active-duty or former service members with admiration and respect. This attitude is only reinforced by the increasing alienation of civilians from the military, which makes the former less inclined and able to criticize the latter. This positive if sometimes unreflective approach is illustrated by the increasingly common use of terms such as "warriors" or "heroes" to designate service members and veterans—words that glorify war making and betray a lack of knowledge of the more routine aspects of military service.[22] Moreover, such expressions of support are often little more than lip service. The fact that almost every presidential election since 1992 has seen candidates with a distinguished war record (from George H. W. Bush to Bob Dole to John Kerry and John McCain) lose to opponents with a far more limited and sometimes even nonexistent one (from Bill Clinton to George W. Bush to Barack Obama) shows respect for veterans and the military in the United States to be both broad *and* shallow. Military service is only one of many criteria that determine Americans' political preferences. There is thus no guarantee that public opinion will not turn against those who served at some point in the future.

It is nonetheless unlikely that the military welfare state will stop growing anytime soon. This is perhaps the essential lesson that we can learn from this study. In the midcentury, many experts predicted that veterans' programs would eventually disappear; they were all proven wrong. It was less the result of the surprising resilience of the veterans' movement than of the fact that all these predictions were based on the faulty assumption that the United States would keep out of future wars, which would have led to the decline and eventual disappearance of the veteran population. Yet far from going away, war has proved a remarkably recurrent pattern in U.S. history. So long as this country continues to engage in conflicts large and small, it will keep on producing new cohorts of veterans, who in turn can be counted upon to defend and expand their separate system of benefits by organizing as a social movement in the same way as their predecessors. As long as there is no end to war in the United States, there will be no end to the military welfare state.

ABBREVIATIONS

AACCCR   All-American Conference to Combat Communism Records, Wilcox Collection, Kansas Collection, RH WL MS 18, Kenneth Spencer Research Library, University of Kansas Libraries, Lawrence, Kansas.

ACLUR   American Civil Liberties Union Records, Public Policy Papers, Department of Rare Books and Special Collections, Princeton University Library, Princeton, New Jersey.

ALA   American Legion Archives, Indianapolis, Indiana.

ALM   *American Legion Magazine*

AMOC   Alvin Mansfield Owsley Collection, University of North Texas Archives, Denton, Texas.

CCREBGR   Citizens Committee for Reorganization of the Executive Branch of the Government records, Hoover Institution Archives, Stanford, California.

CHCPL   Cincinnati and Hamilton County Public Library, Cincinnati, Ohio.

DDEPL   Dwight D. Eisenhower Presidential Library, Abilene, Kansas.

FDR   Franklin Delano Roosevelt Library, Hyde Park, New York.

FFR   Fund for the Republic Papers, Mudd Library, Princeton University Library, Princeton, New Jersey.

HWCC   Harry W. Colmery Ms. Collection, Library and Archives Division, Kansas State Historical Society, Topeka, Kansas.

JBMP   J. B. Matthews Papers, David Rubenstein Library, Duke University, Durham, North Carolina.

KBP   Karl Baarslag Papers, Hoover Institution Archives, Stanford, California.

OETCC   Olin E. Teague Congressional Collection, Cushing Library, Texas A&M University, College Station, Texas.

PCVP   Records of the U.S. President's Commission on Veterans' Pensions, Dwight D. Eisenhower Presidential Library, Abilene, Kansas.

RATP   Robert A. Taft Papers, Manuscript Division, Library of Congress, Washington, D.C.

RFHC   Records of the First Hoover Commission, Herbert Hoover Presidential Library, West Branch, Iowa.

S&S   *Stars and Stripes* (Western Europe, Paris Edition)

SFCP   Stephen Fowler Chadwick Papers, Accession No. 0014–001, Special Collections, University of Washington, Seattle, Washington.

SLP   Samuel Latimer Papers, South Caroliniana Library, University of South Carolina, Columbia, South Carolina.

UAWD   UAW Veterans' Department Collection, 1943–55, Walter P. Reuther Library, Wayne State University, Detroit, Michigan.

USGPO   U.S. Government Printing Office.

VFWNH   Veterans of Foreign Wars National Headquarters, Kansas City, Missouri.

WHS   Wisconsin Historical Society, Madison, Wisconsin.

NOTES

INTRODUCTION

1. See tables Bf196–211 and Ed297–310 in Susan B. Carter et al., eds., *Historical Statistics of the United States: Earliest Times to the Present*, Millennial Ed. (New York: Cambridge University Press, 2006), vols. 2 and 5.

2. Frank Mallen, *You've Got It Coming to You: The Guide for Families, Servicemen [and] Veterans* (New York: D. McKay, 1952).

3. Administrator of Veterans Affairs, *Annual Report for Fiscal Year Ending June 30 1949* (Washington, D.C.: USGPO, 1950), 1–4. The VA employed 200,000 persons in 1949, compared to 455,000 in the Post Office and 1.6 million in the military; see Department of Post Office, *Annual Report of the Postmaster General for the Fiscal Year Ended June 30 1949* (Washington, D.C.: USGPO, 1950), 18; tables Ed26–47 in Carter et al., *Historical Statistics of the United States*, vol. 5.

4. The number of veterans in civilian life grew from 4.2 million in 1940 to 16.6 million in 1945 and 22.5 million in 1960; see tables Ed245–61 in Carter et al., *Historical Statistics of the United States*. At their peak, veterans accounted for 13 percent of the population, compared with 5 percent for the interwar period and 8 percent after the Civil War. See Hugh Rockoff, "Veterans," in Carter et al., *Historical Statistics of the United States*, vol. 5, 343.

5. This figure was advanced by President Harry S. Truman in "Annual Budget Message to the Congress: Fiscal Year 1950," January 10, 1949, Gerhard Peters and John T. Woolley, The American Presidency Project, https://www.presidency.ucsb.edu/node/230146, accessed May 7, 2017. For an example of the "nation of veterans" trope, see "A Nation of Veterans," *New York Times*, June 9, 1953.

6. "The Spreading State of Welfare," *Fortune*, February 1952.

7. John E. Booth, "Veterans: Our Biggest Privileged Class," *Harper's Magazine*, July 1958.

8. Bernard M. Baruch to Ed. C. Johnson, chairman of the Senate subcommittee on Veterans' Legislation, November 21, 1945, in "Comparison of Veterans Benefits for World War Two" (1945).

9. Robert England, *Twenty Million World War Veterans* (Toronto: Oxford University Press, 1950), 6, 9.

10. U.S. General Accounting Office, "Disabled Veterans Programs: U.S. Eligibility and Benefit Types Compared with Five Other Countries," November 1993. The same point was made by a *New York Times* report nearly sixty years earlier; see "Veterans Relief: What Other Nations Do," *New York Times*, June 5, 1932.

11. There is no systematic comparison of veterans' spending in the United States with other countries, but one scholar makes this point for the interwar period; see David Reynolds, *The Long Shadow: The Legacies of the Great War in the Twentieth Century* (London: Simon & Schuster, 2013), 216.

12. See for instance Eveline M. Burns, *The American Social Security System* (Boston: Houghton Mifflin, 1949), 419–20; Lewis Meriam and Karl T. Schlotterbeck, *The Cost and Financing of*

Social Security (Washington, D.C.: Brookings Institution, 1950), 118–19; Committee on Federal Tax Policy, *Financing Defense: Can Expenditures Be Reduced?* 1951.

13. Roy V. Peel, "The 'Separateness' of the Veteran," *Annals of the American Academy of Political and Social Science* 238 (1945): 172.

14. Harry S. Truman, "The President's News Conference on the Budget," January 8, 1949, Peters and Woolley, American Presidency Project, https://www.presidency.ucsb.edu/node/230105, accessed May 7, 2017.

15. For "military caste," see U.S. Congress, Senate, Committee on Civil Service, *Preference in Employment of Honorably Discharged Veterans Where Federal Funds Are Disbursed*, Hearing, May 19 and 23, 1944 (Washington, D.C.: USGPO, 1944), 65. For "special privileges," see Peel, "The 'Separateness' of the Veteran," 167. For "professional patriots," see "The Moon on a Muffin," *Newsday*, Nassau ed., September 4, 1954.

16. For a representative use of the term "hero," see "Remarks by President Trump at the Veterans of Foreign Wars of the United States National Convention, Kansas City, MO," July 24, 2018, https://www.whitehouse.gov/briefings-statements/remarks-president-trump-veterans-foreign -wars-united-states-national-convention-kansas-city-mo/, accessed February 27, 2019. "Wounded Warrior" is the name of a charity for disabled post-9/11 veterans. For "fallen angels," see for instance Jane C. Timm, "Biden Defends His Telling of a Harrowing War Story after Report He Got Facts Wrong," *NBC News.com*, August 30, 2019, accessed January 15, 2020.

17. RAND Health, *"Current and Projected Characteristics and Unique Health Care Needs of the Patient Population Served by the Department of Veterans Affairs"* (Santa Monica, Calif.: RAND Corporation, 2015).

18. For an influential synthesis of the history of U.S. social policy that does not deal with veterans, see Michael Katz, *The Price of Citizenship: Redefining the American Welfare State* (Philadelphia: University of Pennsylvania Press, 2008). Scholarship on the U.S. welfare state is vast, but on the mid-twentieth century in particular, see Romain Huret, *The Experts' War on Poverty: Social Research and the Welfare Agenda in Postwar America*, trans. John Angell (Ithaca, N.Y.: Cornell University Press, 2018); Karen M. Tani, *States of Dependency: Welfare, Rights, and American Governance, 1935–1972* (New York: Cambridge University Press, 2016); Eva Bertram, *The Workfare State: Public Assistance Politics from the New Deal to the New Democrats* (Philadelphia: University of Pennsylvania Press, 2015); Jennifer Mittelstadt, *From Welfare to Workfare: The Unintended Consequences of Liberal Reform, 1945–1965* (Chapel Hill: University of North Carolina Press, 2005); Edwin Amenta, *Bold Relief: Institutional Politics and the Origins of Modern American Social Policy* (Princeton, N.J.: Princeton University Press, 1998); Suzanne Mettler, *Dividing Citizens: Gender and Federalism in New Deal Public Policy* (Ithaca, N.Y.: Cornell University Press, 1998).

19. On the GI Bill, see Sarah F. Rose, "The Right to a College Education? The GI Bill, Public Law 16, and Disabled Veterans," *Journal of Policy History* 24, no. 1 (2012): 26–52; Steven Rosales, "Fighting the Peace at Home: Mexican American Veterans and the 1944 GI Bill of Rights," *Pacific Historical Review* 80, no. 4 (November 2011): 597–627; Laura McEnaney, "Veterans' Welfare, the GI Bill and American Demobilization," *Journal of Law, Medicine and Ethics* 39, no. 1 (2011): 41–47; Kathleen Frydl, *The GI Bill* (Cambridge: Cambridge University Press, 2009); Glenn C. Altschuler and Stuart M. Blumin, *The GI Bill: A New Deal for Veterans* (Oxford: Oxford University Press, 2009); Edward Humes, *Over Here: How the GI Bill Transformed the American Dream* (Orlando: Harcourt, 2006); Margot Canaday, "Building a Straight State: Sexuality and Social Citizenship under the 1944 GI Bill," *Journal of American History* 90, no. 3 (December 2003): 935–57; Suzanne Mettler, *Soldiers to Citizens: The GI Bill and the Making of the Greatest Generation* (Oxford: Oxford University Press, 2005); David H. Onkst, "'First a Negro . . . Incidentally a Veteran': Black World

War Two Veterans and the G. I. Bill of Rights in the Deep South, 1944–1948," *Journal of Social History* 31, no. 3 (April 1998): 517–43; Daniel A. Clark, "'The Two Joes Meet—Joe College, Joe Veteran': The GI Bill, College Education, and Postwar American Culture," *History of Education Quarterly* 38, no. 2 (Summer 1998): 165–89; Theda Skocpol, "The GI Bill and U.S. Social Policy, Past and Future," *Social Philosophy and Policy* 14, no. 2 (1997): 95–115; Michael J. Bennett, *When Dreams Came True: The GI Bill and the Making of Modern America* (Washington, D.C.: Brassey's, 1996); Keith W. Olson, *The GI Bill, the Veterans, and the Colleges* (Lexington: University Press of Kentucky, 1974); Davis R. B. Ross, *Preparing for Ulysses: Politics and Veterans During World War II* (New York: Columbia University Press, 1969). For studies that do not focus on this piece of legislation, see Melinda Pash, "'A Veteran Does Not Have to Stay a Veteran Forever': Congress and the Korean GI Bill," in *Veterans' Policies, Veterans' Politics: New Perspectives on Veterans in the Modern United States*, ed. Stephen R. Ortiz (Gainesville: University Press of Florida, 2012), 222–40.

20. Peel, "The 'Separateness' of the Veteran," 171; Frydl, *The GI Bill*, 69.

21. Friedrich Hayek, *The Road to Serfdom* (Chicago: University of Chicago Press, 1944).

22. U.S. Congress, House, Committee on Veterans' Affairs, *1958 Legislative Programs of the Veterans of Foreign Wars, Disabled American Veterans, the American Legion, and AMVETS*, Hearing, February 4–5, 25, 1958 (Washington, D.C.: USGPO, 1958), 2433.

23. Charles Tilly and Sidney Tarrow, *Contentious Politics*, 2nd ed. (New York: Oxford University Press, 2015), 11.

24. Laura McEnaney, *Postwar: Waging Peace in Chicago* (Philadelphia: University of Pennsylvania Press, 2018); Robert Francis Saxe, *Settling Down: World War II Veterans' Challenge to the Postwar Consensus* (New York: Palgrave Macmillan, 2007); Michael D. Gambone, *The Greatest Generation Comes Home: The Veteran in American Society* (College Station: Texas A & M University Press, 2005); Jennifer E. Brooks, *Defining the Peace: World War II Veterans, Race, and the Remaking of Southern Political Tradition* (Chapel Hill: University of North Carolina Press, 2004); Mark D. Van Ells, *To Hear Only Thunder Again: America's World War II Veterans Come Home* (Lanham, Md.: Lexington Books, 2001).

25. The book that launched this myth is Tom Brokaw, *The Greatest Generation* (New York: Random House, 1998). For critical studies, see Kenneth D. Rose, *Myth and the Greatest Generation: A Social History of Americans in World War II* (New York: Routledge, 2008); Tom Childers, *Soldier from the War Returning: The Greatest Generation's Troubled Homecoming from World War II* (Boston: Houghton Mifflin Harcourt, 2009); John E. Bodnar, *The "Good War" in American Memory* (Baltimore: Johns Hopkins University Press, 2010), chap. 7.

26. Sidney M. Milkis and Daniel J. Tichenor, *Rivalry and Reform: Presidents, Social Movements, and the Transformation of American Politics* (Chicago: University of Chicago Press, 2018), 8.

27. See for instance James A. Thurber, "Dynamics of Policy Subsystems in American Politics," in *Interest Group Politics*, ed. Allan J. Cigler and Burdett A. Loomis, 3rd ed. (Washington, D.C.: CQ Press, 1991), 327; William G. Weissert and Carol S. Weissert, *Governing Health: The Politics of Health Policy*, 4th ed. (Baltimore: Johns Hopkins University Press, 2012), 152. For a different perspective, see Colin D. Moore, "Innovation without Reputation: How Bureaucrats Saved the Veterans' Health Care System," *Perspectives on Politics* 13, no. 2 (June 2015): 327–44.

28. On the NRA, see Scott Melzer, *Gun Crusaders: The NRA's Culture War* (New York: New York University Press, 2009).

29. I borrow this term from the work of historians such as Patrick J. Kelly, *Creating a National Home: Building the Veterans' Welfare State, 1860–1900* (Cambridge, Mass.: Harvard University Press, 1997); Rebecca Jo Plant and Frances M. Clarke, "'The Crowning Insult': Federal Segregation and the Gold Star Mother and Widow Pilgrimages of the Early 1930s," *Journal of American History*

102, no. 2 (September 2015): 406–32. Other scholars have used slightly different terms to refer to the same phenomenon, such as "veterans' exceptionalism" or "martial, or militaristic, patriotism"; see Frydl, *The GI Bill*, 8; Lucy E. Salyer, "Baptism by Fire: Race, Military Service, and U.S. Citizenship Policy, 1918–1935," *Journal of American History* 91, no. 3 (December 2004): 848.

30. Wallace Evan Davies, *Patriotism on Parade: The Story of Veterans' and Hereditary Organizations in America, 1783–1900* (Cambridge, Mass.: Harvard University Press, 1955), 160–63.

31. For an introduction to the vast scholarship on the relationship between gender, sexuality, race, and the U.S. military, see Kara Dixon Vuic, ed., *The Routledge History of War, Gender, and the Military* (New York: Routledge, 2018); Geoffrey Jensen, ed., *The Routledge Handbook of the History of Race and the American Military* (New York: Routledge/Taylor and Francis Group, 2016).

32. Allan Bérubé, *Coming Out Under Fire: The History of Gay Men and Women in World War Two* (New York: Free Press, 1990).

33. This number was arrived at by combining the white share of the total population (89 percent) with the share of men compared to women (49 percent) in 1950; see series A 23–28 in *Historical Statistics of the United States: Colonial Times to 1970*, Bicentennial Ed., part 1 (Washington, D.C.: USGPO, 1975), 9.

34. Robert O. Self, *All in the Family: The Realignment of American Democracy Since the 1960s* (New York: Hill and Wang, 2012).

35. William R. Spear, "The American Scene: 200 Organizations Bid for Favor of Veterans," *Stars and Stripes* (Western Europe, Paris ed.), June 29, 1945.

36. Sam Stavisky, "The Veterans Make Their Choice," *Harper's Magazine*, September 1946, 252.

37. The American Legion, *National Membership Record*, 2012, ALA; Herbert Molloy Mason, Jr., *VFW: Our First Century, 1899–1999* (Lenexa, Kans.: Addax, 1999), 142; Disabled American Veterans, *Wars and Scars: The Story of Compassion and Service for Our Nation's Disabled Veterans; A History of the Disabled American Veterans* (Cincinnati, Ohio: IPR Group American Printing, 2006), 31. The American Veterans Committee counted 100,000 members in 1947, but its membership quickly declined to only 20,000 after the onset of the Second Red Scare; see Saxe, *Settling Down*, chap. 4. The AMVETS approached 125,000 members in the mid-1950s; see Rodney G. Minott, *Peerless Patriots: Organized Veterans and the Spirit of Americanism* (Washington, D.C.: Public Affairs Press, 1962), 109.

38. The Legion maintains an archive of all internal correspondence and publications in its national headquarters in Indianapolis (the archives of its Auxiliary, still mostly untouched, are located in the city's suburbs). As of this project, the only archive available at the VFW National Headquarters in Kansas City, Mo., consists of the past issues of its national magazine. The DAV does not have its own archive, though the public library of Cincinnati and Hamilton County in Ohio has some past issues of its national magazine and the Cincinnati Historical Society has the papers of its founder, Robert S. Marx.

39. Eldon J. Eisenach, *The Lost Promise of Progressivism* (Lawrence: University Press of Kansas, 1994), 18.

40. In 1950 for instance, 63 percent of all VA employees had veterans' preference and 89 percent of male employees were veterans; see Administrator of Veterans Affairs, *Annual Report for Fiscal Year Ending June 30, 1950* (Washington, D.C.: USGPO, 1951), 124–25. On the relationship between the VA and veterans' groups, see Jack A. Underhill, "The Veteran's Administration and the American Legion (1945–1947)" (MA thesis, Columbia University, 1959).

41. "VA Clamps Down on Employees Holding Offices in Vets' Organizations," *ALM*, October 1955, 30.

42. Mallen, *You've Got It Coming to You*, 67–69; *Proceedings of the 32nd National Convention of the American Legion* (Washington, D.C.: USGPO, 1951), 96.

43. *Proceedings of the 25th National Convention of the American Legion* (Washington, D.C.: USGPO, 1944), 229.

44. On the Legion Contact program, see Matthew Cecil, *Branding Hoover's FBI: How the Boss's PR Men Sold the Bureau to America* (Lawrence: University Press of Kansas, 2016), 73–94; Athan Theoharis, "The FBI and the American Legion Contact Program, 1940–1966," *Political Science Quarterly* 100, no. 2 (July 1985): 271–86; Joanne M. Hepp, "Administrative Insubordination and Bureaucratic Principles: The Federal Bureau of Investigation's American Legion Contact Program" (MA thesis, Marquette University, 1985).

45. I borrow this formula from William J. Novak, "The Concept of the State in American History," in *Boundaries of the State in US History*, ed. James T. Sparrow, William J. Novak, and Stephen W. Sawyer (Chicago: University of Chicago Press, 2015), 325–49.

46. *Veterans in Our Society: Data on the Conditions of Military Service and on the Status of the Veteran*, 84 H. Prt. 261 (Washington, D.C.: USGPO, 1956), 115–18.

47. Melanie Martindale and Dudley L. Poston, "Variations in Veteran/Nonveteran Earnings Patterns Among World War II, Korea, and Vietnam War Cohorts," *Armed Forces and Society* 5, no. 2 (Winter 1979): 219–43; Alair MacLean and Meredith Kleykamp, "Generations of Veterans: Socioeconomic Attainment from World War II to the Contemporary Era," *Social Science History* 45, no. 1 (Spring 2021): 83–110.

48. RAND Health, "Current and Future Demographics of the Veteran Population," in *Current and Projected Characteristics*, 31–56.

49. The scholarship on gender and the welfare state is vast, but see for instance Mettler, *Dividing Citizens*; Gwendolyn Mink, *The Wages of Motherhood: Inequality in the Welfare State, 1917–1942* (Ithaca, N.Y.: Cornell University Press, 1995); Linda Gordon, *Pitied but Not Entitled: Single Mothers and the History of Welfare, 1890–1935* (New York: Free Press, 1994); Eileen Boris, *Home to Work: Motherhood and the Politics of Industrial Homework in the United States* (Cambridge: Cambridge University Press, 1994); Linda Gordon, "Social Insurance and Public Assistance: The Influence of Gender in Welfare Thought in the United States, 1890–1935," *American Historical Review* 97, no. 1 (1992): 19–54; Seth Koven and Sonya Michel, "Womanly Duties: Maternalist Politics and the Origins of Welfare States in France, Germany, Great Britain, and the United States, 1880–1920," *American Historical Review* 95, no. 4 (October 1990): 1076–108; Mimi Abramovitz, *Regulating the Lives of Women: Social Welfare Policy from Colonial Times to the Present* (Boston: South End Press, 1988).

50. On big business, see Colin Gordon, *New Deals: Business, Labor, and Politics in America, 1920–1935* (New York: Cambridge University Press, 1994); Gabriel Kolko, *The Triumph of Conservatism: A Re-interpretation of American History, 1900–1916* (New York: Free Press of Glencoe, 1963); Robert H. Wiebe, *Businessmen and Reform: A Study of the Progressive Movement* (Cambridge, Mass.: Harvard University Press, 1962). On farmers, see Adam D. Sheingate, *The Rise of the Agricultural Welfare State: Institutions and Interest Group Power in the United States, France, and Japan* (Princeton, N.J.: Princeton University Press, 2001); Elizabeth Sanders, *Roots of Reform: Farmers, Workers, and the American State, 1877–1917* (Chicago: University of Chicago Press, 1999); John Mark Hansen, *Gaining Access: Congress and the Farm Lobby, 1919–1981* (Chicago: University of Chicago Press, 1991).

51. This nonpartisanship was a departure from the late nineteenth century, when the Grand Army of the Republic acted largely as a subsidiary of the Republican Party. On the GAR, see Stuart Charles McConnell, *Glorious Contentment: The Grand Army of the Republic, 1865–1900* (Chapel Hill: University of North Carolina Press, 1992).

52. On the need to move beyond this binary opposition, see Matthew D. Lassiter, "Political History Beyond the Red-Blue Divide," *Journal of American History* 98, no. 3 (December 2011): 760–64; Brian Balogh, *The Associational State: American Governance in the Twentieth Century* (Philadelphia: University of Pennsylvania Press, 2015); Brent Cebul, Mason B. Williams, and Lily Geismer, eds., *Shaped by the State: Toward a New Political History of the Twentieth Century* (Chicago: University of Chicago Press, 2019).

53. For an introduction to the scholarship on the "carceral state," see the June 2015 issue of the *Journal of American History* (102, no. 1). On the "racial state," see Peggy Pascoe, *What Comes Naturally: Miscegenation Law and the Making of Race in America* (Oxford: Oxford University Press, 2009). On the "warfare state," see Marc Allen Eisner, *From Warfare State to Welfare State: World War I, Compensatory State Building, and the Limits of the Modern Order* (University Park: Pennsylvania State University Press, 2000); James T. Sparrow, *Warfare State: World War II Americans and the Age of Big Government* (New York: Oxford University Press, 2011). On the "straight state," see Margot Canaday, *The Straight State: Sexuality and Citizenship in Twentieth-Century America* (Princeton, N.J.: Princeton University Press, 2009).

54. *Veterans in Our Society: Data on the Conditions of Military Service and on the Status of the Veteran*, 84 H. Prt. 261 (Washington, D.C.: USGPO, 1956), 134.

55. The membership of the Legion, for instance, doubled from 1.6 million in 1945 to almost 3.3 million in 1946, but then experienced a slight decline and remained around 2.7 million for the rest of the 1940s and 1950s. See American Legion, *National Membership Record*, 2012, ALA.

56. *Veterans in Our Society*, 122.

57. On the approach of veterans' groups to race, see Robert F. Jefferson, "'Enabled Courage': Race, Disability, and Black World War II Veterans in Postwar America," *The Historian*, no. 65 (2003): 1120.

58. On the VFW, see Mason, *VFW*, 149.

59. On the attitude of the Legion's official publications toward race and gender, see Steven Trout, *On the Battlefield of Memory: The First World War and American Remembrance, 1919–1941* (Tuscaloosa: University of Alabama Press, 2010), 91–99.

60. Richard Rothstein, *The Color of Law: A Forgotten History of How Our Government Segregated America* (New York: Liveright, 2017), xi.

61. Linda K. Kerber, *No Constitutional Right to Be Ladies: Women and the Obligations of Citizenship* (New York: Hill and Wang, 1998), 221–302.

62. Ira Katznelson, *When Affirmative Action Was White: An Untold History of Racial Inequality in Twentieth-Century America* (New York: W. W. Norton, 2005).

63. Peel, "The 'Separateness' of the Veteran," 172.

64. Henry Ramos, *The American GI Forum: In Pursuit of the Dream, 1948–1983* (Houston: Arte Publico Press, 1998); Maggie Rivas-Rodriguez and B. V. Olguín, eds., *Latina/os and World War II: Mobility, Agency, and Ideology* (Austin: University of Texas Press, 2014); Rosales, "Fighting the Peace at Home."

65. On African Americans, see Thomas A. Guglielmo, "A Martial Freedom Movement: Black GIs' Political Struggles During World War II," *Journal of American History* 104, no. 4 (March 2018): 879–903; Kimberley L. Phillips, *War! What Is It Good for? Black Freedom Struggles and the U.S. Military from World War II to Iraq* (Chapel Hill: University of North Carolina Press, 2012); Christopher S. Parker, *Fighting for Democracy: Black Veterans and the Struggle Against White Supremacy in the Postwar South* (Princeton, N.J.: Princeton University Press, 2009); Onkst, "First a Negro . . . Incidentally a Veteran"; Chad Louis Williams, *Torchbearers of Democracy: African American Soldiers in the World War I Era* (Chapel Hill: University of North Carolina Press, 2010); Adriane

Danette Lentz-Smith, *Freedom Struggles: African Americans and World War I* (Cambridge, Mass.: Harvard University Press, 2009); Salyer, "Baptism by Fire." On Native Americans, see Thomas Grillot, *First Americans: U.S. Patriotism in Indian Country After World War I* (New Haven, Conn.: Yale University Press, 2018). On Asian Americans, see Salyer, "Baptism by Fire."

66. Edwin Amenta, "How to Analyze the Influence of Movements," *Contemporary Sociology* 43, no. 1 (2014): 16–29.

67. On veterans in Japan and Germany in the twentieth century, see Lee Pennington, *Casualties of History: Wounded Japanese Servicemen and the Second World War* (Ithaca, N.Y.: Cornell University Press, 2015); Deborah Cohen, *The War Come Home: Disabled Veterans in Britain and Germany, 1914–1939* (Berkeley: University of California Press, 2001); Jay Lockenour, *Soldiers as Citizens: Former Wehrmacht Officers in the Federal Republic of Germany, 1945–1955* (Lincoln: University of Nebraska Press, 2001); James M. Diehl, *The Thanks of the Fatherland: German Veterans After the Second World War* (Chapel Hill: University of North Carolina Press, 1993); James M. Diehl, "Victors or Victims? Disabled Veterans in the Third Reich," *Journal of Modern History* 59, no. 4 (1987): 705–36.

68. On the veterans' movement in the Vietnam era, see Mark Boulton, *Failing Our Veterans: The GI Bill and the Vietnam Generation* (New York: New York University Press, 2014); Gerald Nicosia, *Home to War: A History of the Vietnam Veterans' Movement* (New York: Crown, 2001).

69. On this same point, see Herbert Obinger et al., "War and Welfare States Before and After 1945: Conclusions and Perspectives," in *Warfare and Welfare: Military Conflict and Welfare State Development in Western Countries*, ed. Herbert Obinger, Klaus Petersen, and Peter Starke (Oxford: Oxford University Press, 2018), 430.

70. "Some Assorted Eggheads," *New Republic,* May 14, 1956, 5.

71. Political scientist James Q. Wilson described this situation as "client politics"; see James Q. Wilson, "The Politics of Regulation," in *The Politics of Regulation*, ed. Wilson (New York: Basic Books, 1980), 369.

72. Paul Pierson, "Increasing Returns, Path Dependence, and the Study of Politics," *American Political Science Review* 94, no. 2 (June 2000): 251–67.

73. On veterans' welfare state prior to the Civil War, see Laura Jensen, *Patriots, Settlers, and the Origins of American Social Policy* (Cambridge: Cambridge University Press, 2003); Emily J. Teipe, *America's First Veterans and the Revolutionary War Pensions* (Lewiston, N.Y.: E. Mellen Press, 2002); John Phillips Resch, *Suffering Soldiers: Revolutionary War Veterans, Moral Sentiment, and Political Culture in the Early Republic* (Amherst: University of Massachusetts Press, 1999); James Warren Oberly, *Sixty Million Acres: American Veterans and the Public Lands Before the Civil War* (Kent, Ohio: Kent State University Press, 1990); James Warren Oberly, "Gray-Haired Lobbyists: War of 1812 Veterans and the Politics of Bounty Land Grants," *Journal of the Early Republic* 5, no. 1 (Spring 1985): 35–58; Minott, *Peerless Patriots*; Davies, *Patriotism on Parade*. On the post–Civil War period, see Peter Blanck and Larry M. Logue, *Heavy Laden: Union Veterans, Psychological Illness, and Suicide* (New York: Cambridge University Press, 2018); Dale Kretz, "Pensions and Protest: Former Slaves and the Reconstructed American State," *Journal of the Civil War Era* 7, no. 3 (September 2017): 425–45; Brian Matthew Jordan, *Marching Home: Union Veterans and Their Unending Civil War* (New York: Liveright, 2014); James Alan Marten, *Sing Not War: The Lives of Union and Confederate Veterans in Gilded Age America* (Chapel Hill: University of North Carolina Press, 2011); Russell L. Johnson, "'Great Injustice': Social Status and the Distribution of Military Pensions After the Civil War," *Journal of the Gilded Age and Progressive Era* 10, no. 2 (2011): 137–60; Barbara A. Gannon, *The Won Cause: Black and White Comradeship in the Grand Army of the Republic* (Chapel Hill: University of North Carolina Press, 2011); Larry M. Logue and Peter David Blanck, *Race,*

Ethnicity, and Disability: Veterans and Benefits in Post–Civil War America (New York: Cambridge University Press, 2010); Donald Robert Shaffer, *After the Glory: The Struggles of Black Civil War Veterans* (Lawrence: University Press of Kansas, 2004); Kelly, *Creating a National Home*; Megan J. McClintock, "Civil War Pensions and the Reconstruction of Union Families," *Journal of American History* 83, no. 2 (September 1996): 456–80; Theda Skocpol, *Protecting Soldiers and Mothers: The Political Origins of Social Policy in the United States* (Cambridge, Mass.: Belknap Press of Harvard University Press, 1992).

74. For overviews of the legal and political framework of veterans' benefits across U.S. history, see James D. Ridgway, "Recovering an Institutional Memory: The Origins of the Modern Veterans Benefits System, 1914 to 1958," *Veterans Law Review* 5, no. 1 (2013): 1–55; James D. Ridgway, "Caring for Those Who Have Borne the Battle: Exploring the Myths and Realities of Veterans' Benefits Since the Revolution," *Journal of the Federal Circuit Historical Society* 6 (2012): 73–88; James D. Ridgway, "The Splendid Isolation Revisited: Lessons from the History of Veterans Benefits Before Judicial Review," *Veterans Law Review* 3 (2011): 135–219.

75. Prior to 1946, veterans' bills fell under the responsibility of four different committees, not all of them veteran focused: the Committee on Pensions, the Committee on Invalid Pensions, the Ways and Means Committee (in charge of all financial matters), and the Committee on World War Veterans' Legislation (created in 1924 to handle all bills related to World War I veterans, and to World War II veterans after January 1944). See Donnald K. Anderson (dir.), *Guide to the Records of the United States House of Representatives at the National Archives, 1789–1989* (Washington, D.C.: USGPO, 1989), 269. The U.S. Senate did not have its own committee on veterans' affairs until 1970.

76. On the "shadow of war," see Michael S. Sherry, *In the Shadow of War: The United States Since the 1930's* (New Haven, Conn.: Yale University Press, 1995).

77. On war in American culture, see George Hutchinson, *Facing the Abyss: American Literature and Culture in the 1940s* (New York: Columbia University Press, 2018), chap. 4; Sherry, *In the Shadow of War*. On veterans and film noir, see Saxe, *Settling Down*, chap. 3. On veterans in postwar U.S. culture, see Andrew J. Huebner, *The Warrior Image: Soldiers in American Culture from the Second World War to the Vietnam Era* (Chapel Hill: University of North Carolina Press, 2008), chaps. 2–3.

78. Justin Gray and Victor H. Bernstein, *The Inside Story of the Legion* (New York: Boni & Gaer, 1948), 99.

79. The poll asked respondents to select the groups whose "ideas" they would "expect to be good on candidates running for office." See Elmo Roper, "Roper Study Indicates Role of Groups in Swaying Voters," *New York Herald Tribune*, May 19, 1952.

80. On the militarization of U.S. state building as a result of World War II and the Cold War, see Bartholomew H. Sparrow, *From the Outside In: World War II and the American State* (Princeton, N.J.: Princeton University Press, 1996); J. Sparrow, *Warfare State*; Frydl, *The GI Bill*, 370–71; Gary Gerstle, *Liberty and Coercion: The Paradox of American Government from the Founding to the Present* (Princeton, N.J.: Princeton University Press, 2015), chap. 8 (the share of federal spending on national defense is quoted on 256).

CHAPTER 1

1. See for instance "Analysis of The American Legion's fight against the recommendations of The Hoover Commission on veterans affairs, February 1950," United States, Reorganization (inc. Hoover Plan), A–Z, ALA.

2. "Legion Declares War," *Taylor Topics* (Chicago), February 1950, United States, Reorganization (inc. Hoover Plan).

3. Jennifer D. Keene, *Doughboys, the Great War, and the Remaking of America* (Baltimore: Johns Hopkins University Press, 2001), epilogue.

4. John M. Kinder, *Paying with Their Bodies: American War and the Problem of the Disabled Veteran* (Chicago: University of Chicago Press, 2015), 180.

5. K. Walter Hickel, "War, Region, and Social Welfare: Federal Aid to Servicemen's Dependents in the South, 1917–1921," *Journal of American History* 87, no. 4 (March 2001): 1362–91.

6. Jennifer Keene, "The Long Journey Home: Federal Veterans' Policy and African-American Veterans of WWI," in *Veterans' Policies, Veterans' Politics: New Perspectives on Veterans in the Modern United States*, ed. Stephen Ortiz (Gainesville: University Press of Florida, 2012), 146–70.

7. See James Alan Marten, *Sing Not War: The Lives of Union and Confederate Veterans in Gilded Age America* (Chapel Hill: University of North Carolina Press, 2011), 14–15; Bernard Rostker, *Providing for the Casualties of War: The American Experience Through World War II* (Santa Monica, Calif.: RAND Corporation, 2013), 101–2.

8. See table I in John F. Miller, "Veteran Preference in the Public Service," in *Problems of the American Public Service*, by Carl Joachim Friedrich et al. (New York: McGraw-Hill, 1935), 276–77.

9. Laura Jensen, *Patriots, Settlers, and the Origins of American Social Policy* (Cambridge: Cambridge University Press, 2003), 213–14.

10. Green B. Raum, "Pensions and Patriotism," *North American Review* 153 (August 1891): 211.

11. Amy E. Holmes, "'Such Is the Price We Pay': American Widows and the Civil War Pension System," in *Toward a Social History of the American Civil War*, ed. Maris Vinovskis (Cambridge: Cambridge University Press, 1990), 172.

12. Richard White, *The Republic for Which It Stands: The United States During Reconstruction and the Gilded Age, 1865–1896* (New York: Oxford University Press, 2017), 28.

13. Marten, *Sing Not War*, 240–41.

14. For the cost, see table Ed298–308 in Susan B. Carter et al., eds., *Historical Statistics of the United States: Earliest Times to the Present*, Millennial Ed. (New York: Cambridge University Press, 2006), vol. 5. For the percentage, see Theda Skocpol, *Protecting Soldiers and Mothers: The Political Origins of Social Policy in the United States* (Cambridge, Mass.: Belknap Press of Harvard University Press, 1992), 65.

15. Isaac M. Rubinow, *Social Insurance: With Special Reference to American Conditions* (New York: H. Holt, 1913), 404.

16. William Pyrle Dillingham, *Federal Aid to Veterans, 1917–1941* (Gainesville: University of Florida Press, 1952), 186.

17. Beth Linker, *War's Waste: Rehabilitation in World War I America* (Chicago: University of Chicago Press, 2011), chap. 1.

18. For a helpful summary of Progressive critiques of the Civil War pension system, see Dale Kretz, "Pensions and Protest: Former Slaves and the Reconstructed American State," *Journal of the Civil War Era* 7, no. 3 (September 2017): 426–27.

19. William Henry Glasson, *Federal Military Pensions in the United States* (New York: Oxford University Press, 1918), 265–66.

20. Quoted in Marten, *Sing Not War*, 214; Stuart Charles McConnell, *Glorious Contentment: The Grand Army of the Republic, 1865–1900* (Chapel Hill: University of North Carolina Press, 1992), 160; Wallace Evan Davies, *Patriotism on Parade: The Story of Veterans' and Hereditary Organizations in America, 1783–1900* (Cambridge, Mass.: Harvard University Press, 1955), 161.

21. Skocpol, *Protecting Soldiers and Mothers*, 128–29.

22. Kinder, *Paying with Their Bodies*, 122–23, 167.

23. Quoted in John F. Cogan, *The High Cost of Good Intentions: A History of U.S. Federal Entitlement Programs* (Stanford, Calif.: Stanford University Press, 2017), 58.

24. Quoted in Paul H. Douglas, "The War Risk Insurance Act," *Journal of Political Economy* 26, no. 5 (May 1918): 463.

25. James D. Ridgway, "The Splendid Isolation Revisited: Lessons from the History of Veterans Benefits Before Judicial Review," *Veterans Law Review* 3 (2011): 170.

26. Samuel McCune Lindsay, "Purpose and Scope of War Risk Insurance," *Annals of the American Academy of Political and Social Science* 79 (1918): 60–61.

27. McConnell, *Glorious Contentment*; "Final G.A.R. Parade," *Washington Post*, September 4, 1914.

28. Herbert Molloy Mason, Jr., *VFW: Our First Century, 1899–1999* (Lenexa, Kans.: Addax, 1999), 142.

29. William Pencak, *For God and Country: The American Legion, 1919–1941* (Boston: Northeastern University Press, 1989), 49–51.

30. Pencak, *For God and Country*, 37–41.

31. Pencak, *For God and Country*, 62.

32. *American Legion Weekly*, July 11, 1919, ALA.

33. Pencak, *For God and Country*, 49.

34. Pencak, *For God and Country*, 30.

35. Mason, *VFW*, 142.

36. Stephen R. Ortiz, *Beyond the Bonus March and GI Bill: How Veteran Politics Shaped the New Deal Era* (New York: New York University Press, 2010), 16–21.

37. Jessica L. Adler, *Burdens of War: Creating the United States Veterans Health System* (Baltimore: Johns Hopkins University Press, 2017), 127–36.

38. On the Auxiliary, see Pencak, *For God and Country*, 296–301; Belle Zeller, *Pressure Politics in New York: A Study of Group Representation Before the Legislature* (New York: Prentice-Hall, 1937), 204–9.

39. Donald Robert Shaffer, *After the Glory: The Struggles of Black Civil War Veterans* (Lawrence: University Press of Kansas, 2004), chap. 6; American Civil Liberties Union, "Race Practices of National Associations," September 1945, Americanism, Tolerance, Segregation, ALA.

40. Equal Justice Initiative, "Lynching in America: Targeting Black Veterans," (Montgomery, Al., 2017); Rebecca Jo Plant and Frances M. Clarke, "'The Crowning Insult': Federal Segregation and the Gold Star Mother and Widow Pilgrimages of the Early 1930s," *Journal of American History* 102, no. 2 (September 2015): 406–32; Chad Louis Williams, *Torchbearers of Democracy: African American Soldiers in the World War I Era* (Chapel Hill: University of North Carolina Press, 2010); Adriane Danette Lentz-Smith, *Freedom Struggles: African Americans and World War I* (Cambridge, Mass.: Harvard University Press, 2009).

41. Pete Daniel, "Black Power in the 1920s: The Case of Tuskegee Veterans Hospital," *Journal of Southern History* 36, no. 3 (1970): 368–88.

42. On the number of black Legionnaires, see Thomas B. Littlewood, *Soldiers Back Home: The American Legion in Illinois, 1919–1939* (Carbondale: Southern Illinois University Press, 2004), 79. On race in the Legion's publications, see Steven Trout, *On the Battlefield of Memory: The First World War and American Remembrance, 1919–1941* (Tuscaloosa: University of Alabama Press, 2010), 91–98.

43. Robert Weldon Whalen, *Bitter Wounds: German Victims of the Great War, 1914–1939* (Ithaca, N.Y.: Cornell University Press, 1984), 162; John N. Horne, "The Living," in *The Cambridge*

History of the First World War, ed. Jay Winter, vol. 3 (Cambridge: Cambridge University Press, 2013), 598.

44. Elizabeth Cobbs Hoffman, *The Hello Girls: America's First Women Soldiers* (Cambridge, Mass.: Harvard University Press, 2017).

45. Mason, *VFW*, 65.

46. Richard Seelye Jones, "The Legion: As We Were," *American Legion Magazine*, May 1947, 41.

47. On the structure of the VFW and the DAV, see George T. Trial, "The American Veterans of Foreign Service and the Veterans of Foreign Wars," *Ohio Archeological and Historical Quarterly* 57, no. 1 (1948): 79–93; Disabled American Veterans, *Wars and Scars: The Story of Compassion and Service for Our Nation's Disabled Veterans: A History of the Disabled American Veterans*, (Cincinnati, Ohio: IPR Group American Printing, 2006), chap. 2.

48. Pencak, *For God and Country*, chap. 4.

49. Littlewood, *Soldiers Back Home*, 32–33.

50. Trial, "The American Veterans of Foreign Service and the Veterans of Foreign Wars," 92.

51. Adam Laats, *The Other School Reformers: Conservative Activism in American Education* (Cambridge, Mass.: Harvard University Press, 2015), 86–95.

52. Dixon Wecter, *When Johnny Comes Marching Home* (Boston: Houghton Mifflin, 1944), 438–39.

53. On the Legion's local activities, see Pencak, *For God and Country*, chap. 10.

54. E. Pendleton Herring, "Scotching the Veterans' Lobby," *North American Review* 236, no. 1 (1933): 51, 54; Pencak, *For God and Country*, 185–87.

55. Pencak, *For God and Country*, chap. 4. For data on the group's membership, see the American Legion, *National Membership Record*, 2012, ALA.

56. "For God, for Country, for Bonus," *Time*, January 21, 1935, 20; Pencak, *For God and Country*, 117–20.

57. William Allen White, *Politics: The Citizen's Business* (New York: Arno Press, 1974), 14–15.

58. John C. Sparrow, *History of Personnel Demobilization in the United States Army* (Washington, D.C.: Department of the Army, 1951), 16.

59. Kinder, *Paying with Their Bodies*, 96.

60. Wecter, *When Johnny Comes Marching Home*, 471.

61. Sparrow, *History of Personnel Demobilization*, 11.

62. Douglas, "The War Risk Insurance Act," 481.

63. Rostker, *Providing for the Casualties of War*, 161–62.

64. Adler, *Burdens of War*, chap. 2.

65. Pencak, *For God and Country*, 178.

66. Rosemary Stevens, *A Time of Scandal: Charles R. Forbes, Warren G. Harding, and the Making of the Veterans Bureau* (Baltimore: Johns Hopkins University Press, 2016), 43; Adler, *Burdens of War*, 164–65.

67. Adler, *Burdens of War*, 158, 162–70; Rosemary A. Stevens, "The Invention, Stumbling, and Reinvention of the Modern U.S. Veterans Health Care System, 1918–1924," in Ortiz, *Veterans' Policies, Veterans' Politics*, 38–62.

68. *Annual Report of the Director of the United States Veterans' Bureau for the Fiscal Year ended June 30, 1922* (Washington, D.C.: USGPO, 1922), 2.

69. Adler, *Burdens of War*, 170–71.

70. Adler, *Burdens of War*, 175.

71. Pencak, *For God and Country*, 185; Mason, *VFW*, 60.

72. See tables Ed297–310 and Bf196–211 in Carter et al., *Historical Statistics of the United States*, vols. 2 and 5.

73. *Annual Report of the Administrator of Veterans' Affairs for the Fiscal Year Ended June 30, 1941* (Washington, D.C.: USGPO, 1941), 49.

74. See table Ed337–50 in Carter et al., *Historical Statistics of the United States*, vol. 5.

75. On Rankin, see Kenneth W. Vickers, "John Rankin: Democrat and Demagogue" (MA thesis, Mississippi State University, 1993).

76. Quoted in Glenn C. Altschuler and Stuart M. Blumin, *The GI Bill: A New Deal for Veterans* (Oxford: Oxford University Press, 2009), 62.

77. Quoted in Davis R. B. Ross, *Preparing for Ulysses: Politics and Veterans During World War II* (New York: Columbia University Press, 1969), 22.

78. U.S. Congress, House, Committee on Un-American Activities, *Investigation of Un-American Propaganda Activities in the United States*, Hearing, March 24–28, 1947 (Washington, D.C.: USGPO, 1947), 5, 7.

79. Herbert Hoover, "The President's News Conference," July 8, 1930, Gerhard Peters and John T. Woolley, The American Presidency Project, https://www.presidency.ucsb.edu/node /211005, accessed May 7, 2017; Ridgway, "The Splendid Isolation Revisited," 175.

80. See for instance Hugh Jedell, "Germany," *New York Times*, June 5, 1932; P. J. Philip, "France," *New York Times*, June 5, 1932.

81. "Veterans Relief: What Other Nations Do," *New York Times*, June 5, 1932.

82. France granted a small old-age pension to all World War I veterans in 1930 over the age of fifty, with an increase at fifty-five, see Antoine Prost, *In the Wake of War: Les Anciens Combattants and French Society* (Oxford: Berg, 1992), 38.

83. "Text of President's Declaration on the Bonus in His Budget Message Sent to Congress," *New York Times*, December 11, 1923.

84. Sidney Howard, "Our Professional Patriots: II. Patriotic Perils," *New Republic*, September 3, 1924, 12–16; Sidney Howard, "Our Professional Patriots: IV. The Patriots and the Peace Seekers," *New Republic*, September 17, 1924, 71–75.

85. Quoted in Brooke Lindy Blower, *Becoming Americans in Paris: Transatlantic Politics and Culture Between the World Wars* (New York: Oxford University Press, 2011), 183.

86. Kinder, *Paying with Their Bodies*, 176.

87. National Industrial Conference Board, *The World War Veterans and the Federal Treasury* (New York: National Industrial Conference Board, 1932), 1–2.

88. Quoted in American Medical Association, *Medical and Hospital Care of Veterans with Non-Service-Connected Disabilities: A Review of American Medical Association Policy* (Chicago: AMA, 1953), 61. See also Adler, *Burdens of War*, chap. 7.

89. Ortiz, *Beyond the Bonus March and GI Bill*, 75.

90. Ross, *Preparing for Ulysses*, 26; Ortiz, *Beyond the Bonus March*, 75; Rostker, *Providing for the Casualties of War*, 171.

91. Herring, "Scotching the Veterans' Lobby," 48.

92. Ross, *Preparing for Ulysses*, 27–28; Ortiz, *Beyond the Bonus March*, chap. 3.

93. Ross, *Preparing for Ulysses*, 28.

94. See tables Ed297–310 and Ed337–50 in Carter et al., *Historical Statistics of the United States*, vol. 5.

95. Rostker, *Providing for the Casualties of War*, 171.

96. Keene, *Doughboys, the Great War, and the Remaking of America*, 201–2.

97. Richard Polenberg, *Reorganizing Roosevelt's Government, 1936–1939: The Controversy over Executive Reorganization* (Cambridge, Mass.: Harvard University Press, 1966), 80–81.

98. Kinder, *Paying with Their Bodies*, 180.

99. Frederic Galbraith, "Men and Women of the Legion," *American Legion Weekly*, June 17, 1921, 5, ALA; emphasis added.

100. Kinder, *Paying with Their Bodies*, 100.

101. Pencak, *For God and Country*, 74–75, 83–84, 197; Kinder, *Paying with Their Bodies*, 181.

102. Quoted in Keene, *Doughboys, the Great War, and the Remaking of America*, 174.

103. For an example of this critique, see William Gellermann, *The American Legion as Educator* (New York: Teachers College, Columbia University, 1938).

104. Pencak, *For God and Country*, 199–200.

105. Anne L. Alstott and Ben Novick, "War, Taxes, and Income Redistribution in the Twenties: The 1924 Veterans' Bonus and the Defeat of the Mellon Plan," *Tax Law Review* 59, no. 4 (Summer 2006): 373–438.

106. For the estimate of veterans eligible, see "Nearly 3,500,000 to Get Cash or Policy: Estimate," *Daily Boston Globe*, May 20, 1924. For the estimate of total cost, see "Text of President's Declaration."

107. See tables Ea10–23 in Carter et al., *Historical Statistics of the United States*, vol. 5.

108. Keene, *Doughboys, the Great War, and the Remaking of America*, 181.

109. Pencak, *For God and Country*, 200–202.

110. Ortiz, *Beyond the Bonus March*, chap. 2.

111. On the Bonus March of 1932, see Roger Daniels, *The Bonus March: An Episode of the Great Depression* (Westport, Conn.: Greenwood, 1971); Donald J. Lisio, *The President and Protest: Hoover, Conspiracy, and the Bonus Riot* (Columbia: University of Missouri Press, 1974); Paul Dickson and Thomas B. Allen, *The Bonus Army: An American Epic* (New York: Walker, 2004); Lucy G. Barber, *Marching on Washington: The Forging of an American Political Tradition* (Berkeley: University of California Press, 2002), chap. 2; Ortiz, *Beyond the Bonus March*.

112. Andrea Louise Campbell, *How Policies Make Citizens: Senior Political Activism and the American Welfare State* (Princeton, N.J.: Princeton University Press, 2005).

113. Franklin D. Roosevelt, "Veto of the Bonus Bill," May 22, 1935, Peters and Woolley, The American Presidency Project, https://www.presidency.ucsb.edu/node/208686, accessed May 7, 2017.

114. Ortiz, *Beyond the Bonus March*, chaps. 4–6.

115. Chris Rasmussen, "'This Thing Has Ceased to Be a Joke': The Veterans of Future Wars and the Meanings of Political Satire in the 1930s," *Journal of American History* 103, no. 1 (June 2016): 84–106; Donald W. Whisenhunt, *Veterans of Future Wars: A Study in Student Activism* (Lanham, Md.: Lexington Books, 2011).

116. Dr. George Gallup, "56% Oppose Paying Widows of Veterans: Many Who Favor Pensions Are Unwilling to Have Taxes Increased in Order to Pay Them," *Washington Post*, February 27, 1938.

117. *Annual Report of the Administrator of Veterans' Affairs for the Fiscal Year Ended June 30, 1941*, 8, 11, 20–21.

118. Keene, *Doughboys, the Great War, and the Remaking of America*, 211.

CHAPTER 2

1. U.S. Congress, Senate, Committee on Finance, Subcommittee on Veterans Legislation, *Increased Benefits for World War Veterans and Their Dependents; Miscellaneous Legislation Relating to Administration of the Veterans' Administration*, Hearing, November 27, 1941 (Washington, D.C.: USGPO, 1941).

2. "Pensions Again," *Time*, December 8, 1941.

3. "Veterans' Pension Grab," *New York Times*, November 26, 1941.

4. "The Veterans' War Against the Treasury," *Reader's Digest*, May 1940.

5. In May 1940, 49 percent of respondents to a Gallup poll disagreed that the widow and children of a World War I veteran who had died of a cause not related to the war should receive a pension, compared to 40 percent who agreed and 11 percent who were without opinion; see Gallup Poll, May 1940: "When a World War veteran dies from causes not connected with the war, should his widow and children be given a pensions by the government?," USGALLUP.40–196.QKT18A, Gallup Organization; Cornell University, Ithaca, N.Y.: Roper Center for Public Opinion Research, iPOLL, accessed June 1, 2017.

6. *Digest of Minutes, National Executive Committee Meeting, November 6–7, 1941*, 52–55, ALA.

7. *Digest of Minutes, Annual Conference of Department Commanders and Department Adjutants, November 15, 16, 17, 1943*, 48, ALA.

8. James T. Sparrow, *Warfare State: World War II Americans and the Age of Big Government* (New York: Oxford University Press, 2011).

9. On the liberal and conservative memories of the GI Bill, see Kathleen Frydl, *The GI Bill* (Cambridge: Cambridge University Press, 2009), 1–12.

10. "Thanks to Hitler," *Foreign Service*, June 1940, 3.

11. Richard Seelye Jones, *A History of the American Legion* (Indianapolis: Bobbs-Merrill, 1946), 60–105.

12. On this program, see Introduction, note 44.

13. Christopher W. Griffin, "Veterans at War: The American Legion and Civilian Mobilization in World War II" (PhD dissertation, Florida State University, 2012).

14. Griffin, "Veterans at War," 21–62.

15. "Varied Groups in D.C. Pledge Loyalty to U.S., President," *Washington Post*, December 8, 1941.

16. Eugene Casey, "Memorandum to the President," October 7, 1943, box 4, folder: American Legion, 1943–45, Official File 64, FDR.

17. *Proceedings of the 25th National Convention of the American Legion* (Washington, D.C.: USGPO, 1944), 229.

18. Operations Letter No. 33, *Foreign Service*, June 1942, 25; "1,000 Pints of Blood," *Foreign Service*, July 1944, 14.

19. National Publicity Division, "Suggested General Address for American Legion Speakers on the Legion's War Contribution," n.d., box 4, Folder: American Legion, 1943–45, Official File 64, FDR.

20. For details, see Edgar I. (Ed) Jersild, "Memorandum to: County Commanders, Post Commanders, Pre-military Training Section," December 20, 1942, box 4, folder: General Files—November–December–Undated, 1942, Records of the Wisconsin American Legion, WHS.

21. *Proceedings of the 25th National Convention*, 229; Paul G. Armstrong, "Numbers by the Fishbowl," *ALM*, October 1941. On the Legion and Selective Service, see George Q. Flynn, *The Draft, 1940–1973* (Lawrence: University Press of Kansas, 1993), 24, 29.

22. Robert J. Havighurst et al., *The American Veteran Back Home: A Study of Veteran Readjustment* (New York: Longmans, Green, 1951), 19.

23. *Proceedings of the 26th National Convention of the American Legion* (Washington, D.C.: USGPO, 1945), 185.

24. Griffin, "Veterans at War," 149–54.

25. Havighurst et al., *The American Veteran Back Home*, 61–62.

26. "Need 10 Million Books for the Armed Forces," *Foreign Service*, January 1943, 30.

27. National Publicity Division, "For Immediate Release," May 2, 1942, reel: 95–1060, Administration and Organization, Membership, World War II Veterans, A-Z, ALA (reel 95–1060, ALA hereafter).

28. DGG to [Ralph B.] Gregg and [Frank] Samuel, n.d. (ca. January 28, 1942), reel 95–1060, ALA.

29. Lynn U. Stambaugh, "Memorandum to Members of NEC ... ," March 13, 1942, reel 95–1060, ALA.

30. William Pencak, *For God and Country: The American Legion, 1919–1941* (Boston: Northeastern University Press, 1989), 307.

31. "Resolution, May 1st 1942," reel 95–1060, ALA.

32. Richard Seelye Jones, "The Legion: As We Are," *ALM*, June 1947.

33. Table Ed245–261 in Susan B. Carter et al., eds., *Historical Statistics of the United States : Earliest Times to the Present*, Millennial Ed. (New York: Cambridge University Press, 2006), vol. 5.

34. "Pro and Con Discussion Reflected in Mails Reaching the National Headquarters of the AL with Reference to Possible Inclusion of Veterans of the Second World War in the AL," n.d. (ca. March 1942), reel 95–1060, ALA.

35. Harry Benoit to Ralph B. Gregg, February 27, 1942, reel 95–1060, ALA.

36. Harry Benoit to Ralph B. Gregg, February 28, 1942, reel 95–1060, ALA.

37. "Shall the American Legion Admit Veterans of World War II?," reprinted from the *Arkansas Legionnaire*, reel 95–1060, ALA.

38. Benjamin L. Alpers, "This Is the Army: Imagining a Democratic Military in World War II," *Journal of American History* 85, no. 1 (June 1998): 129–63.

39. National Planning Resources Board, "Demobilization and Readjustment, Report of the Conference on Postwar Readjustment of Civilian and Military Personnel," 1943, 83; Hadley Cantril, ed., *Public Opinion, 1935–1946* (Princeton, N.J.: Princeton University Press, 1951), 1001.

40. Andrew J. Huebner, *The Warrior Image: Soldiers in American Culture from the Second World War to the Vietnam Era* (Chapel Hill: University of North Carolina Press, 2008), chap. 1.

41. Willard Waller, *The Veteran Comes Back* (New York: Dryden Press, 1944), 13, 191; emphasis original.

42. J. Edgar Hoover, "Is the Army Breeding Criminals?" *Los Angeles Times*, March 11, 1945.

43. Colmery to the Los Angeles Times editor, June 7, 1944, box 56, folder: 223G, HWCC.

44. Hanson to Stambaugh, December 11, 1941, reel 95–1060, ALA.

45. Damon Runyon, "The Brighter Side," *San Francisco (CA) Examiner*, April 1, 1942, reel 95–1060, ALA.

46. "Legion Should Admit World War 2 Veterans," *Hudson (N.J.) Dispatch*, March 30, 1942, reel 95–1060, ALA.

47. Twenty-fourth Annual Convention, the American Department of Wisconsin, Fond du Lac, Wisconsin, July 31, August 1, 2, 3, 1942, reel 4, P82–1868, part 2 (micro 8), Records of the Wisconsin American Legion, WHS.

48. *Digest of Minutes, Annual Conference of Department Commanders and Department Adjutants, November 14, 15, 16, 1944*, 13, ALA.

49. Russell B. Porter, "Legion Gathering in War Solemnity," *New York Times*, September 19, 1942.

50. "Legion Argues Membership: Veterans Can't Agree on Admitting 'Boys' From Present Conflict," *Los Angeles Times*, September 16, 1942; "Veterans Gather for Legion Meet," *Los Angeles Times*, September 19, 1942; Harry W. Colmery to Roane Waring, October 5, 1942, reel 95–1060,

ALA; "Legion Will Accept Soldiers of Today," *Los Angeles Times*, September 21, 1942; "Streamlined for Victory," *ALM*, November 1942.

51. Edward J. Donoghue to Ralph B. Gregg, December 3, 1942; Ralph B. Gregg to Edward J. Donoghue, December 9, 1942; Jack Cejnar to W. Elliott Nefflen, November 30, 1942, reel 95–1060, ALA.

52. "Veterans of World War II," *Pittsfield (Mass.) Berkshire Eagle*, May 8, 1943, reel 95–1060, ALA.

53. Disabled American Veterans, *Wars and Scars: The Story of Compassion and Service for Our Nation's Disabled Veterans; A History of the Disabled American Veterans* (Cincinnati, Ohio: IPR Group American Printing, 2006), 30.

54. William R. Spear, "The American Scene: 200 Organizations Bid for Favor of Veterans," *S&S*, June 29, 1945.

55. On the AVC, see Robert L. Tyler, "The American Veterans Committee: Out of a Hot War and into the Cold," *American Quarterly* 18, no. 3 (October 1966): 419–36; Charles G. Bolté, *The New Veteran* (New York: Reynal and Hitchcock, 1945); Peter D. Hoefer, "A David Against Goliath: The American Veterans Committee's Challenge to the American Legion in the 1950s" (PhD dissertation, University of Maryland, College Park, 2010). On the AMVETS, see Richard Flanagan, *AMVETS: 50 Years of Proud Service to America's Veterans* (Lanham, Md.: AMVETS National Headquarters, 1994).

56. Louis Falstein, "Veterans Welcome," *New Republic*, January 28, 1946, 117–19; A. Victor Lasky, "The Veterans Organizations," *American Mercury*, August 1946, 167–73; John Williamson, "New Organizational Problems of the Communist Party," *Political Affairs*, December 1945.

57. *Proceedings of the 25th National Convention*, 177–81.

58. *Proceedings of the 25th National Convention*, 181.

59. J. Ernest Isherwood to commander, n.d., reel 95–1060, ALA.

60. "Legion Gathers Record Publicity thru War Effort," *Badger Legionnaire*, August 1943, 19, WHS.

61. See resolution no. 333 in *Proceedings of the 25th National Convention*, 112–13; *Proceedings of the 27th National Convention of the American Legion* (Washington, D.C.: USGPO, 1946), 170–71.

62. Justin Gray and Victor H. Bernstein, *The Inside Story of the Legion* (New York: Boni and Gaer, 1948), 18–19.

63. *Proceedings of the 27th National Convention*, 169–73.

64. C. M. Wilson to Lewis Van Wezel, July 23, 1943, Reel 95–1060, ALA.

65. Ben W. Weir, "How One Post Builds Good Will Among Servicemen and Women of World War II," *Digest of Minutes, Annual Conference, November 15, 16, 17, 1943*, 50, ALA.

66. "The Editorial Viewpoint: Together," *ALM*, January 1943.

67. National Public Relations Division, "Suggested Membership Talk for American Legion Speakers Before Community Groups for World War II Enrollment Drive, 1945–1946," reel 95–1060, ALA.

68. Herman Caserta to National Executive Committee, November 22, 1943, Administration and Organization, Organization, Post, "Class" Posts, Black, ALA (Black, ALA hereafter).

69. H. C. Calloway to Franklin D. Roosevelt, September 22, 1942, Black, ALA.

70. For more on this issue, see Olivier Burtin, "Enforcing Conformity: Race in the American Legion, 1940–1960," in *War Veterans and the World After 1945: Cold War Politics, Decolonization, Memory*, ed. Ángel Alcalde and Xosé M. Núñez Seixas (New York: Routledge, 2018).

71. Henry H. Dudley to Elliott Haynes, June 13, 1944, Administration and Organization, Organization, Posts, "Class" Posts, Women, ALA; American Legion, *New Strength for the American Legion: A Picture Story of a New Era in the Legion* (Indianapolis: American Legion, 1945), 46.

72. Letter from Dudley, n.d. (ca. January 1946), Administration and Organization, Membership, Women, ALA.

73. National Publicity Division, "Tip to City Desk," June 1945, reel: 95–1059, Administration and Organization, Membership, World War II Veterans, A–Z, ALA.

74. Herbert Molloy Mason, Jr., *VFW: Our First Century, 1899–1999* (Lenexa, Kans.: Addax, 1999), 65, 149.

75. National Publicity Division, "New Blood for the Legion: Suggested Radio Script for Local Post Production (Timed for 15 Mins.)," March 1945, reel 95–1059, ALA.

76. Drew Pearson, "The Washington Merry-Go-Round," *Washington Post*, August 1, 1944; Mason, *VFW*, 98.

77. James T. Patterson, *Congressional Conservatism and the New Deal: The Growth of the Conservative Coalition in Congress, 1933–1939* (Lexington: University of Kentucky Press, 1967).

78. Davis R. B. Ross, *Preparing for Ulysses: Politics and Veterans During World War II* (New York: Columbia University Press, 1969), 36–38, 148–57.

79. Franklin D. Roosevelt, "Message to Congress on a Veterans' Rehabilitation Service," October 9, 1942, Gerhard Peters and John T. Woolley, The American Presidency Project, https://www.presidency.ucsb.edu/node/209972, accessed May 7, 2017.

80. Ross, *Preparing for Ulysses*, 38–50; Frydl, *The GI Bill*, 79–94; Audra Jennings, *Out of the Horrors of War: Disability Politics in World War II America* (Philadelphia: University of Pennsylvania Press, 2016), chap. 1.

81. "Bills Affecting New War Veterans Before Congress," *Badger Legionnaire*, December 1942, 2, WHS.

82. U.S. Congress, Senate, Committee on Education and Labor, Subcommittee, *Hearings, Vocational Rehabilitation of War-Disabled Individuals*, 77th Cong., 2nd sess. (Washington, D.C.: USGPO, 1942), 58–71, quoted in Jennings, *Out of the Horrors of War*, 40.

83. U.S. Congress, House, Committee on Education, *Hearings, Vocational Rehabilitation Education and Training*, 78th Cong., 1st sess. (Washington, D.C.: USGPO, 1943), 180.

84. Jennings, *Out of the Horrors of War*, 40.

85. U.S. Congress, Senate, Committee on Finance, Subcommittee, *Hearings, Veterans' Legislation*, 78th Cong., 1st sess. (Washington, D.C.: USGPO, 1943), 17.

86. Jennings, *Out of the Horrors of War*, 46–48.

87. Frydl, *The GI Bill*, 106–10; Alan Derickson, "Health Security for All? Social Unionism and Universal Health Insurance, 1935–1958," *Journal of American History* 80, no. 4 (March 1994): 1333–56; Daniel S. Hirshfield, *The Lost Reform: The Campaign for Compulsory Health Insurance in the United States from 1932 to 1943* (Cambridge, Mass.: Harvard University Press, 1970).

88. For the 1933 speech, see Franklin D. Roosevelt, "Address to the American Legion Convention," October 2, 1933; for the 1943 one, see "Fireside Chat," July 28, 1943, Peters and Woolley, The American Presidency Project, respectively https://www.presidency.ucsb.edu/node/207703 and https://www.presidency.ucsb.edu/node/210292, accessed May 7, 2017.

89. Ross, *Preparing for Ulysses*, 71–72, 118–19; Glenn C. Altschuler and Stuart M. Blumin, *The GI Bill: A New Deal for Veterans* (Oxford: Oxford University Press, 2009), 47–48.

90. Samuel I. Rosenman, *Working with Roosevelt* (New York: Harper and Brothers, 1952), 394–95, quoted in Altschuler and Blumin, *The GI Bill*, 44–45.

91. Keith W. Olson, *The G.I. Bill, the Veterans, and the Colleges* (Lexington: University Press of Kentucky, 1974), 15–17; Frydl, *The GI Bill*, 122–24.

92. Stephen R. Ortiz, *Beyond the Bonus March and GI Bill: How Veteran Politics Shaped the New Deal Era* (New York: New York University Press, 2010), 189.

93. Ross, *Preparing for Ulysses*, 79.

94. U.S. Congress, Senate, Committee on Military Affairs, *Mustering-Out Payments*, Hearing, December 1, 1943 (Washington, D.C.: USGPO, 1943), 18–21.

95. "Legion Head Hits Slow Action on Wounded Veterans' Claims," *Washington Post*, December 3, 1943; "Service Claims Delay Stirs Action," *Christian Science Monitor*, December 13, 1943.

96. *Digest of Minutes, National Executive Committee Meeting, November 18–19, 1943*, 39, ALA; *Proceedings of the 26th National Convention*, 17. On Colmery, see Alexander Gardiner, "Colmery of Kansas," *ALM*, January 1937; Altschuler and Blumin, *The GI Bill*, 54.

97. "Chronology of Legion Omnibus Bill, 1943–1944," n.d. (ca. April 1944), box 61, folder 223M, HWCC. See also *Proceedings of the 26th National Convention*, 372–73.

98. *Proceedings of the 25th National Convention*, 14.

99. Frydl, *The GI Bill*, 114; Olson, *The G.I. Bill, the Veterans, and the Colleges*, 7–8. On Canada's "Veterans Charter," see Peter Neary, *On to Civvy Street: Canada's Rehabilitation Program for Veterans of the Second World War* (Montreal: McGill-Queen's University Press, 2011); Peter Neary and J. L. Granatstein, eds., *The Veterans Charter and Post–World War II Canada* (Montreal: McGill-Queen's University Press, 1998).

100. Ross, *Preparing for Ulysses*, 67–69, 82–88.

101. "Muster-Out Pay Facts," *Foreign Service*, March 1944, 21; U.S. Congress, House, Committee on World War Veterans Legislation, *World War Veterans' Legislation*, Hearing, January 11–13, 17–18, February 24, March 9–10, 27–31, 1944 (Washington, D.C.: USGPO, 1944), 23.

102. National Legislative Committee, *Legislative Bulletin*, no. 4 (February 9, 1944), box 4, folder 9, SFCP.

103. Veterans of Foreign Wars, Disabled American Veterans, Regular Veterans Association, and Military Order of Purple Heart to Senator Bennett C. Clark, February 16, 1944, box 61, folder 223F, HWCC.

104. Ortiz, *Beyond the Bonus March*, 192–93; Ross, *Preparing for Ulysses*, 103–4.

105. Omar B. Ketchum, "We Blaze the Trail and Others Strive to Grab the Glory," *Foreign Service*, March 1944, 20.

106. *Proceedings of the 26th National Convention*, 196–99.

107. R. B. Pitkin, "How the First G.I. Bill Was Written," n.d. (ca. 1969), box 66, HWCC.

108. "Petition for 'G. I.' Measure Bears 1,000,000 Names," *Christian Science Monitor*, May 11, 1944; *Proceedings of the 26th National Convention*, 199. The *Monitor*'s estimate of the size of the petition was only half of what the Legion claimed.

109. In June 1943, for instance, 81 percent of respondents to a survey said they would approve of a program to allow a veteran to borrow money to buy a house, farm, or business. Office of Public Opinion Research, Office of Public Opinion Research Roosevelt Survey, June 1943: "In Canada, the government has provided that any solider who wants to can borrow money at a very low interest from the government to buy a house, or a farm, or a business. Would you approve or disapprove of a law of this kind in the United States?," USOPOR.43–012.Q09, Office of Public Opinion Research, Cornell University, Ithaca, N.Y.: Roper Center for Public Opinion Research, iPOLL, accessed March 9, 2017.

110. J. T. Sparrow, *Warfare State*, 14.

111. "Legion Bill Asks Wide Veteran Aid," *New York Times*, January 9, 1944; Karen Hofer Luecke, "'What Shall Be Done When Victory Is Won?' The Cultural Foundations and Implications of the 1944 G.I. Bill of Rights" (MEd thesis, George Mason University, 2005), 177–81.

112. Olson, *The G.I. Bill, the Veterans, and the Colleges*, 20.

113. See speech by Edith Nourse Rogers (Mass.), *Congressional Record* 90, no. 4 (May 15, 1944): H4504.

114. Ortiz, *Beyond the Bonus March*, 196–97.

115. Ross, *Preparing for Ulysses*, 93–98.

116. Harry W. Colmery to Morgan Barnes, April 13, 1944, box 61, folder 223G, HWCC.

117. Quoted in Altschuler and Blumin, *The GI Bill*, 58.

118. Ross, *Preparing for Ulysses*, 107–11; Frydl, *The GI Bill*, 133–42.

119. Ross, *Preparing for Ulysses*, 117.

120. *Proceedings of the 26th National Convention*, 375.

121. *Proceedings of the 26th National Convention*, 326; "President Gives Historic Pen to V.F.W.," *Foreign Service*, July 1944, 11.

122. Altschuler and Blumin, *The GI Bill*, 71–72.

123. Omar B. Ketchum, "President Signs Vet Aid Act," *Foreign Service*, July 1944, 11.

124. Bartholomew H. Sparrow, *From the Outside In: World War II and the American State* (Princeton, N.J.: Princeton University Press, 1996), 63.

125. Ira Katznelson, *When Affirmative Action Was White: An Untold History of Racial Inequality in Twentieth-Century America* (New York: W. W. Norton, 2005), chap. 5.

126. Hilary Herbold, "Never a Level Playing Field: Blacks and the GI Bill," *Journal of Blacks in Higher Education*, no. 6 (Winter 1994–95): 104–8; Edward Humes, "How the GI Bill Shunted Blacks into Vocational Training," *The Journal of Blacks in Higher Education*, no. 53 (Autumn 2006): 92–104; David H. Onkst, "'First a Negro . . . Incidentally a Veteran': Black World War Two Veterans and the G. I. Bill of Rights in the Deep South, 1944–1948," *Journal of Social History* 31, no. 3 (April 1998): 517–43.

127. Quoted in Frydl, *The GI Bill*, 137.

128. This was despite the fact that the language of the law was gender-blind and that congressional debates clearly stated that women veterans were to be included as well as men. See Luecke, "'What Shall Be Done When Victory Is Won?,'" 228–39.

129. On gender discrimination and World War II veterans' benefits, see June A. Willenz, "Invisible Veterans," *Educational Record* 75, no. 4 (Fall 1994): 40; Mary V. Stremlow, "Women as Veterans: Historical Perspective and Expectations," in *A Woman's War Too: U.S. Women in the Military in World War II*, ed. Paula Nassen Poulos (Washington, D.C.: National Archives and Records Administration, 1996), 355–66; Altschuler and Blumin, *The GI Bill*, 118–29.

130. U.S. Civil Service Commission, *History of Veteran Preference in Federal Employment, 1865–1955* (Washington, D.C.: USGPO, 1956).

131. Ross, *Preparing for Ulysses*, 193–96.

132. U.S. Congress, Senate, Committee on Civil Service, *Preference in Employment of Honorably Discharged Veterans Where Federal Funds Are Disbursed*, Hearing, May 19 and 23, 1944 (Washington, D.C.: USGPO, 1944), 12, 43, 46.

133. Bill Mauldin, "Poppa Knows Best," *Atlantic Monthly*, April 1947, 29–36.

134. Samuel A. Stouffer et al., *The American Soldier: Combat and Its Aftermath*, vol. 2, Studies in Social Psychology in World War II (Princeton, N.J.: Princeton University Press, 1949), 622–23.

135. "$64 Question, By Tomorrow's Inquiring Reporter," *S&S*, January 24, 1945, 3.

136. Bolté, *The New Veteran*, 79.

137. John Thomas Taylor to Stephen Chadwick, February 26, 1944, box 17, folder 2, SFCP.

138. "Vet's Problem: Which Group Best," *S&S*, January 24, 1945, 6.

139. Pvt. Robert E. Shaw, Ord., "Four Freedoms," *S&S*, January 10, 1945, 5.

140. Bolté, *The New Veteran*, chaps. 5–7.

141. S/Sgt. Gabe Sanders, Netherlands East Indies, "A Different War," *Yank: The Army Weekly*, February 2, 1945.

142. Sgt. Don E. Williams, "Views to Air," *S&S*, February 21, 1945, 5.

143. Pfc. Bill Fromer, 29 MRU, "Legion Gets a Plug," *S&S*, July 20, 1945, 2.

144. Daniel J. Scarry, "Don't Split Up," *Yank: The Army Weekly*, February 2, 1945.

145. Stouffer et al., *The American Soldier*, 597, 622–23.

146. National Headquarters of the American Legion, "Suggestions for Welcome Home Parties for Members of the Armed Forces," May 21, 1945, reel 95–1059, ALA.

147. Henry H. Dudley to G. H. Stordock, January 11, 1945, reel 95–1060, ALA.

148. Donald G. Glascoff, "Article for Forty and Eighter: New Membership Plasma Revitalizes the Legion," August 1945, reel 95–1059, ALA.

149. Alvin Owsley to Paul Griffith, July 19, 1946, box 607, folder 10, AMOC.

150. N. E. Ekers to national adjutant, April 20, 1945, reel 95–1059, ALA.

151. "American Legion Posts Composed of World War II Veterans," July 27, 1944; "World War II Posts," n.d. (ca. August 1945), Administration and Organization, Organization, Post, "Class" Posts, WWII Veterans, ALA.

152. R. T. Fairey to Frank E. Samuel, May 19, 1943, Administration and Organization, Organization, Post, "Class" Posts, WWII Veterans, ALA.

153. *Proceedings of the 25th National Convention*, 97; *Digest of Minutes, Annual Conference, November 15, 16, 17, 1943*, 55, ALA.

154. *Digest of Minutes, Annual Conference, November 14, 15, 16, 1944*, 14, ALA.

155. Institute of Public Relations, "Building Better Public Acceptance for The American Legion," June 1945, box 757, folder 4, AMOC; emphasis original.

156. *Digest of Minutes, Annual Conference of Department Commanders and Department Adjutants, Indianapolis, Indiana, December 10, 11, 12, 1945*, 29, ALA.

157. Telegram from National Commander Edward N. Scheiberling, August 10, 1945, reel: 95–1059, ALA.

158. "Million War II Vets Have Joined the VFW or Legion," *Army Times*, June 23, 1945.

CHAPTER 3

1. "Fighting Pittsburgh Irishman to Get Nation's Highest Honor," *Christian Science Monitor*, March 9, 1944; "Kelly Calls 'Hero Business' Tougher Job Than Army Life," *Washington Post*, May 6, 1944. For his citation, see "Medal of Honor recipients—World War II (G–L)," Medal of Honor citations, U.S. Army Center of Military History, June 8, 2009, https://www.army.mil/medalofhonor/citations21.html, accessed May 21, 2019.

2. "Mother of Sergt. Kelly to Remain in Own Home," *New York Herald Tribune*, April 15, 1944; "Photo of Kelly's House Jolts Press," *Public Housing* 10, no. 4 (April 1944): 1.

3. "Mrs. Kelly's Doorstep," *New York Times*, April 11, 1944.

4. "Photo of Kelly's House Jolts Press"; "Hero Kelly Disdains Luxury of Hotel for Home with 'Mom,'" *Christian Science Monitor*, April 25, 1944; "Mother of Sergt. Kelly to Remain in Own Home"; "Kelly Editorials Show Working of Free Press," *Public Housing* 10, no. 5 (May 1944): 3.

5. The American Legion, *National Membership Record, 2012*, ALA; Herbert Molloy Mason, Jr., *VFW: Our First Century, 1899–1999* (Lenexa, Kans.: Addax, 1999), 115; Disabled American Veterans, *Wars and Scars: The Story of Compassion and Service for Our Nation's Disabled Veterans; A History of the Disabled American Veterans* (Cincinnati, Ohio: IPR Group American Printing, 2006), 31.

6. Jack S. Ballard, *The Shock of Peace: Military and Economic Demobilization After World War II* (Washington, D.C.: University Press of America, 1983), 92.

7. Ballard, *Shock of Peace*, 73–116; R. Alton Lee, "The Army 'Mutiny' of 1946," *Journal of American History* 53, no. 3 (December 1966): 555–71.

8. Sgt. H. N. Oliphant, "Rackets and Veterans," *Yank: The Army Weekly*, November 2, 1945; Harry Lever, "They're Out to Get You," *ALM*, March 1946.

9. Charles G. Bolté, "The Veterans' Runaround," *Harper's Magazine*, April 1945.

10. Joseph C. Goulden, *The Best Years, 1945–1950* (New York: Atheneum, 1976), 46–47; Robert J. Havighurst and al., *The American Veteran Back Home: A Study of Veteran Readjustment* (New York: Longmans, Green, 1951), 68–89; William M. Tuttle, *Daddy's Gone to War: The Second World War in the Lives of America's Children* (New York: Oxford University Press, 1993), chap. 12.

11. David A. Gerber, "Heroes and Misfits: The Troubled Social Reintegration of Disabled Veterans in 'The Best Years of Our Lives,'" *American Quarterly* 46, no. 4 (December 1994): 545.

12. Charles G. Bolté, *The New Veteran* (New York: Reynal & Hitchcock, 1945), 1–2.

13. John Roy Carlson, *The Plotters* (New York: Dutton, 1946), viii.

14. On veterans' groups after 1945, see Louis Falstein, "Veterans Welcome," *New Republic*, January 28, 1946; J. Donald Kingsley, "Veterans, Unions and Jobs: II. Labor and the Veterans," *New Republic*, November 13, 1944; Victor Riesel, "Fascist Pie for Veterans," *Nation*, April 17, 1943; Sam Stavisky, "The Veterans Make Their Choice," *Harper's Magazine*, September 1946; A. Victor Lasky, "The Veterans Organizations," *American Mercury*, August 1946.

15. *Proceedings of the 27th National Convention of the American Legion* (Washington, D.C.: USGPO, 1946), 29.

16. *Digest of Minutes, National Executive Committee Meetings, October 13, 14 and 18, 1951,* 54–55, ALA.

17. *Proceedings of the 27th National Convention*, 169–73.

18. On the kingmakers, see Robert S. Allen, "Legion GIs Challenge the Brass," *Pic*, October 1948.

19. National Public Relations Division, "Suggested Address for American Legion speakers for World War II Veterans' Welcome Home Parties (1946)," n.d., reel 95-1059, ALA.

20. The American Legion, *New Strength for the American Legion: A Picture Story of a New Era in the Legion* (Indianapolis: American Legion, 1945), 46.

21. McGrath to National Membership Committee Chairman, May 18, 1951, Administration and Organization, Membership, Women, ALA.

22. The *Legion Magazine* claimed a circulation of 2.8 million in 1959, making it the fifteenth largest national publication; see "Suggested Talk on The American Legion for Delivery Before Non-Legion groups: The King-Sized Legion," ca. 1960, ALA.

23. *Digest of Minutes, National Executive Committee Meetings, December 13, 14, 15, 1945, November 17 and 21, 1945,* 47–49.

24. On LaBoon, see *Digest of Minutes, National Executive Committee Meetings, December 13, 14, 15, 1945, November 17 and 21, 1945,* 47–49, ALA. On Swim, see his correspondence with Herbert Hoover in box 232, folder: Swim, H. Dudley Correspondence, 1938–64, Post-Presidential Papers Individual Correspondence File, Herbert Hoover Presidential Library, West Branch, Iowa; John E. Moser, *Right Turn: John T. Flynn and the Transformation of American Liberalism* (New York: New York University Press, 2005), 119–20; *Who Was Who in America with World Notables*, vol. 5, 1969–1973 (Chicago: Marquis Who's Who, 1973).

25. Griffith to Robinson, December 20, 1946, 95-1059, ALA. On Griffith, see *Who's Who In America*, vol. 25 (Chicago: The A.N. Marquis Company, 1948), 980–81; Richard Seelye Jones, "Tough Top Sergeant," *ALM*, January 1947.

26. *Digests of Minutes, National Executive Committee Meetings, September 29, October 4, 1946*, 53, ALA; Joseph C. Keeley, "American Legion College for Leaders," *ALM*, November 1946; Resolution 138 quoted in *Proceedings of the 26th National Convention of the American Legion* (Chicago, 1944), 143.

27. On the school for new DAV officers, see Disabled American Veterans, *Wars and Scars*, 30–31.

28. Keeley, "American Legion College for Leaders"; Donald G. Glascoff, "Orientation," in *Lectures American Legion College First Term, July 8–20, 1946*, ALA.

29. Justin Gray and Victor H. Bernstein, *The Inside Story of the Legion* (New York: Boni and Gaer, 1948), 173.

30. Mark D. Van Ells, *To Hear Only Thunder Again: America's World War II Veterans Come Home* (Lanham, Md.: Lexington Books, 2001), 210. See also Davis R. B. Ross, *Preparing for Ulysses: Politics and Veterans During World War II* (New York: Columbia University Press, 1969), 237–43.

31. Nicholas Dagen Bloom, *Public Housing That Worked: New York in the Twentieth Century* (Philadelphia: University of Pennsylvania Press, 2008), 11.

32. This was the number given by housing official Wyatt to Truman in February 1946; see Wilson W. Wyatt, *Veterans Emergency Housing Program: Report to the President*, February 7, 1946, box 63, folder 5, Wilson W. Wyatt Papers, 1926–92, 95m4, University of Kentucky Special Collections.

33. "The Fortune Survey," *Fortune*, April 1946.

34. National Housing Agency, Statistics and Control Branch, Statistics Division, *Survey of World War II Veterans' Housing Accommodations: September 1945* (Washington, D.C., 1946), 1.

35. Housing and Home Finance Agency, Office of the Administration, Housing Data Staff, *Veterans' Housing Plans and Living Arrangements in 1946 for 108 Survey Areas: By Geographic Region and Division, and by Population Size of Central City*, Statistics Bulletin 2 (Washington, D.C., 1948).

36. Franklin D. Roosevelt Jr., "No Homes for Veterans," *Nation*, November 10, 1945, 486.

37. Gray and Bernstein, *The Inside Story of the Legion*, 112–13.

38. Donald Craig Parson, *Making a Better World: Public Housing, the Red Scare, and the Direction of Modern Los Angeles* (Minneapolis: University of Minnesota Press, 2005), 89.

39. "Veterans Hold Angry Meeting On City Housing," *New York Herald Tribune*, October 25, 1945; Charles G. Bolté, "100,000 Veterans Homeless Unless City Acts," *New York Herald Tribune*, November 11, 1945.

40. "Veterans Occupy Senate Chamber at State Capitol," *New York Times*, October 20, 1946.

41. Hardy to Truman, December 7, 1945; Stack to Truman, December 14, 1945, White House Central Files: Official File 63 (Dec. 1945), box 360, Truman Papers, Truman Library.

42. Quoted in Ross, *Preparing for Ulysses*, 244.

43. Ross, *Preparing for Ulysses*, 249.

44. Richard O. Davies, *Housing Reform During the Truman Administration* (Columbia: University of Missouri Press, 1966), 1–58; Barton Bernstein, "Reluctance and Resistance: Wilson Wyatt and Veterans' Housing in the Truman Administration," *Register of the Kentucky Historical Society* 65 (1967): 47–66; Ross, *Preparing for Ulysses*, 249–59.

45. Ralph E. Flanders, *Senator from Vermont* (Boston: Little, Brown, 1961), 221.

46. Davies, *Housing Reform During the Truman Administration*, 33–37; James T. Patterson, *Mr. Republican: A Biography of Robert A. Taft* (Boston: Houghton Mifflin, 1972), 315–20; J. Joseph Huthmacher, *Senator Robert F. Wagner and the Rise of Urban Liberalism* (New York: Atheneum, 1968), 205–16.

47. Leonard Freedman, *Public Housing: The Politics of Poverty* (New York: Holt, Rinehart and Winston, 1969), 75–78.

48. Ira Katznelson, *When Affirmative Action Was White: An Untold History of Racial Inequality in Twentieth-Century America* (New York: W. W. Norton, 2005); Peter Marcuse, "Interpreting 'Public Housing' History," *Journal of Architectural and Planning Research* 12, no. 3 (1995): 240–58; Kenneth T. Jackson, *Crabgrass Frontier: The Suburbanization of the United States* (New York: Oxford University Press, 1985), chap. 12.

49. Blandford, Jr., to Scheiberling, July 16, 1945; Scheiberling to Blandford, Jr., July 18, 1945; Scheiberling to My Dear Adjutant, n.d., Veteran Welfare, Homes, ALA.

50. Chloe N. Thurston, "Policy Feedback in the Public-Private Welfare State: Advocacy Groups and Access to Government Homeownership Programs, 1934–1954," *Studies in American Political Development* 29, no. 2 (October 2015): 263–65.

51. "The Fortune Survey," 266.

52. "The Veterans' Policy of the Communist Party: An Outline for Discussion in All Clubs . . . ," n.d. (ca. 1948), Communist Party of the United States of America, TAM 132, box 186, folder 48, Tamiment Library/Robert F. Wagner Labor Archives, New York University.

53. Robert Thompson, "Party Policy in the Veterans' Field," *Political Affairs*, January 1946, 47.

54. Gray and Bernstein, *The Inside Story of the Legion*, 25.

55. On the history of the Duncan-Paris Post, see Gray and Bernstein, *The Inside Story of the Legion*, 21–27, 185–190; Walter Bernstein, *Inside Out: A Memoir of the Blacklist* (New York: A. A. Knopf, 1996), 139–43; William Price, "The Veterans' House Divided," *Nation*, May 25, 1946.

56. "For Immediate Release: Kilroy Is Here!!" May 13, 1946; "What Is Operation Housing?" n.d., folder: Operation Housing, ALA; "Duncan-Paris Post The American Legion," November 13, 1946, box 39, folder 1, JBMP; "Congressmen Hear Veterans' Housing Gripes," *New York Herald Tribune*, May 19, 1946.

57. "New Housing Plan Offered to Mayor as Homeless Rally," *New York Times*, May 19, 1946. On the legal battle that followed, see Report of National Judge Advocate to National Executive Committee, May 1951, box 61 (110-7-4-1), folder: 238, no. 795, 1911–75, HWCC; "Duncan-Paris Post Sues," *New York Times*, March 26, 1947; "Legion Post Loses Fight for Charter," *New York Times*, January 14, 1949; "Legion Wins on Post's Appeal," *New York Times*, May 3, 1950; "Legion Drops Duncan-Paris Post," *New York Times*, May 4, 1951.

58. For a detailed history of Gray's work in the Legion, see Dudley to Colmery, July 15, 1948, box 61 (110-7-4-1), folder: 239, HWCC.

59. Robert Francis Saxe, *Settling Down: World War II Veterans' Challenge to the Postwar Consensus* (New York: Palgrave Macmillan, 2007), 117–54; Daniel James, "The Battle of A. V. C," *Nation*, June 14, 1947; Charles G. Bolté, "We're on Our Own," *Atlantic Monthly*, May 1947; Lasky, "The Veterans Organizations."

60. "Minutes, NCULL, Inc., Sunday November 11, 1945–Midland Hotel–Chicago, ILL.," box 5, folder: National Conference of Union Labor Legionnaires (January 1946–February 1946), UAW Veterans' Department Collection, 1943–55, Walter P. Reuther Library, Wayne State University, Detroit, Michigan (UAWVD thereafter).

61. "Minutes, NCULL, Inc., Sunday November 11, 1945"; "So You May Know," n.d., box 62, folder 252: Union Labor, HWCC. For the denials, see "Plot to Destroy Union Posts Is Laid to Legion," *New York Herald Tribune*, May 22, 1946.

62. "Plot to Destroy Union Posts Is Laid to Legion."

63. "Minutes of Veterans Conference," January 11, 1946, box 5, folder: National Conference of Union Labor Legionnaires (January 1946–February 1946); NCULL Convention Headquarters, "Press Release," September 29, 1946, box 5, folder: National Conference of Union Labor Legionnaires (April–November 1946), UAWVD.

64. NCULL, "Newsletter, Special Convention Issue," May 23–24–25–26, 1946, box 5, folder: National Conference of Union Labor Legionnaires (April–November 1946), UAWVD.

65. NCULL, "Newsletter," October 1945, box 2, folder: American Legion (1945–46), UAWVD.

66. Kingsley, "Veterans, Unions and Jobs."

67. Colmery to Dudley, July 3, 1948, box 62 (110-7-4-2), folder 253: Union Labor Legionnaires, HWCC.

68. Progress Report, Colored Posts, May 15, 1944, Administration and Organization, Organization, Post, "Class" Posts, Black, ALA; George N. Craig to Laddell Washington, February 2, 1950, Administration and Organization, Membership, Black Veterans, ALA.

69. "Legion Refuses to Lower Color Bar," *Baltimore Afro-American*, December 1, 1945.

70. Fred Atwater, "Legionnaires Beat Negro Vets," *Chicago Defender*, October 12, 1946.

71. For more details on this topic, see Olivier Burtin, "Enforcing Conformity: Race in the American Legion, 1940-1960," in *War Veterans and the World After 1945: Cold War Politics, Decolonization, Memory*, ed. Ángel Alcalde and Xosé M. Núñez Seixas (Routledge, 2018), 69–82.

72. Lionel Kimble, *A New Deal for Bronzeville: Housing, Employment, and Civil Rights in Black Chicago, 1935–1955* (Carbondale: Southern Illinois University Press, 2015), chaps. 5–6; Martha Biondi, *To Stand and Fight: The Struggle for Civil Rights in Postwar New York City* (Cambridge, Mass.: Harvard University Press, 2003).

73. Alonzo Mead, "Legion Post to Get Action," *Chicago Defender*, February 15, 1947.

74. "Veterans Groups to Protest to Pres. Truman About Bias," *Cleveland Call and Post*, July 27, 1946.

75. P. L. Prattis, "The Horizon," *Pittsburgh Courier*, September 13, 1947.

76. Benjamin Fine, "Facilities in Colleges Taxed By Returning War Veterans," *New York Times*, January 6, 1946.

77. Keith W. Olson, *The GI Bill, the Veterans, and the Colleges* (Lexington: University Press of Kentucky, 1974), esp. 57–78.

78. "Review of the Activities of the Thomas C. Reynolds Post #303 University of Oklahoma, Norman, Oklahoma," n.d.; Don White, memorandum to C. M. Wilson, December 18, 1945, Administration and Organization, Organization, Post, "Class" Posts, Campus, ALA (Campus, ALA hereafter).

79. See for instance Don White, "Report on Visit to Norman, Oklahoma," July 2, 1945, Campus, ALA.

80. C. M. Wilson to R. C. Patterson, May 27, 1945, Campus, ALA.

81. "Digest of Conference Attended by Six College Representatives Called into Session by National Commander John Stelle at Indianapolis, on December 13, 1945," Campus, ALA.

82. *Digest of Minutes, National Executive Committee Meetings, December 13, 14, 15, 1945, November 17 and 21*, 113–14, ALA; Glascoff to Dear Sir, January 15, 1946, Campus, ALA.

83. Hayes to Roy Hickox, n.d., Cooperation, Housing, American Legion Archives, Indianapolis, Indiana (Housing, ALA hereafter).

84. Smith to Stelle, March 27, 1946; Mathews Jr. MC to Glascoff, March 27, 1946, Housing, ALA; Representative [Raymond S.] Springer (IN), "Does the Rank and File of the American Legion Support the Wyatt Housing Bill?," *Congressional Record*, March 28, 1946, H2774–76; Representative [Lawrence Henry] Smith (WI), "American Legion Commander Reverses Stand on Wyatt Housing Plan," *Congressional Record*, April 13, 1946, E2195.

85. For the minutes of the first meeting, see "National Housing Agency—First Meeting of the Veterans Advisory Council," May 9, 1946, Housing, ALA.

86. Charles Hurd, "Few Young Men at Legion Session," *New York Times*, October 6, 1946; Alvin D. Hyman, "American Legion Rolls Out the Barrel," *San Francisco Chronicle*, October 2, 1946; George Draper, "'Lost' Legionnaires," *San Francisco Chronicle*, October 3, 1946. For the membership figure, see American Legion, *National Membership Record*, 2012, ALA.

87. Hyman, "American Legion Rolls Out the Barrel."

88. Stanton Delaplane, "Kilroy Is Here," *San Francisco Chronicle*, September 30, 1946.

89. "Young Vets' Lobby," *San Francisco Chronicle*, October 1, 1946.

90. For unofficial accounts of this event, see Gray and Bernstein, *The Inside Story of the Legion*, 120; John Gates, "Whither the American Legion?" *Political Affairs*, December 1946.

91. *Proceedings of the 28th National Convention of the American Legion* (San Francisco, 1946), 115–16.

92. National Public Relations Division, "Joint Statement of Dudley Swim of Idaho, National Vice Commander (WWII), Richard Marvel, Department Commander of Nebraska (WWII), Wesley Sampier, Department Commander of Arkansas (WWII), William Gallosy, Department Commander of Idaho (WWII)," October 2, 1946, Housing, ALA.

93. Sam Stavisky, "Convention Elects D.C. Publicity Man by Acclamation," *Washington Post*, October 5, 1946; "Remarks of Richard Cadwallader, Chairman of American Legion Housing Committee, on Veterans Housing Panel at National Association of Home Builders Convention, Stevens Hotel, Chicago, February 25, 1947," Housing, ALA.

94. Gray and Bernstein, *The Inside Story of the Legion*, 121. Richard Vail, one of the committee members, would later be indicted for selling houses to veterans in Fresno, California, at prices higher than legally authorized; see Albert Q. Maisel, "Scandals in Veterans' Housing," *Collier's*, July 3, 1948.

95. Letter from Donald G. Glascoff, October 10, 1946, Housing, ALA.

96. Letter from Raymond H. Fields, November 13, 1946; Letter from Jack Cejnar, November 15, 1946; both Housing, ALA.

97. "Tale on Housing by National Commander Paul H. Griffith of the American Legion over Radio Station WYBC, Indianapolis, at 9 pm, November 20, 1946," Housing, ALA.

98. On the booklet, see *Digest of Minutes, National Executive Committee Meeting, November 21, 22, 23, 1946*, 165, ALA.

99. *Digest of Minutes, November 21, 22, 23, 1946*,145–65; "Suggested talk on Housing," n.d, Housing, ALA.

100. "How Veterans Organizations Stand on Housing Issues," *Journal of Housing* 3, no. 12 (December 1946): 279.

101. Davies, *Housing Reform During the Truman Administration*, 50–58.

102. Ross, *Preparing for Ulysses*, 271.

103. On NHA director Raymond Foley's management style, see Davies, *Housing Reform During the Truman Administration*, 60–62.

104. Poston to Cadwallader, December 20, 1946, Housing, ALA.

105. Freedman, *Public Housing*, 17.

106. See for instance Drew Pearson, "The Washington Merry-Go-Round," *Washington Post*, December 12, 1946.

107. Bill Mauldin, "Poppa Knows Best," *Atlantic Monthly*, April 1947, 32, 33, 36.

108. "Roosevelt Jr. Hits Legion on Housing," *New York Herald Tribune*, May 18, 1947.

109. Alexander to Poston, May 26, 1947, Housing, ALA.

110. Freedman, *Public Housing*, 59–75; Davies, *Housing Reform During the Truman Administration*, 15–22; Nathan Strauss, "Why You Can't Get That New Home," *American Magazine*,

December 1947; Tris Coffin, "The Slickest Lobby," *Nation*, March 23, 1946; Leo Goodman, "What Makes the Real Estate Lobby Tick?," *Journal of Housing* 6, no. 12 (December 1950): 423–27.

111. Ben Zdencanovic, "'The Opposite of a European Democracy': The American Real Estate Lobby, French and British Social Housing, and the Making of the Postwar American Welfare State, 1945–1949," *Journal of Transatlantic Studies* 15, no. 1 (January 2017): 77–99; Nancy Kwak, *A World of Homeowners: American Power and the Politics of Housing Aid* (Chicago: University of Chicago Press, 2015), chap. 1.

112. On this campaign, see Wendy Wall, *Inventing the "American Way": The Politics of Consensus from the New Deal to the Civil Rights Movement* (Oxford: Oxford University Press, 2008); Elizabeth A. Fones-Wolf, *Selling Free Enterprise: The Business Assault on Labor and Liberalism, 1945-60* (Urbana: University of Illinois Press, 1994).

113. Griffith to Warner, December 11, 1946, Housing, ALA.

114. "Remarks of Richard Cadwallader, February 25, 1947."

115. "Remarks of Richard Cadwallader, Chairman of American Legion Housing Committee Before NAHB Board of Directors, Stevens Hotel, Chicago, February 24, 1947," Housing, ALA.

116. *Proceedings of the 29th National Convention of the American Legion* (New York, 1947), 265, 269.

117. Hickox to Fields, December 12, 1946, Housing, ALA.

118. Poston to Miller, February 10, 1947, Housing, ALA; *Digest of Minutes, National Executive Committee Meeting, May 5, 6, 7, 1947*, 299-310, ALA.

119. Clarence Woodbury, "Should Veterans Come First in Housing?," *ALM*, January 1948, 48.

120. "Remarks of Richard Cadwallader, February 24, 1947."

121. Cadwallader to Kelly, September 15, 1948, Housing, ALA.

122. "Editorial," *Foreign Service*, December 1947, 9.

123. "For A.M. Release, Jan. 30 (American Legion News Service)," January 28, 1947, Housing, ALA.

124. American Legion, *Operation Housing: Community Programs for Veterans* (Indianapolis: National Headquarters, American Legion, 1947), ALA.

125. Dinger to Dudley, December 2, 1949, Housing, ALA.

126. Joseph C. Keeley, "Three Answers to the Housing Question," *ALM*, July 1947; Bob Richelson, "They Ganged Up to Get Homes," *ALM*, March 1948.

127. U.S. Congress, Senate, Committee on Banking and Currency, Subcommittee on Housing and Rents, *Report on Domestic Cooperative Housing* (Washington, D.C.: USGPO, 1950), 7, 11, 13, 17–19, 27; Harmon Elder, "Rochester Points the Way," *Foreign Service*, March 1947, 16-17.

128. Quoted in Dudley to Nelson, November 4, 1948, Housing, ALA.

129. "Housing Should Come First for Action by the 80th Congress," *Journal of Housing* 4, no. 1 (January 1947): 9.

130. See for instance "City News," *Journal of Housing* 4, no. 8 (August 1947): 228–29.

131. Davies, *Housing Reform During the Truman Administration*, 64–65.

132. Taylor to Fields, June 2, 1947; Kelly to Fields, June 19, 1947, Housing, ALA.

133. Poston to White, July 1, 1947, Housing, ALA; Davies, *Housing Reform During the Truman Administration*, 62–64.

134. Poston to White, July 23, 1947, Housing, ALA.

135. Poston to Cadwallader, July 24, 1947, Housing, ALA.

136. Rollins MacFadyen, "Housing Committee, Department of California, The American Legion," September 16, 1947, Housing, ALA.

137. Woodbury, "Should Veterans Come First in Housing?" 48.

138. "American Legion Votes Against Taft-Ellender-Wagner Bill," *Journal of Housing* 4, no. 9 (September 1947). 255 56.

139. O'Neil to Alessandroni, September 15, 1947, Housing, ALA.

140. Bill Cunningham, "Meet the Commander," *ALM*, April 1948.

141. *Army Times Vet-Letter*, August 23, 1947, Wisconsin Veterans Museum, Madison.

142. Alessandroni to O'Neil, November 21, 1947, Housing, ALA; for his biography, see *Who Was Who in America with World Notables*, vol. 4, 1961–1968 (Chicago: Marquis-Who's Who, 1968).

143. MacFadyen to Comrade Commander, October 22, 1948, Housing, ALA; emphasis original.

144. Drew Pearson, "The Washington Merry-Go-Round," *Washington Post*, November 19, 1947.

145. Alessandroni to O'Neil, September 9, 1947; Alessandroni to O'Neil, November 21, 1947; Alessandroni to Fields, November 24, 1947; all in Housing, ALA.

146. Allen, "Legion GIs Challenge the Brass"; "William H. Doyle, 56, Executive of Legion," *New York Times*, December 4, 1947.

147. Davies, *Housing Reform During the Truman Administration*, 74.

148. Paterson to NPC Members and Al Josephy, George Ebey, Justin Stewart, "National Veterans Housing Conference—March 1st and 2nd," box 174, folder: National Veterans Housing Conference 02/29/1948-03/01/1948, American Veterans Committee Records, Special Collections Research Center, George Washington University; "T-E-W Bill Principles Get Congressional, Vet Support," *Journal of Housing* 5, no. 3 (March 1948): 59–60.

149. *Proceedings of the 30th National Convention of the American Legion* (Washington, D.C.: USGPO, 1949), 214.

150. William S. White, "Big Housing Plan Filed in Congress," *New York Times*, 1948; Flanders, *Senator from Vermont*, 220.

151. *Congress and the Nation, 1945–1964*, vol. 1 (Washington, D.C.: Congressional Quarterly Service, 1964), 1368; "Service Men Get Housing Priority," *New York Times*, November 2, 1944.

152. *Proceedings of the 30th National Convention*, 214.

153. *Digest of Minutes, National Executive Committee Meeting, May 3, 4 and 5, 1948*, 158, ALA.

154. *Proceedings of the 30th National Convention*, 215.

155. Gray and Bernstein, *The Inside Story of the Legion*, 125.

156. "Taft-Ellender-Wagner Bill Before House Committee," *Journal of Housing* 5, no. 4 (May 1948): 123–24.

157. Poston to Taylor, May 18, 1949, Box 4, Folder: Correspondence, 1946-1949, Bradley R. Taylor Papers, WHS. Apparently on the Legion's behalf, Teague introduced the amendment eliminating a five-year limit; see "Housing Act of 1949," *Congressional Record* June 29, 1949, H8647–48; "Washington, D.C.—(ALNS)," July 5, 1949, Housing, ALA.

158. Kelly to Guinivan, June 20, 1949, Housing, ALA.

159. See Sections 302 and 507 of "Housing Act of 1949," Pub. L. No. 81–171, 63 Stat. 338 (1949).

160. "Washington, D.C.—(ALNS)."

161. "We Present . . . ," *Journal of Housing* 7, no. 3 (March 1950): 89.

162. Harry Conn, "Housing: A Vanishing Vision," *New Republic*, July 16, 1951; Jackson, *Crabgrass Frontier*, chap. 12; Parson, *Making a Better World*; Elizabeth Wood, *The Beautiful Beginnings, the Failure to Learn: Fifty Years of Public Housing in America* (Washington, D.C.: National Center for Housing Management, 1982), 44.

163. The percentage decreased from 54.0 in 1949 to 37.1 in 1957; see Robert Moore Fisher, *20 Years of Public Housing: Economic Aspects of the Federal Program* (New York: Harper, 1959), 166.

164. Davies, *Housing Reform During the Truman Administration*, 107–8; Jackson, *Crabgrass Frontier*, chap. 12.

165. Jackson, *Crabgrass Frontier*, chap. 12; Mark I. Gelfand, *A Nation of Cities: The Federal Government and Urban America, 1933-1965* (New York: Oxford University Press, 1975); James T. Patterson, *Grand Expectations: Postwar America, 1945-1974* (New York: Oxford University Press, 1996), 335.

166. Frank D. Morris, "Our Shameful Record in Veterans' Housing," *Collier's*, July 23, 1949, 57.

167. For details on the continuing problem of middle-income veterans' housing, see Frank D. Morris, "Our Shameful Record in Veterans' Housing."

168. *Digest of Minutes, National Executive Committee Meeting, May 3, 4, and 5, 1950,* 208–9, ALA.

169. John N. Popham, "Plattsburg Man New Head of VFW," *New York Times*, August 26, 1949.

170. Richard H. Parke, "World War II Man Named Legion Head," *New York Times*, September 2, 1949.

171. Disabled American Veterans, *Wars and Scars*, 32.

172. *Proceedings of the 32nd National Convention of the American Legion* (Los Angeles, 1950), 89, 96.

173. On Craig, see "George North Craig," June 6, 2005, Biography Reference Bank (H. W. Wilson), EBSCO*host*, accessed January 20, 2015.

174. See American Legion, *National Membership Record*, 2012, ALA; table Ed229-44, in Susan B. Carter et al., eds., *Historical Statistics of the United States: Earliest Times to the Present*, Millennial Ed. (New York: Cambridge University Press, 2006), vol. 5.

175. *Digest of Minutes, October 13, 14 and 18, 1951*, 54–55.

176. James F. O'Neil, "We Spread Ourselves Too Thin," *ALM*, September 1948.

CHAPTER 4

1. Citizens' Committee for the Hoover Report, "Impact! Of the Cracker Barrel Caravan," n.d. (ca. July 1951), box 32, folder: Charles B. Coates, 1950, RFHC.

2. "Caravan Launches Crusade," *Reorganization News*, May 1950, box 2, folder 2, CCREBGR; "Caravan on Tour for Hoover Report," *New York Times*, May 23, 1950; "Cracker-Barrel Caravan Pays Visit to Bay State," *Christian Science Monitor*, June 17, 1950; "Impact! Of the Cracker Barrel Caravan."

3. Susan B. Carter et al., eds., *Historical Statistics of the United States: Earliest Times to the Present*, Millennial Ed. (New York: Cambridge University Press, 2006), vol. 5, series Ed297-310.

4. Charles Stevenson, "How Bureaucracy Swindles the Taxpayer," *Reader's Digest*, March 1949, 61.

5. *Digest of Minutes, National Executive Committee Meetings, August and September 1949,* 36, ALA.

6. On the First Hoover Commission, see Timothy Walch and Dwight M. Miller, eds, *Herbert Hoover and Harry S. Truman: A Documentary History* (Worland, Wyo: High Plains, 1992): Joanna Grisinger, *The Unwieldy American State: Administrative Politics Since the New Deal* (New York: Cambridge University Press, 2012); Ronald C. Moe, *Administrative Renewal: Reorganization Commissions in the 20th Century* (Lanham, Md.: University Press of America, 2003); Peri E. Arnold, *Making the Managerial Presidency: Comprehensive Reorganization Planning, 1905–1996*,

2nd ed., rev. (Lawrence: University Press of Kansas, 1998); William E. Pemberton, "Struggle for the New Deal: Truman and the Hoover Commission," *Presidential Studies Quarterly* 16, no. 3 (Summer 1986): 511–27; Ronald C. Moe, *The Hoover Commissions Revisited* (Boulder, Colo.: Westview Press, 1982); Peri E. Arnold, "The First Hoover Commission and the Managerial Presidency," *Journal of Politics* 38, no. 1 (February 1976): 46–70.

7. "A New Bonus Plan," *New York Times*, September 7, 1949.

8. "Group Seeks to Destroy U.S. Vet's Program in Four Months," *ALM*, February 1952, 30–31.

9. U.S. Congress, House, Committee on Government Operations, *Summary of the Objectives, Operations, and Results of the Commissions on Organization of the Executive Branch of the Government*, 88th Cong., 1st Sess., 1963, 6–7.

10. Asher Achinstein, *The Welfare State*, Public Affairs Bulletin 83 (Washington, D.C.: Library of Congress Legislative Reference Service, 1950), 3, 6.

11. This top-down approach was adopted by the only other historian who studied the battle over the First Hoover Commission's recommendations on veterans' affairs; see Kathleen Frydl, *The GI Bill* (Cambridge: Cambridge University Press, 2009), 179–84.

12. Carter et al., *Historical Statistics of the United States*, vol. 5, series Ed26–47, Ea650–61, Ea636–43, Ea894–903.

13. Harry S. Truman, *Memoirs*, vol. 1 (Garden City, N.Y.: Doubleday, 1955), 12.

14. For a list of these agencies, see U.S. Congress, House, Committee on Expenditures in the Executive Departments, *First Report of the Commission on Organization of the Executive Branch of Government* (Washington, D.C.: USGPO, 1949), 47–50.

15. President's Committee on Administrative Management, *Administrative Management in the Government of United States*, 1937, 36.

16. Grisinger, *The Unwieldy American State*.

17. Michael J. Hogan, *A Cross of Iron: Harry S. Truman and the Origins of the National Security State, 1945–1954* (Cambridge: Cambridge University Press, 2000), 71–72.

18. William E. Pemberton, *Bureaucratic Politics: Executive Reorganization During the Truman Administration* (Columbia: University of Missouri Press, 1979), 21–78.

19. Hogan, *A Cross of Iron*, esp. chap. 3.

20. Quoted in Pemberton, "Struggle for the New Deal," 520.

21. Pemberton, "Struggle for the New Deal," 512–15.

22. Quoted in Pemberton, "Struggle for the New Deal," 518.

23. Webb to Truman, November 5, 1948, White House Central Files: Official File 285-E (1948), box 1059, Truman Papers, Truman Presidential Library.

24. For a factual overview, see "Summary of Reports of the Hoover Commission," *Public Administration Review* 9, no. 2 (April 1949): 73–99.

25. See Committee on Expenditures in the Executive Departments, *First Report of the Commission*, 1–8.

26. *Annual Report of the Administrator of Veterans' Affairs, 1940* (Washington, D.C.: USGPO, 1941), 1–7; *Annual Report: Administrator of Veterans Affairs, 1949* (Washington, D.C.: USGPO, 1950), 1–4, 73–74; *Here's How We Can Get Better Service for Veterans—at Lower Cost*, n.d., box 73, folder 9, CCREBGR.

27. *Annual Report: Administrator, 1949*, 4.

28. Robert England, *Twenty Million World War Veterans* (New York: Oxford University Press, 1950), 94–95.

29. Gladys M. Kammerer, "The Veterans Administration in Transition," *Public Administration Review* 8, no. 2 (Spring 1948): 105–6.

30. Quoted in Omar Nelson Bradley and Clay Blair, *A General's Life: An Autobiography* (New York: Simon and Schuster, 1983), 441.

31. Harry S. Truman, "The President's News Conference," May 15, 1945, Gerhard Peters and John T. Woolley, The American Presidency Project, http://www.presidency.ucsb.edu/ws/?pid=12236, accessed May 7, 2017.

32. On Bradley's tenure as VA Administrator, see Kammerer, "The Veterans Administration in Transition"; Bradley and Blair, *A General's Life*, 446–62.

33. Bradley and Blair, *A General's Life*, 456.

34. Bradley and Blair, *A General's Life*, 453–56.

35. Coates to Smith, June 21, 1951, box 73, folder 9, CCREBGR.

36. U.S. Congress, House, Committee on Expenditures in the Executive Departments, *Report of Commission on Organization of Executive Branch of the Government on Federal Medical Activities*, 81st Cong., 1st Sess. (Washington, D.C.: USGPO, 1949), 2–3.

37. Over half of VA employees worked in hospitals and medical centers; see table 100 in *Annual Report: Administrator, 1949*, 263.

38. Lois Mattox Miller and James Monahan, "Veterans' Medicine: Second to None!," *Reader's Digest*, September 1947.

39. See recommendation no. 6 in U.S. Congress, House, Committee on Veterans' Affairs, *Reorganization of Veterans' Affairs* (Washington, D.C.: USGPO, 1949), 23–24; and recommendation no. 8 in U.S, Commission on Organization of the Executive Branch of the Government, *Report of Commission on Organization of Executive Branch of the Government on Interior Department* (Washington, D.C.: USGPO, 1949), 15.

40. U.S. Congress, House, Committee on Veterans' Affairs, *Report of the Hoover Commission Committee on Veterans' Affairs (Commission Task Force) to the Commission on Organization of the Executive Branch of the Government* (Washington, D.C.: USGPO, 1949), 5–8.

41. John David Skrentny, *The Ironies of Affirmative Action: Politics, Culture, and Justice in America*, Morality and Society (Chicago: University of Chicago Press, 1996), 38.

42. Miriam Roher, "Veterans and the Civil Service," *American Mercury*, December 1946.

43. *Proceedings of the 33rd National Convention of the American Legion* (Washington, D.C.: USGPO, 1952), 173.

44. See recommendations no. 2, 7, 8, 9, and 23 in U.S. Congress, House, Committee on Post Office and Civil Service, *Report of Commission on Organization of Executive Branch of the Government on Personnel Management* (Washington, D.C.: USGPO, 1949).

45. *Annual Report of the Administrator, 1940*, 1–7; *Annual Report: Administrator, 1949*, 1–4, 73–74; *Here's How We Can Get Better Service*.

46. Committee on Veterans' Affairs, *Reorganization of Veterans' Affairs* (Washington, D.C.: USGPO, 1949), 16.

47. For a list, see Committee on Veterans' Affairs, *Report of the Hoover Commission Committee on Veterans' Affairs*, 1.

48. Charles B. Coates, "Memorandum for the Honorable Herbert Hoover," January 5, 1949; "A Program to Promote the Recommendations of the Commission on Organization of the Executive Branch of the Government: The State Program Phase," December 31, 1948; both in box 32, folder: Charles B. Coates, 1948–49, RFHC.

49. On Coates, see Grisinger, *The Unwieldy American State*, 163. On McCormick, see John White, "Did You Happen to See: Robert L. L. McCormick," *Times Herald*, June 22, 1952; McCormick to Weymouth, Laird and Company, September 29, 1950, box 35, folder: Robert L. L. McCormick, June–December, 1950, RFHC.

50. Coates, "Memorandum for the Honorable Herbert Hoover"; Pemberton, *Bureaucratic Politics*, 110.

51. Quoted in Grisinger, *The Unwieldy American State*, 183.

52. "Caravan on Tour for Hoover Report."

53. Citizens Committee for the Hoover Report, *Will We Be Ready? The Job of Reorganizing Our Government Must Be Finished Immediately . . . Before It's too Late!*, United States, Reorganization (inc. Hoover Plan), A–Z, ALA (A–Z, ALA thereafter).

54. "Boston Speech," n.d. (ca. May 7, 1949), box 33, folder: Robert L. Johnson, May 1949–February 1952, RFHC, HHPL.

55. Charles Aikin and Louis W. Koenig, "Introduction," *American Political Science Review* 43, no. 5 (October 1949): 933.

56. Clayton Knowles, "Hoover Warns U.S. Must Halt Waste to Retain Liberty," *New York Times*, December 13, 1949.

57. McCormick to Hoover, October 13, 1950, box 35, folder: Robert L. L. McCormick, June–December, 1950, RFHC; "American Veterans Hail Hoover's GI Plan," *New York Times*, February 27, 1950.

58. "4 Billions Not Saved," *Chicago Tribune*, April 14, 1950; *Washington Post* and *Wall Street Journal* quoted in Grisinger, *The Unwieldy American State*, 181; James MacGregor Burns, "Our Super-Government—Can We Control It?," *New York Times*, April 24, 1949.

59. Pemberton, *Bureaucratic Politics*, 111.

60. Aikin and Koenig, "Introduction," 933.

61. Aikin and Koenig, "Introduction," 933.

62. George Gallup, "Voters Overwhelmingly Back Hoover Commission Report," *Washington Post*, March 8, 1950.

63. Stanley High, "'We're for Government Economy, But—,'" *Reader's Digest*, January 1950.

64. Public Affairs Institute, *The Hoover Report: Half a Loaf*, Occasional Paper Series 3 (Washington, D.C, 1949), 19.

65. Frances T. Cahn, *Federal Employees in War and Peace: Selection, Placement and Removal* (Washington, D.C.: Brookings Institution, 1949), 92–93, 246.

66. "Veterans' Preference," *Washington Post*, December 21, 1949; "Veterans' Report," *New York Times*, February 15, 1950.

67. Ysabel Rennie and Robert Rennie, "Political Economy: Veterans as a Special Interest," *Washington Post*, January 17, 1950.

68. Harry S. Truman, "Annual Budget Message to the Congress: Fiscal Year 1951—January 9, 1950," *Public Papers of the Presidents of the United States* (1950): 68.

69. George Sokolsky, "These Days," *Washington Times-Herald*, October 23, 1949, box 279, folder 5, George Sokolsky Papers, Hoover Institution Archives.

70. Daniel W. Bell, "Economy in Government," *Tax Review* 10, no. 12 (December 1949): 59.

71. "Danger Signals," *Foreign Service*, April 1949, 17; Perry Brown, "The Growing Attack on Veterans' Benefits," *ALM*, July 1949, 14.

72. See for instance Francis M. Sullivan, "Complete Text of Legislative Director Sullivan's Annual Report," *Disabled American Veterans' Semi-monthly*, August 8, 1950, 8, CHCPL.

73. Robert K. Carr et al., *American Democracy in Theory and Practice: National, State, and Local Government* (New York: Rinehart, 1955), 369.

74. V. O. Key, *Politics, Parties, and Pressure Groups*, 2nd ed. (New York: Crowell, 1948), 128.

75. David B. Truman, *The Governmental Process: Political Interests and Public Opinion* (New York: Knopf, 1951), 99.

76. Dayton David McKean, *Party and Pressure Politics* (Boston: Houghton Mifflin, 1949), 510.

77. Elmo Roper, "Roper Study Indicates Role of Groups in Swaying Voters," *New York Herald Tribune*, May 19, 1952.

78. Disabled American Veterans, *Wars and Scars: The Story of Compassion and Service for Our Nation's Disabled Veterans; A History of the Disabled American Veterans* (Cincinnati, Ohio: IPR Group American Printing, 2006), 36.

79. John H. Walsh, "Cold Facts About Legion's Job in Rehabilitation," *ALM*, July 1949.

80. Perry Brown, "Are We Big Enough for Our Job?," *ALM*, August 1949, 39; emphasis original.

81. *Digest of Minutes, National Executive Committee Meetings, October 13, 14 and 18, 1951,* 54–55, ALA.

82. *Digest of Minutes, National Executive Committee Meeting, May 4, 5, 6, 1949*, 169, ALA.

83. *Digest of Minutes, National Executive Committee Meeting, November 4, 5 and 6, 1949,* 169, ALA.

84. Sullivan, "Complete Text of Annual Report"; "Danger Signals."

85. National Public Relations Division, "Suggested 15-Minute Talk for American Legion Speakers: The American Legion and the Hoover Report," n.d. (ca. January 1950), A–Z, ALA.

86. "What Would Happen to the Veteran if These Proposals Became Law," n.d., A–Z, ALA; emphasis original.

87. Omar B. Ketchum, "It's Up to World War II Vets," *Foreign Service*, June 1949, 18.

88. National Public Relations Division, "Suggested 15-Minute Talk."

89. For "divorce all . . . ," see "McCurdy Denounces Economy Movement as a Blow at Disabled War Veterans," *ALM*, January 1950, 29; for "tear down . . . ," see "Legion Declares Privates War," *Badger Legionnaire*, February 1950, 8, WHS.

90. Kraabel to Falcone, April 10, 1952, A–Z, ALA.

91. "Ed Hayes, Talk at Dept Comdrs Conf. at Indpls Jan 8, 1950 [*sic*]," A–Z, ALA.

92. Cejnar to McGinnis, January 26, 1952, United States, Reorganization (inc. Hoover Plan), Operation Victory, ALA. (Operation Victory, ALA hereafter)

93. Brown, "Growing Attack on Veterans' Benefits."

94. "Ed Hayes."

95. Robert B. Pitkin, "Craig Reveals Hoover Commission Ignored Vital Veterans Problems," *ALM*, March 1950, 32.

96. George E. Ijams, "Why H.R. 5182 Should Be Killed," *Foreign Service*, May 1950, 12.

97. "Legion Declares War," *Taylor Topics* (Chicago), February 1950, A–Z, ALA.

98. "Battle Developing over Veteran Unit," *New York Times*, January 20, 1950.

99. "David M. Brown Reports His Year as National DAV Commander," *Disabled American Veterans' Semi-monthly*, August 22, 1950, 7, CHCPL.

100. U.S. Congress, House, Committee on Veterans' Affairs, *Comments of the Veterans Administration on the Recommendations of the Commission on Organization of the Executive Branch of Government as Applied to the Activities of the Veterans Administration*, 81st Cong., 1st Sess., 1949, 4.

101. Donnald K. Anderson (dir.), *Guide to the Records of the United States House of Representatives at the National Archives, 1789–1989* (Washington, D.C.: USGPO, 1989), 270–72.

102. Gallup Organization. Gallup Poll (AIPO), Feb. 1950. USGALLUP.50-453.QK08B, Gallup Organization, Cornell University, Ithaca, N.Y.: Roper Center for Public Opinion Research, iPOLL, accessed May 8, 2017.

103. For a summary of the Hoover Commission legislation introduced in 1949 on veterans' affairs, see *Digest of Minutes, National Executive Committee Meeting, May 3, 4, and 5, 1950,* 35–36, ALA.

104. McCormick to Coates, memorandum, n.d (ca. 1950), box 72, folder 2, CCREBGR.

105. McCormick to Hoover, January 6, 1950, box 35, folder: Robert L. L. McCormick, January–March, 1950; McCormick to Hoover, December 20, 1949, box 35, folder: Robert L. L. McCormick, Robert L. L. Oct–Dec, 1949, RFHC.

106. Coates to Ely, January 13, 1950, box 73, folder 3, CCREBGR, HIA; Thomas A. Rumer, *The American Legion: An Official History, 1919–1989* (New York: M. Evans, 1990), 320.

107. George N. Craig, "(Call to Special Conference of Department Commanders in U.S. Only)," December 1, 1949, A–Z, ALA.

108. Letter from George N. Craig, January 1, 1950, A–Z, ALA.

109. Edward F. McGinnis, "Operation Survival," n.d. (ca. January 8, 1950), A–Z, ALA.

110. "National Rehabilitation Conference, the American Legion: February 6–7–8–9, 1950, Washington, D.C.: Change In Date," December 15, 1949, A–Z, ALA.

111. U.S. Congress, House, Committee on Veterans' Affairs, *1950 Legislative Programs of the American Legion, Veterans of Foreign Wars, Disabled American Veterans, American Veterans of World War II, and United Spanish War Veterans,* Hearing, January 17, 1950 (Washington D.C.: USGPO, 1950); "Truman, Legion Head Talk," *New York Times,* January 26, 1950.

112. "Legion Declares Privates War," *Badger Legionnaire,* February 1950, WHS.

113. "Pass the Ammunition!! What Every Post Should Do," *ALM,* February 1950, 33.

114. "Time for Action," *Badger Legionnaire,* February 1950, WHS.

115. "American Legion Cartoon Hit by Hoover Group," *New York Herald Tribune,* February 12, 1950.

116. Dudley to Gough, February 2, 1950, United States, Reorganization (inc. Hoover Plan), Comments, Departments—AL–WY, ALA (AL–WY, ALA hereafter).

117. Coates to Johnson, February 27, 1952, box 72, folder 1, CCREBGR.

118. U.S. Congress, House, Committee on Expenditures in Executive Departments, *United Medical Administration,* Hearing, March 29, June 13–14, 22, July 12, 1950 (Washington, D.C.: USGPO, 1950), 35–36.

119. "Congress and Legion," *Washington Post,* February 4, 1950; "Veterans' Report," *New York Times,* February 15, 1950; "Play Fair, Legion," *Washington (D.C.) Times-Herald,* n.d. (ca. February 5, 1950), United States, Reorganization (inc. Hoover Plan), Comments, ALA (Comments, ALA hereafter).

120. "Pressure, with Brass Knucks," *Newsday,* February 14, 1950.

121. "Legion Blast," *Washington Post,* February 8, 1950.

122. "Veterans' Report."

123. Sayer to Moorehead, March 22, 1950, Comments, ALA.

124. U.S. Congress, Senate, Committee on Post Office and Civil Service, *Bills To Implement Recommendations of the Commission on Organization of the Executive Branch of the Government (The Hoover Commission),* Hearing, June 30, July 20, 27, 1949, March 1, 14, 21, June 29, July 18, 27, August 7, 1950 (Washington, D.C.: USGPO, 1951), 176–77.

125. Committee on Expenditures in Executive Departments, *United Medical Administration,* 15–16.

126. Monte M. Poen, *Harry S. Truman Versus the Medical Lobby: The Genesis of Medicare* (Columbia: University of Missouri Press, 1979).

127. Pemberton, *Bureaucratic Politics*, 117–20.

128. U.S. Congress, Senate, Committee on Labor and Public Welfare, Subcommittee on Health, *United Medical and Hospital Administration Act*, Hearing, July 10–12, 1950 (Washington, D.C.: USGPO, 1950), 70; U.S. Congress, Senate, Committee on Expenditures in the Executive Departments, *Progress on Hoover Commission Recommendations* (Washington, D.C.: USGPO, 1949), 328–31.

129. Oakey to Kraabel, January 27, 1950, A–Z, ALA.

130. Department Headquarters, the American Legion, Department of Texas, "Release upon Receipt," received January 20, 1950, A–Z, ALA.

131. Deutschle to Craig, January 23, 1950, AL–WY, ALA.

132. Fuecker to Dudley, February 9, 1950, AL–WY, ALA.

133. McAtee to Coates, "Memo re: Veterans," February 15, 1950, box 73, folder 2, CCREBGR.

134. "Hoover Commission Report, Subject: Campaign Being Carried on by American Legion Departments as Requested in National Adjutant's Letter of March 3, 1950," A–Z, ALA.

135. Quoted in James E. Warner, "Hoover Group Asks Apology from Legion," *New York Herald Tribune*, February 12, 1950.

136. "Hoover Commission Report, Subject."

137. National Legislative Commission, *Legislative Bulletin*, no. 5, February 7, 1950, ALA.

138. Thomas and Kerr to the president, February 7, 1950, AL–WY, ALA.

139. Teague to Mehard, April 26, 1950, box 68, folder 221–7, OETCC.

140. Cejnar to Saidt, March 17, 1950, AL–WY, ALA.

141. McCormick to Coates, memorandum: Veterans, January 20, 1950, box 73, folder 2: Correspondence, CCREBGR.

142. McCormick to Pollock, February 9, 1950; Coates to Stuart, February 1, 1950, box 73, folder 2, CCREBGR.

143. Coates to Smith, June 21, 1951.

144. McCormick to Hoover, December 20, 1949. Emphasis original.

145. McCormick to Pollock, February 9, 1950.

146. CCHR, "'Do's and Don'ts,' on Preparing Material about the Hoover Report," n.d. (ca. November 28, 1949), White House Central Files: Official File 285 E Citizens Committee for Reorganization of the Executive Branch of the Government, Truman Papers, Truman Presidential Library.

147. McCormick to Lucas, April 4, 1952, box 72, folder 1, CCREBGR.

148. McCormick to Hoover, November 20, 1950, box 35, folder: Robert L. L. McCormick, June–December, 1950, RFHC.

149. Johnson to Cocke, November 14, 1950, A–Z, ALA.

150. Memorandum to Erle Cocke, Jr., from Leonce Legendre, T. O. Kraabel, Watson Miller, Miles Kennedy, John T. Taylor, Edward McGrail, Ralph Lavers, Norman Lodge, Edward McGinnis, George Kelly, C. H. Olson, n.d. (ca. February 1951), A–Z, ALA.

151. Jack Oakey, "Memorandum to Henry H. Dudley, William E. Sayer," January 4, 1951, A–Z, ALA.

152. Oakey to Irish, May 14, 1951, A–Z, ALA.

153. Rankin to Biddle, June 19, 1951; "Attention, Veterans," *Reorganization News*, October–November 1951, box 2, folder 2, CCREBGR; emphasis original.

154. Coates to McCormick, June 21, 1951, box 73, folder 9, CCREBGR.

155. "Veterans to Spur U.S. Streamlining," *New York Times*, August 19, 1951; "Founding Members, Independent Veterans Committee for the Hoover Report," September 6, 1951, box 73, folder 9, CCREBGR.

156. Coates to McCormick, June 21, 1951.

157. "Group Seeks to Destroy U.S. Vet's Program in Four Months," *ALM*, February 1952, 30.

158. *Proceedings of the 33rd National Convention*, 184, 310.

159. *Digest of Minutes, National Executive Committee Meeting, Indianapolis, Indiana, November 18, 19 and 20, 1951*, 41, ALA.

160. "55% Streamlined," *Washington Post*, February 18, 1952; U.S. Congress, House, Committee on Veterans' Affairs, *Recommendations of Commission on Organization of the Executive Branch of the Government (Hoover Commission) Providing for Reorganization of the Veterans' Administration and Creating a Veterans' Insurance Corporation*, Hearing, May 27–28, June 3–6, 10–12, 1952 (Washington D.C.: USGPO, 1952), 2214.

161. CCHR, "See It Thru in '52: The Unenacted Recommendations of the Hoover Commission Are Essential Steps in Any Program to Halt . . . Unnecessary Non-defense Spending, Avert . . . Inflation, Enable . . . Economical, Efficient Government Operation," n.d. (ca. December 1951), A–Z, ALA.

162. *Digest of Minutes, November 18, 19 and 20, 1951*, 16, ALA; Coates to Smith, March 25, 1952, box 73, folder 9, CCREBGR.

163. *Digest of Minutes, National Executive Committee Meeting, May 5, 6 and 7, 1952*, 39–40, ALA.

164. Operations-chief of staff to the national commander, "Operation Victory," December 10, 1951, Operation Victory, ALA.

165. *Digest of Minutes, May 5, 6 and 7, 1952*, 43–44, ALA.

166. Committee on Veterans' Affairs, *Recommendations of Commission on Creating a Veterans' Insurance Corporation*, 2079.

167. Committee on Veterans' Affairs, *Recommendations of Commission on Creating a Veterans' Insurance Corporation*, 2091.

168. *Proceedings of the 34th National Convention of the American Legion* (New York, 1952), 336.

169. For the statement of the AVC, see U.S. Congress, House, Committee on Post Office and Civil Service, *Recruitment Procedures in the Federal Government*, Hearing, March 25–26, April 1, 3, 8, 24, 29, May 13, 15, 1952 (Washington D.C.: USGPO, 1952), 237.

170. *Digest of Minutes, May 5, 6 and 7, 1952*, 43, ALA.

171. *Proceedings of the 34th National Convention*, 179–80.

172. "Action Sheet—Independent Veterans Committee for the Hoover Report," n.d. (ca. 1952), box 73, folder 9, CCREBGR.

173. *Digest of Minutes, National Executive Committee Meetings, New York City, N.Y., August 24 and 28, 1952*, 5, ALA.

174. See resolution no. 575, *Proceedings of the 34th National Convention*, 65.

175. *Proceedings of the 34th National Convention*, 420.

176. See the planks "Government Reorganization" for the Republican Party and "Streamlining the Federal Government" for the Democratic Party, The American Presidency Project, http://www.presidency.ucsb.edu/platforms.php, accessed May 7, 2017.

177. *Digest of Minutes, National Executive Committee Meeting, October 10, 11 and 12, 1952*, 19, ALA.

CHAPTER 5

1. "Brazil Will Honor New Legion Chief on Nov. 3," *ALM*, November 1949; "Royal Welcome Accorded National Commander Craig by His Home Town," *ALM*, December 1949; Thomas A. Rumer, *The American Legion: An Official History, 1919–1989* (New York: M. Evans, 1990), 302–3.

2. "Royal Welcome Accorded National Commander Craig"; "Baby Guarded as Legion Chief Assails Reds," *Los Angeles Times*, November 4, 1949.

3. "Legion Prestige High with Public," *Detroit District Legion News*, July 12, 1946, 6, ALA.

4. James Q. Wilson, *Political Organizations* (Princeton, N.J.: Princeton University Press, 1995), xx.

5. On the AVC in these years, see Peter D. Hoefer, "A David Against Goliath: The American Veterans Committee's Challenge to the American Legion in the 1950s" (PhD dissertation, University of Maryland, College Park, 2010).

6. Stephen F. Chadwick, "For the Argus," October 25, 1955, Accession No. 1522-002, box 5, folder 5-12, SFCP.

7. Christopher Endy, "Power and Culture in the West," in *The Oxford Handbook of the Cold War*, ed. Richard Immerman and Petra Goedde (Oxford: Oxford University Press, 2013), 323–40.

8. David K. Johnson, *The Lavender Scare: The Cold War Persecution of Gays and Lesbians in the Federal Government* (Chicago: University of Chicago Press, 2004); Landon R. Y. Storrs, *The Second Red Scare and the Unmaking of the New Deal Left* (Princeton, N.J.: Princeton University Press, 2013).

9. The canonical example of the earlier approach is Daniel Bell, ed., *The New American Right* (New York: Criterion Books, 1955).

10. Quoted in Ellen Schrecker, *Many Are the Crimes: McCarthyism in America* (Boston: Little, Brown, 1998), 203.

11. Carl T. Bogus, *Buckley: William F. Buckley Jr. and the Rise of American Conservatism* (New York: Bloomsbury Press, 2011).

12. On Chaillaux, see "Homer L. Chaillaux," *New York Herald Tribune*, February 20, 1946.

13. William Pencak, *For God and Country: The American Legion, 1919–1941* (Boston: Northeastern University Press, 1989), chaps. 6, 9; Christopher C. Nehls, "'A Grand and Glorious Feeling': The American Legion and American Nationalism Between the World Wars" (PhD dissertation, University of Virginia, 2007).

14. Quoted in Alexander Gardiner, "Colmery of Kansas," *ALM*, January 1937, 18. Pencak, *For God and Country*, 250–55.

15. Quoted in Heale, *American Anticommunism*, 136.

16. *Digest of Minutes, National Executive Committee Meeting, May 5, 6, 7, 1947*, 14–15, ALA.

17. *Proceedings of the 28th National Convention of the American Legion* (Washington, D.C.: USGPO, 1947), 160–61.

18. *Digest of Minutes, Annual Conference of Department Commanders and Department Adjutants, November 21, 22, 23, 1948*, 38, ALA.

19. "Week's Legion News in a Nut Shell," April 11, 1947, box 14, folder 773: Press and Public Relations, 1941–75, SLP; Karl Baarslag, "What Has Really Happened to the American Legion?," 7–9, n.d., box 6, folder 1, KBP.

20. On Baarslag's background, see U.S. Congress, Senate, Committee on the Judiciary, Subcommittee To Investigate the Administration of the Internal Security Act and Other Internal Security Laws, *Subversive Infiltration in the Telegraph Industry*, Hearing, May 14–16, June 5–6, 12, 14, 1951 (Washington, D.C.: USGPO, 1951), 1–26; "Karl Baarslag, Author And Ex-Congress Aide," *New York Times*, January 14, 1984.

21. *Proceedings of the 28th National Convention*, 144–45; Baarslag, "What Has Really Happened to the American Legion?," 2.

22. *Proceedings of the 29th National Convention of the American Legion* (Washington, D.C.: USGPO, 1948), 170; *Digest of Minutes, National Executive Committee Meetings, August 24 and 28, 1952*, 22, ALA.

23. National Americanism Commission, the American Legion, *How You Can Fight Communism* (Indianapolis: American Legion, 1949).

24. U.S. Congress, Senate, Committee on the Judiciary, Subcommittee on S. 1194 and S. 1196, *Control of Subversive Activities*, Hearing, April 29, May 4, 6, 18–20, June 10, 1949 (Washington, D.C.: USGPO, 1949), 115–16.

25. National Americanism Commission, American Legion, *Addresses: Counter-subversion Seminar* (Indianapolis: American Legion, 1948), 223.

26. *Proceedings of the 30th National Convention of the American Legion* (Washington, D.C.: USGPO, 1949), 74.

27. Wayne E. Richards, "To Keep Liberty Alive—Outlaw Communism," *V.F.W. Magazine* (May 1954), 12, VFWNH.

28. "Place Communists in Camps, DAV Delegates Insist," *DAV Semi-monthly*, August 22, 1950, 3; "Peace-Time Death Penalty for Traitors Asked," *DAV Semi-monthly*, September 12, 1950, 9, CHCPL.

29. *Proceedings of the 32nd National Convention of the American Legion* (Washington, D.C.: USGPO, 1951), 67.

30. *Proceedings of the 34th National Convention of the American Legion* (Washington, D.C.: USGPO, 1953), 52.

31. American Federation of Labor, *Report of the Proceedings of the Sixty-eighth Convention of the American Federation of Labor* (American Federation of Labor, 1949), 395–96.

32. J. C. McLachlan, "Sound Off: Republicans and Dixiecrats," *ALM*, July 1952, 4. For an example of this kind of article, see William LaVarre, "Is Our Constitution Doomed?" *ALM*, September 1952.

33. Quoted in Alonzo L. Hamby, *Man of the People: A Life of Harry S. Truman* (New York: Oxford University Press, 1995), 566.

34. The most prominent of these were the "Peekskill Riots" in upstate New York; see James Rorty and Winifred Raushenbush, "The Lessons of the Peekskill Riots," *Commentary* 10, no. 4 (October 1950): 309–23.

35. Walter Brooks, "Setting the Stage for Moscow," *ALM*, September 1953; Louis Francis Budenz, "How the Reds Invaded Radio," *ALM*, December 1950; Felix Wittmer, "Now Hear This!," *ALM*, February 1953; Esther Julia Pels, "Art for Whose Sake?" *ALM*, October 1955; William Fulton, "Let's Look at Our Foundations," *ALM*, August 1952.

36. Eugene Lyons, "Our New Privileged Class," *ALM*, September 1951, 39.

37. The *ALM* ranked thirteenth nationwide in terms of circulation by March 1952; see Paul W. Brown, "A Content Analysis of the ALM from 1945 to the Present: Editorial Policy Toward Americanism" (BA thesis, Princeton University, 1953), i.

38. On Matthews, see Howard Rushmore, "'Mr. Anticommunist,'" *American Mercury*, May 1953. For articles by these authors, see J. B. Matthews, "The Commies Go After the Kids," *ALM*, December 1949; Fred Woltman, Victor Riesel, George E. Sokolsky, and Louis F. Budenz, "Watch Out for These Commie Swindles," *ALM*, May 1952; William F. Buckley, Jr., "Sacco-Vanzetti, Again," *ALM*, October 1960.

39. National Americanism Commission, American Legion, *Addresses* 232–33.

40. Willand to Inglis, August 7, 1951, box 649, folder: American Legion, General Papers, 1950, Jan.–Oct. 1958, JBMP.

41. "Counter-subversive Conference Speakers," January 13, 1949, box 39, folder 4, JBMP.

42. *Digest of Minutes, National Executive, August 24 and 28, 1952*, 16. On Manion, see Nicole Hemmer, *Messengers of the Right: Conservative Media and the Transformation of American Politics* (Philadelphia: University of Pennsylvania Press, 2016).

43. *Digest of Minutes, National Executive Committee Meeting, May 2, 3 and 4, 1951*, 128, ALA; *Proceedings of the 34th National Convention*, 14.

44. "Bar Association to Join in Anti-Commie Campaign," *ALM*, February 1951, 36.

45. "Lee Pennington Has Been Assistant Director . . . ," n.d. (ca. May 1958), box 676, folder: Pennington, Lee R., 1955, 1958, JBMP.

46. Justin Gray and Victor H. Bernstein, *The Inside Story of the Legion* (New York: Boni and Gaer, 1948), 211.

47. "Legion News: Americanism," *ALM*, January 1954, 38; U.S. Congress, House, Committee on the Judiciary, Subcommittee No. 1, *Internal Security Legislation*, Hearing, March 18, April 5, 7–8, 12, June 2, 9, 23, 25, 30, 1954 (Washington, D.C.: USGPO, 1954), 201–2; Matthew Cecil, *Branding Hoover's FBI: How the Boss's PR Men Sold the Bureau to America* (Lawrence: University Press of Kansas, 2016), 83–84, 90.

48. See, for instance, *Proceedings of the 26th National Convention of the American Legion* (Washington, D.C.: USGPO, 1945), 87–88.

49. Kathleen McLaughlin, "Rankin Puts Over New Dies Group," *New York Times*, January 4, 1945.

50. On anticommunism as a global phenomenon, see Kyle Burke, *Revolutionaries for the Right: Anticommunist Internationalism and Paramilitary Warfare in the Cold War* (Chapel Hill: University of North Carolina Press, 2018); Marla Stone and Giuliana Chamedes, "Naming the Enemy: Anticommunism in Transnational Perspective," *Journal of Contemporary History* 53, no. 1 (2018): 4–11; Doug Rossinow, "The Dirty War Network," in *Outside In: The Transnational Circuitry of US History*, ed. Doug Rossinow and Andrew Preston (Oxford: Oxford University Press, 2017), 230–46.

51. Robert Pitkin, "How You Made 3,000,000 Kids Happy," *ALM*, August 1950.

52. *Proceedings of the 32nd National Convention*, 45–46, 86, 258–59.

53. "Legion News: Religion," *ALM*, December 1953, 41; H. von Royk-Lewinski, "Curtain of Wooden Churches," *Washington Post and Times Herald*, April 18, 1954.

54. *Proceedings of the 36th National Convention of the American Legion* (Washington, D.C.: USGPO, 1955), 13, 141.

55. Helen Laville and Hugh Wilford, eds., *The US Government, Citizen Groups and the Cold War: The State-Private Network* (New York: Routledge, 2006).

56. D. F. Fleming, "Are We Moving Toward Fascism?" *Journal of Politics* 16, no. 1 (1954): 44.

57. On universal military training, see William A. Taylor, *Every Citizen a Soldier: The Campaign for Universal Military Training After World War II* (College Station: Texas A&M University Press, 2014); Matthew J. Seelinger, "Breaking Ranks: Veterans' Opposition to Universal Military Training, 1943–1948" (MA thesis, Ball State University, 1996).

58. Kevin Kruse, *One Nation Under God: How Corporate America Invented Christian America* (New York: Basic Books, 2015).

59. *Digest of Minutes, Annual Conference of Department Commanders and Department Adjutants, November 14, 15, 16, 1944*, 28, ALA; *Proceedings of the 25th National Convention of the American Legion* (Washington, D.C.: USGPO, 1944), 97.

60. Marion S. Adams, *Alvin M. Owsley of Texas: Apostle of Americanism* (Waco, Tex.: Texian Press, 1971).

61. *Proceedings of the 26th National Convention*, 190–94.

62. "'We've Got to Finish the Job this Time,' Say 'Dead Serious' Members of the Legion," *Indianapolis Star*, May 7, 1943, box 10, folder 592, SLP.

63. *Digest of Minutes, Annual Conference, November 14, 15, 16, 1944*, 14.

64. *Digest of Minutes, Annual Conference, November 14, 15, 16, 1944*, 23–33; *Digest of Minutes, National Executive Committee Meetings, June 5, 6, 7, 1946*, 298, ALA; *Digest of Minutes, National Executive Committee Meeting, November 21–23, 1946*, 93, ALA; Owsley to Griffith, July 19, 1946, box 607, folder 10, AMOC.

65. *Digest of Minutes, National Executive Committee Meeting, October 17 and 21, 1948*, 47, ALA.

66. *Proceedings of the 30th National Convention*, 161. For the comprehensive list of speakers and the text of their lectures, see National Americanism Commission, *Addresses*.

67. National Americanism Commission, *Addresses*, 3.

68. James F. O'Neil, "How You Can Fight Communism," *ALM*, August 1948, 17.

69. *Digest of Minutes, National Executive Committee Meeting, May 3, 4 and 5, 1948*, 103, ALA.

70. *Proceedings of the 30th National Convention*, 161.

71. *Digest of Minutes, Annual Conference, November 21, 22, 23, 1948*, 40.

72. Broad Ripple Post No. 312 and Auxiliary Unit of the American Legion, *Program: Hoosier Counter-subversive Seminar*, Indianapolis, 1954. On Cohn, see Schrecker, *Many Are the Crimes*, 256–60.

73. *Proceedings of the 32nd National Convention*, 135.

74. Baarslag, "What Has Really Happened to the American Legion?," 53.

75. George N. Craig, "Legion Calls Nationwide 'All American' Conference to Organize for Concerted Action Against Communism," *ALM*, February 1950, 29.

76. Jack Little, "'All-American Conference' Welds Eighty Millions into United Front to Destroy Communism in United States," *ALM*, March 1950.

77. Little, "All-American Conference," 29.

78. "$5,000,000 Fund Sought to Fight Reds in America," *New York Herald Tribune*, August 14, 1951; *Digest of Minutes, National Executive, May 2, 3, and 4, 1951*, 176.

79. Fred to George, December 17, 1951, box 1, folder 7, AACCCR.

80. "The All-American Conference to Combat Communism," box 1, folder 17, Edwin Lukas Papers, Historical Society of Pennsylvania, Philadelphia.

81. JGF to Fred, December 13, 1951; Fredman to Fred, December 20, 1951; both in box 1, folder 7, AACCCR; emphasis original.

82. Letter to Dear Fred, September 13 [1952], box 1, folder 10, AACCCR.

83. Baarslag, "What Has Really Happened to the American Legion?" 57–58.

84. "Anti-Red Books to Be Placed in Libraries," *ALM*, July 1952, 33; *Proceedings of the 34th National Convention*, 138.

85. "Legion Starts Memorial Book Plan to Honor Men Who Died in Korea Fighting Communism," *ALM*, June 1952, 31.

86. *Digest of Minutes, National Executive Committee Meeting, October 10, 11 and 12, 1952*, 47, ALA.

87. Baarslag, "What Has Really Happened to the American Legion?," 38.

88. *Digest of Minutes, National Executive Committee Meeting, April 29–30, May 1, 1953*, 44, ALA.

89. See the last two pages of the American Legion, *Counter-subversive Manual*, 1955, box 11, folder 3, Lee R. Pennington Papers, Hoover Institution Archives.

90. *Proceedings of the 33rd National Convention of the American Legion* (Washington, D.C.: USGPO, 1952), 144.

91. Baarslag, "What Has Really Happened to the American Legion?," 14.

92. *Proceedings of the 30th National Convention*, 42, 162.

93. From 1945 to 1950, see *Digest of Minutes, National Executive Committee Meetings, October 13, 14 and 18, 1951*, 54–55, ALA. From 1951 to 1960, see the report of the national treasurer in the *Proceedings* of the following year's national convention.

94. *Proceedings of the 34th National Convention*, 136.

95. *Digest of Minutes, Annual Conference, November 21, 22, 23, 1948*, 40.

96. *Digest of Minutes, National Executive Committee Meeting, November 17, 18, and 19, 1950*, 5–6, ALA.

97. "Memo from American Legion: No Letdown Against Reds," *U.S. News and World Report*, July 24, 1953.

98. *Digest of Minutes, National Executive, April 29–30, May 1, 1953*, 54.

99. *Proceedings of 36th National Convention*, 436.

100. For the percentage, see *Digest of Minutes, National Executive, October 13, 14 and 18, 1951*, 54–55.

101. McCarthy addressed the Security Commission at the 1953 convention but never the full convention; see "... When Good Fellows Get Together," *ALM*, October 1953, 37. The 1957 convention passed a resolution to "regret" his passing and to praise his record, but stopped short of asking the Senate to lift its censure of him; see *Proceedings of 39th National Convention of the American Legion* (Washington, D.C.: USGPO, 1958), 58. For more, see Wayne Edwin McKinley, "A Study of the American Right: Senator Joseph McCarthy and the American Legion, 1946–1955" (MS thesis, University of Wisconsin, 1962); Morten Bach, "None So Consistently Right: The American Legion's Cold War, 1945–1960" (PhD dissertation, Ohio University, 2007), 142–45.

102. "Memo from American Legion."

103. *Digest of Minutes, National Executive, May 2, 3 and 4, 1951*, 130–31.

104. For Baarslag's version of this episode, see "What Has Really Happened to the American Legion?" 38, 62–63, 65–68. The firing was covered in the press a few months later; see "Legion's 'Red Chase,'" *U.S. News and World Report*, June 12, 1953. For the Legion's response, see "Memo from American Legion."

105. C. P. Trussell, "Bolters Spurn McCarthy Plea For Return to Inquiry Group," *New York Times*, July 17, 1953.

106. *Digest of Minutes, National Executive Committee Meeting, October 15, 16 and 17, 1953*, 59–60, ALA.

107. Baarslag, "What Has Really Happened to the American Legion?," 68.

108. *Proceedings of 37th National Convention of the American Legion* (Washington, D.C.: USGPO, 1956), 13.

109. Quoted in Gary P. Henrickson, "Minnesota in the 'McCarthy' Period: 1946–1954" (PhD dissertation, University of Minnesota, 1981), 159–60, 173. See also Dale R. Sorenson, "The Anticommunist Consensus in Indiana, 1945–1958" (PhD dissertation, Indiana University, 1980), 212–13, 216; Ronald W. Johnson, "The Communist Issue in Missouri, 1946–1956" (PhD dissertation, University of Missouri–Columbia, 1973), 20, 144–45, 181; Richard J. Loosbrock, "The History of the Kansas Department of the American Legion, 1919–1968" (PhD dissertation, University of Kansas, 1968), 350–59.

110. Research Division, *The Freedom of the Public-School Teacher* (Washington, D.C.: National Education Association of the United States, 1951), 53.

111. See subseries 3A.5, box 763, folder 25, ACLUR.

112. Quoted in Schrecker, *Many Are the Crimes*, 15.

113. Richard Seelye Jones, *A History of the American Legion* (Indianapolis: Bobbs-Merrill, 1946), 349.

114. KB to JB, June 13, 1946, box 591, folder: Baarslag, Karl, General Papers, 1946–51, JBMP.

115. Baarslag, "What Has Really Happened to the American Legion?," 60.

116. Samuel A. Stouffer, *Communism, Conformity, and Civil Liberties: A Cross-section of the Nation Speaks its Mind* (Garden City, N.Y.: Doubleday, 1955), 235.

117. American Legion Membership Survey, Winter 1954–55, reel #96–10, pp. 20, 60, ALA.

118. S. E. Graham, "The (Real)politiks of Culture: U.S. Cultural Diplomacy in Unesco, 1946–1954," *Diplomatic History* 30, no. 2 (April 2006): 238, 240.

119. On Lyons and UNESCO, see Michelle Nickerson, *Mothers of Conservatism: Women and the Postwar Right* (Princeton, N.J.: Princeton University Press, 2012), 89–97; Glen Warren Adams, "The UNESCO Controversy in Los Angeles, 1951–1953: A Case Study of the Influence of Right-Wing Groups on Urban Affairs" (PhD dissertation, University of Southern California, 1970).

120. *Proceedings of the 31st National Convention of the American Legion* (Washington, D.C.: USGPO, 1950), 24.

121. J. B. Matthews, "The United Nations—Boon or Boondoggle?" *ALM*, November 1952.

122. *Digest of Minutes, National Executive, April 29–30, May 1, 1953*, 123–24.

123. "Report from Los Angeles," *V.F.W. Magazine*, September 1952, 17, VFWNH.

124. *Digest of Minutes, National Executive, April 29–30, May 1, 1953*, 47–48; "Report of Special Committee to Study the Covenant of Human Rights and to Act as Liaison with the Standing Committee on Peace and Law Through United Nations of the American Bar Association," n.d., box 62, folder 248, HWCC.

125. Frank Miles, "The Name Is Murphy," *American Legion Monthly*, December 1935; Pencak, *For God and Country*, 253; Bach, "None So Consistently Right," 214.

126. Ray Murphy, "The American Legion and UNESCO," *America*, November 26, 1955; Ray Murphy, "Which Constitution Do We Want?" *ALM*, February 1954. On the American Bar Association and the National Lawyers Guild, see Schrecker, *Many Are the Crimes*, 301–2.

127. Graham, "The (Real)politiks of Culture."

128. Allen Drury, "Legion Ranks Are Split over the UNESCO Issue," *New York Times*, September 18, 1955.

129. *Digest of Minutes, National Executive Committee Meeting, May 2, 3 and 4, 1954*, 187–95, ALA.

130. *Proceedings of 36th National Convention*, 100–101; *Digest of Minutes, National Executive Committee Meeting, October 5, 6 and 7, 1954*, 88–89, ALA.

131. Letter from Joe C. Jenkins, "Hi Ya," August 12, 1954; Lyons to Jenkins, July 14, 1954; both in box 605, folder 7, AMOC.

132. MacFarland, Jr., to Dear fellow Patriot, July 15, 1954, box 605, folder 7, AMOC.

133. For the Murphy Committee's report, see *Digest of Minutes, National Executive Committee Meeting, May 4, 5 and 6, 1955*, 112–76, ALA. For the National Americanism Commission's report, see National Americanism Commission, *Report on the United Nations Educational, Scientific and Cultural Organization*, May 1, 1955, box 541, folder 4, JBMP.

134. "Which Legion Is the Real Legion?" *Christian Century*, September 28, 1955.

135. Drury, "Legion Ranks Are Split."

136. Ben H. Bagdikian, "How the Legionnaires Were Duped," *Atlantic Monthly*, July 1956, 54.

137. Roscoe Drummond, "Legion Committee Defends UNESCO," *Washington Post and Times Herald*, September 10, 1955.

138. "Challenge for the Legion," *Life*, September 12, 1955, 48.

139. Dwight D. Eisenhower, *The Papers of Dwight David Eisenhower*, ed. Louis Galambos and Daun Van Ee, vol. 16 (Baltimore: Johns Hopkins University Press, 1996), 1832–33; Telephone Call

from the President, Monday, August 29, 1955 11:38 a.m., box 10, folder: Telephone Conv.—White House Mar. 7, 1955 to Aug. 29, 1955 (1), John Foster Dulles Papers, Telephone Conversations Series, Eisenhower Presidential Library.

140. *Digest of Minutes, National Executive, May 4, 5 and 6, 1955*, 168.

141. "Seeks to Upset Legion's Anti-UNESCO Stand," *Free Men Speak*, May–June 1955, box 541, folder 3, JBMP.

142. Merwin K. Hart, "How About It, Legionnaires!" *Economic Council Letter*, no. 368 (October 1, 1955), box 62, folder 246, HWCC.

143. Hon. H. R. Gross (IA), "American Legion Members, Again Called upon to Fight Endorsement of UNESCO . . . ," *Congressional Record*, August 2, 1955.

144. The evaluation is quoted in exhibit 5 of Gross, "American Legion Members."

145. Stark to Collins, "Report on U.N.E.S.C.O. by Ray Murphy's Committee," June 8, 1955, box 541, folder 5, JBMP. The same letter can be found in box 62, folder 245, HWCC.

146. "Warns Peril for U.S. Lies in UNESCO," *Florida Legionnaire*, August 15, 1954, box 5, folder 5–2, accession no. 1522-002, SFCP.

147. Anti-subversive Chairman, Department of Washington, *A Refutation of the Report of the American Legion Special Committee on Covenent [sic] of Human Rights and United Nations Herein Referred to as the Murphy Committee*, n.d. (ca. October 1955), box 541, folder 5, JBMP.

148. Bagdikian, "How the Legionnaires Were Duped."

149. Jenkins to Murphy, January 28, 1955, box 5, folder 5–2, accession no. 1522-002, SFCP.

150. Murphy to Owsley, August 11, 1954, box 605, folder 7, AMOC; "Statement by Ray Murphy Before Subcommittee . . . ," March 9, 1956, p. 8, box 62, folder 247, HWCC.

151. McKinley to Members of National Executive Committee and Members of the National Americanism Commission, March 10, 1955, box 62, folder 245, HWCC.

152. Millis to Ferry, "Memorandum on the Miami Convention of the American Legion, October 10–13, 1955," box 16, folder 6, FFR.

153. *Proceedings of 37th National Convention*, 13.

154. For the final text of the joint committee resolution, see *Proceedings of 37th National Convention*, 55–56. For a description of the debate within the committee and on the floor of the convention, see "News of The American Legion: Two Convention Echoes; Press Garbled UNESCO Story; Legion to Seek Pension Gains," *ALM*, December 1955; Murphy, "The American Legion and UNESCO"; "The Legion Is Disgraced," *Life*, October 24, 1955.

155. Murphy to Quinn, August 8, 1957, box 63, folder 308, HWCC.

156. "UNESCO and the Legion," *Newsday*, Nassau ed., October 14, 1955.

157. "The Legion Is Disgraced," 44.

158. "The Legion and UNESCO," *New York Times*, October 14, 1955.

159. Bert Collier, "The Reckless Legion," *Nation*, October 22, 1955.

160. "Press Reaction to American Legion Action on UNESCO," *Michigan Legionnaire*, December 1955, Bentley Historical Library, University of Michigan.

161. See for instance J. Addington Warner, "Another Look at UNESCO," *ALM*, August 1956.

162. U.S. Congress, House, Committee on Foreign Affairs, Subcommittee on International Organizations and Movements, *The United Nations Specialized Agencies* (Washington, D.C.: USGPO, 1957), 7, 26.

163. Reitman to Thomas, August 8, 1958, box 610, folder 4, ACLUR.

164. Intra-Office Buck Sheet: from A.R. to PMM, September 8, 1958, box 610, folder 4, ACLUR.

165. *Proceedings of the 40th National Convention of the American Legion* (Washington, D.C.: USGPO, 1959), 5–6.

166. Resolutions no. 75 and 421 in *Proceedings of the 38th National Convention of the American Legion* (Washington, D.C.: USGPO, 1957), 49, 51.

167. George Lewis, *The White South and the Red Menace: Segregationists, Anticommunism, and Massive Resistance, 1945–1965* (Gainesville: University Press of Florida, 2004).

168. "Legion Head on Spot," *Baltimore Afro-American*, April 30, 1955; "Negro Legionnaires in 5 States Protest Commander Race Slur," n.d., Administration and Organization, Membership, Black Members; "Biloxi, Miss., July 10 (AP) . . . ," Americanism, Tolerance, Segregation, ALA.

169. Breakstone to Hutchins, March 16, 1956, box 16, folder 5, FFR.

170. Hoefer, "A David Against Goliath," 180–91.

171. Hoefer, "A David Against Goliath," 196–211.

172. Harvey Glickman, "The Legion Dies Laughing," *Nation*, September 7, 1957, 103.

173. Lisle H. Alexander, "Department Adjutant and Welfare Committee," *Michigan Legionnaire*, July 1958, Bentley Historical Library, University of Michigan.

CHAPTER 6

1. "FBI Seizes Two in $300,000 Fraud," *New York Times*, December 3, 1950; Edward Ranzal, "199 Veterans Among 205 Indicted in $250,000 Beauty School Fraud," *New York Times*, January 13, 1951; "$300,000 Fraud in GI Education Gets Fines, Jail," *Washington Post*, June 7, 1951; *House Select Committee to Investigate Educational, Training, and Loan Guaranty Programs Under GI Bill*, 82 H. Rpt. 1375, 1952, 94; "4 Ex-GI's Get Jail for Tuition Fraud," *New York Times*, May 30, 1952.

2. On the role of scandal in the 1944 GI Bill, see Kathleen Frydl, *The GI Bill* (Cambridge: Cambridge University Press, 2009), chap. 4.

3. Gary Gerstle, *Liberty and Coercion: The Paradox of American Government from the Founding to the Present* (Princeton, N.J.: Princeton University Press, 2015), chap. 8; Michael J. Hogan, *A Cross of Iron: Harry S. Truman and the Origins of the National Security State, 1945–1954* (Cambridge: Cambridge University Press, 2000); Aaron L. Friedberg, *In the Shadow of the Garrison State: America's Anti-statism and Its Cold War Grand Strategy* (Princeton, N.J.: Princeton University Press, 2000); Mary Ann Heiss and Michael J. Hogan, eds., *Origins of the National Security State and the Legacy of Harry S. Truman* (Kirksville, Mo.: Truman State University Press, 2015).

4. See for instance Hogan, *A Cross of Iron*, 365.

5. *Proceedings of the 34th National Convention of the American Legion* (Washington, D.C.: USGPO, 1953), 59.

6. U.S. Congress, House, Committee on Veterans' Affairs, *Education and Training and Other Benefits for Veterans Serving on or After June 27, 1950*, Hearing, February 6–7, 13–14, 19–21, 26–28, March 4–6, 11, 1952 (Washington, D.C.: USGPO, 1952), 1327.

7. Sec. 800 (a) (2) of Servicemen's Readjustment Act of 1944, Pub. L. No. 78-346, 58 Stat. 284.

8. "Veterans on the Dole," *Chicago Daily Tribune*, March 12, 1947.

9. Quoted in U.S. Congress, Committee on Labor and Public Welfare, Subcommittee on Veterans' Affairs, *Amend Servicemen's Readjustment Act*, Hearing, June 23, 1949 (Washington, D.C.: USGPO, 1949), 28; Glenn C. Altschuler and Stuart M. Blumin, *The GI Bill: A New Deal for Veterans* (Oxford: Oxford University Press, 2009), 154.

10. "LI Vets Warned on Home Frauds," *Newsday*, May 19, 1952.

11. R. K. McNickle, "Benefits for Korean Veterans," Editorial Research Reports 1952, vol. 1 (Washington, D.C.: CQ Press, 1952).

12. "A Service to Veterans," *New York Times*, June 17, 1945.

13. A. J. Angulo, *Diploma Mills: How For-Profit Colleges Stiffed Students, Taxpayers, and the American Dream* (Baltimore: Johns Hopkins University Press, 2016), 59.

14. Homer A. Ramey, "Let's Stop Abuses in Veterans' Schools," *Collier's*, May 8, 1948.

15. Albert Q. Maisel, "What's Wrong with Veterans' Schools?," *Collier's*, May 1, 1948, 24. For a reprint, see Albert Q. Maisel, "Veterans' Training: The $500,000,000 Boondoggle," *Reader's Digest*, June 1948.

16. Maisel, "What's Wrong with Veterans' Schools?"

17. *Committee to Investigate Educational, Training, and Loan Guaranty Programs*, 105–9.

18. Ramey, "Let's Stop Abuses in Veterans' Schools." For the hearings, see U.S. Congress, House, Committee on Veterans' Affairs, Subcommittee on Education, Training, and Rehabilitation, *Veterans' Education and Training Program in Private Schools; Part 1: Relating to Education and Training Program at Columbia Technical Institute, Washington, D.C.*, Hearing, January 23, 1948 (Washington, D.C.: USGPO, 1948); U.S. Congress, House, Committee on Veterans' Affairs, Subcommittee on Education, Training, and Rehabilitation, *Veterans' Education and Training Program in Private Schools. Part 2: Relating to Education and Training Programs in Private Schools under the Servicemen's Readjustment Act*, Hearing, January 30, February 6, 1948 (Washington, D.C.: USGPO, 1948).

19. Ramey, "Let's Stop Abuses in Veterans' Schools," 27.

20. There were eight major amendments to the 1944 GI Bill between 1945 and 1950: Pub. L. No. 79-268, 59 Stat. 623; Pub. L. No. 79-679, 60 Stat. 934; Pub. L. No. 80-377, 61 Stat. 791; Pub. L. No. 80-411, 62 Stat. 19; Pub. L. No. 80-512, 62 Stat. 208; Supplemental Independent Offices Appropriation Act of 1949, Pub. L. No. 80-862, 62 Stat. 1196; Independent Offices Appropriation Act of 1950, Pub. L. No. 81-266, 63 Stat. 631; Veterans' Education and Training Amendments of 1950, Pub. L. No. 81-610, 64 Stat. 336.

21. Charles Hurd, "Legion, VFW Seek Pensions for All," *New York Times*, January 28, 1949.

22. *Congress and the Nation, 1945–1964*, vol. 1 (Washington, D.C.: Congressional Quarterly Service, 1964), 1345.

23. U.S. Congress, House, Committee on Veterans' Affairs, *Pensions for Veterans of World Wars I and II—Legislative Programs of the American Legion, Veterans of Foreign Wars, Disabled American Veterans, and American Veterans of World War II*, Hearing, January 27, February 1–3, 8–9, 1949 (Washington, D.C.: USGPO, 1949), 46; John D. Morris, "Veteran Pensions Opposed by Truman," *New York Times*, February 2, 1949; "100 Billion Pension Seen," *New York Times*, February 27, 1949.

24. Robert C. Albright, "Uproar Reigns as House Group Reports Veteran Pension Bill," *Washington Post*, February 16, 1949.

25. "$90 Veterans' Pensions Under Attack in House," *New York Herald Tribune*, February 17, 1949.

26. *Congress and the Nation*, 1: 1345.

27. Sam Stavisky, "After Pensions—the Bonus?," *Collier's*, July 23, 1949.

28. Stavisky, "After Pensions."

29. "Bay State Among 16 to Approve Veterans' Bonus," *Daily Boston Globe*, March 13, 1949; "Taxpayers, Including Veterans, Survey High Cost of Bonuses," *Saturday Evening Post*, July 2, 1949.

30. "Payment of Bonus Urged by Amvets," *New York Times*, January 17, 1949; "Vets Groups Ask Billions for Pensions, Adjusted Pay (Bonus)," *Daily Boston Globe*, January 28, 1949. For federal

spending, see table Ea636–43 in Susan B. Carter et al., eds., *Historical Statistics of the United States: Earliest Times to the Present*, Millennial Ed. (New York: Cambridge University Press, 2006), vol. 5.

31. "Mr. Rankin's 'Bonus,'" *New York Times*, July 31, 1949.

32. "Veterans' Bonus May Become Hot Congress Issue," *Los Angeles Times*, January 9, 1950; "Bonus for Vets Likely to Form Hot 1950 Issue," *Chicago Daily Tribune*, January 9, 1950.

33. Gallup Organization, Gallup Poll (AIPO), February 1947: "Do you think that veterans' benefits are adequate at present?," USGALLUP.47–390.QKT15A, Cornell University, Ithaca, N.Y.: Roper Center for Public Opinion Research, iPOLL, accessed May 29, 2017.

34. Gallup Organization, Gallup Poll (AIPO), February 1947: "Do you think the Government in Washington should provide a Federal bonus this year for veterans of World War II?," USGALLUP.47–390.QK14A; Gallup Organization. Gallup Poll (AIPO), March 1949: "A bill has been introduced in Congress to pay a pension of $90 a month—or about a $1,000 a year—to all U.S. (United States) veterans of World Wars I and II when they reach 65. Do you approve or disapprove of this?," USGALLUP.49–438.QKT12; both at Cornell University, Ithaca, N.Y.: Roper Center for Public Opinion Research, iPOLL, both accessed May 29, 2017.

35. "Danger Ahead," *New York Times*, February 17, 1949.

36. "A New Bonus Plan," *New York Times*, September 7, 1949.

37. Stavisky, "After Pensions."

38. "Allies Against Grab," *Christian Science Monitor*, August 22, 1949.

39. See table Bf188–95 in Carter et al., *Historical Statistics of the United States*, vol. 2.

40. Lewis Meriam and Karl T. Schlotterbeck, *The Cost and Financing of Social Security* (Washington, D.C.: Brookings Institution, 1950), 97.

41. Harry S. Truman, "Annual Budget Message to the Congress: Fiscal Year 1952," January 15, 1951, Gerhard Peters and John T. Woolley, The American Presidency Project, http://www.presidency.ucsb.edu/ws/?pid=13810, accessed May 7, 2017.

42. Harry S. Truman, "Annual Budget Message to the Congress: Fiscal Year 1950," January 10, 1949, Peters and Woolley, The American Presidency Project, http://www.presidency.ucsb.edu/ws/?pid=13434, accessed May 7, 2017.

43. Harry S. Truman, "The President's News Conference," June 29, 1950, Peters and Woolley, The American Presidency Project, http://www.presidency.ucsb.edu/ws/?pid=13544, accessed May 7, 2017.

44. Quoted in Marilyn B. Young, "Hard Sell: The Korean War," in *Selling War in a Media Age: The Presidency and Public Opinion in the American Century*, ed. Kenneth Osgood and Andrew K. Frank (Gainesville: University Press of Florida, 2010), 130; Andrew J. Huebner, *The Warrior Image: Soldiers in American Culture from the Second World War to the Vietnam Era* (Chapel Hill: University of North Carolina Press, 2008), chap. 4.

45. Survey Research Center, University of Michigan, Minor American Election Study 1951, June 1951: "Do you think we did the right thing in getting into the fighting in Korea last summer (1950) or should we have stayed out?," USCPS.51PRE.Q38; Gallup Organization, Gallup Poll, October 1951: "A United States senator says that the Korean war is an utterly 'useless war'. Do you agree or disagree with this?," USGALLUP.110551.RK05; both Cornell University, Ithaca, N.Y.: Roper Center for Public Opinion Research, iPOLL, both accessed April 7, 2016.

46. Howard A. Rusk, "Public Apathy to Korea G.I.'s Slows Their Benefit Claims," *New York Times*, September 27, 1953.

47. "Truman Stand in Korean Crisis Endorsed by V.F.W.," *Foreign Service*, August 1950, 6.

48. "Universal Military Training Made First Objective in New Policy Formed by National Exec. Committee," *ALM*, September 1950, 29.

49. "Legion Commander in Korea," *New York Times*, March 10, 1951; "National Commander Gough Makes Trip to Far East; Gets First Hand View of Korean Front," *ALM*, December 1952,33.

50. "Veteran Newsletter: Legion Called On to Step Up Blood Program," *ALM*, March 1951, 38.

51. "North Dakota Post Collects Clothes for Korea," *ALM*, January 1952, 31.

52. "Seattle Chapters Sell Stickers," *Disabled American Veterans' Semi-monthly*, December 19, 1950, 3, CHCPL.

53. *Digest of Minutes, National Executive Committee Meeting, November 17, 18, and 19, 1950*, 71; *Digest of Minutes, National Executive Committee Meeting, May 2, 3 and 4, 1951*, 84; both ALA.

54. *Proceedings of the 33rd National Convention of the American Legion* (Washington, D.C.: USGPO, 1952), 61, 311; *Proceedings of the 34th National Convention*, 331.

55. "A Preview of the Garden of Stars," *Disabled American Veterans' Semi-monthly*, September 12, 1950, 2, CHCPL.

56. "National Executive Committee Sets Schedule for 1952 at October Meeting; Names Must Legislative Program," *ALM*, December 1952, 31.

57. "Chicago City and Legion Has Honor for New Vets," *ALM*, November 1952, 36.

58. *Digest of Minutes, National Executive Committee Meeting, April 29–30, May 1, 1953*, ALA,118.

59. "'Hometown, U.S.A.' Details Simple," *Michigan Legionnaire*, December 1952, 5, ALA.

60. "'Hometown USA' Gets Big Mail," *ALM*, June 1953, 32.

61. National Public Relations Commission, "Hometown USA Memorandum," n.d. (ca. September 3, 1953), box 61, folder 232, HWCC.

62. *Proceedings of 35th National Convention of the American Legion* (Washington, D.C.: USGPO, 1954), 229.

63. Cocke, Jr., to the President of the United States, December 6, 1950, International Affairs, Korea, War, 1950, A–Z, ALA.

64. "Affairs of Legion Reviewed in Meeting of National Executive Committee; Strong Foreign Policy Stated," *ALM*, June 1951, 30.

65. "Legion Chief Says MacArthur Has to Fight With Hands Tied," *Christian Science Monitor*, April 9, 1951.

66. Edward T. Folliard, "Truman Cancels Date with Legion Head," *Washington Post*, April 11, 1951.

67. "Following Statement Was Released by Commander Cocke to Wire Services and Washington Papers at 5 a.m. EST This Morning (April 11)," International Affairs, Korea, War, 1950, Dismissal of MacArthur, ALA.

68. See "Following Statement Was Released."

69. Miles Frederick, "Loyalty on the March," *V.F.W. Magazine*, June 1951, VFWNH.

70. Joyce Mao, *Asia First: China and the Making of Modern American Conservatism* (Chicago: University of Chicago Press, 2015).

71. Larry Blomstedt, *Truman, Congress, and Korea: The Politics of America's First Undeclared War* (Lexington: University Press of Kentucky, 2016).

72. "Head of Legion Demands All-Out Effort in Korea," *New York Times*, May 13, 1951; "St. Louis Mayor Boycotts Talk by Legion Head," *New York Herald Tribune*, May 13, 1951.

73. National Broadcasting Company, Roper Commercial Survey, May, 1952: "Which do you think most leaders of the American Legion/Veterans of Foreign Wars/etc. will probably favor for the president this year (1952)—the Republicans or the Democrats?," USROPER.RCOM52–059. Q21E, Cornell University, Ithaca, N.Y.: Roper Center for Public Opinion Research, iPOLL, accessed May 29, 2017.

74. Erle Cocke, Jr., "Who Is Letting Our GIs Down?" *ALM*, May 1951, 30.

75. "Suggested Reply Re: Clarkson Letter," October 26, 1951; Wilson to Clarkson, December 12, 1951; both in International Affairs, Korea, War, 1950, A–Z, ALA.

76. Richard H. Parke, "Legionnaires Ask That War in Korea Be Left to Military," *New York Times*, August 29, 1952.

77. Robert A. Bedolis, "Legion's Head for Bombing of Manchuria," *New York Herald Tribune*, September 18, 1952; "Legion Chief Urges Ultimatum on Korea," *New York Times*, October 26, 1952; "Full-Scale War in Korea Urged by Legion Chief," *Los Angeles Times*, November 10, 1952.

78. *Rehabilitation Memorandum*, no. 35 (August 4, 1950), International Affairs, Korea, War, 1950, Manpower, Benefits, ALA.

79. Melinda Pash, "'A Veteran Does Not Have to Stay a Veteran Forever': Congress and the Korean G.I. Bill," in *Veterans' Policies, Veterans' Politics: New Perspectives on Veterans in the Modern United States*, ed. Stephen R. Ortiz (Gainesville.: University Press of Florida, 2012), 222.

80. Rankin to Kennedy, July 13, 1950, International Affairs, Korea, War, 1950, Manpower, Benefits, ALA.

81. Quoted in *Proceedings of the 32nd National Convention of the American Legion* (Washington, D.C.: USGPO, 1951), 239.

82. Hon. Harry P. Cain (WA), "Extension of Certain Benefits to American Forces in Korea," *Congressional Record* July 10, 1950, 9790–91.

83. "Extension of All War II Benefits Asked by DAV," *Disabled American Veterans' Semimonthly*, September 26, 1950, 1, CHCPL; see resolution no. 292 in "Resolutions Adopted by the 51st National Encampment," *Foreign Service*, October 1950, 35.

84. "Truman Quoted in Favor of Veterans' Benefits," *The Sun* (Baltimore, Md.), November 15, 1950.

85. "Sponsors Abandon G.I. Rights in Korea," *New York Times*, September 5, 1950.

86. "Veterans Newsletter: Proposed Benefits for Korean Vets," *ALM*, November 1950, 25.

87. Harry S. Truman, "Annual Budget Message to the Congress: Fiscal Year 1951," January 9, 1950, Peters and Woolley, The American Presidency Project, http://www.presidency.ucsb.edu/ws/?pid=13765, accessed May 7, 2017.

88. Harry S. Truman, "Special Message to the Congress Transmitting Report on the Training of Veterans Under the Servicemen's Readjustment Act," February 13, 1950, Peters and Woolley, The American Presidency Project, http://www.presidency.ucsb.edu/ws/?pid=13706, accessed May 7, 2017.

89. H.R. Doc. No. 466, 81st Cong., 2d Sess., 1950, 11–12.

90. U.S. Congress, House, *Report of the House Select Committee to Investigate Educational and Training Program Under G.I. Bill*, 81 H. Rpt. 3253, 1951, 13.

91. Alec Philmore Pearson, Jr., "Olin E. Teague and the Veterans' Administration" (PhD dissertation, Texas A&M University, 1977), 3–5, 8–10; Mark Boulton, *Failing Our Veterans: The G.I. Bill and the Vietnam Generation* (New York: New York University Press, 2014), 35.

92. Teague to Slauson, April 7, 1949; Teague to Hoyt, April 12, 1949; both in box 64, folder 207-9, OETCC.

93. Stavisky, "After Pensions," 51.

94. Dudley to Darbell, August 4, 1950; Huddleston, Jr., to Dudley, August 10, 1950; Dudley to Huddleston, Jr., August 15, 1950; all in Administration and Organization, Membership, Eligibility, Korean War, ALA.

95. *Proceedings of the 32nd National Convention*, 63–64.

96. Pub. L. No. 81-895, 64 Stat. 1122.

97. Pub. L. No. 81–894, 64 Stat. 1121. Technically, the act was an amendment to make those serving on or after June 27, 1950, eligible under Public Law 16—the original vocational rehabilitation law passed in 1943 for World War II veterans.

98. Harry S. Truman, "Annual Budget Message to the Congress: Fiscal Year 1950," January 10, 1949, Peters and Woolley, The American Presidency Project, http://www.presidency.ucsb.edu/ws/?pid=13434, accessed May 7, 2017.

99. Cejnar to Kelly, September 12, 1950, International Affairs, Korea, War, 1950, Manpower, Benefits, ALA.

100. "GI Course Costs to Be Investigated," *Washington Post*, December 10, 1950; *Committee to Investigate Educational, Training, and Loan Guaranty Programs*, 13.

101. The Legion bills in the House and the Senate were H.R. 1217 and S. 714; see *Digest of Minutes, May 2, 3 and 4, 1951*, 66–67.

102. "Legion Rehab Program Includes Full Rights for Korea Veterans, Cocke Tells Committee," *ALM*, June 1951, 34.

103. U.S. Congress, House, Committee on Veterans' Affairs, *1951 Legislative Programs of the American Legion, Veterans of Foreign Wars, Disabled American Veterans, and American Veterans of World War II*, Hearing, April 25, 1951 (Washington, D.C.: USGPO, 1951), 104, 110, 114, 117.

104. Pub. L. No. 82–23, 65 Stat. 33. See also Edwin B. Patterson, "'Free' Insurance,'" *Washington Post*, March 11, 1951; Rufus H. Wilson, "Insurance For GIs," *Washington Post*, March 15, 1951.

105. "Korean Vet Denied Treatment—It's Not Right War," *Newsday*, May 10, 1951.

106. "Loophole in the Law," *Newsweek*, May 21, 1951.

107. "Congress Says It's a War in Korea," *ALM*, July 1951, 29–30.

108. "Congress Says It's a War in Korea."

109. Mollett, Bloss, and Beans to Sir, May 15, 1951, box 1077, folder: Veterans, Legislation (1951), RATP.

110. Kash to Taft, May 4, 1951, box 1077, folder: Veterans, Legislation (1951), RATP.

111. Benjamin Fine, "14 Billions Spent in 7 Years to Educate 8,000,000 G.I.'s," *New York Times*, July 22, 1951.

112. U.S. Congress, Senate, Committee on Labor and Public Welfare, *Certain Educational and Training Benefits to Veterans*, Hearing, September 17–19, 1951 (Washington, D.C.: USGPO, 1951), 23–25.

113. Committee on Veterans' Affairs, *Benefits for Veterans Serving on or After June 27, 1950*, 1431.

114. UCommittee on Labor and Public Welfare, *Certain Educational and Training Benefits*, 58, 63.

115. "GI Bill for Korea Veterans Shelved," July 11, 1950, International Affairs, Korea, War, 1950, Manpower, Benefits, ALA; "Korea G.I. Bill Put Off," *New York Times*, July 12, 1950.

116. U.S. Congress, House, Select Committee to Investigate Educational, Training, and Loan Guaranty Programs Under GI Bill, *Investigation of Veterans' Educational Program*, Hearing, June 4–6, 18–19, July 12–13, 18–19, 24, August 7, 9–10, 20–22, September 25–26, 1951 (Washington, D.C.: USGPO, 1951), 704.

117. "Revamped GI Training Bill Sought," *Los Angeles Times*, November 25, 1951.

118. For the select committee's separate report on the GI Bill's loan guaranty benefits published in August 1952, see House Select Committee to Investigate Educational, Training, and Loan Guaranty Programs Under GI Bill, *Veterans' Loan Guaranty Program*, 82 H. Rpt. 2501, 1952.

119. House Select Committee to Investigate Educational, Training, and Loan Guaranty Programs Under GI Bill, 6–8, 12, 93, 101.

120. Committee to Investigate Educational, Training, and Loan Guaranty Programs, *Veterans' Loan Guaranty Program*, 1, 10.

121. U.S. Congress, House, Committee on Veterans' Affairs, *Education and Training and Other Benefits for Veterans Serving on or After June 27, 1950*, 82 H. Rpt. 1943, 1952, 25.

122. Committee to Investigate Educational, Training, and Loan Guaranty Programs, *Veterans' Loan Guaranty Program*, 80.

123. Committee to Investigate Educational, Training, and Loan Guaranty Programs, 12.

124. Committee on Veterans' Affairs, *Benefits for Veterans Serving on or After June 27, 1950*, 1622.

125. "GI Bill Graft," *Los Angeles Times*, February 12, 1952.

126. Sidney Shalett, "How Our Tax Dollars Are Wasted," *Saturday Evening Post*, May 24, 1952.

127. "The New Veterans Education Bill," *New York Herald Tribune*, March 12, 1952.

128. Committee on Veterans' Affairs, *Benefits for Veterans Serving on or After June 27, 1950*, 1497–549.

129. Committee on Veterans' Affairs, *Benefits for Veterans Serving on or After June 27, 1950*, 1467.

130. Committee on Veterans' Affairs, *Benefits for Veterans Serving on or After June 27, 1950*, 1469.

131. Committee to Investigate Educational, Training, and Loan Guaranty Programs, 101.

132. Committee on Veterans' Affairs, *Benefits for Veterans Serving on or After June 27, 1950*, 1469, 1474, 1478.

133. Committee on Veterans' Affairs, *Benefits for Veterans Serving on or After June 27, 1950*, 1511.

134. These bills were, respectively, H.R. 5040, H.R. 6425, and H.R. 6377. See Benjamin Fine, "Education in Review," *New York Times*, March 16, 1952.

135. The memorandum from June 22, 1951, is reproduced in Committee on Veterans' Affairs, *Benefits for Veterans Serving on or After June 27, 1950*, 926.

136. Committee on Veterans' Affairs, *Benefits for Veterans Serving on or After June 27, 1950*, 1387.

137. U.S. Congress, Senate, Committee on Labor and Public Welfare, Special Subcommittee on Veterans Education and Rehabilitation Benefits, *Veterans Readjustment Assistance Act of 1952*, Hearing, June 10–13, 17, 1952 (Washington, D.C.: USGPO, 1952), 156.

138. Subcommittee on Veterans Education and Rehabilitation Benefits, *Veterans Readjustment Assistance Act*, 159.

139. John D. Morris, "Dispute on Tuition Snags New G. I. Bill," *New York Times*, May 28, 1952.

140. C. P. Trussell, "New G.I. Rights Bill Is Passed by House," *New York Times*, June 6, 1952.

141. No survey of Korean War veterans or service members was made on this issue, but three surveys of World War II veterans indicate that they were generally content with the provisions of the original GI Bill and disapproved of Teague's changes; see *Committee to Investigate Educational, Training, and Loan Guaranty Programs*, 27; Roy N. Chelgren, "An Attitude Survey Concerning the Provision of Educational Benefits for Korean Veterans," *School and Society* 76, no. 1969 (September 13, 1952): 169–71; Committee on Veterans' Affairs, *Benefits for Veterans Serving on or After June 27, 1950*, 1179.

142. *Legislative Bulletin*, May 17, 1952, International Affairs, Korea, War, 1950, Manpower, Benefits, ALA.

143. U Subcommittee on Veterans Education and Rehabilitation Benefits, *Veterans Readjustment Assistance Act*, 25, 28, 154.

144. "G. I. Korea Bill Gains," *New York Times*, June 25, 1952.

145. "Congress Passes Korea Vet GI Bill," *ALM*, August 1952, 29.

146. "Veterans' Readjustment Assistance Act of 1952," *Congressional Record*, June 28, 1952, 8421.

147. Harold B. Hinton, "New G.I. Bill Voted as Congress Works to Adjourn Today," *New York Times*, July 5, 1952; "Korea G. I. Bill of Rights Sent to White House," *New York Herald Tribune*, July 5, 1952; "New Veteran Bill Signed by Truman," *New York Times*, July 17, 1952.

148. Hon. Alvin E. O'Konski (WI), "Veterans' Readjustment Assistance Act of 1952," *Congressional Record*, July 4, 1952, 9401.

149. For details on the features of the law, see "The New GI Bill: Who Gets What?," *Changing Times* May 1953, 21.

150. Trussell, "New G.I. Rights Bill Is Passed by House."

151. Subcommittee on Veterans Education and Rehabilitation Benefits, *Veterans Readjustment Assistance Act*, 36–38, 150.

152. Melinda L. Pash, *In the Shadow of the Greatest Generation: The Americans Who Fought the Korean War* (New York: New York University Press, 2012), 212.

153. Marcus Stanley, "College Education and the Midcentury GI Bills," *Quarterly Journal of Economics* 118, no. 2 (May 2003): 675.

154. Melanie Martindale and Dudley L. Poston, "Variations in Veteran/Nonveteran Earnings Patterns Among World War II, Korea, and Vietnam War Cohorts," *Armed Forces and Society* 5, no. 2 (Winter 1979): 219–43.

155. For the 1944 percentage, see Elaine K. Swift, Robert G. Brookshire, David T. Canon, Evelyn C. Fink, John R. Hibbing, Brian D. Humes, Michael J. Malbin, and Kenneth C. Martis, Database of [United States] Congressional Historical Statistics, 1789–1989, ICPSR03371-v2 (Ann Arbor, Mich.: Interuniversity Consortium for Political and Social Research, 2009-02-03): http://doi.org/10.3886/ICPSR03371.v2. For the 1952 percentage, see Member Profiles Results (Washington: CQ Press), dynamically generated March 30, 2016, from CQ Press Electronic Library, CQ Congress Collection, http://library.cqpress.com/congress/memberanalysisresults.php?congress2=202&yearlimit=0&milservice=Did not serve.

156. *Digest of Minutes, April 29–30, May 1, 1953*, 161.

157. "Cut in Appropriations for VA Vital Service Blow Below Belt, Gough Tells the President," *ALM*, July 1953, 31.

158. *Proceedings of 35th National Convention*, 9–10.

CHAPTER 7

1. Kennedy to Dudley, April 14, 1950, Veteran Welfare, Pensions, A–Z, ALA (A–Z, ALA hereafter).

2. "Veterans' Newsletter: Vet Population in these United States," *ALM*, October 1953, 26; John Kenneth Galbraith, *The Affluent Society* (Boston: Houghton Mifflin, 1958).

3. Field to Cocke Jr., April 11, 1951, A–Z, ALA.

4. For a summary of pension rates between 1945 and 1964, see *Congress and the Nation, 1945–1964*, vol. 1 (Washington, D.C.: Congressional Quarterly Service, 1964), 1354. For the historical poverty threshold ($1,101 in 1953), see Table Be85–94 in Susan B. Carter et al., eds., *Historical Statistics of the United States: Earliest Times to the Present*, Millennial Ed. (New York: Cambridge University Press, 2006), vol. 2.

5. Temple to Craig, March 9, 1950, A–Z, ALA.

6. Schevon to Dear Commander, August 8, 1952, A–Z, ALA.

7. Carlson to Dear Sir, January 21, 1950, A–7, ALA.

8. On the use of the term in the 1930s, see John M. Kinder, *Paying with Their Bodies: American War and the Problem of the Disabled Veteran* (Chicago: University of Chicago Press, 2015), 210–12.

9. "VA's New Boss Is in the Middle," *New York Herald Tribune*, August 30, 1953.

10. See works cited in Chapter 6, n. 3.

11. American Legion News Service, "For Immediate Release," May 5, 1959, A–Z, ALA.

12. Bradley's autobiography failed to mention the commission; see Omar Nelson Bradley and Clay Blair, *A General's Life: An Autobiography* (New York: Simon and Schuster, 1983). His most recent biography makes the same omission: Steven L. Ossad, *Omar Nelson Bradley: America's GI General, 1893–1981* (Columbia: University of Missouri Press, 2017). For a study of the commission that focuses on disability ratings, see Keith Wailoo, *Pain: A Political History* (Baltimore: Johns Hopkins University Press, 2014), chap. 1.

13. Prior to 1946, when the distinction between these two benefits was made official, the term "pension" was commonly used to refer to both service-connected and non-service-connected payments. See *Congress and the Nation*, 1: 1336.

14. See table Ed297–310 in Carter et al., *Historical Statistics of the United States*, vol. 5.

15. For an overview of the legal background of medical and hospital benefits for non-service-connected veterans after World War I, see U.S. Congress, House, Committee on Veterans' Affairs, *Veterans' Administration Hospitals*, Hearing, July 8, 15–18, 22–24, 29–30, August 6, 1958 (Washington, D.C.: USGPO, 1958), 4020–25.

16. For pension figures, see table Ed 337–50 in Carter et al., *Historical Statistics of the United States*, vol. 5; for a breakdown of VA hospital patient figures in 1950, 1955, and 1960, see Administrator of Veterans Affairs, *Annual Report for Fiscal Year Ending June 30, 1950* (Washington, D.C.: USGPO, 1951), 147; Administrator of Veterans Affairs, *Annual Report for Fiscal Year Ending June 30, 1956* (Washington, D.C.: USGPO, 1957), 194; Administrator of Veterans Affairs, *Annual Report, 1961* (Washington, D.C.: USGPO, 1962), 207, 210.

17. They represented 80 percent of those on the rolls in 1957. See table no. 38 in Administrator of Veterans Affairs, *Annual Report for Fiscal Year Ending June 30, 1957* (Washington, D.C.: USGPO, 1957), 218–19.

18. James L. Sundquist, *Politics and Policy: The Eisenhower, Kennedy, and Johnson Years* (Washington, D.C.: Brookings Institution, 1968), 292–95; Christy Ford Chapin, *Ensuring America's Health: The Public Creation of the Corporate Health Care System* (New York: Cambridge University Press, 2015); Jennifer Klein, *For All These Rights: Business, Labor, and the Shaping of America's Public-Private Welfare State* (Princeton, N.J.: Princeton University Press, 2003).

19. On the history of Social Security, see Andrew Morris, "Eisenhower and Social Welfare," in *A Companion to Dwight D. Eisenhower*, ed. Chester J. Pach (Malden, Mass.: Wiley-Blackwell, 2017), 246–63; Daniel Béland, Edward D. Berkowitz, and Larry DeWitt, *Social Security: A Documentary History* (Washington, D.C.: CQ Press, 2008), 1–30; Steven Greene Livingston, *U.S. Social Security: A Reference Handbook* (Santa Barbara, Calif.: ABC-CLIO, 2008), chap. 1.

20. Sheryl R. Tynes, *Turning Points in Social Security: From "Cruel Hoax" to "Sacred Entitlement"* (Stanford, Calif.: Stanford University Press, 1996), 151.

21. Gilbert Y. Steiner, *The State of Welfare* (Washington, D.C.: Brookings Institution, 1971), 238.

22. See table Bd294–305 in Carter et al., *Historical Statistics of the United States*, vol. 2.

23. Klein, *For All These Rights*, esp. chap. 6.

24. Gregory P. Guyton, "A Brief History of Workers' Compensation," *Iowa Orthopaedic Journal* 19 (1999): 106–10.

25. A 1954 VA survey found that "nearly one-half of the aged veterans of the 'new wars' who were on the pension roll were also receiving OASI benefits," as a result of average OASI payments being relatively low and of income limits for veterans' pensions being high enough "that even the maximum OASI payment falls below them." See U.S. Congress, House, Committee on Veterans' Affairs, *Findings and Recommendations of the President's Commission on Veterans' Pensions (Bradley Commission)*, Hearing, April 23, May 8–11, 16–18, 22, 1956 (Washington, D.C.: USGPO, 1956), 364.

26. John Jay Corson and John W. McConnell, *Economic Needs of Older People* (New York: Twentieth Century Fund, 1956), 260.

27. Lewis Meriam and Karl T. Schlotterbeck, *The Cost and Financing of Social Security* (Washington: Brookings Institution, 1950), 118–19.

28. Committee on Federal Tax Policy, *Financing Defense: Can Expenditures Be Reduced?* (New York, 1951), 20–21; Eveline M. Burns, *The American Social Security System* (Boston: Houghton Mifflin, 1949), 419–20.

29. "Veterans Are Citizens," *New York Times*, April 14, 1953. See also "A Nation of Veterans," *New York Times*, June 9, 1953; "Veterans as Citizens," *New York Times*, September 4, 1954.

30. Stanley Frank, "We Licked the Veteran Problem," *Saturday Evening Post*, November 5, 1955, 156.

31. "Veterans Hospital Abuses," *Chicago Daily Tribune*, March 29, 1953.

32. "Veterans Pensions," *Mattoon (Ill.) Daily Journal-Gazette*, February 3, 1956, Veteran Welfare, Pensions, War Veterans Security Bill, 1956, ALA (WVSB, ALA thereafter).

33. Opinion Research Corporation, ORC Public Opinion Index, September 1952: "How about benefits for veterans—should they (the next administration) do more for veterans, or less?," USORC.52NOV.R23, Cornell University, Ithaca, N.Y.: Roper Center for Public Opinion Research, iPOLL, accessed February 6, 2017.

34. Gallup Organization, Gallup Poll (AIPO), August 1953: "Do you think the government should or should not be required to give a war veteran free care and treatment at a veterans' hospital if his injury or illness was not caused by being in the service?," USGALLUP.53–519.Q15A, Gallup Organization, Cornell University, Ithaca, N.Y.: Roper Center for Public Opinion Research, iPOLL, accessed February 6, 2017.

35. *Veterans in Our Society: Data on the Conditions of Military Service and on the Status of the Veteran*, 84 H. Prt. 261 (Washington, D.C.: USGPO, 1956), 119–28.

36. Dwight D. Eisenhower, "Annual Budget Message to the Congress: Fiscal Year 1955," January 21, 1954, Gerhard Peters and John T. Woolley, The American Presidency Project, https://www.presidency.ucsb.edu/node/232149, accessed May 7, 2017.

37. Morris, "Eisenhower and Social Welfare."

38. Michael J. Hogan, *A Cross of Iron: Harry S. Truman and the Origins of the National Security State, 1945–1954* (Cambridge: Cambridge University Press, 2000), chap. 9.

39. Samuel A. Lawrence, "My Notes on Sam Hughes' Comments . . . ," May 23, 1957, box 2, folder: Memoranda of Conferences, Records of the U.S President's Commission on Veterans' Pensions, Dwight D. Eisenhower Presidential Library.

40. Irving Breakstone, "Payments to Veterans? Right or Gratuity?," *Chicago Daily Tribune*, July 2, 1959.

41. Wayne E. Richards, "A Call to Action," *VFW Magazine*, March 1954, 14, VFWNH.

42. Lewis K. Gough, "Who Is Being Treated in the VA Hospitals?" *ALM*, February 1953.

43. Timothy Walch, ed., *Herbert Hoover and Dwight D. Eisenhower: A Documentary History* (New York: Palgrave Macmillan, 2013), 133–34; Ronald C. Moe, *The Hoover Commissions Revisited* (Boulder, Colo.: Westview Press, 1982), chap. 3.

44. Commission on Organization of the Executive Branch of Government, *Hoover Commission Report on Federal Medical Services*, 84th Cong., 1st Sess., H. Doc. 99, 1955, 36–38.

45. On VA hospitals and the disability ranking system, see recommendations no. 5, 6, and 13 in Commission on Organization, 33–34, 41–43. On civil service, see recommendations no. 12 and 13 in U.S. Congress, House, Committee on Post Office and Civil Service, *Hoover Commission Report on Personnel and Civil Service*, 84th Cong., 1st Sess. (Washington, D.C.: USGPO, 1955), 36–39.

46. "Gypping the Government," *Wall Street Journal*, February 15, 1956; "Reforms in Civil Service," *New York Times*, February 15, 1955; "Veterans' Medical Care," *New York Times*, March 2, 1955; "Hoover Savings," *Newsday, Nassau Ed.*, March 1, 1955; "Federal Health Service," *Washington Post and Times Herald*, February 28, 1955.

47. Omar B. Ketchum, "The Hoover Commission Report," *VFW Magazine*, April 1955, 23, VFWNH; "Few Tears as Hoover Board Quietly Expires," *Disabled American Veterans' Semimonthly*, July 21, 1955, 1, CHCPL; "Hoover Medical Report Released," *ALM*, April 1955, 29; "Rehabilitation: Questions and Reports," *ALM*, February 1956, 43; "Hoover Report: A Public Service?" *ALM*, May 1955, 34–35.

48. Walch, *Herbert Hoover and Dwight D. Eisenhower*, 133–34.

49. *Proceedings of the 39th National Convention of the American Legion* (Washington, D.C.: USGPO, 1958), 320; Moe, *The Hoover Commissions Revisited*, 109.

50. On this fight, see Monte M. Poen, *Harry S. Truman Versus the Medical Lobby: The Genesis of Medicare* (Columbia: University of Missouri Press, 1979).

51. See resolution no. 196 in *Proceedings of the 27th National Convention of the American Legion* (Chicago, 1945), 88.

52. American Medical Association, *Medical and Hospital Care of Veterans with Non-Service-Connected Disabilities: A Review of American Medical Association Policy* (Chicago: AMA, 1953), 61.

53. For an account of this breakdown, see Wallace Croatman, "That Veterans' Lobby," *Medical Economics*, November 1953.

54. American Medical Association, *Medical and Hospital Care of Veterans*, 7–12.

55. Louis M. Orr, "To Socialized Medicine and Socialism by Way of the Veterans Administration," *Journal of the American Medical Association* 162, no. 9 (October 27, 1956): 860.

56. *Digest of Minutes, National Executive Committee Meeting, October 15, 16 and 17, 1953*, 107, ALA.

57. Drew Pearson, "Legion, AMA Gird for Battle," *Washington Post*, January 5, 1954.

58. Holman Harvey, "Must We Follow the VA Route to Socialized Medicine?," *Reader's Digest*, March 1954, 49.

59. "End Something-for-Nothing," *Newsday*, Nassau ed., June 5, 1953.

60. "Joe Burke Gives AMA New Meaning in Address to Astoria Chapter," *Disabled American Veterans' Semi-monthly*, August 10, 1954, 2, CHCPL; "VFW Attacks 'Old Dodos' of AMA on Vets," *Washington Post*, August 3, 1953. For the Legion's reaction, see "Rehabilitation: AMA Plays a Lone Hand," *ALM*, December 1953.

61. D. Pearson, "Legion, AMA Gird for Battle."

62. U.S. Congress, House, Committee on Veterans' Affairs, Subcommittee on Hospitals, *Entitlement and Eligibility of Veterans for Hospital Care and Outpatient Dental Treatment*, Hearing, July 8–10, 13–17, 20–21, 1953 (Washington, D.C.: USGPO, 1953), 2481.

63. Quoted in Colin D. Moore, "Innovation Without Reputation: How Bureaucrats Saved the Veterans' Health Care System," *Perspectives on Politics* 13, no. 2 (June 2015): 333.

64. "60 Listed as Abusers of V. A. Hospitalization," *New York Herald Tribune*, July 14, 1953.

65. "V.A. Tightens Rule for Hospital Care," *New York Times*, November 6, 1953. A 1956 General Accounting Office report found no cases "in which a veteran was denied hospitalization because of his financial status . . . if he had sworn that he was unable to pay for hospitalization." See *Abuses of Veterans Administration Outpatient Program (Part 1); Report of the General Accounting Office on the Ability of Veterans to Pay for Hospitalization Involving Non-Service-Connected Disabilities (Part 2)*, 84 H. Prt. 232 (Washington, D.C.: USGPO, 1956), 166.

66. Samuel to Randall, March 28, 1940, A–Z, ALA.

67. Cejnar to Bane, December 15, 1948, A–Z, ALA.

68. A survey carried out by the Bradley Commission in the mid-1950s found that a quarter of all World War I veterans favored service pensions, compared to only 10 percent of World War II veterans and 14 percent of Korean War veterans. See *Veterans in Our Society*, 125.

69. Cronenwett to Wilson, June 24, 1952, A–Z, ALA.

70. Ahrends to National Commander, April 3, 1957, A–Z, ALA.

71. Grunning to Collins, July 19, 1955, A–Z, ALA.

72. *Congress and the Nation*, 1: 1347, 1353.

73. Weber to Taft, n.d. (ca. February 1951), box 1077, folder: Veterans, Legislation (1951), RATP.

74. Sam Stavisky, "Vets Demand Pensions for All," *Nation's Business*, April 1956, 34.

75. "War I Veterans Choose 1st Chief," clipping, n.d. (ca. November 14, 1953), A–Z, ALA.

76. "Veterans Newsletter: Pensions, Compensation Get Cost-of-Living Hike," *ALM*, November 1954, 27.

77. Richard H. Immerman and Robert R. Bowie, *Waging Peace: How Eisenhower Shaped an Enduring Cold War Strategy* (New York: Oxford University Press, 1998).

78. Dwight D. Eisenhower, "Statement by the President upon Signing Bills Increasing Payments to Veterans or Their Dependents.," August 28, 1954, Peters and Woolley, The American Presidency Project, http://www.presidency.ucsb.edu/ws/?pid=10009, accessed May 7, 2017.

79. "Veterans' Pension Study Unit Named," *New York Herald Tribune*, January 15, 1955.

80. "Bureau of the Budget Briefing," July 18, 1955, box 2, folder: Memoranda of Conferences, PCVP.

81. For a list of the commissioners and staff, see the President's Commission on Veterans' Pensions, *Veterans' Benefits in the United States: Findings and Recommendations* (Washington, D.C.: USGPO, 1956), title page.

82. "Minutes of First Meeting of the President's Commission on Veterans' Pensions, Monday, 28 March 1955—10:45 a.m.," box 17, folder: Meeting of March 28, 1955 Minutes (1), PCVP.

83. For a complete list of all the staff reports, see the finding aid for the records of the Bradley Commission at the Eisenhower Presidential Library, https://eisenhower.archives.gov/Research/Finding_Aids/pdf/US_Presidents_Commission_on_Veterans_Pensions.pdf, accessed on February 15, 2017.

84. Commission on Veterans' Pensions, *Veterans' Benefits*, 3, 9. For "backward-looking," see the letter of transmittal in the preface.

85. Commission on Veterans' Pensions, *Veterans' Benefits*, 128.

86. Commission on Veterans' Pensions, *Veterans' Benefits*, 79.

87. Commission on Veterans' Pensions, *Veterans' Benefits*, 92–97.

88. *Veterans in Our Society*, 98–99.

89. Commission on Veterans' Pensions, *Veterans' Benefits*, 134–36.

90. Commission on Veterans' Pensions, *Veterans' Benefits*, 137–38.

91. Commission on Veterans' Pensions, *Veterans' Benefits*, 375–76.

92. Commission on Veterans' Pensions, *Veterans' Benefits*, 139, 319.

93. "Bureau of the Budget Briefing."

94. "For Sacrifice, Not Just Service," *Christian Science Monitor*, April 24, 1956.

95. "A New Look," *Time*, May 7, 1956, 38.

96. "Veterans Everywhere," *Washington Post and Times Herald*, April 24, 1956.

97. "U.S. Group Urges Deep Cut in Vets' Pension Benefits," *Newsday*, Nassau ed., April 23, 1956.

98. "Veterans' Benefit Cuts Attacked," *New York Herald Tribune*, May 9, 1956.

99. "Some Assorted Eggheads," *New Republic*, May 14, 1956, 5.

100. Committee on Veterans' Affairs, *Findings and Recommendations of the President's Commission*, 3685.

101. "Bradley Report, 40&8 Troubles Highlight Legion NEC Meetings," *ALM*, June 1956, 37.

102. National Public Relations Division, "For Immediate Release," December 16, 1955, A–Z, ALA.

103. National Public Relations Division, "For Immediate Release," November 1955, A–Z, ALA.

104. Davis to Wilson, November 1, 1955, A–Z, ALA.

105. Taylor to Hass, February 18, 1956, box 6, folder: Correspondence, 1956, Jan.–Aug., Bradley R. Taylor Papers, WHS.

106. Committee for the War Veterans Security Bill, "How about 'Freedom from Want' for America's Disabled Veterans?," n.d., WVSB, ALA.

107. National Public Relations Division, "For Immediate Release," January 12, 1956, A–Z, ALA.

108. Wagner to My Fellow War Veterans, January 23, 1956, WVSB, ALA; emphasis original.

109. National Public Relations Division, "For Immediate Release," November 1955.

110. "Legion Opens Drive to Pass War Veterans Security Bill," *ALM*, March 1956, 31.

111. Stavisky, "Vets Demand Pensions for All"; U.S. Congress, House, Committee on Veterans' Affairs, *Legislation Relating to Non-Service-Connected Pensions for Veterans and Their Dependents (All Wars)*, Hearing, February 27–March 1, 1956 (Washington, D.C.: USGPO, 1956), 2779.

112. "House Votes Next Week on Bill to Aid Veterans," *New York Herald Tribune*, June 19, 1956.

113. Teague to McChesney, June 4, 1956, box 64, folder 207-7, series 1, OETCC.

114. Sam Stavisky, "After Pensions–the Bonus?," *Collier's*, July 23, 1949.

115. Teague to Slauson, April 7, 1949; Teague to Newsome, May 26, 1949; both in box 64, folder 207-9, series 1, OETCC.

116. Teague to Nickelson and Hardy, March 22, 1956, box 64, folder 207-6, series 1, OETCC; Olin E. Teague, "How Veterans Can Help Protect Veterans' Benefits," *VFW Magazine*, June 1956, 19, VFWNH.

117. Teague to Nickelson and Hardy.

118. Teague to Lawson, May 13, 1960, box 52, folder 91B-23, series 18; Teague to McCaskill, March 27, 1956, box 64, folder 207-6, series 1; both in OETCC.

119. Alec Philmore Pearson Jr., "Olin E. Teague and the Veterans' Administration" (PhD dissertation, Texas A&M University, 1977), 154; "Drive for Easy-to-Get Pensions Draws Volley of Counter Fire," *BusinessWeek*, July 14, 1956; "Find Veterans' Free Care Abuse," *New York Herald Tribune*, April 9, 1956; "GI Pension Abuses Outlined," *Washington Post and Times Herald*, April 17, 1956.

120. "Vets Security Bill: Pull All Stops," *ALM*, June 1956.

121. Hauck to Stelle, March 27, 1956, WVSB, ALA.

122. Irving Leibowitz, "Legion Has Its Hand Out," *Indianapolis Times*, March 5, 1956, A–Z, ALA; "One-Eighth of a Nation," *New York Times*, March 7, 1956.

123. "The Greedy Legion," *Chicago Daily Tribune*, February 1, 1956.

124. Committee on Veterans' Affairs, *Findings and Recommendations of the President's Commission*, 3607.

125. Committee on Veterans' Affairs, *Findings and Recommendations of the President's Commission*, 3612, 3636, 3646, 3696–97.

126. "The American Legion Comments on Recommendations of the President's Commission on Veterans' Pensions," n.d. (ca. December 1956), A–Z, ALA.

127. Committee on Veterans' Affairs, *Findings and Recommendations of the President's Commission*, 3649–50.

128. "Vets Security Bill Delayed; All-Out Mail Support Urged," *ALM*, May 1956, 31.

129. Lawrence M. Fornia, memorandum to Department Chairmen, Committee for the War Veterans Security Bill, March 16, 1956, WVSB, ALA.

130. Lawrence H. Fornia, memorandum to Department Chairmen, War Veterans Security Bill Committee, May 23, 1956, WVSB, ALA.

131. De Pew to Wagner, April 23, 1956, A–Z, ALA.

132. Finlay to Commander Wagner, n.d. (ca. April 25, 1956), A–Z, ALA.

133. Van Dyke, "Pensioner's Plaint," n.d. (ca. April 10, 1956), WVSB, ALA.

134. "Belated Action Gives HR7886 Chance of Approval in House," *ALM*, July 1956, 31.

135. "Ayres and Teague Rebuked by House Passage of War Vet Security Bill," *ALM*, August 1956.

136. "Pension Increase," *New York Times*, June 29, 1956.

137. Kraabel to Sherling, August 15, 1956, WVSB, ALA.

138. "Pension, Compensation Bills Stranded as Congress Quits," *ALM*, September 1956.

139. A. Pearson, "Olin E. Teague and the Veterans' Administration," 169.

140. For the number and the total cost of World War I veterans and their survivors receiving pensions as of June 30, 1956, and June 20, 1960, see table 34 in Administrator, *Annual Report for June 30, 1956*, 228, and table 30 in Administrator of Veterans Affairs, *Annual Report 1960* (Washington, D.C.: USGPO, 1961), 212. For the total World War I veteran population and the VA expenditures, see tables Ed 245–61 and Ed297–310 in Carter et al., *Historical Statistics of the United States*, vol. 5.

141. Blackmore to Falkenberg, February 8, 1957, A–Z, ALA.

142. Olson to Logan, May 7, 1957, A–Z, ALA.

143. "Legion Drafts WW1 Pension Bill Again," *ALM*, March 1957, 27; "Programs, Lawmakers Keep Legion Busy on Many Fronts," *ALM*, May 1957.

144. "Text of President's Talk in Oklahoma City Citing Need for Rise in Funds for Science," *New York Times*, November 14, 1957.

145. "Cuts to Be Asked in Veterans' Aid," *New York Times*, December 15, 1957.

146. William H. Becker and William M. McClenahan, *Eisenhower and the Cold War Economy* (Baltimore: Johns Hopkins University Press, 2011), 85.

147. Alan J. Otten and Ted Lewis Jr., "Back to the Capitol," *Wall Street Journal*, January 6, 1958; Edwin L. Dale Jr., "Budget Cutters Foresee No Chance of Big Saving," *New York Times*, December 2, 1957.

148. For these letters, see Correspondence re: Cutting Veterans' Benefits, box 1, Bulk Mail Files, White House Central Files, DDEPL. The box contains between five hundred and six hundred of these letters, including some from local posts of the American Legion, DAV, and VFW, all dated from between December 1957 and March 1958.

149. U.S. Congress, House, Committee on Veterans' Affairs, *1958 Legislative Programs of the Veterans of Foreign Wars, Disabled American Veterans, the American Legion, and AMVETS*, Hearing, February 4–5, 25, 1958 (Washington, D.C.: USGPO, 1958), 2433–34.

150. "Washington Outlook," *BusinessWeek*, August 2, 1958, 34.

151. Lester Tanzer, "Administration Maps Retreat from Plan for Veterans' Benefit Cut," *Wall Street Journal*, March 25, 1958.

152. U.S. Congress, Senate, Committee on Finance, *Veterans Pensions*, Hearing, July 28–29, 1959 (Washington, D.C.: USGPO, 1959), 79.

153. *Congress and the Nation*, 1: 1353.

154. See resolution no. 331 in *Proceedings of 40th National Convention of the American Legion* (Chicago, 1958), 51–52.

155. McGrail to Anderson, November 7, 1958, A–Z, ALA.

156. Dwight D. Eisenhower, "Annual Budget Message to the Congress: Fiscal Year 1960," January 19, 1959, Peters and Woolley, The American Presidency Project, https://www.presidency.ucsb .edu/node/234819, accessed on February 17, 2017.

157. The bill proposed to include the spouse's income as well as the veterans' estate (hitherto taken into account only through the annual income test). See "Administration Offers Bill to Overhaul Veterans' Pensions," *Wall Street Journal*, April 17, 1959.

158. "Politicians and Veterans," *Wall Street Journal*, April 20, 1959.

159. "Drastic Government Bill to Restyle Pensions Pushed in the Congress," *ALM*, June 1959.

160. Jack Z. Anderson, memorandum for Mrs. Whitman, November 7, 1958, box 37, folder: Staff Notes Nov. 1958, DDE Diary Series, Papers of Dwight D. Eisenhower as President, 1953–61, DDEPL.

161. "Washington Outlook," *BusinessWeek*, December 6, 1958, 34.

162. "Legion Drafts Bills for Its Three-Point Pension Program," *ALM*, February 1959.

163. For the testimonies of the Veterans of World War I, USA, and the Legion, see U.S. Congress, House, Committee on Veterans' Affairs, *Operation of Pension Program*, May 9, June 4–5, 9–10, 1959 (Washington, D.C.: USGPO, 1959), 325–27, 479–87.

164. "National Executive Committee Rejects Proposed Pension Bill," *ALM*, June 1959, 27.

165. For a detailed list of the bill's provisions, see "First Major Pension Chance in Decade Passes House," *ALM*, August 1959.

166. For a detailed estimate of the bill's future cost produced by Teague's committee, see U.S. Congress, House, Committee on Veterans' Affairs, *Non-Service-Connected Pensions for Veterans of World Wars I, II, Korean Conflict and Their Widows and Children*, 86 H. Rpt. 537 (Washington, D.C.: USGPO, 1959), 9–10.

167. "Veterans Newsletter: A Look at the New Pension Bill," *ALM*, August 1959.

168. Omar B. Ketchum, "The Voice of the VFW," *VFW Magazine*, October 1959, 19, VFWNH.

169. "Revised Pensions Would Cost More," *New York Times*, June 18, 1959.

170. "Veterans' Pensions," *New York Times*, June 17, 1959; "The Insult to Veterans," *Wall Street Journal*, June 18, 1959; "The Results of Hasty Debate," *Los Angeles Times*, June 21, 1959; "The Catch in the Veterans' Bill," *Chicago Daily Tribune*, June 27, 1959.

171. Committee on Finance, *Veterans Pensions*, 13, 16.

172. "Senate Unit Votes Veterans Pension Bill, Puts Cost Below House-Passed Measure," *Wall Street Journal*, August 11, 1959; "New Veterans Pension Law and What To Do About It," *ALM*, November 1959.

173. "Senate Approves War Pension Rise," *New York Times*, August 14, 1959.

174. "President Gets Bill to Raise G. I. Pensions," *New York Herald Tribune*, August 19, 1959; "Eisenhower Signs Veterans Pension Bill," *Wall Street Journal*, August 31, 1959.

175. *Congress and the Nation*, 1: 1355.

176. *Proceedings of 41st National Convention of the American Legion* (Minneapolis, 1959), 19.

177. Administrator of Veterans Affairs, *Annual Report 1963* (Washington, D.C.: USGPO, 1963), 242; for a breakdown of the veteran population by generation, see table Ed245–61 in Carter et al., *Historical Statistics of the United States*, vol. 5.

178. Thacker to McDonald, May 31, 1961, A–Z, ALA.

179. Kockler to National Adjutant, October 23, 1959, A–Z, ALA.

180. Wilhelm to McKneally, March 16, 1960, A–Z, ALA.

181. Paul Duke, "World War I Veteran's Drive for a Special Pension Gains Ground," *Wall Street Journal*, June 26, 1962.

182. "Where U.S. Debt to Veterans Ends," *Nation's Business*, May 1961, 98.

183. American Legion, *National Membership Record*, 2012, ALA.

184. Gates to Moore, March 25, 1959, A–Z, ALA.

185. See for instance Suffron to McKneally, November 2, 1959; Ross to Randall, August 8, 1960; Gafford to McKneally, August 18, 1960; Thacker to McDonald, May 31, 1961; Opp to Bacon, August 11, 1962, A–Z, ALA.

186. Casparie to National Commander of the American Legion, October 22, 1959; Reveal to Burke, February 28, 1961, A–Z, ALA.

187. Strong to National Commander, March 19, 1960, A–Z, ALA.

188. Wilhelm to McKneally, April 14, 1960, A–Z, ALA.

189. Bennett to Burke, May 4, 1961, A–Z, ALA.

190. Kennedy to Miller, March 17, 1962, A–Z, ALA.

191. Olson to Bullen, Jr., June 9, 1964, A–Z, ALA.

192. *Congress and the Nation*, 1: 1361–63.

193. Disability pension rolls peaked at 1.2 million in 1964 and remained on a course of steady decline thereafter. Death pension rolls (which represented not veterans but their survivors) peaked at 1.2 million in 1973. See table Ed337–50 in Carter et al., *Historical Statistics of the United States*, vol. 5.

194. Steiner, *The State of Welfare*, 237.

EPILOGUE

1. Paul Starr, *The Discarded Army: Veterans After Vietnam; The Nader Report on Vietnam Veterans and the Veterans Administration* (New York: Charterhouse, 1974), 48.

2. On the passage of this law, see Mark Boulton, *Failing Our Veterans: The GI Bill and the Vietnam Generation* (New York: New York University Press, 2014), chap. 2.

3. For the percentage of veterans in the total population, see figure Ed-E in Hugh Rockoff, "Veterans," in Susan B. Carter et al., eds., *Historical Statistics of the United States: Earliest Times to the Present*, Millennial Ed. (New York: Cambridge University Press, 2006), vol. 5, 340-349, 343.

4. Theda Skocpol, *Diminished Democracy: From Membership to Management in American Civic Life* (Norman: University of Oklahoma Press, 2003).

5. Alan S. Murray and Jeffrey H. Birnbaum, *Showdown at Gucci Gulch: Lawmakers, Lobbyists, and the Unlikely Triumph of Tax Reform* (New York: Random House, 1987), 79–80.

6. Quoted in Gerald Nicosia, *Home to War: A History of the Vietnam Veterans' Movement* (New York: Crown, 2001), 52.

7. Quoted in Andrew E. Hunt, *The Turning: A History of Vietnam Veterans Against the War* (New York: New York University Press, 1999), 52.

8. Starr, *The Discarded Army*, 41–42.

9. Nicosia, *Home to War*, 348, 507.

10. Patrick Hagopian, *The Vietnam War in American Memory: Veterans, Memorials, and the Politics of Healing* (Amherst: University of Massachusetts Press, 2009), 108.

11. Nicosia, *Home to War*, 592–95; Wilbur J. Scott, *The Politics of Readjustment: Vietnam Veterans Since the War* (New York: Aldine De Gruyter, 1993), 203–6.

12. See tables Bf196–211 in Carter et al., *Historical Statistics of the United States*, vol. 2.

13. On Kennedy, Johnson, Nixon, and Ford's views of veterans' benefits, see Boulton, *Failing Our Veterans*, 53, 64, 123–26, 177–78.

14. Boulton, *Failing Our Veterans*, chap. 6.

15. Boulton, *Failing Our Veterans*, 108–11, 148–49.

16. Elizabeth Cobbs Hoffman, *The Hello Girls: America's First Women Soldiers* (Cambridge, Mass.: Harvard University Press, 2017); Molly Merryman, *Clipped Wings: The Rise and Fall of the Women Airforce Service Pilots (WASPs) of World War II* (New York: New York University Press, 1998); June A. Willenz, *Women Veterans: America's Forgotten Heroines* (New York: Continuum, 1983); Mary V. Stremlow, "Women as Veterans: Historical Perspective and Expectations," in *A Woman's War Too: U.S. Women in the Military in World War II*, ed. Paula Nassen Poulos (Washington, D.C.: National Archives and Records Administration, 1996), 355–66.

17. Jennifer Mittelstadt, *The Rise of the Military Welfare State* (Cambridge, Mass.: Harvard University Press, 2015); Beth L. Bailey, *America's Army: Making the All-Volunteer Force* (Cambridge, Mass.: Belknap Press of Harvard University Press, 2009).

18. For instance, the Continental Congress passed the first invalid pension law in 1776 largely to encourage enlistments; see William Henry Glasson, *Federal Military Pensions in the United States* (New York: Oxford University Press, 1918), 20–21.

19. Meredith Kleykamp and Crosby Hipes, "Social Programs for Soldiers and Veterans," in *The Oxford Handbook of U.S. Social Policy*, ed. Daniel Béland, Christopher Howard, and Kimberly J. Morgan (Oxford: Oxford University Press, 2015), 570.

20. See for example Sabrina Tavernise, "Civilian-Military Gap Grows as Fewer Americans Serve," *New York Times*, November 24, 2011.

21. For a recent example of such criticism, see James T. Bennett, *Paid Patriotism? The Debate over Veterans' Benefits* (London: Routledge, Taylor and Francis Group, 2017).

22. The Wounded Warrior Project, for instance, is a charity organized in 2003 to help disabled veterans. For examples of the use of "heroes," see Carl Forsling, "If You Call All Veterans Heroes, You're Getting It Wrong," Task & Purpose, August 5, 2014, https://taskandpurpose.com /call-veterans-heroes-getting-it-wrong, accessed June 25, 2017.

ACKNOWLEDGMENTS

This book would not have been possible without the help of many individuals and institutions.

First, I would like to thank the several libraries, museums, historical societies, and archives whose staff kindly gave me access to their documents for my research: the American Jewish Archives in Cincinnati, Ohio; the American Legion Auxiliary Library and the American Legion Library in Indianapolis, Indiana; the Bentley Library in Ann Arbor, Michigan; the Cincinnati and Hamilton County Library in Cincinnati, Ohio; the Cushing Library at Texas A&M University; the David Rubenstein Library at Duke University; the Eisenhower Presidential Library in Abilene, Kansas; the FDR Presidential Library in Hyde Park, New York; the Firestone Library and the Seeley G. Mudd Special Collections in Princeton, New Jersey; the Gelman Library at George Washington University; the Hagley Library in Wilmington, Delaware; the Historical Society of Pennsylvania, Philadelphia; the Hooks Central Library in Memphis, Tennessee; the Hoover Institution Archives at Stanford University; the Hoover Presidential Library in West Branch, Iowa; the Indiana Historical Society and Indiana State Library in Indianapolis, Indiana; the Kansas State Historical Society in Topeka and the Kenneth Spencer Library at Kansas University in Lawrence, Kansas; the Library of Congress in Washington, D.C.; the Minnesota Historical Society in St. Paul, Minnesota; the National Archives in Washington, D.C.; the Notre Dame University Archives in South Bend, Indiana; the Reuther Library at Wayne State University; the South Caroliniana Library at the University of South Carolina; the Special Collections Library at the University of Kentucky, Lexington; the Special Collections at the University of Washington, Seattle; the Syracuse University Library; the Tamiment Library at New York University; the Harry Truman Presidential Library in Independence, Missouri; the University of North Dakota in Grand Forks; the University of North Texas in Denton; the University of the Pacific in Stockton, California; the University of Virginia Special Collections in Charlottesville; the Veterans of Foreign Wars National

Headquarters in Kansas City, Missouri; the Wayne County Public Library in Goldsboro, North Carolina; and the Wisconsin Historical Society as well as the Wisconsin Veterans Museum in Madison, Wisconsin.

This project received generous financial support from several sources: the Organization of American Historians, the University of North Texas at Denton, the Bentley Library, the Wisconsin Veterans Museum, the Herbert Hoover Presidential Library, the Society for Military History, the Eisenhower Library Foundation, the Harry S. Truman Library Institute, the Roosevelt Institute, and the American Studies Program and Department of History at Princeton University. This project has also received funding from the European Union's Framework Programme for Research and Innovation Horizon 2020 (2014–2020) under the Marie Skłodowska-Curie Grant Agreement No. 754388 and from the Ludwig Maximilian University at Munich's Institutional Strategy LMUexcellent within the framework of the German Excellence Initiative (No. ZUK22).

Portions of this research were previously published in somewhat different form: "Veterans as a Social Movement: The American Legion, the First Hoover Commission, and the Making of the American Welfare State," *Social Science History* 44, no. 2 (Summer 2020), and "Enforcing Conformity: Race and the American Legion, 1940–1960," in *War Veterans and the World After 1945: Cold War Politics, Decolonization, Memory*, ed. Ángel Alcalde and Xosé M. Núñez Seixas (Routledge, 2018). I would like to thank Cambridge University Press and Routledge for permission to reprint this material.

Princeton University was the ideal place to start this project. Julian Zelizer constantly prodded me to think bigger while providing a model of scholarly rigor and professional commitment. I also learned immensely from my regular interactions with other faculty, including Kevin Kruse, Margot Canaday, Beth Lew-Williams, Joe Fronczak, Philip Nord, David Bell, and Paul Miles. I cannot thank enough our departmental staff—Kristy Novak, Jaclyn Wasneski, Judy Hanson, and Judy Miller—for having solved so many logistical issues throughout the years. I was also nurtured all along this adventure by friends who kept me going: Richard Anderson, José Argueta, Michael Barany, Dan Barish, Benjamin Bernard, Katlyn Carter, Matthew Chan, Alex Chase-Levenson, Sarah Coleman, Peter Conti-Brown, Teresa Davis, Andrew Edwards, Merle Eisenberg, Margarita Fajardo, Seyi Fasoranti, Chris Florio, Christian Flow, Kellen Funk, Josh Garrett-Davis, Joppan George, Dylan Gottlieb, Casey Hedstrom, Maximilian Hirschberger, Saarah Jappie, Emily Kern, Anne Kerth, Abigail Kret, Meg Leja, Molly Lester, Patrick Luiz de Oliveira, Andrea Oñate Madrazo, Jane Manners, Martín Marimón, Kathryn McGarr, Diana Andrade Melgarejo, Nikhil Menon,

David Moak, Lee Mordechai, Iwa Nawrocki, Emily Prifogle, Sudhir Raskutti, Ronny Regev, Joan Ricart-Huguet, Morgan Robinson, Ingrid Rocket, Benjamin Sacks, Marcia Schenck, Will Schultz, Mark Sholdice, Paris Spies-Gans, Joel Suarez, Fidel Tavarez, Mathura Umachandran, Veronica Valentin, Sean and Sara Vanatta, Jan Van Doren, Paula Vedoveli, and Marc Volovici. For helping me stay sane throughout these years, I owe a special debt to the Delaware and Raritan Canal State Park, the Institute Woods, and the Billy Johnson Mountain Lakes Preserve, which provided perfect outlets for countless runs in all seasons.

In Munich, my discussions with Michael Hochgeschwender, Uwe Lübken, Andreas Etges, Charlotte Lerg, Wiflried Mausbach, Anke Ortlepp, Delia Gonzalez de Reufels, Herbert Obinger, Teresa Huhle, Jessica Gienow-Hecht, Axel Schäfer, and Simon Wendt helped me think about the project in larger terms. Outside of academia, Lieke Asma and Edwin, Katie Fitch, Magda Hirschberger (and the entire Hirschberger family), Maria Withrow, Aude Barraud, Vincent Tirehote, Kerstin Hartung, Christoph Spicker, Lion Waaser, Ambre Nicolle, Erika Lansberg, Clemens Van Loyen, Renate Krakowczyk, Dayela Valenzuela, Golf Graspy, and Katharina all provided sustenance. I am also thankful to Oxford University's Rothermere American Institute for giving me the chance to spend one term there as a visiting fellow in the fall of 2020, which gave me the chance to present my research and exchange with their thriving scholarly community.

At various points, I received invaluable advice from a number of scholars who helped improve this project tremendously. I was lucky to meet James Sparrow early on, and I am still in awe of the time and work he devoted to helping transform what was then still a very narrow chapter draft into something much more ambitious. Equally helpful were Steve Ortiz, Laura McEnaney, Jessica Adler, Bruno Cabanes, Jennifer Keene, Mark Wilson, Ellen Schrecker, G. Kurt Piehler, Hugh Wilford, Marc Selverstone, Jennifer Mittelstadt, Andrew Preston, Beth Bailey, Sarah Myers, Tim Naftaly, John Kinder, Kyle Burke, Ángel Alcalde, Paul Huddie, Nick Witham, Gary Baines, Jonathan Fennell, Grace Huxford, Mark Edele, Erwan Le Gall, Gwendal Piégais, Damien Accoulon, Ben Zdencanovic, Colin Moore, and Julilly Kohler-Hausmann. My editor Bob Lockhart also provided helpful guidance in the later stages.

In France, the support of a number of scholars was key in getting this project started and seeing it to its end: Elsa Devienne, Romain Huret, Stephen Clay, Nicolas Delalande, Nicolas Roussellier, Andrew Diamond, Claire Zalc, Mario del Pero, and Pauline Peretz.

I owe the greatest debt to my family and especially my parents, whose constant support was key to making this project imaginable and feasible.